Continuum Companion to Second Language Acquisition

Continuum Companion to Second Language Acquisition

Edited by

Ernesto Macaro

continuum

Continuum International Publishing Group

The Tower Building   80 Maiden Lane
11 York Road   Suite 704, New York
London SE1 7NX   NY 10038

www.continuumbooks.com

British Library Cataloguing-in-Publication Data
A catalogue record for this book is available from the British Library.

ISBN: 978-0-8264-9506-8 (hardback)

Library of Congress Cataloging-in-Publication Data
A catalog record for this book is available from the Library of Congress.

Typeset by Newgen Imaging Systems Pvt Ltd, Chennai, India
Printed and bound in Great Britain by the MPG Books Group

To my son Jamie

Contents

Notes on Contributors

Paul Seedhouse is Professor of Educational and Applied Linguistics in the School of Education, Communication and Language Sciences, Newcastle University, UK. His monograph *The Interactional Architecture of the Language Classroom* was published by Blackwell in 2004 and won the Modern Languages Association of America Mildenberger Prize. He also co-edited the collections *Applying Conversation Analysis* (Palgrave Macmillan 2005), *Language Learning and Teaching as Social Interaction*, (Palgrave Macmillan 2007) and *Conversation Analysis and Language for Specific Purposes* (Peter Lang 2007). He currently has a second grant from the IELTS consortium to look at topic development in the IELTS speaking test.

Susan M. Gass is University Distinguished Professor of Linguistics and Languages, Director of the English Language Center, Director of the Second Language Studies Ph.D. programme, Co-Director of the Center for Language Education and Research, Co-Director of the Center for the Support for Language Teaching, all at Michigan State University. She received her undergraduate degree from University of California at Berkeley, an M.A. from U.C.L.A. and her Ph.D. from Indiana University. She has published widely in the field of second language acquisition and is the author of numerous articles and books. She is the winner of numerous awards, including the Distinguished Faculty Award at Michigan State University, the Ralph Smuckler Award for International Studies at Michigan State University, Paul Pimsleur Award for Outstanding Research from ACTFL (American Council for the Teaching of Foreign Languages) and the Michigan Association of Governing Boards Award. She has served as the president of the American Association for Applied Linguistics and and of the International Association of Applied Linguistics (AILA). She is also on numerous editorial boards and is the current Associate Editor of *Studies in Second Language Acquisition*.

Andrew D. Cohen (Professor in Second Language Studies, University of Minnesota) served as a Peace Corps Volunteer on the High Plains of Bolivia, as a Fulbright Scholar in Brazil, and as a professor of language education at the Hebrew University of Jerusalem in Israel for 17 years. He has written numerous research articles on language teaching, language learning, language testing, and research methods, as well as books on bilingual education, language learner strategies, language assessment and research methods. His recent efforts include co-editing *Language Learner Strategies* (Oxford University Press, 2007) with Ernesto Macaro, writing of an online course, 'Assessing Language Ability in Adults and Young Adults' in the ELT Advantage series with Heinle Cengage Learning, and co-authoring a teachers' guide to pragmatics, *Teaching and Learning Pragmatics: Where Language and Culture Meet* with Noriko Ishihara (Pearson Education, in press).

Zoltán Dörnyei is Professor of Psycholinguistics at the School of English Studies, University of Nottingham. He has published widely on various aspects of individual differences and second language acquisition, and is the author of several books, including, *Motivational Strategies in the Language Classroom* (2001, Cambridge University Press), *The Psychology of the Language Learner* (2005, Lawrence Erlbaum/Routledge), *Research Methods in Applied Linguistics* (2007, Oxford University Press), *Motivation, Language Identity and the L2 Self* (2009, Multilingual Matters, co-edited with Ema Ushioda), *The Psychology of Second Language Acquisition* (2009, Oxford University Press) and *Teaching and Researching Motivation* (2nd edition, in press, Longman, co-authored with Ema Ushioda).

Vivian Cook is a Professor of Applied Linguistics Sciences at Newcastle University in England. He is mostly known for his work developing the idea of multi-competence and for his books on Chomsky and on the applications of SLA to language teaching. Recently he has also taken up writing books on writing systems and popular books on spelling and vocabulary. His current research interest is the study of bilingual cognition, and has a book to appear in 2010 *Language and Bilingual Cognition*. He was a founder and first President of the European Second Language Association and is joint founder and editor of the new journal *Writings Systems Research*.

Victoria A. Murphy studied Linguistics and Psychology at undergraduate and graduate levels and obtained her DPhil from McGill University. She is now a University Lecturer in Applied Linguistics/Second Language Acquisition in the Department of Education, University of Oxford and is a Fellow at Kellogg College. Her work focuses mostly on aspects of children's second language learning, with a specific focus on lexical and morphological development and reading comprehension. Her research is primarily directed towards understanding the linguistic development of children learning their second languages within primary school contexts, both when the L2 is taught as a subject (Modern Foreign Languages) and when it is the medium of instruction for language minority children.

Ernesto Macaro is Professor of Applied Linguistics in the Department of Education at the University of Oxford where he teaches courses in second language acquisition and language teacher education. His main research interests are in language learner strategies and in teacher codeswitching behaviour. Much of his research is conducted in real classroom contexts and with adolescent language learners. He has published books with Oxford University Press (a book on strategies with Andrew D. Cohen) and with Continuum. His research has appeared in a number of international journals including *Modern Language Journal*, *Applied Linguistics* and *Language Learning*.

Robert Vanderplank is Director of Oxford University Language Centre and a Fellow of Kellogg College, Oxford, where he is also Director of the Kellogg College Centre for the Study of Lifelong Language Learning. His current research interests are broad and include second language maintenance and attrition, technology in language learning and teaching, first language development at school, second language listening comprehension, self-assessment and attribution in adult language learners. He is Reviews Editor of *System* and author of the well-reviewed *Uglier than Monkey's Armpit: Untranslatable Insults, Put-downs and Curses from Around the World* (2007, Boxtree).

Paul Meara is professor of Applied Linguistics at Swansea University, where he leads a group of PhD students working on vocabulary acquisition. He is currently working on very simple computational models of how bilingual lexicons work, and ways of assessing productive vocabulary in L2 speakers. He also moonlights as Baritone Saxophone player for the City of Swansea Concert Band.

Acknowledgements

I am deeply grateful to the following people for their careful reading of the sections of this book but for which I am of course directly responsible. Suzanne Graham, Rosa Manchòn, Robert Woore. Andrew Cohen and I would also like to express our thanks to the team of people who painstakingly went through six years' worth of research journals in order to make possible the information we have provided in Chapters 1 and 3 of this book. They are: Tor Lindbloom, Sabina R. Cohen, Yuen Yi Lo and Jang Ho Lee.

Part 1

The Second Language Acquisition Landscape

1 Second Language Acquisition: The Landscape, the Scholarship and the Reader

Ernesto Macaro

In the twenty-first century the majority of people in the world speak more than one language. A considerable number speak three languages or more. In the first quarter of the century the second language that the majority of non-anglophones speak is, undoubtedly, English. There are at least two languages, other than English, which are spoken as first languages by billions of people: Mandarin Chinese and Spanish. These languages may well come to rival English as second languages that people aspire to learn as the century progresses. Already, in the USA there are indications that more television programmes are watched in Spanish than in English.[1]

Second languages are learnt in school, at university, in the workplace and in the street. They are learnt at home by speaking to families, carers and friends. Some are learnt alone, through formal self-study. Some are learnt informally, simply by reading a book or newspaper on the train. As an object of learning, a second language has no rival. No other subject is learnt by so many people over such long periods of time. Some people may decide or are compelled to change the second language that they are learning, upgrade or downgrade the intensity with which they are learning a language or simply 'use' a second language with no real intention of making any noticeable progress with it. But even if someone is simply using a second language in order to conduct their everyday business, the process of noticing something new, the questioning of something already known, and the process of language maintenance, are in themselves forms of learning.

Second language learning is neither cumulative nor neat and tidy. And it is in that messy, non-linear, but semi-permanent process of learning the subject, and in the myriad situations in which a second language is engaged, that the complexity of second language learning resides.

I would like to make an initial note to the reader. In this chapter, a number of concepts and technical terminology will be introduced. Most are explained in the 'compendium of key concepts' provided in the next chapter. However it should be possible for the reader new to the field of second language acquisition to get a reasonably satisfying impression of the landscape I am about to describe without having to constantly refer to the explanations of these key terms. But of course it's up to you how you decide to read this chapter. A principle of applied linguistics is that the reader is the boss, not the writer!

Second Language Acquisition

What is second language acquisition (SLA)? Is it different from second language learning? Absolutely not. SLA is simply a term given to the methodical study of second language learning or, for that matter, third language learning. SLA scholars are 'applied linguists'. Unlike scholars of general linguistics their prime objective is not to describe a language. Rather, they look for relationships between a language and the people who are speaking it or attempting to speak it. They wonder what might be the complex influences that contribute to the huge range of second language learning outcomes. They ask themselves why some learners learn faster than others and why some learners achieve ultimately higher levels than others. They investigate why some learners have a burning desire to learn a language while others do it simply because they are forced to. SLA researchers want to know whether there is something about the second language that causes this variation or whether it is something inherent in the learner's first language. Like other 'social scientists' SLA researchers also investigate the 'old chestnut' about the balance between nature and nurture. Is second language learning ability something we are born with or is it the case that aspects of the society we are in enable some people to learn better than others? All these questions, then, are of interest to SLA scholars.

Nor is a distinction nowadays being made (as Stephen Krashen once attempted to make) between acquisition, which was supposedly subconscious, and learning which was supposedly conscious. It is now generally accepted that totally subconscious acquisition/learning could really only take place when you are asleep, in a coma or through some kind of subliminal device such as is sometimes (illegally) attempted in advertising.

Thus the study of SLA is not different from the study of second language learning. There is no suggestion that what scholars are interested in is drawing a clear line between some kind of idealized mental process, sanitized by the laboratory setting, and the complex, often chaotic linguistic environment where those other humans present might influence one's thoughts, one's emotions and one's ability to learn. Well, at least not many scholars would *admit* to wanting to draw that clear line! Perhaps some, in their heart of hearts, would love to operate like natural scientists and isolate their subjects in cages, bring them out from time to time onto the laboratory bench, feed them a particular language diet and then see the progress their subjects made. But they know that they would be ridiculed, not to say imprisoned. So instead SLA researchers, like other social scientists, try to control for as many factors as possible when studying humans' relationship with language, while accepting that they have to take account of a human being's relationship with other human beings around them, and the situation in which they are in.

Whatever, the operational parameters of SLA researchers, stated or otherwise, all would agree that the SLA phenomenon exists – people do learn a second language. They also agree that it is worth the effort of trying to explain how the phenomenon occurs and what predicts that it will occur in a particular way. In other words, researchers are convinced that it is worth studying the fact that people are able to learn a language in addition to the one they are confronted with from the moment of birth and that some learn this second language (L2) to a level at which it is, to all intents and purposes, indistinguishable from a native speaker of that language; others do not reach those lofty heights. The latter, of course, may well have a perfectly valid reason for not wishing to do so.

Origins of the Study of SLA

When did the study of SLA begin? That's a tricky question. Some would point out that it has been informally studied for centuries. Others might argue that its birth was not noticed until the beginning of the twentieth century when links between language learning and the description of a language were first being made. However, with far greater conviction, we can pinpoint the late 1960s as a time when authors first began to draw on many fields of learning including the fields of linguistics, language teaching, sociology and psychology, and in doing so started a process of systematic reflection on language learning, based on collecting research evidence and theory building. Then in the 1980s the production of SLA research underwent a veritable explosion, in part linked to the expansion of English language teaching world-wide (both as a second and as a foreign language) and in part as a result of a perceived need to establish an equilibrium between those who saw second language learning as merely a continuation of first language learning and those who saw it as a completely different enterprise. In fact this debate about whether learning to speak an L2 is as natural as learning to speak the first language, or whether it involves radically different mental capacities and processes, has remained at the heart of SLA research to the present day and is extensively discussed by Vivian Cook in this volume.

Interestingly, it is around the late 1980s and 1990s that a growing rift can be observed between researchers working in first language acquisition and development, and those working in SLA. The reason for this was probably that first language researchers detected two problems that needed solving. First, the overwhelming majority of children learn the oral form of their first language without difficulty, and therefore the researchers presumed the remaining few must be undergoing some kind of language deficit or difficulty which needed to be treated – that is, these children were considered to have specific learning impairments and these required examination by speech experts. Secondly while the overwhelming majority of children learn the oral form of their L1 without difficulty, a considerable minority either have delayed literacy (the development of reading and writing) with their L1 or indeed have persistent difficulties well into adolescence and beyond (dyslexia). Neither of these two themes appears to be of immediate concern to most SLA researchers who seem more concerned with difficulties experienced in the L2 by learners who have had no signs of difficulty in the L1.

Books on Second Language Acquisition

How has the study of SLA been documented and disseminated? Largely it has been done through books and academic journals, although more recently online information services and 'Centres' have been posting findings of research on line. Let us first take the case of books. It is almost impossible to enumerate and list with any certainty all the volumes that have been dedicated to SLA. It is however possible to categorize their objectives and their readership. For example, there has recently been a trend to produce and publish 'handbooks of SLA' (e.g., Doughty and Long 2003) which are primarily intended to offer the student of SLA or language teachers a brief introduction by experts in the field to an area of SLA study. These publications should be handled with care by students and practitioners alike as they are both highly selective and often subjective summaries of years of research endeavour, summaries which might appear to be providing the ultimate judgement on the trustworthiness of a particular theory or body of research.

A much longer history can be traced in those books which propound a particular theory of how L2s are learnt, offer some research evidence for that theory and propose a future agenda for testing and refining the theory. Most of these are edited books, but some might also be single-authored books (e.g., Kramsch 2002; Krashen 1981; Lantolf and Appell 1994; Robinson 2001; VanPatten 1996). All claim to offer either a total or partial explanation for the phenomenon that is SLA through some kind of unifying theory. The student who wishes to develop an in-depth understanding of how, historically, different authors have taken these different 'positions' on SLA and how they have come from different disciplines in order take those positions, would do well to read all these in the original. Similarly there are edited books that explore an area rather than a theoretical framework. Often these are books which attempt to bring together a community of practitioners all working in the same area (Cohen and Macaro 2007; Cook and Bassetti 2005; Muñoz 2006; Schmitt 2004). Here the reader will find chapters written by different experts in the field, usually offering a single study that they have carried out, or a synthesis of a cluster of studies.

Books which attempt to make theories easily accessible to the student of SLA are the following: Cook (2001); Lightbown and Spada (1993/2006); McLaughlin (1987); Mitchell and Myles (1998); Sharwood-Smith (1994); VanPatten and Williams (2006). These are books which give brief explanations of a number of theories of SLA and discuss them in the light of the evidence available. Similarly there are books which are, as it were, compendiums of recent and relevant research to SLA. The focus here is less on what the theory is but more on the accumulation of evidence around a theme (Chaudron 1988; Ellis 1994/2008; Macaro 2003).

Lastly, there are books which are written with the SLA student specifically in mind. For example De Bot, Lowie and Verspoor (2005) and Gass and Selinker (2008), can be considered as coursebooks in that they have a planned curriculum of SLA learning, and some with activities for the student to undertake.

A Companion to SLA

So what kind of a book is a 'Companion to SLA'? I don't think there is really an established definition of what a Companion is but I can tell you what this one is trying to do. This book tries to cater essentially for students of SLA, whether at undergraduate or postgraduate level, but also for practitioners wishing to update their knowledge of some of the principles underlying language teaching. It tries to strike a balance between making theories and research findings clear and accessible and not being condescending to its reader through oversimplification of complex ideas. First, the Companion offers an overview of the field. This is what this chapter is attempting to do at the moment and will continue to do after a brief deviation. Providing an overview is an objective shared by Chapters 2 and 3 of Part 1. Chapter 2 (written by Ernesto Macaro, Robert Vanderplank and Victoria Murphy) offers explanations of key concepts in SLA thus making them accessible to someone first embarking on the subject. These key concepts are cross-referenced, demonstrating the strong interconnected nature of SLA research. The objective in this collection of key terms was to go beyond the brief definition of a concept and to provide what we might call an 'exposition' of an idea, hypothesis or theory which has been of interest to SLA researchers. In this chapter the authors limited themselves to between 200 and 300 words for each exposition, attempting to provide where possible both an initial definition and a brief account of how the concept has been tackled or has developed over time as well as offering the reader one or two key references to follow up.

Chapter 3 on research methods (written by Andrew Cohen and Ernesto Macaro) does not provide the reader with a handbook guide to carrying out research. A comprehensive explanation of research methods would be beyond the scope of a single chapter. Instead, first the reader is guided to those authors who have approached applied linguistics research methods in a number of different ways. Secondly the chapter provides an overview of the types of research methods that have been used by SLA researchers in the early years of the twenty-first century. Thirdly it offers some critiques and observations on these methods and argues for certain improvements that could be made and that the novice SLA researcher may want to take on board.

The last section comprises seven chapters written by different authors with a strong interest in a particular field of SLA. These chapters are meant to be challenging for any reader interested in language acquisition. For each chapter the author was asked to tackle not a single concept or domain but the possible relationships between two concepts or domains and I shall refer to these themes and authors as this introductory chapter progresses.

I hope that this combination of approaches is a suitable interpretation of what a 'Companion' to an academic subject is. Personally I like my academic companions to be both informative and challenging. The reader will have to judge whether the book lives up to these two aspirations.

Journals of Second Language Acquisition

Having communicated to the reader the intentions of this volume we can now return to providing the landscape of SLA. We have touched on its historical development and seen how different authors have approached book writing on the subject. Let us now turn to research journals. *Language Teaching* used to list more than 50 journals from which it created its 'abstracts'.

For the purposes of this book I and some colleagues[2] documented the research carried out in the early years of the twenty-first century and published in 5 journals: *Applied Linguistics, Language Learning, Language Teaching Research, Modern Language Journal* and *Studies in Second Language Acquisition*. I consider these to be among the most influential journals in SLA. By identifying and documenting the aims of each paper, usually through the research questions, we can begin to have a vision of the landscape of SLA.

One way of making sense of the SLA landscape is to divide it up into four broad areas:

1. The acquisition of the rules system and the acquisition of vocabulary
2. The development of language skills
3. The beliefs that teachers and learners hold about second language learning
4. The practice of teaching and learning

These four areas no doubt fail to capture the totality of the landscape, and they certainly overlap in places, but they certainly will help us to observe its main perspectives and aspirations. Let us consider each of these broad areas in turn.

Second Language Lexis and Second Language Rules

There has been, in the early years of the twenty-first century, a continued interest in how L2 rules (morphology and syntax) are acquired. I detect no increase or diminution of interest to that shown in the previous two decades. On the other hand, vocabulary acquisition research has grown enormously in recent years and it would be difficult for anyone to claim (as happened in the 1980s and 1990s) that it is still a neglected area. Both rule-system and vocabulary research are concerned with some of the main ingredients in the language

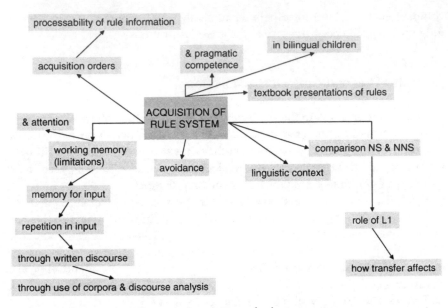

Figure 1 Acquisition of rule system

competence cake mix. That is, relative knowledge of both is the necessary although not sufficient requisite for being able to communicate.

If we consider Figure 1, we notice certain keywords which are closely associated with acquiring the grammar of the L2: acquisition orders, processability, bilingual children, working memory limitations, role of L1, avoidance. These areas of interest are, in many respects, concerned with *constraints* being placed on the acquisition of the L2 rule-system. The questions being asked are what is stopping the learning of morpho-syntactic patterns? Is there a fixed order of learning certain features of grammar? Is there something about the human brain that impedes learning and does that 'something' vary from human to human? Do younger bilinguals have more freedom to learn, or more access to the acquisition of rules, than older bilinguals? This last area, whether age is in fact an important factor in SLA and therefore whether language learning should start in the primary school, is thoroughly examined by Victoria Murphy in this volume.

Two over-arching theories of acquisition underpin these research questions. The first is a theory of the relationship between language and the human brain; because languages have universal properties (things which are the same in all languages), the human brain may, at birth, already be 'set up' to learn all languages in a particular way. However, the evolutionary link between the nature of language and the nature of language learning is, to my knowledge, never adequately explained. The second theory compares the human brain, or rather human memory, to an extremely powerful and intelligent computer which

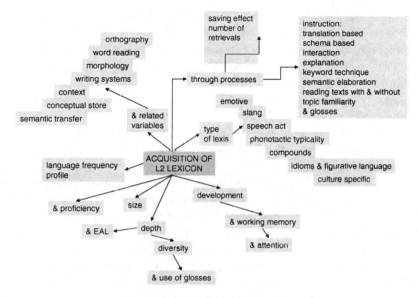

Figure 2 Acquisition of L2 lexicon

processes incoming information and thereby develops patterns of language as it is used by others and acquires the rules therein.

While there are still numerous attempts to validate one of these theories against the other in the realm of morpho-syntax, in the realm of vocabulary acquisition it is generally accepted that intensive processing in the conscious memory system, and relating this information to what the memory system already knew, is how the meaning of words is acquired. Figure 2 attempts to demonstrate the considerable effort currently being exerted in order to better understand how the meaning (semantics) and the form (phonology and morphology) of words and short phrases is perceived, processed, stored and eventually retrieved for use. Some of the questions being asked are: is the size of the lexical store related to the development of proficiency? A related question is explored by Paul Meara in this volume who outlines the difficulties inherent in a relationship between vocabulary knowledge and vocabulary use. Researchers have also asked whether knowledge of formulaic language allows learners to sound more fluent. Are words learnt better implicitly or explicitly? Are new words in an L2 text learnt better if they are highlighted in some way? How do learners build 'word families'? What are the best strategies for learning vocabulary? How much vocabulary of a text do you need to know to understand it and what is the maximum vocabulary you don't need to know before it is impossible for you to correctly guess the meaning of unknown words? What is the relationship between being able to retain sounds in your head and vocabulary learning? Does reading something, the topic of which you are familiar with, make learning its vocabulary easier?

The reader of journal articles may come to the same conclusion that I have arrived at in recent years, namely that the study of vocabulary acquisition appears to relate more directly to research on the development of language skills than does research on the acquisition of the rule-system of the L2. This is not to say that research on acquisition of rules is not capable of providing powerful insights into language skill development (quite the contrary), but that researchers seem to have drawn up their agendas more narrowly and focused more on acquisition per se than on linking it to skills. On the other hand researchers in the rule-system field have attempted to make frequent links between their findings and possible teaching methods, usually in a couple of paragraphs at the end of long articles. It seems to me, and of course this may be a highly subjective impression, that this group of researchers is much more inclined to see their research as providing prescriptions for teaching methods than those working in the vocabulary field. To put it simply, some researchers working on grammar acquisition appear to want to promote explicit grammar teaching albeit at different levels of intensity, while researchers working with vocabulary acquisition appear to be less concerned with the teaching method as with what are the options available to the learner for learning vocabulary and for furthering the use of that vocabulary in real-life contexts.

Second Language Skills

There is a general acceptance that the categorization of the four language skills (reading, listening, speaking and writing) is conceptually appropriate. Some may argue, with some justification, that we rarely use these skills in complete isolation, for example when writing a report on a series of documents we have read and interviews we have conducted. Nevertheless this multi-skill approach still has underlying it a recognition that the four-skills categorization holds water even if real-life L2 use is more complex than that categorization might imply.

So how have SLA journals covered the four skills? First we should note that, to my knowledge, there is no journal specifically dedicated to either L2 speaking or L2 listening (nor for that matter to L2 interaction), yet there are journals (*Journal of Second Language Writing*; *Reading in a Foreign Language*) which only admit papers on skill-specific research. I cannot say for sure why this should be the case. Perhaps it is entirely a product of history and the interests and drive of certain individuals.

I have divided up the research papers we scrutinized into productive skills (speaking and writing) and receptive skills (listening and reading). There is

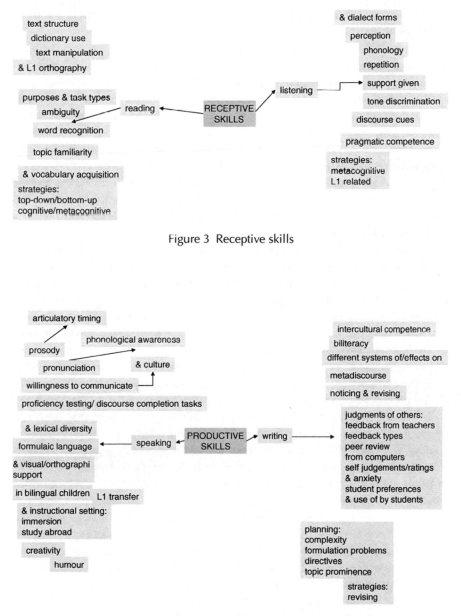

Figure 3 Receptive skills

Figure 4 Productive skills

general consensus now that the words 'productive' and 'receptive' are more appropriate than 'active' and 'passive'.

If we consider the diagrammatic overview of receptive skills, and if I have succeeded in faithfully portraying the research interests of recent years, we notice considerable areas of overlap between listening and reading. Both areas of research demonstrate an interest in the role of metacognition (planning, predicting, monitoring, evaluating) to further the process of comprehension. Both suggest that top-down and bottom-up strategies provide the means of overcoming L2 comprehension problems by compensating, complementing, and confirming each other. In both skills, researchers have spotted difficulties to do with decoding and perceiving the sounds and symbols of the language the learner is studying. In both skills, the extent to which a learner is familiar with the topic of the texts may be influencing whether he or she is having difficulty understanding the intended meaning or not.

On the other hand there are also divergences in research aims brought on by the different modalities. In listening, authors have been interested in whether repeating an item of information increases comprehension or not; whether different varieties or dialect forms have an impact on listening; whether listeners listen out for cues in the text in order to focus their attention on what the speaker intended. In contrast, in reading, there has been a very strong interest in the text structure. How do the structures of different written texts vary? Are readers able to access the structure that is apparent in the text? Can readers spot the main proposition of a text and its supporting propositions? Can they deal with any ambiguities inherent in a text and if so how?

Unlike the case of receptive skills, if we consider the diagrammatic overview of productive skills we notice that speaking is not necessarily a mirror image of writing. Even though both may draw on similar theories of language production, the areas of interest diverge considerably. Perhaps the most obvious illustration of this is in the area of feedback. While in writing research there is a huge effort made to document the effects of feedback to learners, or what we might call 'judgements on their writing outputs', this does not figure prominently in the speaking literature. This may be because the theme of feedback to speaking has been considered more under the broad category of teacher-learner and learner-learner interaction (see below). However, I would propose that this distinction on the issue of feedback is not an arbitrary one brought on by my artificial categorization, but by substantive differences in perspectives on the purpose of feedback. To make myself clearer: in the case of feedback on learner writing the research aims have been more focused on how feedback develops the skill of writing, and less with the extent to which writing develops the underlying rule-system (through analysis of developing accuracy). In the case of feedback to speaking, the research aims have been almost entirely related to whether the feedback furthers the acquisition of the rule-system and vocabulary, not with whether it furthers the skill of speaking. In sum, researchers into feedback in writing are interested in performance (the skill of writing for effective communication); researchers into feedback in speaking appear to be interested in competence (the underlying knowledge of a second language that the learner has and is developing). This is why feedback on speaking is more appropriately categorized under 'interaction', but this tendency does leave an important gap in the literature which could be summarized by the research question: 'to what extent does feedback on spoken productions promote fluency, complexity, and accuracy?'

Apart from feedback, the following are other questions which researchers investigating productive skills have sought to answer. In writing they have asked: do writers notice the difference between their own writing and that of a native speaker writer carrying out the same writing task, and does this then lead the learner to revise their own text effectively? What causes writing anxiety or 'writer's block'? What are the problems and problem-solving strategies associated with writing when the writing system in L2 is completely different from the writing system in L1? How quickly do young writers progress in an immersion setting? Does the skill of writing progress in parallel with a learner's more general proficiency? Can intercultural competence be enhanced through computer mediated instruction? Does planning a task in a particular way lead to differences in the complexity of the written product?

In speaking they have also asked about the effects of planning. For example, what are the effects of planning a task before carrying it out on the subsequent performance in that task? Other questions have included: what makes some learners unwilling to communicate? In what way does a person's creativity impact on narrative speaking tasks? To what extent do different learners' L1s affect their pronunciation of an L2? What factors lead to an improvement in pragmatic ability? Does providing different types of information or support improve spoken productions? What kinds of tasks best capture how native-like an L2 learner sounds? How does the use of formulaic language enhance fluency?

In asking and answering these questions, the main focus has been on the individual speaker, writer, listener or reader. In these studies generally there is little consideration of the interlocutor. The presence of the interlocutor is however very visible in interaction studies.

Interaction

In interaction studies, as we noted above, the research endeavour has been largely to discover how the process of talking to others (usually with someone more proficient in the L2) furthers the acquisition of a competence in which grammatical rules and the breadth and depth of vocabulary are central. These

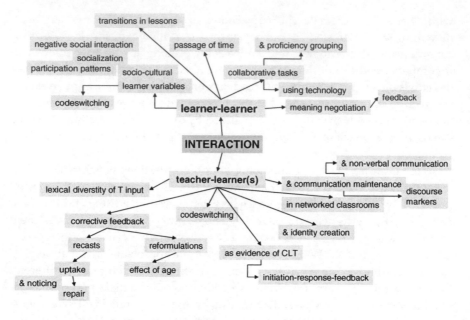

Figure 5 Interaction

aims have been largely pursued through two distinct approaches. The first is to set up pairs of speakers in fairly isolated conditions where one of the interlocutors is the native speaker, and the other is the learner or non-native speaker. Some of these studies have used participants in formal instructed contexts, others have used participants from 'naturalistic' contexts, that is, people using the L2 for their work, leisure, for socializing, but not in the context of learning it in class. The second (and it is fair to say less used) approach has been to observe teacher-to-whole-class interaction and record certain aspects or critical moments.

The answers that researchers were looking for were, for example: does interaction lead to more meaning negotiation than just listening to modified native speaker (or teacher) talk, and thence to comprehension and acquisition?; does interaction that forces the learner to say something new further acquisition?; does teacher feedback cause the learner to notice problems in his or her linguistic knowledge and put them right? As these issues are dealt with at length by Susan Gass later in this book I will not elaborate on them here. Other areas of teacher-student interaction have been:

1. What part does non-verbal communication play in the acquisition of vocabulary during interaction?
2. To what extent does codeswitching facilitate comprehension and more general learning?

3. How is communication maintained in the L2 classroom?
4. Are identities created through classroom discourse?
5. How does technology play a part in teachers interacting with students?
6. Is interaction in the classroom the same as interaction in a 'laboratory setting'. That is, when learners are pulled out of the classroom and the situation is more controlled, are the same results obtained?
7. To what extent can we deduce that a particular teaching approach is being pursued from the interaction observed?

When it comes to the interaction between learners, some of the same themes are explored although often with different outcome variables. For example codeswitching among learners is considered from the perspective of how far this resembles naturalistic codeswitching, whereas in the teacher-learner scenario it is more to do with how the teacher might use the first language to focus on the form of the language and take a break from communicating. Other areas in learner-learner interaction that research has centred on are: how socio-cultural variables affect the discourse; participation patterns where one learner might be more dominant than another or more proficient than another; how collaborative tasks might result in different outcomes through the use of technology; whether children interact and negotiate meaning differently from adults; whether interaction is different if the participants are using an L2 they also speak at home from the interaction used by L2 speakers who are studying it as a foreign language.

All the categories within the landscape that we have surveyed so far have been centred on the L2 learner's progress. They have studied L2 learners in terms of their knowledge, their performance and their behaviour and asked what factors relate or influence those three areas of progress. A fairly separate area of interest has been one which has explored what participants, in the process of learning and teaching, themselves think about what is involved in learning; in other words their perceptions and beliefs.

Belief Systems

Language teacher beliefs are linked to what theories they hold about their own practice. This of course is not surprising and this area of study is the theme pursued by Paul Seedhouse in a chapter in this book comparing the discourse of the classroom with the intended pedagogy of the teacher. The intended pedagogy of the teacher is, we presume, indirectly related to the beliefs, values and theories that teachers hold about the way languages are learnt and, by inference, the best way to teach the learners. Often this exploration of teacher beliefs is undertaken within the constructivist paradigm which is an umbrella

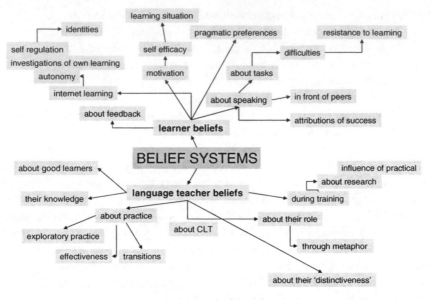

Figure 6 Belief systems

term for a series of propositions about what 'reality' is and how we can access it, observe it and discuss it. For constructivists reality is that which exists, and is created by, the shared perceptions that we humans have of the world and things that occur in the world. For them reality is not something external and independent of human beings, but perceived and constructed by human beings.

As we can see from Figure 6, language teacher beliefs have been explored through, at least, three approaches. First, there has been an exploration of how they see themselves as teachers; what their role is in the classroom. Often this is depicted in terms of metaphor. Teachers ask themselves (or are asked by probing researchers) am I a 'transmitter' of linguistic knowledge?; am I the 'scaffolding' necessary for the construction of the language learner's performance and confidence; am I the 'lubrication' in the machine of learning, the 'facilitator' in the transition from novice to expert? Related to this metaphorical representation of the teacher is the notion of there being something distinctive about the language teacher himself or herself, something which sets them apart from teachers of other subjects.

Not all types of research on teacher beliefs systems are as figurative or indirect. Some have centred on how teachers acquire their beliefs about pedagogy; for example, how an understanding of 'focus on form' comes about and what it means to them. How does teacher knowledge affect the beliefs that teachers report over time and particularly where does this knowledge come from? Does it come from their pre-service education programme? Does it come from their reading of the research literature? Are their decisions affected by the particular context they are working in and, if so, which agencies in that context (e.g., governments, school headteachers) are the most influential?

Running alongside many of these questions is the approach that interested parties (such as teacher trainers or policy makers) should take in changing language teacher behaviour in the classroom. Should it be via 'action-research', that is, teachers investigating their own classrooms guided or unguided by an experienced researcher external to the context? Should it be via 'exploratory practice' which, unlike action-research does not presume that a problem exists to be solved but asks teacher to 'puzzle' over classroom events and phenomena and, moreover, involve the learners in solving the puzzle?

Lastly, there have been some researchers who have asked what teachers think about learners, particularly what is their image of the motivated learner or, more commonly, about what the good language learner's characteristics are.

Fortunately this interest in teacher beliefs has been balanced by an interest in learner beliefs. As we can see from Figure 6, much of this research has involved identifying why learners are reluctant to speak in the classroom. Is it connected to the kinds of tasks they are asked to undertake, perhaps because they are too difficult or too alien to the pedagogical approaches they have been used to in the past? Or is reluctance more related to the presence of their fellow students (their peers) who make them feel shy, nervous or uncomfortable?

These are important questions which help us understand better the kinds of results that are obtained in studies which simply measure psycholinguistic learner variables (e.g., their ability to process information) on learner performance. By combining questions on performance with questions on learner beliefs and perceptions, researchers can identify possible causes and effects which might otherwise escape the research design net. In these types of studies, researchers have asked: what factors affect the motivational intensity of learners? Is it their self-confidence in specific tasks (known as self-efficacy) or is it their ability to control their own language learning destinies (self-regulation)? How is teacher feedback perceived by learners? Somewhat related to these questions is the role of technology. Does the internet or computer mediated communication enhance perceptions of self-confidence and drive motivation? Is the use of technology an aid to the approach taken by the teacher in the face-to-face classroom or is it a teaching approach in itself.

What learners feel about themselves and the potential sources of these feelings is the theme of Zoltán Dörnyei's chapter in this book where he argues for a more multi-layered and multi-faceted approach to our understanding of motivation.

Teaching Approaches

Very rarely in the SLA literature do authors still use the term 'teaching method'. I imagine this is because one would be at pains to identify, and overtly prescribe, a method of teaching that always works in every type of learning circumstance. Such a method would have to involve a clear series of steps which teachers must follow, one in which the outcomes predicted at the beginning of the series of steps would be the outcomes obtained. Some would argue that the 'last of the methods' was the 'audio-lingual method' and that since then we have opted for less prescriptive 'broad approaches'. Such an approach is 'communicative language teaching', which is based more on a series of principles than on a specific series of steps to follow. Yet, in some of the concepts contained in the teacher behaviour section of Figure 7 we do discern some fairly prescriptive stages which in the end could be described as a method rather than an approach. The presentation, practice, production (PPP) guidelines, often proposed on CELTA[3] courses seem to me to add up to a method in everything but name. Theories underlying 'input processing' almost invariably translate into a fairly rigid series of steps for the teacher to take in order to see whether input, which is manipulated in a certain way, leads to acquisition of the rule-system.

Other concepts expressed in Figure 7 are indeed less prescriptive. The phrase 'focus on form' was coined in a deliberately (I would imagine) vague manner in order to allow for teacher judgement as to when and how much 'form' to focus on.

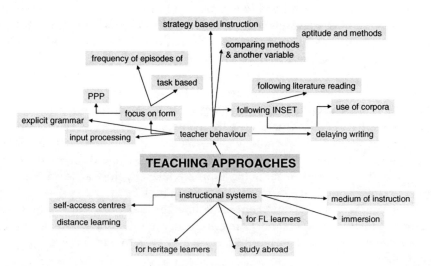

Figure 7 Teaching approaches

The word 'based' in task-based learning is equally (and sometimes provocatively) vague in order to give teachers plenty of leeway in how much the task leads the lesson plan rather than the content that the teacher would like the learners to acquire might lead the lesson. Studies which have been slightly tangential to these concerns have been those which have enquired whether some methods suit some learners more than others. For example research has attempted to find out whether certain profiles of aptitude are best served by communicative or more grammar-based teaching approaches.

There has been considerable interest in terms of whether teacher behaviour (as opposed to teacher beliefs, see above) changes as a result of in-service training or teacher development programmes, and which programme type is most effective. For example should novice teachers collaborate more with experienced teachers and how does that affect classroom pedagogy? Do the latest findings from the exploration of 'real language' (usually through the study of corpora) filter through teacher development programmes and from there into classroom practice? How sustainable are programmes of teacher development? Do changes in teacher behaviour last or do teachers revert to their original practice after a certain time has elapsed?

Finally, and taking a more bird's eye view of teaching approaches, there has been a continued interest in the value of different instructional systems. These are usually linked to policy decisions in particular countries with regard to language (almost invariably English language) learning. For example, do second language 'immersion' systems work? If the medium of instruction for all subjects on the curriculum is the L2, does this affect the learning of those subjects and does the L2 improve sufficiently to make this educational initiative justifiable?

Some research questions are, in a sense, being forced into the SLA arena. For example, the increase in the number of students going into higher education has prompted the use and the evaluation of self-access centres and also of more distant forms of learning. Another question has been to what extent does studying abroad, in the country where the target language is spoken, prove beneficial not only in terms of developing fluency and accuracy in the L2 but also in terms of developing intercultural understanding?

The above, then, is a brief 'tour d'horizon' of the landscape of SLA. It attempts to capture in relatively few words the huge output of research and theorizing that the student of SLA or the practising language teacher can tap into. I have tried to build up and categorize this landscape mostly by referring to recent research and to a limited number of research journals. However, the interested student or teacher will be faced with the daunting task of selecting, obtaining and attempting to come to grips with this vast output. Without some assistance from more experienced scholars this may become a demotivating experience. Particularly the last challenge, getting to grips with what the studies are reporting, can be an enormous one if the reader is not experienced in the metalanguage, the research traditions, the writing conventions and, perhaps most of all, the statistical information contained in these articles. Hopefully by reading this Companion, or by coming back to it from time to time, you will be enabled to access some of these articles more easily. However to finish off this introductory chapter, the following section provides you with some advice as to how to understand some of the more difficult journal reports of studies undertaken.

Advice to the Reader of SLA Literature

A question I am often asked by my students (either students on a teacher training programme or students embarking on an applied linguistics course) is, should I read books first or journal articles first? My answer is usually, 'it depends', which naturally students find very unhelpful and frustrating. But it *does* actually depend on a number of factors: how much you have already read about SLA in general, whether you have read some professional literature (teachers writing about their practice and beliefs), whether you want to start with a specific area and work outwards or whether you want to get an overview of the main themes and then look more deeply at some, whether you already feel confident with some of the terminology, whether you have already studied a related discipline such as linguistics or psychology and so on.

Nevertheless, the categories of books I have outlined above do all, in their different ways, give you an introduction to the field and, for most people new to SLA, this is a good place to start. But (most) books will not teach you how to become what we might call an 'independent reader' of SLA. They will give you a basic understanding of some of the theories and often a global summary of the findings, but they will not help you to make up your own mind about what the literature is telling us. In order to build up the layers of evidence for yourself, and with your own perfectly valid personal theories as sounding boards, you have to go, sooner rather than later, to the journal articles.

There are of course many different reasons that you may have for reading a research article in second language acquisition. You may simply want to find out the latest research evidence on a particular theme or answers to just one of the questions penned above. You may be quite satisfied with simply obtaining a summary of the results and be perfectly prepared to accept at face value what the authors of the article are saying they found. In which case you can probably do two things. Read the 'abstract' at the beginning of the article and then flick (or scroll) through to the conclusion at the end. Both will have summaries of the findings in a few sentences and, with a bit of luck, these two sets of sentences will be saying roughly the same thing. However, if that is your intention and purpose, beware! Therein lie dragons!

Whether you are a student of SLA charged with writing an essay or dissertation on a theme, a teacher wishing to inform their classroom practice, or a policy maker intent on finding solutions to perceived problems in their language learning context, beware that the summaries of findings, in any single report, may not be worth a can of beans. Without reading the whole article and considering at least some of the issues below you may be accepting as evidence some highly doubtful and untrustworthy assertions.

So let's start with the abstract. Have a really good look at what it's telling you and how it does this. Is each sentence clear to you even though you may not be an expert in the area they are researching? They should be! The writer should not be so arrogant as to assume that only experts in his or her field will be perusing abstracts in order to find out if the whole article is relevant to their line of enquiry. Does the abstract tell you: the aims of the study, why it was carried out, who the participants were, what research methods were used, what the main results were? The abstract may also tell you what the implications of the findings might be. If it tells you all that, and it is clear and understandable to you, then, in my view, it has pressed the first 'trust the findings' button and a green light has come on.

Next should come the Introduction to the study. This introduction should clearly set the scene for you by giving you some minimal but important information. When roughly was the study carried out? Was it fairly recently, or are the authors using data from many years ago? There may be perfectly valid reasons for using old data, but the world of SLA may have moved on since then and the way it was collected may not have taken into account these changes in perspectives. In which country was the study carried out? It helps to know this right from the start because it sets the findings in a real context, and not all learning contexts are the same. Does it then tell you why it was carried out at this point in time and in this particular context? Does it say (usually in a footnote) whether the study was funded by a particular body and who that body might be? Was it an independent body that would not put pressure on the researchers to come up with a particular set of findings or slant the conclusions in order to pursue a desired educational policy? Hopefully another green light will now appear!

Normally the review of previous literature comes next as a separate section. Occasionally it is embedded in the introduction but I find this makes the job of distinguishing the context of the study from what other researchers in other parts of the world have done, somewhat difficult.

Try to identify the theory or group of theories that the study is linked to. A theory is a rational and logical explanation of an event or a phenomenon which has emerged from prolonged and methodical study of that event or phenomenon. A theory also predicts (or at least claims to predict) that if certain circumstances apply, then a certain result will be observed. So *explanation* and *prediction* are the key functions of a good theory. Is the theme of the article linked to a well established theory? Or is it an emerging theory for which as yet there is little evidence? Or indeed is it just the author's own personal theory? All these are acceptable to varying degrees but they must be clearly stated. Does the author also try to analyse what might be problematic about the theory and therefore why further research might strengthen the explanation/prediction and what might in fact undermine it?

In terms of empirical evidence, how much is presented? Is it mainly primary evidence (the author has gone to the original study), or mainly secondary evidence (the author appears to be relying on the interpretation of others). Is the research evidence coherently grouped so that an argument is gradually being built up? Does the review of the literature end with a summary and does the summary match what you have just been reading?

The research questions normally follow the literature review. Ask yourself whether the review, at face value, actually invites those research questions. In other words, given what we know so far, is it a good idea to ask these questions now? Think about the research questions carefully and ask yourself if they are actually stated as questions. You should also consider if there are too many questions or too few given the general direction of the study so far. Sometimes authors present research questions as hypotheses to be tested. This is fine provided it's not just trying to 'dress up' the study as super-scientific when in fact it is not. Hypotheses should only be used instead of research questions if the researcher is trying to test the predictive power of the theory. The hypothesis will be that if X is the condition, then Y will be the result.

At this point the author will normally introduce the research methods used. Ask yourself if the broad thrust of the methods used was quantitative, qualitative or both (see Chapter 3) and whether the methods adopted appear to be appropriate in answering the research questions. Another way to consider the appropriateness of the study design is whether it is a descriptive study, an exploration of relationships or some sort of intervention (again, for further explanation see Chapter 3). The key issue is whether the appropriate design was adopted given what we already know about the theme. Be suspicious of studies where the researcher introduces a treatment for a particular group of learners without some prior knowledge from previous studies which describes the event or the phenomenon in some way, and which has established the possible variables (sometimes called factors) which may be influencing that event or phenomenon. Also ask yourself whether the data was collected at a single point in time or whether it was longitudinal – collected from the same sample of participants over a period of time. Sometimes studies which collect data at a single point in time do so from different age groups (cross-sectional data) and from that try to extrapolate how the younger learners would develop into the older learners. This may not necessarily be the case. Only a longitudinal study using the same learners over time can really tell you this.

Is it clear what the dependent and independent variables are? Are these actually stated as in 'the independent variables for this study was/were. . . .'? It helps if they are stated and you don't have to go rummaging around to find them or infer them from the rest of the method section. Dependent variables are sometimes called 'outcome variables' because these are what the researcher is interested in measuring and finding out how they are influenced by the independent variables. Next ask yourself if the study has controlled for possible confounding variables? The basic idea is that what you are trying to establish is that the only thing that could be influencing the outcome is the independent variable not some other variable that perhaps nobody has thought of. For an example of the problems with variables in research see my chapter in this book on strategic behaviour and success. Hopefully you are still getting green lights coming on at this stage. However, now we come to a major problem in the SLA literature, the sample of participants.

The Introduction to the study should have already told you what the population was that was being studied. Was it adult aid workers with mixed L1s trying to learn a tribal language in the Amazon jungle or young Flemish-speaking children first exposed to English in a classroom in Belgium? Can we assume that they all learn an L2 in the same way? Probably not! Putting sensible boundaries round populations is important, although by no means an easy task. There are often overlaps (although not in the extreme example just cited!) and examples where you might say, 'well why should they be any different'? The important thing is for the researcher to at least ask the question and try to answer it for you. It's important because if the author does not establish the 'population boundaries' then how can you as a reader gauge whether the sample they have chosen represents that population? And if it doesn't represent the population then the findings are not *generalizable*, no matter what the author tries to tell you at the end of the article! Findings don't *have* to be generalizable, but (a) it helps if at least some studies are generalizable and (b) the author should, at least, tell you that they are not seeking to establish generalizability.

OK, so let's be optimistic and assume that the author has told you what the population was and you are satisfied that it makes sense. How did they choose their sample? Our Flemish-speaking Belgian kids amount to maybe over 50,000 *possible* participants (I don't actually have a clue!) and we can't expect the researcher to have surveyed them all. So what 'sampling frame' has the researcher used? How has s/he ensured that the sample takes into account all the possible (sensible) variations in the population. Does the sample include children from various socio-economic backgrounds, from various geographical locations, different school types, equal numbers of boys and girls? Not everyone in that part of Belgium speaks Flemish at home and/or to both parents so that they may not actually be 'Flemish-speaking kids'. All these things have to be considered in the sampling frame. Some things we can discard. We need not have in our sample some children who prefer chocolate ice cream and an equal number who prefer strawberry – at face value that does not seem to make sense! But be very suspicious of researchers who do not tell you how the sample was chosen. Moreover, they should state, at least as a footnote, how permission was obtained from the participants to carry out the research.

If the sample was then divided into more than one group for whatever reason, how was this done, and does the way it was done match the reason for doing it? Did the participants know that they were being divided up and for this reason? Does it matter whether they were told or not? The way that they are divided up is important because usually researchers want to make sure that there isn't in one group a preponderance of different types of participants to the other group. In order to achieve this researchers either use 'randomization' or 'matching'. Space doesn't allow a discussion here of the advantages and disadvantages of these two forms of creating groups but once again, the authors should be telling you their decision-making process.

When it comes to the research instruments used, what you should be looking for is a clear description of how they went about validating them, making sure that they would consistently be getting the answers that match the questions they were asking. In Chapter 3 we provide a critique of the way that a number of tests and tasks are used in the SLA literature with little or no explanation of this piloting or validation process. Ask yourself, moreover, whether enough data was collected to answer the research questions. There is no hard and fast rule here. It is a judgement that you will have to make and some may disagree with you but nevertheless it helps to ask the question.

You should also welcome a brief explanation of how the data collection procedures were carried out to ensure that they were consistently reliable and that, if a different researcher had done it, the procedures would have been exactly the same and not affected the outcomes. The same applies to the way the data was then analysed. If a different researcher (for example you!) were analysing the data would you come up with the same results as the author? So, has there been any 'intra-rating' or 'inter-rating' of the analysis?

Now we come to the reporting of the results. This is often the section where the inexperienced reader of SLA starts to reach for the sedatives. The important thing is that in the results section there should be at least a couple of sentences that tell you what the results actually were and that these are crystal clear. In the case of a quantitative study, the author may feel that they need to tell you all about the different statistical procedures they went through, and indeed many editors and peer reviewers demand this. So if you are not familiar with statistics you will have to search in the murky mathematical waters for at least those sentences which tell you what they found. Once you have these, try, at the very least, to match them to the 'descriptive results' which are usually presented in a table. In that table you should be able to locate the average scores (the Mean) and compare these. Elsewhere in the text you should also look for the significance value represented by the letter '*p*'. A value of less than 0.05 (presented as $p < .05$) will reassure you that the difference between the 'means' was not a chance occurrence but a real difference that is likely to be found in the population. If you have understood the last three sentences then you are well on the way to getting to grips with basic statistics and it should all be plain sailing from now on!

After the results (or 'findings') section there is usually a 'discussion' section. This sometimes blurs into a 'Conclusions'. However, what you should look for in the discussion section is how the author is matching the findings to two things: (a) previous research findings and (b) the theory or theories that they stated they were relating their theme to. It is well worthwhile spending time on this section. It will give you a real flavour of the layers of evidence building up. It is from this section that you should make up your mind about what to do as a result of the findings, *not* from the author's conclusions. The reason is that the conclusions may be biased. The sample may be unrepresentative and the results may be very tentative but the conclusion is sometimes blown up like a giant ageing puff ball. And the thing about ageing puff balls is that if you tread on them their insides are instantly reduced to a powder-like substance. So personally I wouldn't ever go off and change my entire way of teaching or redesign a curriculum merely from reading the conclusions. And if I were a policy maker (which fortunately I am not) I wouldn't impose guidelines or directives on language teachers based only on an author's conclusions.

Which is where we started this section; on the dangers of just reading abstracts and conclusions. I hope I have convinced you to take a little time and look for certain essential features of a study that makes the conclusions trustworthy.

We have taken an initial journey though the SLA landscape. It is now time to let you explore it on your own. I hope that I and my colleagues in this volume have produced an attractive Companion to take with you on that journey of exploration and that you will not only find what you see there interesting but of real practical value for teaching and learning a second language.

Notes

1. Reported in *The Week*, 24 January 2009. Viewer hours are now higher in Spanish than English as a result of viewer interest in 'soaps' broadcast from Columbia and Mexico.
2. By 'we' is meant a team comprising Andrew D. Cohen, Ernesto Macaro, Tor Lindbloom, Sabina R. Cohen, Yuen Yi Lo and Jang Ho Lee.
3. Certificate in English Language Teaching to Adults.

2 A Compendium of Key Concepts in Second Language Acquisition

Ernesto Macaro, Robert Vanderplank and Victoria A. Murphy

Chapter Overview	
Introduction	29
Key Concepts	30

Introduction

In this chapter we build on the overview of SLA areas of interest provided in Chapter 1 by identifying more than 150 key concepts (or 'constructs') that researchers have used in order to attempt to understand language acquisition. These are much more than simple glossary definitions, which we did not believe would be helpful to the reader in a Companion of SLA. Rather we would describe them as brief 'expositions' of a concept which includes not only an attempt at a definition, but possible problems associated with that definition, an elaboration of the opposing positions taken by scholars on the concept, as well as some references that the reader could follow up. These references are kept to a minimum because of space constraints.

Inevitably this is a highly selective list and one which has been governed by our own subjective impressions of what constitutes 'key' or 'essential' for understanding the SLA landscape.

Our original plan was to exclude concepts and terminology which are normally covered in the 'theoretical linguistics' literature, that is where a language or languages are described scientifically, and to only include applied linguistics terms in the sphere of SLA. However, we soon realized that to exclude all terms which describe language would mean that some SLA areas of research would be rendered incomprehensible to the reader. We have therefore included expositions of such concepts as 'phoneme' and attempted to demonstrate how these have been 'applied' in SLA research.

Certain items from the assessment literature have been included. Once again these are highly selective. First we have kept in mind that the book contains a chapter on SLA methodology and secondly we have targeted those assessments and tests which we believe are important to understand in terms of what precisely they are trying to test about L2 competence or performance.

In summary, this compendium has been formed by our intuitions of what we think students and other readers of this book need as more formalized descriptions of second language acquisition constructs.

Key Concepts

Accessibility Hierarchy. The Noun Phrase Accessibility Hierarchy is closely associated with Keenan and Comrie (1977). According to them, all languages that form relative clauses form subject relative clauses; all those that can form direct object relative clauses can also form subject relatives, and so on down the hierarchy. In addition, certain relative clauses will be more difficult to process and to acquire in certain roles; the variation will be both systematic and hierarchical. The Hierarchy predicts universal constraints on the **order of acquisition** of relative clauses by means of an implicational scale which 'expresses the relative accessibility of relativization of NP positions in a simplex main clause' (p. 66).

The ordering of relative clauses in the hierarchy is:

Subject > Direct Object > Indirect Object > Oblique > Genitive > Object of comparison

Subject	That's the woman [who drove away].	The boy [who asked the time] is my brother.
Direct object	That's the woman [I met last week].	The boy [John saw] is my brother.
Indirect object	That's the woman [to whom I gave the parcel].	The boy [who I sent a post-card to] is my cousin.
Oblique	That's the woman [I was complaining about].	The boy [who I was complaining about] is my cousin
Genitive	That's the woman [whose face I recognise].	The boy [whose pet was lost] told me he was sad.
Object of Comparison	That's the woman [I am older than].	The boy [who John is older than] is my cousin.

Researchers such as Gass (1979) have used the accessibility hierarchy to test whether relative clauses in L2 learners' interlanguage are influenced by transfer from L1 or other languages and/or by language universals which are independent of the learners' native languages. Studies testing the claims of the hierarchy have indicated that it is not necessarily applicable to the acquisition of languages such as Cantonese, Japanese and Korean.

Acculturation. In SLA this term is closely associated with John Schumann's acculturation or pidginization model (1978, 1986). In simple terms, SLA is compared to the way in which pidgin languages become more complex as they move towards becoming nativized (i.e., 'native' languages) or becoming creoles and this process is linked to the degree of acculturation of second language learners. Schumann describes acculturation as the social and psychological integration of second language learners with the target language group. Within this model, social adaptation is an integration strategy which involves second language learners' adjustment to the lifestyles and values of the target language group while maintaining their own lifestyle and values for use within their own group. Schumann contends that learners will succeed in second language acquisition only to the extent they acculturate into the group that speaks the target language natively. The closer they feel to the target speech community, the better learners will become 'acculturated' and the more successful their language learning will be. Instruction is set apart from acculturation in this model and is less important in the SLA process than acculturation. Schumann's acculturation model includes seven social variables and four affective variables such as *Congruence*: the more similar the culture of the two groups, the more likely there will be social contact and thus language acquisition; and *Enclosure*: the more the second language learning group shares social institutions such as schools, churches, workplaces and clubs with the target language group, the more favourable the conditions will be for acquiring the target language.

Achievement, in relation to L2 learning, is a term most closely associated with language testing but looks at tested performance through a particular lens. For example it is used in the sense of 'achievement rate', that is the relation between retention of newly encountered words and the amount of time invested. It is also used to describe more generally the progress that learners have made over a period of time (e.g., MacIntyre et al. 2001). Measurements of second language achievement can be operationalized through the exercise of professional judgement, with or without the aid of testing instruments. Although often used synonymously, achievement can be differentiated from 'proficiency' in that the latter does not take into account background information on the learner, does not examine a learner's learning trajectory, nor a learner's rate of progress. Achievement, moreover, is often associated with individual progress against an expected national or local benchmark (e.g., Brindley 1998) and is therefore more often used in recognizable educational contexts than in international measures of performance. For example, a low-achieving language learner may be one who is performing below the expected average for a particular population. The underlying assumption is that a number of educational factors have been controlled for, including the number of years the learner has been learning the language, the number of hours of language learning they have been exposed to and the type of instructional programme they have experienced. Once these factors have been controlled for, researchers may investigate low-achievement on the basis of socio-economic status, or psychological factors. None of these considerations are normally taken into account when measuring language proficiency. Because of the international nature of much of the publications in second language acquisition, achievement is a construct which is under-researched in favour of language proficiency.

Acquisition see **Language Acquisition**.

Acquisition orders is a theory that claims that L2 learners acquire the **morphology** and syntax of the target language in a predictable order and irrespective of their L1. The theory has its origins in L1 research which provided evidence that children acquire certain morphemes before others, for example in English, the progressive '–ing' before the irregular past. The theory adopts, therefore, a **nativist** perspective asserting that certain aspects of language are neurologically pre-programmed in human brains. However, although L2 orders were consistently found in a clutch of 'morpheme studies' (Dulay and Burt 1974) these by no means mapped perfectly onto L1 orders and as a consequence the claim of universality of orders of acquisition was undermined, and the lack of mapping partly attributed to more advanced cognition in L2 learners. Analysis of data in the morpheme studies was criticized for not accounting for **variation** in some of the features observed, for its coarse ranking of elements and for restricting itself to a narrow range of elements which fell short of explaining the acquisition of the entire rule-system. Furthermore, some authors have argued that what was being measured was **performance** accuracy rather than acquired **competence**. The reasons why some features should be acquired before others has remained in dispute with some authors arguing that, rather than complexity or **saliency,** it is the frequency in the input that may affect the order. As a result of this lack of consensus, attention has turned more to **developmental readiness**, that is, how each element is acquired. Examples of features studied are 'questioning' in English (Spada and Lightbown 1999), and 'possessives' in French (Zobl 1985). Evidence of fixed sequences has given credence to a **teachability** hypothesis.

Adaptive Control of Thought Model (ACT*). ACT* (pronounced Act-Star) is a cognitive model (of memory) developed by Anderson (1976, 1983) which attempts to describe how humans store and retrieve knowledge. The model combines ideas related to both how knowledge is represented in memory and how information is processed. **Procedural knowledge** [knowing how to follow different procedural steps to perform an action (i.e., if X then Y)] is encoded in the form of production systems, while **declarative knowledge** [knowing facts about different things (i.e., knowing 'that')] is encoded in the form of highly inter-connected propositional or semantic networks. An experienced driver uses procedural knowledge to brake suddenly when faced with a hazard but uses declarative knowledge to explain how a car's braking system works. A production system is the set of rules which need to be followed in order to perform the action or execute a skill. Procedural skills develop in 3 different stages: cognitive (thinking about explicit rules for implementing a procedure) associative (practising these rules) and autonomous (using the rules automatically). Anderson intended his theory to be sufficiently broad as to provide an overarching theory of the architecture of cognition, and different cognitive processes (memory, language comprehension, reasoning, etc.) are all considered to fall under the same underlying cognitive system. A number of researchers in SLA have used the model to help understand how knowledge of L2 develops and within this view, the development of linguistic skill is considered the development of a complex cognitive skill. Language learning then is considered a form of skill learning that must develop both in terms of developing declarative knowledge of the language, but also in developing automaticity which leads to more fluent language performance. DeKeyser (1997, 2001, 2007) and others (McLaughlin 1987; McLaughlin et al. 1983) have considered L2 learning to be an example of learning a complex cognitive skill. For example, DeKeyser (1997) discusses the development and automatization of L2 grammar skills within the ACT* model.

Affective factors are usually regarded in SLA as being the individual, learner-internal factors such as anxiety, motivation, attitude, interest, value, effort, perceived competence, lack of pressure and sense of belonging which contribute in some way to success in second language learning.

Our understanding of the role of affective factors in SLA was greatly enhanced by the work of David Krathwohl and Benjamin Bloom in the early 1960s (Anderson and Krathwohl 2001; Krathwohl et al. 1964) on taxonomies of educational objectives which illustrated the relationship between factors falling within the cognitive domain (e.g., recall, recognition, understanding, skills of application, analysis and evaluation) and factors falling within the affective domain (e g, receiving, responding, valuing, organizing and characterizing values).

The term 'affective filter' is usually associated with Stephen Krashen and linked to his Monitor Theory (1982). It is often used to describe the 'blockage' caused by negative emotional attitudes (such as anxiety, boredom or low self-esteem) towards learning a second language in general or some particular aspect of learning that language. The 'affective filter hypothesis' asserts that a learner's emotional state acts as an adjustable filter which permits or hinders the language input necessary for acquisition to take place. While the hypothesis remains unproven, the term is much used by teachers and learners to characterize specific individual difficulties in learning a foreign language.

Aptitude is a measurement of a learner's attributes which are claimed to predict the rate of learning and relative ease of learning an L2. These attributes (or components) are phonemic awareness/phonemic coding ability (the capacity to encode unfamiliar sounds for the purpose of retention and processing); sensitivity to grammar (the capacity to identify how words behave in sentences); inductive language learning ability (the capacity to identify patterns in the input and use this information to create new utterances); associative memory (the capacity to form links in memory). These four attributes are measured independently of the language being studied and via decontextualized instruments, the best known of which is the Modern Language Aptitude Test (originally devised by Carroll and Sapon 1959). Aptitude, it is claimed, is stable and not particularly amenable to instruction. Its stability and predictability of success has not endeared the construct to (some) researchers and practitioners alike who see it as an unhelpful obstacle for learners with low aptitude and who are concerned with its use as a language course recruitment criterion. Moreover, some authors have claimed that low aptitude can be countered by high **motivation** (but see Drönyei this volume) and that 'successful learning' is a slippery construct in which environmental factors as well as learner internal factors need to be considered (see Macaro this volume). Thus, recently, aptitude has been examined to determine which instructional methods most correlate with each of the above attributes, to determine which components best predict success with particular task types, and to establish whether successful learners from different age groups draw more on one component than another (i.e., the memory component in young children and the analytical components in adults). These inquiries have led some researchers (Robinson 2002) to propose a much more complex model of aptitude.

Attainment see **Proficiency**.

Attrition. Language attrition refers to the gradual forgetting of a first or second language. It may be distinguished from the term *language shift,* where the focus is on groups of speakers, and from *language loss,* a term applied to the decline of linguistic skills in individuals or speech communities. A common typology for research in attrition (De Bot & Weltens 1995) lists four categories of natural language attrition (rather than pathological conditions such as aphasia):

1. attrition of first language skills (L1) in an L1 environment (e.g., ageing, dialectal loss)
2. attrition of L1 skills in an L2 environment (e.g., fading L1 in migrant populations)
3. attrition of L2 in an L1 environment (e.g., decline in school-learnt L2) or decline in L2 following return to home country (e.g., returning expatriate workers or their children)
4. attrition of L2 skills in an L2 environment (e.g., loss of L2 skills when ageing)

Language attrition is recognized as a normal part of changes in language proficiency over time, as distinct from changes caused by accident or disease. The degree and rate of language attrition may be affected by any or all of the following factors: proficiency, age, attitude, motivation and frequency of language use.

Various hypotheses have been proposed to explain language change during periods of disuse: the Regression Hypothesis maintains that the sequence of language loss is the mirror image of the sequence of acquisition, so that forms acquired late are the most vulnerable to attrition; the Threshold Hypothesis holds that there may be a level of proficiency that, once attained, enables the language learnt to remain fairly stable and resist attrition for some time; the Retrieval Failure Theory and the Savings Paradigm both suggest that language which has been learnt is not lost but is only difficult to retrieve (i.e., forgotten) and in the latter case, may be quickly re-learnt for productive use.

The Audiolingual method of L2 teaching drew from two theoretical sources: structural linguistics (the way that phonological units relate to both grammatical and lexical units, and how these, in turn, can be manipulated in sentences) and **behaviourism**. The objective of the method was the mastery of both the units and their relationship via a process of habit-formation. Through instruction, bad habits (essentially L1-related habits) were eliminated and replaced with good (L2-related) habits. Good habits were encouraged by the repetitive use of a stimulus such as a question from the teacher or a signal on a tape recorder. Reinforcement of accurate productions was encouraged via positive feedback either from the teacher or from recorded repetitions of the correct model (the language laboratory being a device closely associated with the audiolingual method). Incorrect productions received negative feedback. Analysis and creative construction were discouraged in favour of association and analogy. Attempts were made to situate the language models in semi-realistic contexts, oral language was given prominence over written language, and the L1 was almost entirely excluded from the learning process. A typical learning sequence involved: hearing a model sentence (or turn in a dialogue); repeating the model; substituting words or phrases in the model; either the teacher or learners themselves confirming that the substitution was a correct one. 'Audio-visual' has at times been used synonymously with 'audio-lingual' thus empha-sizing the associative nature of the method (i.e., matching a picture with a phrase). The method fell into disfavour less on the basis of research evidence of its ineffectiveness and more because of the theoretical attacks on behaviourism. Elements of the method persist in language pedagogy even today, particularly for the teaching of pronunciation. Indeed, exponents of more nuanced forms of behaviourism would claim that its potential for learning has been misrepresented (see Castagnaro 2006).

Authenticity is a term that has come to be most closely associated with **communicative language teaching**. Authenticity in instructed SLA contexts can be divided into two broad areas: authenticity of materials used, and authen-ticity of the discourse among the class participants. There has been considerable debate about the value of both of these areas. In the case of authentic materials, the definition usually applied is 'text produced by a native speaker for a native speaker reader' where there is no intention to match text difficulty to learners' L2 proficiency level. A criticism of using authentic materials has been that the kinds of tasks devised to aid comprehension of authentic text have, of necessity, tended to be of low cognitive demand. More recently the use of corpora has come to be viewed as authentic text but this too has come in for criticism: 'unfil-tered' examples of words and phrases in use have not yet proved themselves as promoting SLA. Authenticity of discourse has provoked even more debate and a definition of authentic classroom discourse is hard to come by. The argument is centred around whether discourse in an L2 classroom can ever be considered as 'authentic' and that therefore, rather than simulating the outside world (through role plays for example) we should be considering whether the talk encountered is 'authenticated' (Van Lier 1996) by its participants. Authenticity is not in the nature of a piece of text, but rather is the property of a speaker's intention and a hearer's interpretation. This view consolidates earlier positions (e.g., Breen 1985) who considered that the only 'valid language' in the classroom is the language needed to perform everyday classroom tasks.

Automatic Processing see **Declarative Knowledge**.

Autonomy is a construct often associated with and sometimes used synony-mously with independent learning. The main thrust of the concept is that the more a learner is able to learn a language without the direct help or direction of the teacher (1) the better s/he is prepared for lifelong learning of that language and other languages and (2) the more motivated s/he will be to pursue learning. Taking responsibility for one's own learning, and making choices in every area of learning and assessment were key principles in early representations of language learner autonomy (see Holec 1981). However, even supporters of autonomy admit that the term continues to lack precision. Little consensus has been achieved on whether autonomy is an individual learner trait or whether it is a state that manifests itself in reaction to institutional contexts; whether autonomy is a psychological phenomenon that can be nurtured by teachers or whether it is an inevitable product of the socio-cultural situation in which the learners find themselves (see Benson 2001). Most recently, there has been a focus on learner autonomy's interdependence with teacher autonomy (i.c., freedom from institutional and national constraints to develop reflective and experimental practice – see Lamb and Reinders 2008). Despite more than two decades of researcher and practitioner interest in autonomy, the construct has failed to achieve a high status in the research evidence (see its absence from research questions in Chapter 1 Part 1, this volume) and internationally has not made much headway in terms of influencing pedagogy. Some authors argue that this lack of progress is possibly due to the threat autonomy poses to the educational status quo.

Avoidance is a term most often used in the context of **learner strategies** and particularly as a communication strategy in that it is a conscious mental act with a language use goal. There are two basic types of avoidance strategies adopted by learners: avoidance of topic and avoidance of formulations (the choice of certain words, phrases or language structures to express ideas). However the two types can be interrelated. Topic avoidance is usually a result of lack of cultural knowledge required for that topic to be discussed adequately. In that sense it results from a conceptual deficiency. However, it can also result from an L2 speaker's belief that s/he does not have the required language resources to put across an idea that s/he could easily communicate in L1. Scovel (2000) argued that avoidance of certain formulations is likely to occur when a particular linguistic structure in the L2 is very different from that which a speaker has acquired in the L1. Consequently, through avoidance of formulations, very few mistakes are made and for this reason it is difficult to measure instances of avoidance as well as to have a true understanding of the learner's current interlanguage. However, formulation avoidance, when combined with appropriate circumlocution, can be a very effective way of keeping a conversation going, thus possibly attracting input from a native speaker or more proficient L2 learner.

Behaviourism is a psychological theory of learning dominant in the 1950s and 1960s, most closely associated with B. F. Skinner, but originating with Pavlov's well-known *classical conditioning* experiments with dogs. The behaviourist approach attempts to understand learning without reference to the mental processes that may underlie them. Behaviourists feel that in studying learning, the focus should be on the relationship between the environmental input and an organism's behaviour, since this relationship is the only measurable observable relationship. Therefore, an important tenet of Behaviourist theory is that all learnt behaviour is based upon specific stimulus relationships in the environment. Skinner (1957) extended his theory of *Stimulus-Response (S-R) learning* to Language in his book *Verbal Behavior*. This book was heavily criticized by Noam Chomsky (1959) who argued against such an approach, triggering the 'cognitive revolution'. The debate continues as to the relative role of the linguistic environment in language learning, as opposed to more innate and internally driven processes as exemplified by **Universal Grammar**. From a behaviourist approach, L2 learning can be seen as the process of replacing L1 verbal behaviours (learnt from the environment in response to linguistic input, reinforcement and contingencies) with newly learnt L2 behaviours. Lado's (1957) **'Contrastive Analysis Hypothesis'** was influenced by Behaviourism by considering the potential difficulties encountered when replacing L1 behaviours with newly learnt L2 behaviours. The **audiolingual method** is based on some basic precepts of Behaviourism such as providing the correct 'model' (stimulus) for the L2 learner to help them replace their L1 behaviours by *reinforcing* correct linguistic behaviour and correcting incorrect L2 behaviour.

Bilingual education refers to an educational policy whereby primary (and sometimes secondary) school children are educated through more than one language. The National Association for Bilingual Education (NABE) proposes that, in the USA,the term Bilingual Education refers specifically to educating *minority language* children for whom English, the *majority language*, is not the native language, and where the most significant first exposure to the majority language is through schooling. However, bilingual education programmes can be found throughout the world and therefore do not always imply *English Language Learners* (ELLs) or *English as an Additional Language* (EAL) learners. Typical *developmental bilingual education* programmes (in the USA. for example) are developed for *minority language* students where both English and the native language are used for instruction during several primary grades. *Two-way Immersion Programmes* are those where both minority and majority language children are taught in the same class in both the minority L1 and the majority L2 in literacy and more general academic subjects. *Transitional bilingual programmes* are aimed at language minority children where support in both the L1 and majority L2 is offered in the early years of primary education, with the child being *transitioned* into the majority-language only programmes later on. **Immersion** is also a form of bilingual education, but focused towards majority language students where the focus is on academic content delivered in a second language, usually an L2 that has some relevance to the wider community (such as French in Canada). Bilingual education programmes throughout the world differ with respect to how much they support education in both the child's L1 and L2. For example, developmental bilingual programmes typically aim to support full bilingual proficiency and grade-appropriate standards in academic subjects whereas transitional programmes attempt to promote proficiency within the majority L2. Much of the research that has been carried out investigating the relative impact on different bilingual education programmes illustrates that supporting the L1 in bilingual education is important as it is positively related to L2 literacy development and grade-appropriate academic standards (Genesee et al. 2006) among other positive effects.

Bilingualism is the term used to describe the speaking and understanding of more than one language but can also include knowing many languages (also referred to as **multilingualism**). Therefore, a person who is bilingual is someone who speaks at least two languages, though it should be noted that it is rare if not impossible to find perfectly *balanced bilinguals*, where all aspects of linguistic knowledge and performance are equally developed and fluent in both languages. Individuals are therefore, often *dominant* in either one or the other language. Some researchers consider someone with even limited amounts of L2 skill as a bilingual, whereas others only consider individuals who are highly proficient in more than one language as bilingual (see Baker 2006 for a discussion of different definitions). Bilingualism is an over arching construct that has given rise to research in diverse areas including: child language development, educational policy and cognitive neuroscience. From a developmental perspective, researchers are interested in how children, growing up in bilingual communities, learn more than one language at the same time (*simultaneous bilinguals*) a phenomenon also referred to as *bilingual first language acquisition*. From this perspective bilingualism is often differentiated from L2 learning in that the bilingual child is one growing up with two (or more languages) whereas the L2 learner is one who learns and develops knowledge of the L2 after an L1 has become more established. A *sociolinguistic* view of bilingualism is concerned with understanding issues such as language and identity and language choice. Researchers adopting a *psycholinguistic* perspective consider how bilinguals store, represent and process information within multiple languages. Bilingualism can also refer to communities or societies in which multiple languages are spoken (e.g., in Canada, Belgium) and the promotion of bilingualism can therefore be a source of controversy among educational policy makers (see *bilingual education*).

Bottom-up and top-down processing are two terms most often associated with listening and reading. They each refer to the set of cognitive and metacognitive

strategies that learners may be able to deploy when trying to access the meaning of an L2 text. Bottom-up processes include (in alphabetic languages): decoding from phoneme to grapheme (in listening) and from grapheme to phoneme (in reading); whole word recognition; noticing morphemes and/or segmenting words into morphemes; identifying or assembling short phrases in order to analyse them, syntactically and as units of meaning (parsing); translating individual words, collocations and phrases into L1 (perhaps using glossaries or dictionaries); linking pronouns with their referents; linking subordinate clauses with the main clause; noticing textual clues (prosody, punctuation etc.). Thus, bottom-up processes include all text-based resources which the listener/reader appropriates in order to carry out further processing. Top-down processing involves **schema** (see **schema theory**) and script (conventionally recognized sequences of events). A reader or listener will almost inevitably trigger schema and script when the first content word of a text is understood (e.g., 'snow'). As the reading/listening progresses the different schematic subsets *should be* activated, informed by the text-based resources being appropriated (sledge, children, fun [rather than] blizzard, frostbite, despair). In L2 text access, the two processes act in compensatory fashion (resorting to schema in order to compensate for not recognizing words; resorting to careful text analysis in order to compensate for unfamiliarity with the text topic), and confirmatory fashion (using later text information to confirm earlier established predictions of what the text is about). Therefore, an interactive-compensatory model of text access is now generally accepted (Stanovich 1980).

Brainstorming see **Graphic Organizers**.

CALP/BICS (Cognitive Academic Language Proficiency vs Basic Interpersonal Communication Skills). A controversial area of studies in language acquisition usually associated with Jim Cummins (1979). Cummins and others differentiate between the acquisition of language for social purposes (relatively undemanding in cognitive terms) and acquisition for schooling and further education (cognitively much more demanding) particularly in immigrant contexts in Canada and the USA. While acquiring social language for daily interactions may take from six months to two years from time of arrival, acquiring the necessary language proficiency for success in school or further education may take from five to seven years. Teachers may be slow to grasp that fluency in social skills may mask underlying weaknesses in academic language performance. Cummins has argued that there is a common underlying proficiency (CUP) between two languages. It is possible to transfer skills, ideas and concepts which students learn in their first language into the second language. The notion of the CALP/BICS distinction has been attacked on a number of grounds, most notably that it promotes a 'deficit theory' since it attributes the academic failure of bilingual/minority students to low cognitive/academic proficiency rather than to inappropriate schooling. The on-going controversy highlights the absence of consensus regarding the relationship of language proficiency to academic achievement.

Child language is the term used to describe the language young children produce and therefore specifically refers to the language produced by a child who is still developing their native language [or in the case of *bilingual first language acquisition*, developing their knowledge of their first languages]. Child language is distinguishable from adult language in a number of ways. Phonologically, there are a number of sounds that young children find it difficult to articulate (e.g., a child might say *pasghetti* for *spughetti*) as initial consonant clusters are difficult for young children to produce. Child language also contains a variety of morphosyntactic errors. For example, young children typically over-extend their knowledge of rules to forms and produce items such as *goed* or *wented*. Different syntactic structures also characterize child language such as *Why not you coming?* instead of *Why aren't you coming?* Young children also make a number of semantic errors such as over-extending the meaning of specific forms to other related forms. For example, a child might use the form *ball* to refer to a picture of a ball in a book and then use it to mean any round object. *Developmental psycholinguists* are interested in studying the development of child language and have found in a number of different domains predictable stages of acquisition with regard to linguistic knowledge. For example Brown's (1973) corpus illustrated that there was considerable similarity in how young English children learnt about different English grammatical morphemes. Other similar sequences of development have been observed in children learning other linguistic forms. Thus while there may be some idiosyncratic errors that children make, many errors that young children make are indicative of the process of working out the linguistic system and developing native-like linguistic knowledge, a theory that was then adopted by researchers working in SLA (see **acquisition orders**).

Child directed speech (CDS) is the term used to refer to the speech used towards young children by 'caregivers'. CDS is considered the more appropriate term than the originally used term *motherese*. Characteristics of CDS include a slower speech rate, frequent repetitions, phonetic emphasis of content words, high prevalence of question forms and shorter and more simplified utterances. An interest in CDS originated when researchers began trying to understand language development from an *interactionist* point of view. Within this perspective of language learning, researchers have investigated the extent to which CDS is important in guiding the child towards ultimate attainment of their native language, potentially making specific features of language more salient to the child (e.g., by segmenting the speech stream). There is some evidence to support a relationship between CDS and the child's developing linguistic system since research has shown that expansions and extensions are positively correlated with language development. It has been argued that recasts of children's language errors help children to converge on the correct form of their native language (Farrar 1992). However, other researchers have argued that CDS cannot be a vital ingredient in the development of child language since in some respects features of CDS are more complex (e.g., imperatives and questions) (Newport et al. 1977). Moreover, other researchers have argued that not all features of CDS can be found in all languages (Bohannon and Warren-Leubecker 1988), which would be expected if CDS was indeed a driving force underlying successful L1 development.

Chunking is a term which has come from cognitive psychology and mnemonics and refers to our tendency or our ability to recode information in memorable 'chunks' as a means of holding them in long-term memory. Long strings of numbers, for example, may be grouped into easily memorized and recalled units.

In language learning, the terms 'chunks' and 'chunking' are used to refer to the way in which words are often found in groups such as collocations, fixed and semi-fixed expressions and other lexical phrases, for example, 'by all accounts', 'it's a figment of his imagination', 'the findings dealt a mortal blow to his case'. Native speakers hold many such prefabricated chunks in their memories. The Lexical Approach (Lewis 1993, 1997) holds that language fluency and accuracy is achieved largely by retrieving and combining ready-made chunks of language.

Classroom-centred research in language learning is often posited in contrast to 'laboratory-based' SLA research (where participants are extracted and isolated from their normal learning environment) and the issue centres around whether data on the same theme collected in these two diverse settings can be comparable or whether findings in laboratories can be extrapolated to real classroom contexts. The advantage of laboratory studies is that as many confounding variables as possible can be eliminated, thus the situation can be highly 'controlled'. The advantage of classroom-centred research is that it has ecological validity, in that it studies phenomena that occur in the everyday lives of learners with all their complexities both **cognitive** and **affective**. Some theoreticians argue that this 'representativeness' or 'naturalness' is the main validity that classroom-centred research bestows on data, and is more important than generalizability, whether a particular (and usually small) sample can accurately reflect a larger population. An example of research on this issue is in the field of interaction (Gass, Mackey and Ross-Feldman 2005) where the two settings were compared and few differences were found in the interactional outcomes. A more extreme conceptualization of classroom-centred research is one where teachers themselves are considered to be best placed to obtain representative or natural data regarding their learners but this view is countered by notions of participant-researcher bias. Despite the debate at a theoretical level, in SLA there have been few attempts to replicate, in classrooms, studies that have been carried out in laboratory settings in order to compare findings and explore methodologies.

Classroom discourse is the observed interaction between teacher and learners and between learners and learners. It is often claimed to constitute a distinct discourse domain. That is, it contains content features, structural relationships, and rituals which make it distinct from, for example, day-to-day informal conversation or the discourse of interviews. Classroom discourse is of interest to SLA researchers because:

1. the L2 (in broadly **communicative** classrooms) represents both the content of the lesson and the medium through which the content is understood (thus it differs from other subjects on the curriculum);
2. in many contexts teacher input is the main exposure to the L2 that learners receive, thus the interaction represents a unique opportunity for learning;
3. teacher talk often contains the pedagogical intentions of the teacher which may not be obvious to observers or understood by learners (see Seedhouse this volume);
4. classroom discourse is highly complex in that it often operates on several 'planes' and utterances can be directed at any number and combinations of participants in the interaction.

Analysis of classroom discourse has been proposed as a tool for language teacher development. Research has centred on: how teachers modify their speech to make it **comprehensible** (see Chaudron 1988); the use of controlling mechanisms which teachers deploy (e.g., through topic selection and **turn-taking** patterns); the cognitive demands of teacher questions; how communication breakdown is repaired; how teachers provide feedback to learner errors; how learners become socialized via the interaction. These diverse research themes reflect different research traditions adopted and there is disagreement as to which analytical methods best explain the phenomenon – socio-cultural (how interaction shapes society), psycholinguistic (how the interaction leads to learning) or 'neutral-descriptive' (the quantification and classification of talk).

Cloze procedure is a 'method of systematically deleting words from a prose selection and then evaluating the success a reader has in accurately supplying the words deleted' (Robinson 1973, p. 89). Words are deleted from a passage according to a word-count formula (e.g., every fifth word) or various other criteria (e.g., every fifth noun or verb). Readers are then asked to replace the deleted words in the spaces left in the text. Scoring can be exact (only the deleted word is correct) or acceptable (any word which fits is marked correct).

Cloze procedure was originally described by Wilson L. Taylor as a method of measuring the 'readability', or difficulty, of a text (1953) and later (1956) as a measure of reading comprehension for native speakers. Taylor based the cloze procedure on the idea of 'closure', the notion in Gestalt psychology which describes the human capacity to close gaps in a familiar but unfinished pattern. In applied linguistics, cloze tests are now considered as 'reduced redundancy' tests along with **C-tests,** and are based on the assumption that adult educated native speakers of a language can, in general, make use of the redundancy of their language to restore incomplete messages through their knowledge of the rules, patterns and idiom of their own language and culture, while a learner or non-proficient user will be less able to make use of redundancy to complete the message.

Cloze tests are integrative and there is still disagreement on exactly what skills are brought to bear on filling a blank in a cloze test and, thus, exactly what is being measured by cloze tests.

Codeswitching is the practice of alternating between two languages (or dialects) during communication. There are a number of principles underlying this switching although exceptions or violations of these principles have been recorded:

1. it is normally accepted that one language is the dominant language ('matrix language'. Myers-Scotton 1989) and the other the embedded language;
2. that switching can take place intra-sententially or inter-sententially (the latter sometimes known as code-mixing);
3. that the grammar of either language is not violated.

In uninstructed settings codeswitching is considered to be a bilingual competence, not a symptom of language deficiency, and one of a series of communication strategies through which meaning can be expressed. Functions of codeswitching include its use for socio-cultural effect, for establishing social relationships, for signalling utterances on different textual planes, for communicating more precisely a concept not existing in the matrix language, and for using appropriate metalanguage among professionals. Use of codeswitching in formal bilingual classrooms is somewhat contentious and even more so in monolingual foreign language classrooms where it is sometimes considered pejoratively as 'resorting to L1 use' due to its effect of reducing exposure to L2, undermining the communicative orientation of the classroom, and depriving learners of the opportunity to infer meaning. Supporters of codeswitching in instructed settings argue that, on limited occasions, communicative tasks can be advanced via judicious teacher codeswitching, and learning can be enhanced by making reference to the learner's L1. They posit, moreover, that SLA instruction should be concerned with creating bilinguals not emulating native speakers, and that to prohibit learners from using their own L1 can be a form of linguistic imperialism. Researchers are currently trying to establish a series of principles for judicious use of codeswitching (or 'optimal' use – see Macaro 2005) which might inform practice.

Cognitive psychology is the study of human behaviour and processes which includes investigating how people perceive, learn, remember and think. Issues of attention and consciousness, how knowledge is represented in the human mind, how humans process information, how memory is organized, how people reason and make decisions and solve problems are all areas that fall within the broader discipline of Cognitive Psychology. Cognitive Psychology is therefore a highly inter-disciplinary domain which draws from research and literature in psychology, neuroscience, linguistics, computer science and biology (among others). An important sub-domain within Cognitive Psychology is language, and questions on how language is learnt, how knowledge of language is represented and retrieved from memory, how language is produced and understood are prominent issues in Cognitive Psychology. Therefore, theories within the study of both first and second language learning and processing draw heavily from key issues within Cognitive Psychology. Robinson (2001) is but one example of a volume which identifies and discusses how various issues within Cognitive Psychology such as memory, attention and automaticity can shed insights on how second languages are learnt, and the implications these findings have for L2 teaching.

Cognitive style is a term more often found in educational literature than in SLA but is equally situated in the more general field of **cognitive psychology**. It refers to an individual's preferred or habitual approach to processing information and by extrapolation, to the different ways they learn. There has been a plethora of different proposals for ways of classifying the different cognitive styles, from simple (or bipolar) to highly complex (or multi-dimensional). For example, a bipolar explanation of cognitive styles is the difference between **field-dependent** and field-independent individuals where the latter are more able to distinguish between figures in the foreground of a picture from its background. Well-known multi-dimensional models having complex inter-relationships have been proposed by, for example, Riding (see Riding and Sadler-Smith 1992) (e.g., verbalizer/visualizer; analytical/holistic). It is perhaps the last of these explanations of cognitive style differences that has been the most favoured by SLA researchers. For example Littlemore (2001) investigated the relationship between communication strategies (see **language learner strategies**) preferred by L2 learners and their styles on the holistic/analytical dimension. As well as some doubts about the psychometric reliability of some of the instruments developed from these theories, concern has been expressed about how they could be and have been adopted in language teaching practice. For example, Multiple Intelligences Theory (Gardner 1993), where 'intelligences' are posited as similar to cognitive styles, has led to a practitioner and policy maker view that every lesson should contain something visual, something auditory and something kinaesthetic, in order to 'cater' for each individual's cognitive style, a trivialization of the theory that Gardner himself now, apparently, rejects.

Coherence. Henry Widdowson provides the clearest and most practical explanations of coherence and cohesion in his book *Teaching Language as Communication* (1978). In his terms, text has cohesion while discourse has coherence. In other words, for a string of words to be regarded as a text it must have surface syntactic and semantic markers (such as pronouns) providing anaphoric or cataphoric reference linking the words, phrases, sentences and paragraphs.

Discourse, on the other hand, (both written and spoken) may show a complete absence of cohesion and have no surface linking elements but may still be perfectly comprehensible to readers or interlocutors as in Patricia Carrell's (1982, p. 484) example:

The picnic was ruined. No one remembered to bring a corkscrew.

The underlying relationship between the two sentences which is one of causality is not reflected in the surface structure of the text. There are no **cohesive** markers to link the two sentences which are coherent as the shared background information or 'mutually accessible concepts and relations which underlie the surface text' (de Beaugrande and Dressler 1981, p. 4) make it easy to understand what is meant.

Widdowson explains our ability to understand discourse in terms of the illocutionary (unspoken) act or value in a speaker's utterances or writer's sentence. Thus, when a speaker says 'It's cold in here', on the surface a statement about how a room or other place feels to the speaker, it may contain the unspoken request to close a window or switch on the heating. The illocutionary force is in this case one of a polite request. In both speech and writing, illocutionary acts in discourse may often give rise to ambiguity.

Cohesion see **Coherence**.

Communicative competence was a term first used in the late 1960s (e.g., by Hymes 1972) but perhaps is most associated with a seminal paper by Canale and Swain (1980). Communicative competence is the knowledge that native speakers have acquired which enables them to interact *effectively* with one another. Thus it is in relative juxtaposition with Chomsky's original concept of competence where the focus was on an idealized native speaker's knowledge of grammar in a single homogeneous linguistic community. In Canale and Swain's account, grammatical knowledge is conceptualized as evidence of having sufficiently acquired the rule-system of the language for the purpose of use – i.e. grammatical competence. Other competences in their model were 'sociolinguistic competence', the knowledge of how a language is linked to the cultural conventions of a particular speech community, and 'strategic competence' (see also **language learner strategies**), how linguistic resources are maximized in order to facilitate communication. Thus communicative competence became a framework in which to develop a notion of L2 proficiency. However, both the framework and the notion of proficiency were, albeit implicitly, modelled on the native speaker. Native speaker-likeness remained the ultimate goal for all L2 learners. It is now argued that native speaker-likeness lacks the '**intercultural communicative competence**' dimension, one which does not ignore the social identity and cultural competence of the learner. Nevertheless, the communicative competence framework has consistently been used as a basis for assessing the communicative orientation of classroom pedagogy and for language testing.

Communicative language teaching developed in the 1970s from work (by David Wilkins 1976, for example) on communicative **functions** (e.g., asking the time, giving directions, making polite requests) and grammatical **notions** (e.g., time, definiteness, reference) and ESP (English for Specific Purposes). It was an approach to language teaching distinct from methods being used at this time such as grammar-translation, structural language teaching, the audio-lingual method or the audio-visual method. The goal of **communicative competence** is often said to underlie the communicative approach to language teaching.

At the heart of CLT is the idea that we learn a foreign or second language in order to be able to communicate with others. Learners need to be engaged in the pragmatic, functional use of language for meaningful purposes in addition to gaining grammatical or linguistic competence. Therefore the CLT classroom tries to simulate the outside environment by adopting negotiation of meaning, information gap activities, role-play, language games and authentic materials. Fluency and accuracy are viewed as complementary. As in the earlier Direct Method, CLT tries to avoid the use of the L1 as a means of language comparison.

In the 1980s, proponents of communicative language teaching tended to divide into two camps: those who focused entirely on learning to communicate through interaction in the target language (e.g., the Natural Approach) with little or no explanation of grammar, and those who continued to advocate the explicit presentation of language structures (often in terms of notions and functions which mapped onto-morpho-syntactic structures) during a 'pre-communicative' phase of teaching (e.g., Brumfit and Johnson 1979; Littlewood 1981).

Competence refers to an individual's knowledge of language, irrespective of whether that knowledge is explicit or implicit, which allows them to produce, and distinguish the difference between, grammatical and ungrammatical forms. **Performance** refers to the individual's actual language use. For example, a mature speaker of a language (e.g., English) might make an error and produce an utterance such as '*I will be home yesterday*'. The adult speaker of English who makes this error knows that this constitutes an ill-formed utterance, and can easily recognize it as such. However, *performance* errors like these are fairly common in adult speech and can result from higher levels of stress, fatigue and/or lapses of attention and memory, for example. While many researchers both within L1 and L2 research (see **interlanguage** in the case of L2), are interested in understanding the nature of a learner's underlying competence, all language behaviour is ultimately performance, and therefore a tension exists between measures of linguistic knowledge (i.e., competence) which necessarily have to rely on human behaviour (i.e., performance). Researchers interested in understanding linguistic competence need to be diligent therefore to use measures which minimize performance errors.

(The) Competition model (CM) is a theoretical framework, developed by MacWhinney (1987; Bates and MacWhinney 1987) for understanding both first (L1) and second (L2) language learning. A fundamental assumption about the model is that language is learnt through the relationship between the linguistic input/environment and the cognitive processes inherent in all humans (e.g., attention, memory, etc.). Language learning within the view of the CM is therefore driven by the input and not by a set of pre-specified internal linguistic constraints as in **universal grammar**. Learners have to detect linguistic 'cues' which are distributed within the linguistic input and by detecting these cues will be able to learn language. Whether the cues are reliable, consistent and available in the input will influence the probability that different linguistic form-function mappings will be learnt. An example of an important cue is 'agent identification' i.e., who is doing the action expressed in an utterance. In the sentence '*The boy is annoying the parrots*' there are a number of different cues available which signal who the agent of the action is: (1) in the Noun Phrase (NP), 'the boy' is placed before the verb, (2) the verb agreement between 'is' and 'the boy', (3) the sentence initial position of the NP 'the boy' and (4) the use of the article 'the'. All of these cues work together to signal to the language learner that the agent of the action is 'the boy'. The 'competition' in the CM comes from the fact that there is a competition between which NP, in the sentence ('the boy' or 'the parrots') will 'win' at being identified as the agent. This view of language learning therefore relies heavily on specific features of the input and therefore learning different languages with different cues and cue reliability will have to follow different developmental paths.

Comprehensible input is a term most closely associated with Krashen (1985) who proposed the 'comprehensible input hypothesis' (CIH) which claimed that new grammatical or lexical elements in the input (from the teacher or other sources) would be subconsciously acquired by the L2 learner provided s/he could understand the *meaning* they conveyed. Understanding unknown items was dependent on the learner being able to infer their meaning from the context – a notion formulated as 'i + 1' (current knowledge/**competence** + the new item). CIH therefore predicts acquisition (i.e., moving beyond current competence) simply by listening and understanding and only (and additionally) requiring a low **affective filter** in the hearer. Krashen claimed that the learner's *output* is a result of acquisition. It does not lead to acquisition. The hypothesis was predicated on **nativist** theory and on L1 development, claiming evidence for a similar silent period, similar **acquisition orders,** and similarly using the **language acquisition device.** That comprehensible input predicted acquisition was highly attractive to some theorists and many practitioners, avoiding the need for **explicit** grammar teaching or repetitive drilling, making reference to the learner's L1 unnecessary, and providing further theoretical support for **communicative language teaching**. It led to researcher and practitioner interest in teacher input modification as a way of facilitating comprehensible input. CIH has been widely and persistently attacked by theorists for its ill-defined terms, lack of rigorous empirical evidence, circularity of argument (McLaughlin 1987), and with counter evidence (from immersion programmes) that aspects of grammar are difficult to acquire subconsciously. Moreover, for practitioners in input poor environments, a theory of acquisition which placed so much importance on input was difficult to accept.

Computer assisted language learning (CALL) is an area of research that has been undertaken to describe the ways that computers can provide additional individualized learning, allowing learners to control the pace of their learning. It also permits individual learners to interact with the computer such that they can obtain feedback on their understanding of language or their productions of language. Many other similar terms have been used such as Technology Enhanced Language Learning and Computer Accelerated Language Instruction. CALL software can be 'stand alone' as in individual CDrom packages, supplements to textbooks, and internet-based software which can be regularly updated by the designers.

CALL (see ReCALL journal) can be differentiated from Computer Mediated Communication in that the latter is an umbrella term for any kind of software which facilitates L2 interaction between volunteer participants. Critics of CALL have pointed to its fragmented approach to language learning and an over-emphasis on consolidation of language knowledge rather than skills. CALL supporters have argued that the virtual environments that it creates are motivating, simulate real-world situations and develop critical thinking skills. Although proponents of CALL have rarely seen it as a substitute for face to face but rather complementary to it, there is still insufficient quality research which has established its long-term benefits.

ReCall Journal is a publication of the European Association for Computer-Assisted Language Learning (ISSN 0958-3440).

Connectionism. Developments in neuroscience have shown that the brain consists of billions of neurons which are inter-connected and which excite and inhibit each other. Language learning, like all **cognitive** processes, must *emerge* from an interaction between processing in the brain (with its neural architecture), and the environment. Connectionist models, therefore, are an attempt to model learning within a network which in essence is a metaphor for the human brain. It must be noted, however, that connectionist models do not even begin to approximate the complexity of the neural architecture of the human brain. An assumption underlying connectionist models and investigations of learning within these systems is that a greater understanding of both (i) learning mechanisms responsible for (language) learning, and (ii) the relevant contribution of different input factors, will emerge from carrying out research within connectionist architectures. Indeed there have been a number of models which have investigated the acquisition of morphology, phonological rules, novel word repetition, prosody and semantic and syntactic structure (see Plunkett 1998). These models have shown that even very crude models of how the brain might work can extract patterns out of the input and demonstrate a kind of rule-like behaviour, even without rules as such being a part of the system. Researchers have suggested that these findings are indicative that traditional models of how language knowledge is learnt, ones that rely on rule-abstraction and rule-representation, may not be the most plausible, nor indeed accurate, accounts. Importantly, connectionist modelling allows researchers to investigate the kind of representations or 'knowledge' which develops as a function of experience with the input. As connectionist models are ultimately complex computer-based models, researchers can manipulate the input (e.g., the frequency of occurrence of different items) in a highly controlled manner that is not possible in research with human beings. Connectionist models have also attracted the attention of SLA researchers interested in trying to explain these important underlying cognitive mechanisms responsible for language learning (e.g., Ellis 2001). [Note: connectionist models are also referred to as *artificial neural network* models.]

Constructivism is a theory of knowledge (epistemology) concerned with how humans come to understand the world (Kelly 1955) and differentiate between justified belief and opinion. It is often regarded as the opposite of positivism (see Chapter 3 this volume for a lengthier explanation), and proposes that reality only exists as seen through the filter or lens of the human mind operating both individually and collectively. Aside from the way in which learners 'construe' their learning or learning environment, its application to SLA has been principally in the area of construing the L2 rule-system. In a sense this reflects the explicit/implicit divide where a positivist view of grammar would be that rules exist as 'realities external to the human mind'. A constructivist account, on the other hand, would propose that rules only exist as 'creations of human minds' interacting with one another. Constructivism has at times been related (see Larsen-Freeman 1997) to chaos-complexity theory (how order gradually emerges, via non-linear processes, from disorder). A specific example of a constructivist perspective of grammar learning is given by Blyth (1997) with respect to the very complex (not to say chaotic) rules governing 'aspect', where he proposes that only through a learner experiencing the input which contains information and exemplars of aspect can they begin to construe an understanding of the phenomenon of aspect and thus incorporate it into their interlanguage.

Content-based instruction (CBI) in second or foreign language learning contexts focuses on the subject matter to be learnt rather than on the form of the language. The rationale behind CBI is that natural language acquisition takes place in context and CBI provides a context in which meaningful language can be acquired; students learn best when there is an emphasis on relevant, meaningful content rather than on the language itself (e.g., Met 1991; Spada and Lightbown 1993).

For example, while core subjects such as Maths may be taught in the learners' first language, other subjects such as Geography may be taught through the second/foreign language. CBI has links with such approaches as 'languages across the curriculum' which emphasizes the integration of language learning within the wider curriculum, especially in foreign language contexts. CBI may also be seen as a continuum from immersion, where the focus is entirely on the content, to classes where the focus is on language practice but there is substantial topic- or subject-specific content. Research has suggested that CBI has some limitations for language learners unless it is complemented by teaching which focuses on language form, especially for lower-level learners.

Different models of CBI are applied in different learning contexts. For example, the so-called theme-based model is often found in EFL settings, where language can be taught through a topic or series of topics. 'Sheltered' and 'adjunct' models are regarded as suitable for learners who are more proficient in the target language. In the 'sheltered' model, a class may be team-taught by a specialist in the subject together with a language teacher. In the 'adjunct' model, language preparation classes are given which focus on the needs of learners in terms of specific language and vocabulary, such as the language needed to follow lectures in science subjects.

Context see **Schema Theory**.

Contrastive analysis (CA) is the systematic comparison of two languages or two linguistic systems. The Contrastive Analysis Hypothesis (Lado 1957) was developed as an attempt to apply structural linguistics to language teaching. The main assumptions behind this hypothesis were that difficulties in learning a second language come from interference from the first, and importantly, that these difficulties can be predicted by systematically different comparing the structural properties of the two languages. Where languages are more distinct and different from each other, the more interference (*negative transfer*) would arise and thus make learning the L2 form more difficult. However, where the two languages were similar, *positive transfer* would result and thus the L2 form was predicted to be easier to learn. These assumptions led to a *hierarchy of difficulty* which is an attempt to formalize the predictions of contrastive analysis. One of the most cited examples compares English and Spanish (Stockwell et al. 1965) as follows:

Correspondence	x = x	'-ing' = '-ndo'
Coalescence	x and y = x	'His/her' realized as 'su'
Absence	x = 0	'do' as a tense carrier
New	0 = x	marking for grammatical gender
Split	x = x and y	For = 'por' or 'para'

The predicted easiest learnt features are those which *correspond* while the most difficult are those which are *split*. CA fell out of favour as it failed to predict all errors that L2 learners make, and sometimes predicted errors which L2 learners do not tend to make. Weaker versions of the CA led to **Error Analysis** where learners' errors are analysed with a view to identifying whether the source of the error can be attributed to L1 interference.

Conversation analysis is usually considered a research methodology rather than a concept in SLA (see Markee 2000; see also Seedhouse, this volume), a methodology which approaches SLA events as being on-line, contextualized and socially constructed phenomena. In that respect it has an affinity with social-**constructivism**. Conversation Analysis explores utterances and turn-taking patterns in great detail, taking care not to disregard possible important information including non-verbal information relating these data to the possible intentions of participants. It is distinguished from its **discourse analysis** counterpart which eschews the socio-cultural dimension when examining classroom language. Conversation analysis has been used effectively in language teacher education settings where aspects of their interaction (e.g., turn-taking, discourse control and pragmatic content) are analysed by teachers seeking to improve their practice. In that sense conversation analysis is at the intersection of SLA research and language teaching pedagogy and is considered by some as more than simply a research method (Mori 2001).

Corpus Linguistics. The aim of corpus linguistics is to establish a path between large quantities of naturally occurring samples of spoken and written language and a theory of language. In this endeavour it runs counter to the belief that there exists an idealized perfect language but rather that the rules governing a language are generated by the speech communities that use it. Once a corpus of language has been collected it can be annotated according to some sort of scheme.

Perhaps its best-known use is in the compilation of dictionaries; for example The Collins COBUILD dictionary was designed and compiled using the Bank of English Corpus (the University of Birmingham allows access to the corpus). However, analysis of large corpora of language in use is increasingly being promoted as a tool for teaching and learning a second language (McEnery et al. 2006). Lexical frequency lists, uses of collocations and idiom, and even nuances of grammar can all be exploited by teachers through the use of corpora.

Use of corpora in second language teaching has been criticized in that it gives the impression that only **authentic** language (i.e., that spoken by native speakers) should be taught in the classroom whereas some would argue (see Seidlhofer 2003 for an extensive review of the controversy) that what should be taught is language that engages the learners and allows them to learn from it and this may not necessarily be authentic language.

Creative Construct Hypothesis. This term is used to describe how learners, particularly younger learners, use subconscious processes in order to acquire a second language (Dulay and Burt 1974; for a critical discussion see Sharwood-Smith 1994). The hypothesis posits that acquisition occurs through the same processes as L1 acquisition in that the learner's innate internal mechanisms are ready to select only that information from the input which they need to further develop their competence in the rule-system. Learners analyse from what they already know about the target language plus new input and construct a creative idea as to its morphosyntax. The hypothesis differs from **interlanguage** theory in that there is no claim that learners have systematic intermediate grammars in their heads and in that there is a denial of any L1 **transfer** in performance errors. In this creative construct process the internal representations of the target language rule-system are 'weak' in the sense that they lack sufficient positive input data and this leads to the formulation of creative errors such as 'I broked the cup'. Because the creative construct process is independent of the learners' L1, patterns of development are common to all learners of a particular target language irrespective of their first language background. The notion of creative construction was the theoretical impulse for the **morpheme studies**. A pedagogical implication of the hypothesis is that an externally imposed curriculum of grammar learning will interfere with this creative construct process and either derail the learning or result in no real learning at all.

(The) Critical period hypothesis (CPH) is a theory of development that stipulates that for a specific behaviour to develop, the organism must be exposed to the relevant input within a specific and definable time frame. It is a construct often discussed in the L1 and L2 literature as a potential explanation for why older learners have more apparent difficulty learning a (second) language than younger learners. For example, Herschensohn (2007) notes that late L1 (after 5 years old) seems to be 'incomplete' with increasing 'incompleteness with increases in Age of Acquisition (AofA)'. CPH was first related to language development by Penfield and Roberts (1959) and later by Lenneberg (1967) who argued that the human brain loses its capacity for language learning as maturation proceeds. Penfield and Roberts (1959) argued that after the age of nine the human brain becomes 'progressively stiff' while Lenneberg (1967) argued that the critical period for language learning was between the ages of 2 years and puberty, a period of time which corresponds to when brain function becomes associated with specific brain regions (lateralization). Singleton (2007) has demonstrated that there are many different versions of the CPH and many disagreements in both the L1 and L2 literature concerning whether it is applicable either to L1 or L2 development, and when the onset and the offset of the 'critical period' might be for different aspects of linguistic knowledge. The term **sensitive period** has often been used in lieu of CPH to accommodate the idea that unlike other animal learning paradigms, human language development (either L1 or L2) does not seem to be subject to such a tightly defined time frame but rather suggests a time frame where the effects of a particular stimulus (i.e., linguistic environment) on behaviour (i.e., learning) are particularly strong.

Cross-linguistic. The basic definition of 'cross-linguistic' is limited to statements such as 'relating to different languages'. In the SLA literature, cross-linguistic is often to be found as the preferred term (over contrastive analysis or contrastive linguistics, for example) where concepts and theories of second language acquisition are tested in a variety of languages (hence 'across languages') in order to provide models which are valid in broad environments, both monolingual and multilingual.

The term first came to prominence in studies of child language development with cross-linguistic (rather than cross-cultural) comparisons carried out by researchers such as Slobin in the 1970s and 1980s (e.g., 1985). In studies of children learning a wide variety of languages, data were used to formulate and test theories about how children acquire different languages and how difficulties in acquisition are related to differences in the languages being learnt.

The term 'cross-linguistic influence' also came into use in the 1980s in part to replace the somewhat stigmatized term 'interference' (owing to its association with **behaviourism** and **audio-lingualism**) to describe the influence of first or other previously learnt languages on the target language to be learnt. It is often used synonymously with 'language transfer' and 'language mixing', so we may talk about positive and negative transfer under cross-linguistic influence when discussing, for example, language learners' errors.

The C-Test, developed by Ulrich Raatz and Christine Klein-Braley, was presented in 1981 as a means of overcoming weaknesses which had been identified in **cloze tests,** notably the variability in validity and reliability. Like cloze tests, the C-Test is an integrative written test of general language proficiency based on the principle of reduced redundancy, that is, that speakers of a language are able to supply missing linguistics items or understand well enough without them (e.g., in the presence of noise or other interference).

A C-Test consists of five to six short authentic texts to provide variety. Each text should be complete in itself. The first sentence of each text is unmodified. Then the 'rule of two' is applied: beginning at word two in sentence two the second half of every second word is deleted. In a word with an odd number of letters, the bigger part is omitted. One letter words are ignored. Numbers and proper names are usually left without deletions, but otherwise the deletion is an entirely mechanical process until about 100 items are produced. The text is then allowed to run on to its natural conclusion. Texts are arranged in order of difficulty with the easiest text first. Only exact scoring is used.

Native speakers should score 90% or higher. If native speakers cannot make scores higher than 90%, then the text should not be used for non-native speakers.

The C-Test has been shown to be a strong predictor of overall second/foreign language proficiency (Babaii and Ansary 2001; Raatz and Klein-Braley 1998).

As with other integrative tests such as cloze, it has been criticized for its poor construct validity in that it is not clear which skills are being tested.

<u>**Declarative knowledge**</u> is one of the types of knowledge described in Anderson's (1983) **ACT* model** of memory. Declarative knowledge consists of knowing 'that', that is, knowing about different facts and events. For example, knowing that London is the capital of the United Kingdom is an example of declarative knowledge. Declarative knowledge also includes *episodic* and *semantic* knowledge. Episodic knowledge is declarative knowledge about events. For example, information about who you were with or what you were doing during an event (e.g., a birthday party) would be considered episodic knowledge. Semantic knowledge is knowledge about the world, such as knowing that grass is green or that there are 12 months in each calendar year. Declarative knowledge is contrasted against **procedural knowledge** which is the second component in Anderson's ACT* model, and which is knowing 'how to do something'. For example, knowing how to drive a car would be an example of procedural knowledge. Both types of knowledge are integral to Anderson's ACT* model. Within the field of SLA a number of researchers have considered L2 knowledge within the framework of the ACT* model and declarative and procedural knowledge.

<u>**Decoding**</u> is literally to convert information from one format to another. For example, to convert body language into verbal language, or a cryptic message into an intelligible one. In second language acquisition research it is most commonly used to refer to the relationship between the written form of the language and the spoken form: in English, between the grapheme and its phonemic representation; in Chinese, between the written character and both its spoken syllabic and tonal representations. There is considerable evidence that second language learning is linked to first language phonological-orthographic ability (Meschhyan and Hernandez 2002), at least at beginner and lower-intermediate level, and that even advanced L2 speakers use different decoding strategies at the word level from native speakers (Zuckernick 1996). A related term is encoding which technically means converting information into some sort of code for someone else to decode. However, the two terms in SLA are sometimes used to suggest a difference in the conversion process between receptive conversion (decoding for understanding) and productive conversion (encoding an idea into a word or phrase).

<u>**Developmental readiness**</u> is a concept which forms part of the larger theory of **processability** which attempts to predict which grammatical structures are able to be processed by a learner at a certain stage in his/her development. It has its origins also in **acquisition orders**. Its main thesis is that a learner's L1 may

inhibit the acquisition of certain L2 structures. As a consequence the brain will not be 'ready' to acquire a structure until sufficient exposure to **input** (both positive and negative) has occurred. However, certain complex structures (such as question forms in English or negatives in German) may be acquired in stages with each stage requiring the learner to be 'ready' for the next stage. For example, in the case of English questions the following stages were identified and the notion of readiness to move up a stage was noted (Mackey and Philp 1998):

1. single words or fragments (without verb): 'spot on the dog'?
2. SVO with rising intonation: 'a boy throw ball'?
3. Fronting: 'do the boy is beside the bus'?
4. Wh- with copula; yes/no questions with auxiliary inversion: 'where is the space ship'?; 'Is there a dog on the bus'?
5. Wh- with auxiliary second: 'what is the boy throwing?'

Spada and Lightbown (1999), however, argued that counter-evidence to the need for readiness may be found in a learner's ability to subsume earlier stages of a sequence if s/he is exposed to sufficient later (more difficult) stages of that sequence.

What 'readiness' may mean in psychological or biological terms remains open to question and the practical applications of developmental readiness may only be evident with very small classes where individual differentiation may be achievable.

Dialect usually applies to the vocabulary, grammar and pronunciation characteristic of specific geographic localities or social classes. Traditionally, dialects have been regarded as variations from a 'standard' form of the language. However, it is often the case that standard forms are themselves dialects which have come to predominate for social and political reasons. The study of variations between different dialects is known as *dialectology*.

The German-Dutch speech community provides an interesting example of how dialects may form a continuum in which adjacent dialects are mutually intelligible, while those which are not in contact may be mutually unintelligible. Adjacent dialects tend to differ more in pronunciation than in grammar or vocabulary.

Diglossia is a very useful term for describing the linguistic situation in countries or regions where two forms of the same language or even two languages are used for different social and economic purposes. The term is used to distinguish a functional bilingualism which applies to a society from individual bilingualism (Ferguson 1959). Ferguson identified languages as falling into the H category (having high prestige) and L category (having low prestige).

Examples of diglossic situations include the use of Swiss German dialects and Standard German in Switzerland and the use of regional dialects alongside Standard Italian in Italy. Local or regional dialects tend to be low prestige, restricted to local and family spoken use, while Standard forms having high prestige, being used for official and other formal documents for public speaking, sermons, political broadcasts, etc.

In terms of language acquisition, children in diglossic situations may encounter reading difficulties. For example, in some Arabic-speaking countries, the local dialect and literary Arabic, and the language of school books and instruction, differ greatly.

(The) Direct method as an approach to language teaching grew out of a reaction to formal grammar-translation teaching towards the end of the nineteenth century. Its originality lay in the proposal that speaking and listening should be at the heart of language learning. It is usually associated with linguists and phoneticians such as François Gouin, Paul Passy and Wilhelm Viëtor. It was most famously applied in the language schools of Maximilian Berlitz , where Direct Method also implied no L1 use in the classroom, with communication through mime and gesture if necessary to introduce new vocabulary.

Its two fundamental tenets were that the learner should be isolated as much as possible from his/her L1 and that the act of speaking rather than written text should be central to learning. Typical classroom activities were repetition, oral drills, intensive sequences of questions and answer around a visual stimulus and corrective feedback focusing on developing accuracy of pronunciation and grammar. The Direct Method can only be considered a pseudo-communicative method because the interaction used full sentences not utterances and the teacher knew what the student was going to answer (in fact directing the student to a particular sentence response). Moreover, the syllabus was organized structurally, not around the functions of language (see **communicative language teaching**).

The five principles of the Direct Method are good pronunciation, oral work, inductive teaching of grammar, real reading and realia. Reading and writing were delayed until speaking and listening were established, mirroring the L1 acquisition process. Indeed, the model of the foreign language learning in the Direct Method was that of first language acquisition.

Many of the techniques found in the Direct Method were adopted by the audio-lingual method in the late 1940s and 1950s and certain aspects of Communicative Language Teaching share much in common with Direct Method.

Discourse Analysis. While both 'discourse' and 'discourse analysis' have a wide range of different meanings to scholars in different fields (see, for example,

Schiffrin, Tannen and Hamilton 2003, p. 1), in SLA, discourse analysis (DA) has tended to mean the study of language in use. DA is important in SLA because, in some respects, **communicative language teaching** was built on the increased awareness of what people actually said in communication in different domains, as highlighted by pioneering work in fledging discourse analysis in the 1970s in such diverse fields as doctor-patient interaction, classroom talk, business negotiation and service encounters. The choice of the word 'discourse' is significant, signalling that what is being analysed is beyond the word or sentence and involves context, shared knowledge between interlocutors, assumptions, intended meaning and interpretations.

Discourse markers (DMs), sometimes called 'discourse connectives', are lexical expressions in speech and writing such as 'so', 'then', 'nevertheless', 'moreover', 'therefore', 'however', 'in conclusion' . Deborah Schiffrin (1987, p. 328) describes them as 'sequentially dependent elements that bracket units of talk'. In her terms, they have a **coherence**-building function at the local level. They also have to be syntactically detachable from the sentence in which they occur, be commonly used in the initial position of a sentence or utterance, have a range of prosodic contours, be able to operate at both local and global levels of discourse and be able to operate on different planes of discourse.

Bruce Fraser (1999), refining Schiffrin's definition, describes DMs as being drawn from three syntactic classes: conjunction, adverbs and prepositional phrases. A DM relates different parts of a discourse together but does not contribute to their propositional meaning and could be deleted without altering the propositional content. Fraser (1999, p. 944) gives the following example:

a. I want to go to the movies tonight. **After all**, it's my birthday.
b. John will try to come on time. **All the same**, he is going to be reprimanded.
c. A: Harry is quite tall. B: **In contrast**, George is quite short.

In addition, DMs have a procedural meaning rather than a conceptual meaning: they signal how the sentence or utterance which they introduce is to be interpreted in the light of what has been written or said prior to it. While each DM has a core meaning, the interpretation of the DM depends on both the linguistic and conceptual context.

Within SLA, DMs have often been treated as 'gambits'. Müller's (2005) work sheds light on the relevance of DM research for SLA in the context of German speakers learning to use 'so', 'well', 'you know' and 'like'.

English as an additional language (EAL) is a term typically used to identify school-aged students who come from a home linguistic background that is not English but who are being educated in English schools (i.e., in communities where English is the language spoken and used by the majority of the population). The term EAL is analogous to the term 'English Language Learners' (ELLs) which is the term used in North America. EAL learners typically tend to be a heterogeneous group, coming from a range of different language backgrounds, cultures and socio-economic status bands. While some EAL learners go on to excel academically and become highly proficient in their two languages (home language and English), on the whole, EAL children tend to lag behind their native English-speaking peers on a range of academic and linguistic achievements. A range of factors have been identified as contributing to the success EAL (ELL) students have at both learning English and achieving expected-level performance on academic outcomes. These variables include the level of literacy development in the home language, and the level of education and socio-economic status of the caregivers (parents) of the EAL (ELL) child. Additionally, the quality of the educational experience and the kind of educational programme the EAL (ELL) child receives has also been shown to play a significant role in how successfully the EAL (ELL) child is able to learn English and perform at the expected level academically (August and Shanahan 2008; Genesee et al. 2006, for examples of comprehensive reviews of the language, literacy and academic development of EAL (ELL) students).

Error analysis in SLA is concerned with identifying and describing language errors made by learners in terms of linguistic level (pronunciation, grammar, lexis, style, etc.) and with attempting to ascribe the causes of errors to particular sources, such as the application of conventions and rules in a learner's mother tongue (interference) or faulty application of target language rules. It enjoyed a heyday in the late 1960s and the 1970s when scholars such as Pit Corder, Jack Richards and William Nemser attempted to link the study of learners' errors to the mechanisms, procedures and strategies involved in both first and second language acquisition. Errors were seen as evidence of a built-in syllabus significant, according to Corder, in three respects: informing the teacher what needed to be taught; providing the researcher with insights into how learning proceeded; and providing the learners with a means of testing their hypotheses about the target language. Within the strong form of this paradigm, and distinguishing it from contrastive analysis, it was intended that errors could be described fully in terms of the target language, without reference to the L1 or another language known by the learner.

A notable broadening in the scope of EA was provided by Lennon (1990) in identifying that errors may not only be located at a 'local' level in a word or a few words, but may also be found at a 'global' level, affecting a sentence or even a text.

While EA may have been superseded by the study of learners' **interlanguage** as a focus of interest for SLA, it remains as Cook (1993: 22) puts it, 'a methodology for dealing with data', valued by language teachers for its relevance to their daily work.

Error Treatment see **Feedback, Focus on Form, Error Analysis**.

Experience of language learning is usually measured in two ways: the number of languages previously learnt when embarking on a new language course, and the number of years spent previously learning an L2. A further consideration is whether the previous language learning was a **heritage** language. Experience is sometimes associated with *expertise*, but this is problematic (see Johnson 2005). It is believed that *expert* language learners/users (or more generally multilinguals) have an advantage over second language learners because of what McLaughlin and Nayak (1989) call a 'positive transfer hypothesis' in that they are able to adjust their strategic approach to a particular task. Moreover, *expert* learners are said to possess greater metalinguistic awareness and communicative sensitivity. Thus Rivers (2001: 2) defines *experts* as 'learners with sufficient experience of language learning and sufficient awareness of that experience to make conscious use of it in their third language courses'. However, it is open to question whether an *experienced* language learner may be someone who has 'tasted' a variety of languages but not been particularly successful at any of them.

Explicit knowledge has given rise to considerable theorizing as to the nature of its construct, its measurement and its role in language learning. It is generally accepted that the explicit knowledge of an L2 that a learner has is accessible in working memory and is knowledge of which the learner is consciously aware and can articulate. This does not mean that explicit knowledge is necessarily correct. According to Rod Ellis (2004) explicit knowledge takes place on two planes: the breadth of facts a learner has about language and the depth of refinement about each of those facts. Thus an L2 learner may be able to articulate a number of rules of English but at a superficial or unsophisticated level. It is also hypothesized that explicit knowledge is stored in **declarative** long-term memory but the nature of that storage is as yet unclear. Moreover, its relationship with implicit knowledge (that which can be articulated 'by feel' as in 'that feels right to me') remains an area for investigation. It is likely that a learner will resort to explicit knowledge when 'feel' proves insufficient to accomplish a language task and that a learner will draw more on implicit knowledge when examining a grammatical sentence and on explicit knowledge when examining an ungrammatical one. A variety of grammaticality judgement tests have been used to measure and distinguish explicit knowledge, and it is believed (Bialystock 1979; Ellis 2004) that the less time a participant has to judge the correctness of a sentence the less likely s/he is to be using explicit knowledge. A number of studies have shown that correctness is not necessarily dependent on explicit knowledge. However, the evidence suggests that explicit knowledge gives, as it were, added value in a variety of language tasks where some reflection is possible.

Explicit learning of second language morpho-syntactic patterns and the semantic properties of a lexical item entails conscious reflection on that information in its declarative form, for example: 'in French, some adjectives are placed before a noun but most come after'; 'in some cultures "pig" has a different meaning to ours'; 'in the present tense "she" is a subject pronoun which has an effect on the verb's ending'. Thus explicit learning *may* include the involvement of metalinguistic information. In explicit language learning, a learner arrives at an understanding of a rule through a global explanation involving logical reasoning (deductively), followed by examples which give credence to that explanation. In implicit (or inductive) learning a learner arrives at an understanding of a rule through being exposed to multiple but varying instances of a 'pattern in use' and then infers (or creates) a rule that appears to account for all the different instances so far encountered. The term is sometimes wrongly associated with intentional learning (see **incidental learning**) but there are clear differences in that one may learn something intentionally without it being explicit. An additional complication with this term is that it is sometimes used synonymously with **explicit knowledge** (that a learner has or demonstrates) but if one adopts the **interface position**, then that which has been learnt through explicit processes may well become implicit knowledge (see **explicit knowledge**) which may no longer be easily articulated (and vice-versa). In classroom-based research few comparisons have been made between explicit and implicit learning. However, Erlam (2003) did find minor advantages of explicit learning in the short term with regard to French pronouns.

Feedback is a general term used in both SLA research and L2 pedagogy for the information that a teacher provides in response to a learner production (spoken or written) and is most commonly associated with inaccuracy rather than with praising interesting or accurate productions. It thus subsumes more specific concepts such as **recasts**, error correction and reformulations. In oral interaction it represents the third part of the well documented IRF sequence (Initiation, Response, Feedback) and is considered by many researchers to promote acquisition by helping a learner to notice the gap between what they said and the target language model. One consideration in giving corrective feedback is that, in **communicative** classrooms, the more extensive the feedback (and any subsequent learner **uptake**) the more it interrupts the meaning-based interaction.

Another is that the extent of overlap between a teacher's intention in providing oral feedback and a learner's perception of that feedback has not been sufficiently established. Feedback to written productions has given rise to much more disagreement among researchers. Some (e.g., Truscott 1996) argue that there is little or no evidence that it improves written accuracy while others (e.g., Bruton 2007; Ferris 2003) argue that (a) alternative interpretations of these studies are possible and (b) lack of evidence lies in problems with previous research designs and (c) treatment of error cannot be dissociated from a more general 'response to writing'. There is also evidence that feedback to written errors requires the learner to take responsibility for acting purposively on that feedback.

Field dependence/independence is often associated with **cognitive styles,** in itself a branch of **individual differences**. Field independent learners are able to focus on the relevant details and their attention will not be attracted to unnecessary contextual features. Field dependence/independence stems from that branch of psychology which explains why some people can see a picture in a mass of dots of different colours on a card and some cannot, or the ability to spot an elf in a tree in a forest, an activity found in some children's books. Field independence/dependence does not have to be visual. It can also be auditory or even abstract. It is perhaps in the domain of auditory field independence that might lie the most interest for SLA researchers in that being able to distinguish one sound from another in the incoming speech stream would be a feature of phonological ability and awareness. The evidence of the impact of field dependence/independence on SLA is inconclusive although it may influence different types of learning. Alptekin and Atakan (1990) suggested some relationship between field independence and grammar-orientated learning tasks whereas Johnson, Prior and Artuso (2002) found evidence of a link between field dependence and performance in communicative productions.

First Language. The term 'first language' (L1) is often used synonymously with 'native language' or 'mother tongue' and generally refers to the language a child began learning at the moment of birth and which the child continues to develop and master. Usually, individuals are most highly proficient linguistically in their L1 however, in certain specific contexts, L2 learners can lose aspects of their L1 through **attrition**. There is a further issue within bilingualism research more specifically and that is how to define or identify an L1 if a child is learning more than one language at the same time. If a child is exposed to two languages from birth they are sometimes considered to be developing two first languages. In applied linguistics research, the term L1 can often refer to L1 developmental issues in children. L1-based research, for example seeks to understand the linguistic, developmental, social, psychological and educational aspects of children's first language (L1) development (e.g., Karmiloff and Karmiloff-Smith 2001). Many of the ideas that have been developed within L1 research have been explored within the L2 framework, such as whether or not principles of **universal grammar** which are argued to constrain L1 development, are influential or important in some way in understanding L2 development (see White 1989) or whether specific types of linguistic input are more or less facilitative in fostering linguistic proficiency. For example, basic elements of Krashen's theory (1982) of second language acquisition assume key concepts from L1 research such as the notion that fluent language is largely implicit and acquired.

Fluency, in spoken production, can be investigated either in a holistic and subjective sense ('not very fluent' [to] 'near native') or in a narrow, usually quantitative and highly objective sense (Lennon 1990). It is the latter that has most interested researchers who have experimented with various components of fluency including:

1. speech rate (usually the number of syllables uttered per minute)
2. repetitions
3. false-starts
4. self-corrections
5. pauses ('number of' and 'length of'; 'filled' and 'unfilled')
6. average length of uninterrupted 'runs' between pauses.

It is particularly the last of these that appears to correlate with increased general proficiency, amount of exposure to the L2 and with holistic judgements of fluency (Towell et al. 1996). Various theories have been considered as affecting these measures. For example different components of Levelt's model of speech production may adversely affect fluency because of problems: in the conceptualizer (lack of ideas slowing down expression), in the formulator (lack of vocabulary or grammar slowing down expression), in the articulator (difficulties related to the speech organs), and through use of the monitor (thinking about the accuracy of the previous utterance or rehearsing the next utterance before articulating it). An alternative theoretical approach is to examine the relative use of **formulaic language** or chunks of language that have become automatized, this being a characteristic which is believed to distinguish native and non-native speakers. Researchers are currently investigating the effectiveness of technology for measuring fluency as the implications for language testing (in which fluency plays an important part) could be considerable.

Focus on form (FonF) is an expression used to describe either a type of restricted pedagogical intervention or a full-blown teaching method. Usually attributed to Long (1991), FonF adheres to the principle that L2 teaching should essentially both involve and promote communication of meaning but that, at certain moments in the lesson when learners reveal a gap in their knowledge, the focus should switch from communicating messages to drawing the learners' attention to formal aspects of the language, particularly its grammar. By adhering to the communicative principle it distances itself from what Long labelled 'Focus on Forms' which is a teaching method that begins with and is governed by an analysis of the formal properties of the L2, essentially **grammar-translation**. Proponents of FonF, therefore, argue that positive input (see **input hypothesis**) alone is not sufficient to promote acquisition of the whole of the L2 morpho-syntactic system and that even **negotiation of meaning** may in some instances not allow sufficient attentional resources to be directed at the new language element, simply because of the demands of understanding the message. FonF may be proceduralized in many ways by the teacher, ranging from a simple **recast** to a full (but brief) explanation of how a rule works in the L2 or is different from the L1. Problems with FonF reside in: how to decide that a learner is developmentally ready (see **developmental readiness**) to attend to a new form; how to choose which elements are most likely to be amenable to treatment of this kind; and how to decide what level of treatment is likely to produce the best results while not deviating too far from the communicative principle.

Focus on Forms see **Focus on Form.**

Form to Function Relationship. In talking about language, it is often stated that form and function do not have a one-to-one relationship. As Nunan (1992, p. 169) says, 'the linguistic form of an utterance does not necessarily coincide with the functional intention of that utterance.' A language form may express a number of (communicative) functions: 'your son is hanging from the branch', declarative in form, may function as both a descriptive statement or as, for example, a warning. Similarly, a language function may be expressed in a number of forms. Questioning the truth of a statement such as 'There won't be any ice left at the North Pole in five years time', may be expressed, for example, by a simple declarative: 'What you are saying is totally untrue' or by an interrogative, 'How can you say such a thing?' or an imperative, 'Get out of here!'

An important distinction is also to be made between linguistic form and grammatical function (sometimes called grammatical role). A noun (a linguistic form) may have as its grammatical function: subject of verb, object of verb, indirect object of verb, etc.

In SLA studies, significant attention has been paid to 'form-function mapping', the way in which second language learners map the relationship between linguistic forms and grammatical functions from their native language to their target language, especially within the framework of the **competition model** (Bates and MacWhinney 1982). Interesting cross-linguistic differences have been found within this model. Su (2001), for example, found that Chinese EFL learners became increasingly more sensitive to word order with increased proficiency, and while English CFL learners conversely showed stronger sensitivity to animacy as proficiency increased, their performance did not match that of the Chinese EFL learners.

Formulaic Language. While definitions vary, all share a similar emphasis on formulaic language being prefabricated or stored and retrieved as an unanalysed chunk. Alison Wray (2002, p. 9), for example, defines formulaic language (FL) as 'a sequence, continuous or discontinuous, of words or other elements, which is, or appears to be, prefabricated: that is, stored and retrieved whole from memory at the time of use, rather than being subject to generation or analysis by the language grammar.' Regina Weinert (1995, pp. 182–183) sees FL as 'multi-word collocations which are stored and retrieved holistically rather than being generated *de novo* with each use. Examples of formulaic language include idioms, set expressions, rhymes, songs, prayers, and proverbs; they may also be taken to include recurrent turns of phrase within more ordinary sentence structures'.

In SLA research, formulaic expressions are difficult to identify because we may not know how a certain phrase was produced. However, a number of criteria help us with identification: they are produced fluently and without hesitation; they are morpho-syntactically above the level one would expect of the learner; they are used frequently/repeatedly and in particular situations; they may be used erroneously with respect to the meaning intended (see Schmitt 2004; Wray 2002). Formulaic phrases permit even beginner learners to express themselves despite a poor command of grammar. For example, a learner can say '*I'd like* a return ticket' without needing to have been taught the conditional tense, modal verbs or rules governing contractions. Formulas learnt in early stages can be analysed later and/or 'slots' in them changed to convey different meaning. Alternatively, constructed phrases, when frequently used over a period of time, can become FL in that they are stored and produced automatically as chunks thus freeing up working memory capacity.

Fossilization. Fossilization in the second language learner's language was first introduced as a construct in SLA research in 1972 by Larry Selinker. It has become widely accepted as a psychologically real phenomenon of theoretical and practical importance, though is often used as a cover term for the cessation of language learning. Since 1972, it has undergone a number of revisions and is now generally accepted as referring to both the stabilized deviant linguistic forms in the learner/user's **interlanguage** and to the underlying cognitive mechanisms which have produced deviant stabilized forms (Han 2004, p. 20).

From the first perspective, fossilization refers to incorrect linguistic forms that seem to have become permanent in the second or foreign language of the learner or user, even after long exposure to or instruction in the target language. For example, /l/ and /r/ errors in the speech of Japanese learners of English in spite of lengthy training, word order errors in English speakers learning German. In Selinker and Lakshmanan (1992), for example, fossilization is defined as persistent non-target-like structures in the learner/user's **interlanguage**. From the second perspective, it is also used to characterize and explain a foreign language learning process which has come to a halt and as such, is often used to describe the inability of a learner or user to attain or produce a native-like ability in the target language.

Free variation is a term believed to have been first used by Rod Ellis (1985) to demonstrate that 'variability' in **interlanguage** is not necessarily systematic. Systematic variation (e.g., the same learner using both 'I went'; '*I goed') has been hypothesized as being due to factors such as formal/informal speech, to analysed/non-analysed speech, to performance rather than competence or to some aspect of the immediate linguistic context which the learner believes influences the grammatical element. In free variation the learner produces more than one type for a particular grammatical element, *without any apparent reason*. Ellis' explanation of free variation is that a number of different rules in the learner's head are competing with one another. However, because humans always try to be as economical as possible with their information processing (the economy principle) they look for clues in subsequent input which favour one rule over another and eventually they discard the redundant rule. It is because free variation is possible that learning can take place as systematic variation might accommodate more than one rule in perpetuity. Opposition to the concept of free variation has been proposed in **processability theory**, which argues that an interlanguage has to be assumed to be 'steady' at any single point in its development – i.e. its variation is constrained.

Frequency effect examines how, in the input that a learner receives, it is how often a particular feature occurs, and its degree of salience, which affects development and acquisition (for a review see N. Ellis 2002). It is therefore a theory based on language use, where language learning is related not to an innate capacity or mechanism for learning language but to the linguistic environment surrounding the language learner whose natural tendency is to attempt to extract patterns and regularities from that highly complex input data that s/he receives. However, in this account, the learner is sensitive to the frequency with which linguistic features occur and each instance of their occurrence is, as it were, a confirmation that the information contained in that feature is important, that it should be attended to and recorded in the neural networks of the brain (see also **connectionism**). This is somewhat in contrast to an inductive account of rule formation whereby the learner hypothesizes a rule from even a limited amount of input. Frequency effect has been adopted as an underlying theory mostly in the study of morphosyntax acquisition (e.g., word order), but also in the acquisition of collocations (Durrant 2008) where frequency is hypothesized to be an important variable in a comparison between native and non-native speakers of a language.

Full transfer/full access (FTFA) can be conceptualized as a standpoint that a theoretician may take on two issues: whether the L1 **transfer** plays a role in L2 acquisition; whether the innate framework provided by **universal grammar** (UG) is still available to adult L2 learners. The FTFA standpoint proposes that the starting point for generating L2 utterances is the learners' first language grammar which, during acquisition, has itself been constrained by UG principles. When the learner realizes that the L1 grammar can no longer fully explain the L2 input s/he is receiving, and is no longer sufficiently serving the purpose of generating L2 utterances, s/he turns to UG, which is still available, in the expectation of finding principles and parameters which will guide accurate generation of the L2. Neither of these two processes guarantees accurate generation nor do they guarantee ultimate attainment of the L2 rule-system (for a defence of this 'model' see Schwartz and Sprouse 1996).

Functions and Notions see **Communicative Language Teaching**.

Gender see **Individual Differences**.

Generative Grammar. The notion of generative grammar originated with Chomsky (1957) and this approach has been the focus of a considerable amount of work within theoretical linguistics resulting in different versions of grammatical theory. Underlying this idea is the notion that, in acquiring language, children cannot be simply memorizing the sentences to which they are exposed in the input (as implied by Skinner 1957) but must rather be more actively generating novel sentences out of a knowledge of the grammatical principles of their (native) language. The assertion is that all languages have an infinite number of possible sentences, and therefore, these sentences would be impossible to memorize. Rather, a finite set of phrase structure rules are acquired which allows the language user to *generate* an infinite number of sentences from a finite set of grammatical rules. Associated with this idea of generative grammar is the notion of **universal grammar** which claims that the ability to acquire this necessary grammatical knowledge is innately specified for the human species. A significant branch of research within second language acquisition is situated within a generative grammar framework, and attempts to understand the grammatical knowledge available to the L2 learner and the extent to which universal grammar is available and/or accessible to L2 learners (e.g., Gass and Schachter 1989; White 1989).

Genre. While a typical general dictionary definition of 'genre' might be along the lines: 'A category of artistic composition, as in music or literature, marked by a distinctive style, form, or content', in SLA, the use of the term is more restricted to the membership of texts to specific discourse communities of speech or writing which share regularities in the form, function, content and expression of their writings. John Swales stresses the aspect of shared communicative purposes in bringing together texts as a genre (1990, p. 46). For example, Swales' (1990) work on research articles showed that articles across a wide range of fields shared commonalities at a wide range of levels, including discourse and rhetorical, which marked them out as belonging to a particular type of written text. In this approach, genre is described in terms of functionally defined stages, moves and steps. Genre studies have revealed the strong cross-cultural influence of expert discourse communities such as in medical and professional settings, or, in contrast, the scope for cross-cultural mis-communication, as in business settings.

While both genre and register refer to varieties of language use, register tends to be used in the sense of, for example, *writing in a scientific register*, where a writer might choose to use a botanical name for a plant rather than its common name.

Good Language Learner see **Language Learner Strategies**.

(The) Grammar-Translation method of L2 teaching can be categorized as a broad approach with a long historical tradition dating back to at least the middle ages, and the translation of classical texts into the vernacular, and probably before. However, it was probably not recognized as a 'pedagogy' until the eighteenth century. It holds two basic principles: first the L2 can be learnt by comparing it to the L1; secondly, by analysing the component parts of the L2, the overall system of rules of the L2 will be learnt. These two principles, it is believed, are best served by explicit *reflection on* the language and this, in turn, is best achieved through the written rather than the spoken mode. A typical (but by no means the only possible) set of pedagogical activities in a grammar-translation lesson would be the following:

1. The learner is provided, through the L1, with an explicit account of an L2 grammatical rule.
2. S/he is exposed to a series of L2 sentences in which the selected grammatical element features prominently.
3. S/he translates the sentence into L1.
4. The learner is given a series of L2 sentences with gaps into which s/he inserts the target element provided in (e.g., in the case of verbs) the infinitive.
5. S/he then translates a series of related sentences into the L2.
6. S/he translates a whole text in which the target element features prominently into L1 and then translates a (similar) whole text from L1 into L2.

Grammar-translation can be said to lie at the extreme end of a continuum with 'pure' **communicative language teaching** at the opposite end and with various intermediate approaches such as **focus on form** in the middle. It survives to this day in many classrooms although it is usually combined with more communicative activities.

Grammaticality Judgement see **Explicit Knowledge**.

A **grapheme** is the smallest meaningful unit, in the writing system of a particular language (see Cook and Bassetti 2005). In English, the letters 't' and 'h' can be graphemes but so can the combination of letters 'th'. Thus, in English, graphemes are the written equivalents of phonemes. By contrast in Chinese a grapheme is a character and represents a larger meaning of unit – roughly equivalent to a morpheme. In opaque languages such as French and English, a number of graphemes will represent the same phoneme. For example, 'f' (as in 'four') 'ff' (as in 'sniff'), 'ph' (as in 'philosopher') and 'gh' (as in 'trough') are all written equivalents of the phoneme 'f'. This opaqueness leads to **decoding** and pronunciation problems for L2 learners of English.

Graphic organizers are a specific type of 'advance organizer' and are usually applied to listening and reading comprehension pre-task activities. The idea is that access to the text will be facilitated if the listener or reader prepares their mind (more specifically their **schema**) before being faced with the text. This can be achieved by the teacher presenting a 'concept map' (words connected in meaning radiating out from a central word) or by the teacher conducting an initial elicitation activity, producing a graph on the board in the middle of which is the central core word (e.g., 'famine') and from which a mind-map is formed linking all possible connecting words to it (e.g., 'hunger, starvation, poverty, drought'). This activation of schema is said to allow the student to predict what words are likely to occur in the text and therefore reduce the cognitive load by, as it were, having done some of the comprehension beforehand, or by re-grouping the input into more manageable chunks. Other types of advance organizers are 'structural overview' (predicting 'who/what/when/how'), text related questions (Teichert 1996) or feasible 'statements' about the text (Herron et al. 1998). Although there is some evidence that these organizers facilitate comprehension in the immediate task, there is as yet little evidence that they transfer to other tasks or result in long-term improvement of comprehension.

Heritage Language (minority language). Heritage Language is the term used to refer to a language spoken in a child's home or home community which is different from the language spoken in the majority of the community (*majority language*). Heritage language and minority language are therefore largely synonymous. However, the term heritage language does not have associated with it any potentially offensive or pejorative aspects associated with the societal standing of the child's home language and heritage language is often associated with a language that may have originated in the country in which it is no longer the majority language (e.g., Mohawk in Canada). Issues concerning children's heritage language development are most commonly considered within the domain of **bilingual education**, as there have been a number of different educational programmes around the world which promote heritage language education. Heritage language education is a 'strong form' of bilingual education (Baker 2006) where children use their heritage, or native/home language in the school as a medium of instruction – in addition to learning the L2 or majority language. Examples of heritage language education programmes include education through Navajo and Spanish in the USA, Basque in Spain, Welsh in Wales (Great Britain) and Maori in New Zealand. The primary aim of these programmes is to promote additive bilingualism, and protect and promote the child's development and use of their heritage or home language.

Majority Language: The majority language, in contrast to the above, is the language spoken by the wider community, society and/or country and is the language most often used for educational, business and governance. Examples of majority languages are English in the USA and French in France.

Hypothesis Testing see **Ouput Hypothesis**.

Idiolect. The language individuals speak and which may differ from the language of other members of the speech community or shared dialect in many smaller or larger ways is referred to as one's idiolect. We all have an idiolect with particular characteristics. As part of my idiolect, I may say 'there's nice' (commonly found in English speech in South Wales but sounding odd elsewhere) while all around people say 'that's nice'. In my idiolect, I may have other variations in my pronunciation, use of words and grammar which have developed over the years and which all mark my own speech out as unique to me.

The apparently simple notion of idiolect hides a controversy. Is a standard language an overlapping of idiolects or is language a social institution (with social shared meanings) and idiolects are merely the individual's imperfect expression and understanding of it?

Immersion is a term used to denote a type of **bilingual education** programme that was developed in Canada in the 1970s (Lambert and Tucker 1972) where children were educated within the medium of a second language and therefore 'immersed' in this L2 with a view to becoming a competent user of that language with no cost to their academic achievement. The focus of the immersion classroom was not on the L2 per se, but rather on the content of the academic curriculum. The L2 in the immersion setting is therefore not the subject matter, but rather the medium of instruction. As it was originally formulated in Canada, immersion was developed for English-speaking children to learn French. The aims of the original programmes in Canada were to encourage the students involved in immersion programmes to become competent in French in both speaking, reading and writing, to develop an appreciation of different cultural aspects of the L2 community and to reach expected-level academic achievement. The original French immersion classes proved to be highly successful and have led to successful immersion education programmes throughout the world (e.g., Australia, Finland, Hong Kong, South Africa). There are different types of immersion education programmes which vary with respect to two different variables: age and amount of time spent in immersion. For example, in *early total immersion* a child begins their experience in the immersion classroom at a young age (early) and spends 100%–80% of their time within the L2. Immersion education programmes have proved to be highly successful at promoting *additive* bilingualism (namely, where the bilingual individual develops a high level of competence in both languages). (See Baker 2006 for a comprehensive review of international research on immersion education.)

Implicit Knowledge see **Explicit Knowledge**.

Implicit Learning see **Explicit Learning**.

Incidental Learning. Often proposed in contrast to intentional learning, incidental learning may occur when learners' attention is focused predominantly (but not exclusively) on the message contained in an utterance or a text rather than the form through which that message is being conveyed. That attention cannot be focused exclusively on the message is argued on the basis that some awareness of the form of a new word, or unfamiliar grammatical element, must occur in order for 'noticing' (and subsequent processing of that word or element) to take place and leading to possible acquisition. For example, when reading a text containing an unknown word an L2 learner may be able to understand (or think they understand) the meaning of the sentence in which that word is contained without stopping, reflecting on and inferring the word's possible meaning from its context. However, in order for the new word to be acquired, some processing in working memory must occur which links the word's shape or components to its meaning. Hence, although generally accepted that incidental learning may arise spontaneously (i.e., without any prior planning), the idea that incidental learning is totally unmotivated and unintentional, has been challenged. This notion has formed the basis of some pedagogical practice (see Loewen 2005) in which focus on form episodes arise incidentally during interaction the pedagogical intention of which is predominantly communicative. Studies suggest that incidental learning is less effective for both vocabulary and grammar than intentional learning but the lack of a precise definition of 'incidental' makes synthesis of these studies untrustworthy. Research into incidental learning has been carried out almost exclusively within a psycholinguistic framework although a few authors have adopted a socio-cultural perspective by situating it within activity theory (McCafferty et al. 2001).

Individual differences in SLA is an area which has generated increasing research interest since the 1980s (for introductory volumes see Dörnyei 2005; Skehan 1989). They are the personal characteristics that, it is hypothesized, all learners have but which may measurably differ from learner to learner. ID research thus explores aspects of an individual that could logically affect L2 learning and can be contrasted with *group differences* such as ethnicity, L1 background, nationality, and sex/gender. However, the research is by no means characterized by case studies (as one might expect) but by quantitative methods and test batteries through which, although the findings are scalar, the conclusions ultimately, 're-categorize' individuals into broad groups. Thus researchers have classified individuals as being of low/high **aptitude**, as frequent/ infrequent users of **strategies**, as being of introvert/extrovert personality, as having convergent/divergent **cognitive styles**, as being susceptible/not susceptible to levels of anxiety, as being **autonomous**/not autonomous, as having high/ low **motivation**. While these categorizations are not as dichotomous as sex/ gender they are nevertheless categories which serve as independent variables for examining their relationships with success in L2 learning. Conversely, some might argue that group differences such as gender (in the socio-cultural meaning of the word) are not much more watertight than individual differences.

Whether 'age' is classified as a group or an individual difference is also open to debate and probably relates to the research question being asked. Thus it is increasingly evident, particularly to socio-cultural theorists, that there is a constant interaction between the two types of 'differences'.

Initiation Response Feedback see **Questioning** see **Turn-taking**.

Inner speech, also known as silent self-directed speech, is the faculty that humans possess to think using words and phrases. Inner speech is linked, but also different from, sub-vocalization in that the latter is language which is articulated through the speech organs albeit at a very low volume. Inner speech is also distinguished from private speech which technically is not private in that the speaker may say 'right, so what I need to do now is X' in front of other people but will be doing so in order to regulate his/her thinking in carrying out that task. In SLA inner speech has often been interpreted from a **socio-cultural** perspective (for a review see De Guerrero 2005), drawing on the work of Vygotsky, and is concerned with, for example, whether the L1 is used in preference to the L2 in L2 problem-solving tasks; whether inner speech is used in order to maintain, in working memory, recently seen or heard language; planning processes in writing; rehearsing prior to speaking; the relationship between inner speech and (outward) gestures or facial expressions. One of the obvious problems in researching inner speech is that it can only be mediated through spoken or written language and therefore the validity of using stimulated recall or think-aloud procedures (see Cohen and Macaro, this volume) is called into question. There is some evidence that bilingual children develop different characteristics of inner speech than do adults learning an L2 in more formal environments.

Input Hypothesis see **Comprehensible Input**.

Input processing (IP) is a theory of SLA in instructed contexts associated originally with the work of Bill VanPatten (for a comprehensive account see VanPatten 1996). The theory attempts to explain why grammar acquisition does not automatically result from comprehensible input by proposing that the natural tendency is to listen for meaning rather than to attend to form and that it is difficult for both to happen simultaneously because of processing limitations. Moreover, listeners tend to focus on content words rather than function words or morphemes (because many of these are redundant for meaning) and in particular on the first noun of an utterance (the first noun principle). Therefore in instructed contexts the teacher will have to manipulate the input in such a way that the listener cannot arrive at meaning without attending to grammatical clues in the input. For example, Benati (2001), attempting to teach the Italian future tense, removed the temporal markers (tomorrow, next year, etc.) from the input thereby forcing the learners to pay attention to the verb endings in order to determine whether the utterance was about future action. Benati obtained positive results for this fairly easy grammatical feature. Less conclusive results have been found (Allen 2000) for more complex features (e.g., the French causative). A problem with IP instruction is that VanPatten proposes that IP sequences should begin with some explicit instruction making it difficult to completely distinguish IP classes from traditional grammar teaching classes. A further criticism comes from DeKeyser et al. (2002) who argue that there is evidence that attentional capacity is not as limited as is suggested and therefore learners can attend to both form and meaning.

Intake is the term normally used to describe those parts of the comprehended input which are, at least in part, attended to and processed by the learner. They are the samples of the comprehended input which actually influence 'the learner's evolving sense of the language' (Guthrie 1983: 36). It is the process during which the input is compared to existing knowledge. For Gass and Selinker (2008) it is the stage at which hypotheses are formed, tested and, if necessary, rejected. As well as differing itself from input, intake is in a differential relationship to *acquisition*, in that not all that is 'taken in' will be acquired.

(The) Interaction hypothesis is an amalgam of emergent theoretical positions which have come to form part of a recognizable and coherent research tradition which began in the 1980s. It comprises (1) **modified input**, (2) **negotiation of meaning**, (3) forced output (see **output hypothesis**) and (4) **feedback** to learner errors. The over-arching claim of the hypothesis is that interaction in the L2 furthers acquisition as well as the exchange of information (i.e., there is focus on form as well as focus on meaning). There is general consensus that these four aspects of L2 interaction jointly contribute to acquisition in some way. It is less clear if they do so incrementally (each one adding value to the other) or whether they contribute to different aspects of interlanguage development. For example, Ellis et al. (1994) found that interactionally modified input led to better acquisition of *vocabulary* than pre-modified input which in turn led to better acquisition than un-modified input. Pica et al. (1987) found evidence of the superiority of output over modified and interactionally modified input in the acquisition of *vocabulary*. This set of studies, then, suggest an incremental contribution to vocabulary learnings. However, numerous feedback-to-error studies have shown a contribution to *grammar* suggesting that the hypothesis does not have a unified contribution to interlanguage development. Moreover, because researchers in this tradition have worked almost exclusively in L2-only contexts, it is unclear what the position of the hypothesis is to the role of the L1 in acquisition – is it considered merely an irrelevance, or a relationship which simply has not yet been studied?

Intercultural communicative competence is considered to be the knowledge, understanding and skills needed to communicate successfully with members of a different social group. Intercultural communicative competence recognizes the lingua franca status of English and celebrates the fact that successful bilinguals possess intercultural insights (Alptekin 2002). However, many consider intercultural competence to go beyond the simple transmission and acquisition of these attributes, arguing that it involves not only the communication of culture-laden meaning (as in *pragmatic competence*) but also its interpretation and co-construction between interlocutors. In other words, it requires the setting up of encounters between one's own culture and that of the 'other'. The argument is that shared knowledge between interlocutors is relative rather than fixed and it is in the 'third space' (Kramsch 1993) between culture and language that learning, through experience, takes place. Theories of intercultural competence draw from many fields including psychology and anthropology. Approaches to teaching intercultural competence are many, as are the controversies that surround them. In ELT particularly, the notion of a fixed target culture has been greatly undermined by the globalization of the English language and the approach of modelling according to a native speaker widely discredited. The cultural contrast approach is also criticized for operating at too superficial a level and risking developing stereotypical views. Computer mediated communication is currently seen as a facilitator of intercultural competence (Kern, Ware and Warschauer 2004) as it shifts the locus of learning from the teacher and language learning material to the social participants themselves in the act of communicating.

Interface/Non-interface Position (see also language acquisition). The Interface/Non-interface argument concerns whether there can be any crossover (the interface) between aspects of a second or foreign language that are taught/learnt explicitly and consciously (e.g., grammatical constructions or vocabulary items) and the sub-conscious or automatic second language acquisition process. In its most extreme form, advocated by Stephen Krashen (1982, 1985), there is no possibility of learning becoming acquisition or vice-versa. Consciously learnt language knowledge does not lead to acquisition and can only be used as a 'monitor' or corrective mechanism.

The Interface position, especially in its strong form, maintains that the two systems are not separate and that there is a role for **explicit learning** and practice. In this view, the role of practice is to allow learnt language knowledge to become fluent and automatic language use. In its weaker form, its advocates claim that explicit learning of rules may have no more than a facilitating effect on language acquisition and may aid the learner to grasp comprehensible input.

Interference see **Contrastive Analysis**.

Interlanguage is a term broadly adopted to describe the language of the L2 learner in its current state, that is, at any one moment in a trajectory from zero competence to native speaker competence. Interlanguage theory (the term coined by Selinker in 1972) proposes a number of principles. First, the language system that the learner possesses at any moment in time is not one based on the notion of deficit. Errors are not the result of laziness or stupidity. Secondly, the learner is actively engaged in construing the target language system on the basis of the evidence that s/he has available at any one time. That evidence includes the learner's first language and elements of the L2 that s/he has already acquired. Thus the learner is constantly seeking and adopting a structure for his/her internalized linguistic system. A metaphor for this structure could be that learners have an individualized grammar book inside their heads. Some of the grammar entries are wrong but they are nevertheless formed on the basis of (albeit limited) evidence. Thirdly, and as a consequence, the interlanguage is systematic. Learners do not produce the entries in a random way. Although there is considerable variation in the system (see **free variation**), there appear to be, nevertheless, constraints on the variations in learner productions around a particular grammatical element. Interlanguage theory is central to the study of SLA because of the need to understand the system in its own right. Researchers are interested in the origins of the 'grammar entries' (how they came about), how a particular structure develops or, alternatively, **fossilizes**, whether there are sequences of development of a structure which learners go through, and whether and how intervention or instruction impacts on interlanguage development.

Intralingual Error see **Contrastive Analysis**.

Language acquisition is a term juxtaposed with language learning by some authors and used more or less synonymously by others. Probably the author most noted for making the distinction was Stephen Krashen (see Krashen 1981). His basic argument was that acquisition was the only process that children adopted to learn their first language. Adults on the other hand had two possible processes available to them, acquisition and learning. Acquisition was a subconscious process whereby new linguistic information was absorbed by the learner whereas learning was a conscious process in which the explicit learning of rules featured prominently. Acquisition was almost certainly slower than learning but resulted in more secure **competence**. Linguistic knowledge which has been acquired is 'felt' by the learner to be correct whereas linguistic knowledge that has been learnt is logically argued by the learner as being correct or incorrect. Only once learners have acquired a certain structure will they be able to produce it, whereas with a learnt structure they can produce it without having first acquired it. Probably Krashen's strongest claim was that the two processes were not compatible (see [non-] **interface position**). The distinction has been criticized by several authors (e.g., McLaughlin 1987) on the grounds that there is no evidence either biological or psycholinguistic for two separate processing systems in the human brain and that, in any case, Krashen did not provide the experimental situations or tools where such a hypothesis could be tested. More recently some support for the distinction has surfaced (e.g., Zobl 1995) in that certain linguistic domains such as markedness as well as relative levels of computational complexity, could give some credence to the existence of two systems.

The Language acquisition device (LAD) was hypothesized by Chomsky (1957, 1965) and refers to children's putative 'innate' ability to learn their native (first) languages. All children throughout the world seem to be able to learn and master their native language in a relatively straightforward manner, regardless of the context in which the child is developing (e.g., rich/poor, literate/illiterate, etc.). The main factors necessary for language acquisition in children seem to be a healthy brain and exposure to linguistic input. The reason for proposing the LAD stemmed from the following observations by Chomsky which contributed to his development of the *Nativist* or *Innate* view of language acquisition. First, all neurologically healthy children pass through similar stages of developmental progress with respect to how their L1 develops; babbling precedes the first word stage, which is then followed by the two-word stage etc. This observation seems to be independent of which L1 is being learnt by the child and the socio-economic, linguistic and cultural circumstances surrounding the child's development. Second, children seem capable of learning their L1 despite the fact that much of the natural language input that they are exposed to is not itself perfectly grammatical (i.e., people make performance errors when they talk). Finally, children acquire their L1s despite the fact that they receive no *negative evidence* – an indication of what is not grammatically possible in their L1. These observations, in conjunction with work in neuroscience demonstrating that language knowledge and processing seems to be under the jurisdiction of specific brain regions (e.g., Broca and Wernicke's areas) led Chomsky to propose that language acquisition in children must be *innate* (**Nativism**) and that there must be some sort of centre, or 'device' in the child's developing brain which facilitates linguistic development, hence the LAD. The LAD in the child's brain therefore consists of innate knowledge about what language could possibly consist of and enables them to develop their competence in their L1.

Language Awareness. The term 'awareness of language' appears to have been first used with its present meaning by Michael Halliday in 1971 when introducing new English language teaching materials for use in English schools (*English in Use*, Doughty 1971) during a period when there were concerns about levels of literacy in English schools and there was an intense debate about the need to teach English (L1) 'across the curriculum'. During the 1980s, Language Awareness (LA) was carried forward through the work and writing of Eric Hawkins, with books such as *Awareness of Language. An Introduction*, Cambridge University Press, 1984.

The Association for Language Awareness defines LA as 'explicit knowledge about language, and conscious perception and sensitivity in language learning, language teaching and language use'. LA projects in schools may introduce into the curriculum languages which are not usually taught in schools such as the mother tongues of some of the pupils, local regional languages which are not recognized in schools or any other language including the school language. The approach has moved on from its early days to be global and comparative as well as cross-curricular.

LA issues include exploring the benefits that can be derived from developing a conscious understanding of how languages work, of how people learn them and use them, of perceiving the differences and similarities between one's own language and that of others. It includes critical perspectives and consciousness-raising, extends to literary awareness, and integrates awareness of other (i.e., non-linguistic) areas of human communication. LA projects often include cultural components to make learners aware of similarities not only in language but also across peoples and cultures.

Language distance is a term used to describe a set of criteria that researchers use in order to see how similar or different languages are to one another. It is linked to the notion of language universals (features of languages which are common to all) and language typology (the categorization of different languages). Corder (1981) suggested a language distance hypothesis. Children learning any language will take approximately the same amount of time to master its oral form; however the learning of second languages takes different amounts of time. The extent to which the L1 and the L2 are similar will determine how easy it is to learn an L2 and how long it will take. This hypothesis has, to some extent, contributed to the establishment of criteria for the length of different second language courses. The problem however lies in the interpretation of 'similarity' and how one, as a consequence, might go about grouping the world's languages. For example is English more similar to Mandarin than French because they share relatively simple morphologies or are they distant because of their very different **writing systems**. In other words, if typological factors allow languages to be members of different groups, which typological differences should be considered as causing the greatest problems. Thus the general consensus seems to be that while one cannot deny language distance as a potential variable in SLA, it cannot be considered in isolation from other variables sufficiently to allow policy or pedagogical decisions to be made on the basis of language typology alone.

Language education is a broad term adopted for the study of any type of (mostly second) language learning. It is less concerned with theories of second language acquisition, more with providing an overview of language teaching and learning from an historical, policy, or pedagogical methodology perspective. In other words it is concerned with language learning in its socio-political and cultural context rather than an abstracted understanding of how the human mind processes language, although it certainly does not exclude the latter. There is some disagreement as to whether language education rather than SLA should form the basis of Language Teacher Education, that is the theories and research evidence (e.g., on teacher beliefs, decision making and action) that inform the language teaching profession whether at novice or experienced level.

Language Learner Strategies. The seeds of strategies research were sown during the search for the characteristics of the 'good language learner' (GLL) (Rubin 1975). These characteristics were the series of behaviours a learner adopted in order to both maximize his/her limited linguistic resources (in language use tasks) and to further develop those linguistic resources (language learning). Such characteristics (e.g., an active approach to learning, willingness to experiment), clearly broad and trait-like, later became 'strategies' which Oxford (1990: 8) defined as 'a plan, step, or conscious action towards achievement of an objective', making them *both* highly specific actions in a learning situation *and* broader general behaviours which included *both* overt motor behaviour *and* inner cognitive behaviour, as reflected in Oxford's widely used strategy elicitation instrument (the SILL). This inclusive approach has been attacked as being a-theoretical. A more recent conceptualization of strategies (Macaro 2006) involves them being considered *only* as a cognitive or metacognitive mental action which, when used as part of a 'strategy-cluster', against a learning goal and, in relation to a language learning or use task, can be effective (if appropriately selected) in maximizing existing linguistic resources. The controversy as to whether strategies are internal or external, large or small, specific or abstract continues and some authors have argued for abandoning the concept in favour of 'self-regulation' (Tseng et al. 2006), again with trait-like characteristics, but adherents to strategies research remain (see Cohen and Macaro 2007) as does the belief that strategies can be taught (strategy instruction) in order to develop more effective learners. Another remaining issue is whether some learners are able to use different strategies simply because they are more proficient, or whether different strategic behaviour among learners of equal linguistic resources leads to increased rate of progress, eventual attainment or both.

Language teacher education (LTE) is one of a variety of terms which refer to the process that individuals undergo (and/or the courses they enrol on) in order to become teachers of languages or, if they are already language teachers, to develop as professionals (see Tedick 2004 for an introduction to the area). Although sometimes used synonymously with 'teacher training' and 'in-service training' respectively, LTE attempts to emphasize that teaching an L2 is a complex and intellectual activity requiring knowledge and reflection (sometimes known as the 'reflective practice' model of LTE) rather than simply copying the behaviour of the more experienced practitioner (the 'apprenticeship' model). It is generally recognized that individuals bring a rich resource of knowledge, beliefs and values to LTE programmes and that in the process of learning they 'shape and are shaped by the activity of teaching' (Freeman and Richards (1996: 353). However, it has also been observed that personal theories often outweigh the impact of pre-service LTE. One of the keenest areas of research interest has been into how language teachers make decisions and their evaluations of the results of those decisions together with a related area which is the gap between declared beliefs and private beliefs. There has been surprisingly little research to date on the impact that different types of LTE programmes (whether reflective practice or 'training') have on language learning outcomes.

Learnability see **Teachability**.

Learning Styles see **cognitive Styles**.

Lexical Segmentation see **Phonotactics**.

(The) Lexicon is a kind of mental-dictionary – a mental representation which consists of all the knowledge individuals have about the words of their language. This knowledge includes phonological, morphological, orthographic, syntactic, semantic and pragmatic characteristics of words. It can be more implicit (i.e., word recognition) or more explicit (e.g., more overt, verbalizable knowledge about the word such as being able to provide a definition). Lexis (or vocabulary) is the term used to describe the vocabulary of a language (in contrast to the grammar, for example). Vocabulary makes up a significant component of one's knowledge of language and as a result researchers have long been interested in trying to understand the precise nature of how knowledge of words is represented, how words are acquired and how the lexicon might be structured and organized. Additionally, retrieval of word knowledge (lexical access) is also an important element in research on lexical processing.

For example, Sunderman and Kroll (2006) investigated the extent to which models of lexical processing were relevant to L2 lexical knowledge of L2 learners. Studies such as these speak to the issue of how L1 and L2 lexical knowledge are related in the mental lexicon and the extent to which knowledge of other aspects of language (e.g., grammar) are implicated in the structure of the L2 mental lexicon. Fitzpatrick and Barfield (2009) present a collection of papers illustrating how issues concerning lexical processing, acquisition and storage are currently being considered within SLA research.

Lexis see **Lexicon**.

Linguistic Universals see **Language Distance**.

Majority Language see **Heritage Language**.

Memory see **Working Memory**.

Metalanguage see **Metalinguistic Terms**.

Metalinguistic terms (or metalanguage) are those shared terms used to describe language. Thus 'preposition', 'adverb', 'relative clause' and so on are all metalinguistic terms. These terms are a sub-component of more general metalinguistic knowledge, which is any conscious knowledge about language (e.g., in French some endings of words are silent). The main interest in SLA has centred on whether metalinguistic knowledge in general and the knowledge of terms in particular predicts better acquisition of the rule-system of the L2 than no metalinguistic knowledge. The theory would explain this mainly in terms of the difference between first language acquisition and SLA. Very young children rely less on metalinguistic knowledge of their L1, and have no knowledge of terms, yet manage, in overwhelming numbers, to learn to speak it perfectly well. In contrast, L2 learners post-**Critical Period** mostly do not. It is therefore hypothesized that possessing metalinguistic knowledge might act as a short-cut to learning. An often cited study that tested this was by Green and Hecht (1992) who tested secondary school students who had received metalinguistic information and found that most could correct an incorrect sentence even though they could not recall the rules related to the incorrect feature. More recently Roehr (2008), however, did find a link between being able to correct and describe errors in sentences, suggesting that the debate continues among researchers. The debate is also alive among practitioners some of whom argue that knowing the terminology helps to understand the patterns they are exposed to, while others see learning metalanguage, at least for some learners, as a difficult undertaking, especially when one considers the opaqueness of some of the terminology (e.g., 'indirect object pronoun').

Mistake see **Error**.

Minority Language see **Heritage Language**.

(A) **Modern language** is any language that is still currently spoken by a recognizable speech community. Thus Latin and Ancient Greek are not modern languages. 'Modern language' is a term that is sometimes used synonymously with foreign language although the phrase 'modern language learning' is rarely used. Occasionally modern languages is used as a term to differentiate it from English as a global second language. It is a term used in the curricula of some Anglophone countries both at secondary school level (e.g., the National Curriculum of England and Wales) or at tertiary level where students may describe themselves as 'learning a modern language'. It is sometimes used in preference to 'foreign languages' because of the negative connotations that the word 'foreign' may conjure up. In SLA journals 'modern languages' is rarely used even though, probably for historical reasons, one of the best-known SLA journals is *The Modern Language Journal*.

Modified Input see **Comprehensible Input**.

Modified Interaction see **Interaction Hypothesis**.

Monitoring in SLA is a general term used to describe the mental processes involved in verifying that what one has spoken, written or even temporarily rehearsed (i.e., practised before speaking) is correct. Macaro (2003) makes a clear distinction between monitoring and checking where the former relies on learner-internal resources and the latter is a recourse to external sources such as dictionaries or glossaries. Krashen's 'monitor theory' was used as a means of differentiating between the learnt system and the acquired system whereby only the conscious learnt system could monitor speech production. There is a continued interest in the role of attention in the monitoring process. For example Kormos (2000) analysed how speakers monitored their speech productions by analysing self-repairs and correction rates and noted that the higher the proficiency, the more monitoring focused on higher level aspects of the productions such as discourse level considerations.

Morphology. A *morpheme* is the smallest meaning-bearing unit in a language. *Lexical* morphemes are usually concrete, while *grammatical* morphemes mark some grammatical function. A *free* morpheme is a morpheme that can stand on its own and count as a word. A *bound* morpheme is one that must be attached to a word stem. Examples of free lexical morphemes therefore are words such as *table* and *car*. Free grammatical morphemes are typically function words such as articles (*the, an*). Bound lexical morphemes are derivational affixes (prefixes, suffixes or in some languages, infixes) such as *natio<u>nal</u>*. Bound grammatical morphemes are inflectional affixes (e.g., *wal<u>ked</u>*). *Allomorphs* are variations of a morpheme, usually required by some trigger in the immediately surrounding linguistic environment. For example, the allomorphs of the English indefinite article *a* are *a/an* (<u>*a*</u> *horse*, <u>*an*</u> *apple*) while the allomorphs of the English regular plural inflectional morpheme are *s/z/es* (*cat<u>s</u>, dog<u>s</u>, hous<u>es</u>*). *Morphology* is the study of these morphemes and allomorphs, with a specific focus on how they combine together to form new words: *teach + er = teacher*. Knowledge of morphology is an important component of vocabulary knowledge, with proficient users of a language showing that they have knowledge of possible morphological derivations of different words (e.g., happy, happiness, unhappy). A classic study in child L1 research by Brown (1973) followed the developmental trajectory of English-speaking children's morphological development by looking at when grammatical morphemes appeared in their language. Brown's study identified that while the children varied as to the exact age at which different grammatical morphemes started to emerge in their spoken language, the children in his study all seemed to follow a similar sequence of development. Brown's original research paradigm was extended into the L2 domain where both adult and child L2 learners' morphological development was studied and argued to also consist of specific developmental or acquisition sequences (see Dulay et al. 1982 and Goldschneider, and DeKeyser 2001 for a more recent discussion of this evidence).

Motivation, as related to L2 learning, has undergone considerable development in the past 40 years. It was originally closely associated with the attitudes of learners towards the L2 and/or the target culture. Early work begun by Gardner and Lambert (1959) offered a distinction between *integrative* and *instrumental* motivation where an integrative motive for learning signalled an intention to be associated with the country and culture where the L2 was spoken, whereas an instrumental motive signalled an intention to derive personal benefit from learning (e.g., exam grades, job opportunities, practical communication needs). A widely used self-report instrument, the Attitude and Motivation Test Battery (Gardner 1985) was originally modelled on the bilingual Canadian context and this, together with the naturalistic population on which it was normed led to a realization that it was insufficient for instructed contexts and for 'foreign' language learning populations. Moreover it masked the dynamic nature of the motivational impulse and its interaction with progress and learning success. Its dynamic nature has become central to subsequent waves of motivation research (see Dörnyei, this volume) where attribution (that to which learners attribute success and failure), self-efficacy (learners' beliefs about their ability to successfully achieve specific tasks in the future), expectation (whether learners believe they will achieve their longer-term goals) and the ideal self (that to which you aspire to be) provide an intricate web of factors influencing that which initiates and sustains the learning effort. These new directions have not yet answered the crucial question of whether motivation leads to success or whether the perception that progress is being made leads to sustained motivation, not least because few studies have adopted a longitudinal methodology.

Multi-competence is a theory most closely associated with the work of Vivian Cook (1992) who proposes that second language acquisition involves not the learning of one language but the gradual development of two or more languages (see Cook this volume). Multi-competence theory is as much a philosophical statement as a theory of language acquisition. It argues (Cook 2007) that we wrongly conceive of monolingualism as the default position given that the majority of human beings are, to some extent, bilingual or multilingual. This therefore has implications for the importance that we attach to the native speaker (for which read monolingual) as the model for second language learners to aspire to. Language teachers' over-arching objective should therefore be the creation of bilinguals not monolinguals of a second language. From a psycholinguistic perspective multi-competence offers a variation on the theory of **interlanguage** where any given psychological state in a learner is on a continuum between the L1 and native speaker-like L2 competence. Rather, the L1 and the L2 are in a constant state of inter-dependence. Support for this proposition can be found in evidence that: L2 speakers have a different type of knowledge of their L1 than monolinguals; that, in fact, learning an L2 can affect the L1; that in bilinguals codeswitching can occur without problems; that bilinguals are more cognitively flexible; that there is no separation in the mental lexicon between one or more languages; and that L2 processing cannot isolate (switch off) L1 processing.

Multilingualism see **Bilingual**, see **Experience**.

Native Language see **First Language** see **Non-native Speaker**.

Native Speaker see **Non-native Speaker**.

Nativism see **Language Acquisition Device**.

Natural language acquisition is a term very often associated with the hypotheses put forward by Stephen Krashen (see **comprehensible input**). Underlying the notion is the belief that SLA can occur in very much the same way as first language acquisition, even among adults, provided that the right learning environment can be created. It contains the notion of the silent period – not expecting L2 learners to speak before they are ready to speak – because a silent period occurs in the early developmental stages of babies. Consequently it argues for the primary importance of input as the key ingredient in the acquisition of the L2 and that correction of grammar is unnecessary because generally parents do not correct the accuracy of their children's utterances. These beliefs lead to the proposition that acquisition takes time but in the long run it is more secure than 'unnatural' instructed language learning. Practical teaching guidelines are given in Krashen and Terrell (1983) and these approaches recommend avoiding any form of grammar exercises, homework, use of dictionaries, translation and any activity which treats language as object rather than language as communication. Undermining these propositions is the fact that, at least in adolescent or adult instructed SLA, the amount of exposure to the target language is too limited compared to that of a child, for input alone to be sufficient, and that adults possess greater analytical strategies than very young children, and therefore can take short-cuts in learning. The biggest difference is, of course, that adults learning an L2 already have an L1 with which to compare and contrast the L2 (see Cook this volume).

Negative evidence is an indication of what is not grammatically possible in a child's developing L1. Despite the fact that there are potentially numerous possibilities for how language might be structured, children seem to readily learn the linguistic features of their native language without ever being formally taught or without any indication of what is and is not 'allowed' in the language. The notion here is that when/if children are ever corrected on their linguistic utterances it is mostly in consideration of the truth value of the utterance, without reference to the grammatical accuracy of the utterance. If for example a child were to say '*I putted the giraffe on the table*', the adult caregiver would be more likely to comment on whether that event actually occurred as opposed to pointing out to the child that *putted* is not correct in English. Chomsky (1965) argued, therefore that such negative evidence either is non-occurring in the environment or occurs so infrequently and so inconsistently as to be useless to the child in learning language (see Marcus 1993 and for a counter-argument, Farrar 1992; Saxton 2000). If negative evidence is not available to children while learning their L1, the question posed by Chomsky is how do they actually learn to discriminate between what is grammatically possible from what is grammatically impossible in their language? Chomsky's answer to this question is that children acquire language through **universal grammar**.

Negotiation of meaning is a term attributed to Michael Long (for early work see Long 1981) and now widely used in the interactional research literature (see Gass, this volume). It stems from Long's conviction that modified input (as proposed by Krashen in his **input hypothesis**) was necessary but not sufficient for L2 acquisition. Originally using the term 'modified interaction', Long proposed that negotiation of meaning occurred when teacher-learner interaction (or non-native speaker – native speaker interaction) broke down, or when one participant in the interaction sensed that a breakdown may have occurred. In order that the speaker's meaning might be co-constructed a number of negotiation moves were possible:

a clarification request – 'I'm sorry could you explain that'
a comprehension check – 'do you understand? Is that clear?'
a confirmation signal – 'oh right you mean X'

The idea is that negotiation of meaning goes beyond the benefits of communication repair. Whereas **modified input** is a pre-emptive measure not necessarily targeted at an individual's **interlanguage**, negotiation of meaning allows the interaction to focus on precisely the elements in the interlanguage which the learner needs in order to move on. Thus it furthers acquisition in a more individually supportive manner. Although there is evidence that negotiation of meaning enhances comprehension, and to a certain extent aids the acquisition of lexis, the evidence for it furthering acquisition of the rule-system is less convincing and this has led to the development of the broader **interaction hypothesis**.

Non-native Speaker (NNS). This term, along with its supposed opposite, **native speaker (NS)**, is one of the most contentious terms in SLA literature (see Canagarajah 1999). The fundamental challenges to the construct (and therefore to the dichotomous nature of the two terms) are that the language one is exposed to at birth may not necessarily be the language(s) one feels most confident in as an adult (e.g., due to **attrition**) and that some **bilinguals** are exposed to two languages simultaneously at birth. However, the psycholinguistic, socio-cultural (and indeed philosophical) ramifications are much wider. Psycholinguistically, the dichotomy is challenged because studies have demonstrated that 'NSs' cannot differentiate between NSs and NNSs even in the area of pronunciation, thereby undermining the objective of having the NS as the learner's role model (see also **multicompetence**). Socio-culturally, the dichotomy has been accused of underwriting an imperialistic attitude to language leaning in that certain (especially anglophone) nations are able to exert unjustified power over others through their majority language. This power, it is claimed, has percolated into all areas of language education (see Moussu and Llurda 2008) from learner beliefs, to teacher feelings of inadequacy for not being NSs, to programme administrators and policy makers who only employ NSs. An argument in favour of maintaining some sort of NS-NNS distinction has been made by Long and by Gass (in Seidlhofer 2003) in that, while acknowledging that both the dichotomy and the notion of NS as ultimate goal to be attained are no longer entirely valid, they are nevertheless useful tools in researching SLA in that a fundamental objective of the discipline is to study how learners acquire a new language.

(The) Noticing hypothesis states that 'what learners notice in the input is what becomes **intake** for learning' (Schmidt 1995: 20). By noticing is meant that learners first perceive some kind of external feature and allow working memory to attend to it (in the case of SLA a linguistic feature of some kind), spotlight it and process it to varying levels of intensity thereby bringing about a change in long-term memory. It is only if these preliminary stages have been gone through that learners can compare what they have attended to and spotlighted to their previous knowledge and 'notice a gap'. According to the hypothesis, since the outside world and long-term memory are mediated by working memory processing, then nothing can be learnt without noticing it first, at least to some degree. By this account subliminal or subconscious learning is impossible. Schmidt proposes that noticing is influenced by the frequency that a feature occurs in the input, the salience of that feature, the developmental readiness of the learner to that feature, and the demands of the task which may or may not allow sufficient attention to spotlight the feature and then process it. Critics of the hypothesis (e.g., Truscott 1998) have pointed out that to notice (in this way) everything about an L2 would be impossible and that some learning must take place without conscious effort and that perhaps it is more the metalinguistic aspects of an L2 that are learnt only by noticing.

Obligatory context is a term given to the conditions created for a particular kind of language test, usually associated with a grammar test. An obligatory context is one in which a writer or speaker has to 'supply' a particular linguistic form in that particular phrase or utterance and one in which an avoidance strategy cannot be used. Thus it is a way of determining whether they have acquired that particular linguistic form. Obligatory contexts tasks were used in the series of morpheme studies (**morphology**). However, this technique or test type is not without its controversies. Pica (1983) demonstrated that obligatory context analysis failed to capture those instances of when a correct form was used in an *inappropriate* context. Therefore the notion of 'target-like use' is more reliable in that it measures all incidences both of suppliance in obligatory and non-obligatory contexts. However, obligatory contexts might still be appropriate if one's aim is to measure development rather than final acquisition. For example, in French the verb phrase *j'ai pris* (I took) would show development of the perfect tense (Macaro and Graham 2008) because it would be correct in a context where it was obligatory to use a past completed action, even though this measure would not confirm acquisition of aspect (perfect/imperfect distinction) since the same form might be used in a context requiring 'I was taking medicine every morning at that time'.

Optimality Theory. The central idea behind Optimality Theory (OT) (Prince and Smolensky 1993) is that surface forms of language reflect resolutions of conflicts between competing underlying constraints. A surface form is 'optimal' if it incurs the least serious violations of a set of constraints, taking into account their hierarchical ranking. So for example, in phonology, there may be a conflict in the ranking of syllable onset alongside morpheme boundaries which will affect how a word is pronounced. Violations must be minimal and languages differ in the ranking of constraints, which may account for errors in the interlanguage of L2 learners. OT also allows for the incorporation of general principles of markedness into language-specific analyses.

While OT has been generally developed within a generative phonology and/ or computational linguistics framework, a number of researchers have attempted to apply it to issues arising in SLA studies. Eckman (2004), for example, has applied OT to explaining the appearance of the resumptive pronoun in Swedish learners of English when neither the learners' L1 nor English has resumptive pronouns in their respective relative clause constructions. Escudero and Boersma (2004) have looked at the perception and pronunciation of /I/ and /i/ (the 'sheep vs ship' problem for EFL learners) by Spanish L1 speakers within an OT frame-work. They argue that L2 learners, like L1 learners, build perception categories on the basis of the distribution of the acoustic properties in the input, which may or may not correspond to the optimal perceptions of native speakers.

(The) Output hypothesis is attributed to the work of Merryll Swain who first proposed it in Swain (1985) and further developed it in Swain (1995). It is part of the general interaction research tradition (see **interaction hypothesis**) which also includes **modified input** and **negotiation of meaning** both of which Swain claimed were necessary but not sufficient for acquisition. Swain's basic premise is that 'forcing' learners to speak in the L2 (i.e., putting them in a situation where they have to construct an utterance which they know *may* be wrong) furthers acquisition, and is in direct contrast to Krashen's (see **comprehensible input**) claim that output is the result of acquisition not its cause. Swain's 'forced output' furthers acquisition because:

1. it encourages **'noticing'** – learners may notice the gap between what they want to say and what they believe they know
2. it encourages hypothesis testing – which in turn may result in either a communication breakdown 'forcing' the learner to reformulate the utter-ance, or simply in useful feedback from a native speaker

3. it operates as a metalinguistic function – encouraging learners to think about linguistic information. This contributes to consolidating knowledge.

Whereas modified input and negotiation of meaning may only result in learners focusing on the messages being exchanged in interaction, all these three functions of output serve to focus the learner on form as well as meaning.

Over-generalize/Over-extend see **Child Language**.

Paralinguistic features refer to those features of communication which are non-verbal, that is, do not refer to words/phrases themselves and their meanings and therefore cannot be linguistically segmented. Prosodic features, a sub-category of paralanguage, involve conscious or unconscious aspects of speech which give additional meaning to the words and utterances themselves, for example, intonation, word stress, word pitch, rhythm, loudness and so on. Another category of paralanguage is what we might call body language and encompasses communicative signals such as gestures, coughing, crying, clearing one's throat and facial expressions. Both prosodic features and gestures have been the subject of considerable research in second language acquisition contexts. An obvious rationale for such research is that many of the features of both sub-categories are language or culture specific and therefore may be difficult for L2 learners to acquire. For example Trofimovich and Baker (2007) examined how stress timing and peak alignment contributed to the degree of foreign accent among young Korean L1 learners of English L2. Additionally paralinguistic features may lead to miscommunications. A recent comprehensive work on gesture is by McCafferty and Stam (2008).

Peer reviewing is a practice connected with L2 writing which has received considerable research attention. There are a number of claimed advantages of fellow students reading the written output of L2 learners including the following: it provides an alternative readership to the teacher; it is less threatening and less evaluative in nature; it encourages a focus on communication rather than accuracy; it may be pitched more at the level of the learner. Results, in terms of furthering the skill of writing, or more thorough revisions, however, have so far been mixed. Peers appear to respond to surface errors just as much as teachers and are not always able to give as effective advice as teachers. Students do not always feel confident that peer comments are valid. Thus when studies have compared peer reviewing with teacher feedback (e.g., Paulus 1999; Tsui and Ng 2000) it appears that writers are more likely to revise as a result of teacher feedback than peer feedback.

Performance see **Competence**.

(A) Phoneme, in a given language, is the smallest unit of sound used to distinguish between different spoken words. The consonant sounds /t/ and /p/ are phonemes in English, because they distinguish between the 'minimal pair' *tan* and *pan*. The word *pan* has three phonemes: /p/, /a/ and /n/.

In reality, however, a word's spoken form is produced by continuous movements of the speech organs and reaches our ears as a continuous stream of sound. Moreover, individual phonemes can be analysed into smaller units of sound: for example, both /t/ and /p/ are 'voiceless' consonants; both /p/ and /m/ are produced by closing the lips. However, the abstract unit of sound known as the phoneme is useful in representing the pronunciations of words.

A further complication is that, within a given language, phonemes may be pronounced differently depending on where they occur in a word, and in what combination. For example, the English phoneme /t/ is 'aspirated' (followed by a puff of air) in the word *top*, but not in *stop*. However, this contrast in /t/ is never used to distinguish between different words in English: therefore, these two sounds are not distinct phonemes of the language. Because the difference between them is purely *phonetic* rather than phonemic, native speakers may not even be aware that they differ. However, differences that are purely phonetic in one language may be phonemic in another. For example, Mandarin does have minimal pairs of words where the only difference between them is that one has an aspirated /t/, and the other an unaspirated /t/.

It has been claimed that L2 learners find it difficult to discriminate between L2 phonemes that do not contrast phonemically in their L1 (Best et al. 2001). Moreover, phonological deficits (see **aptitude**) are considered by some to be at the root of poor L2 learning (Ganshow and Sparks 2001).

Phonological Awareness see **Phoneme** see **Aptitude**.

Phonology/Phonetics see **Phoneme**.

(The study of) Phonotactics aims to describe the combinations of **phonemes** which are admissible in any given language. For example in English the phoneme combination of 'g' and 'n', as in 'ignore' are permissible; In Italian they are not. In German 'pf' is a legal combination at the beginning of a word (pfeffer, pfennig) but it is not legal in English. In second language research our understanding of phonotactic constraints can be used to study the impediments that L2 learners may have in understanding L2 speech as well as in their own speech production . A particularly important application is in lexical segmentation (the identification of word boundaries in the speech stream), where a listener's knowledge of phonotactic rules can be used as cues in order to locate the beginnings of words. Knowledge of phonotactic constraints in the L1 in adults can cause problems with identifying word boundaries in an L2 which allows different groups of phonemes. Weber and Cutler (2006) compared English native speakers with advanced German EFL learners and found that words were spotted fastest by the learners when their boundaries were common to both English and German. Al-jasser (2008) part-replicated the study with Arabic learners of English and obtained similar results. Additionally the latter researcher investigated the efficacy of teaching English phonotactic rules over an 8-week period and reported significant gains in lexical segmentation ability.

Politeness see **Intercultural Communicative Competence**.

Positive Transfer see **Contrastive Analysis**.

Priming is a theory which attempts to explain some of the morpho-syntactic development in SLA through a particular feature of the interaction the learner is involved in. This feature is described (e.g., by McDonough and Mackey 2008) as a tendency for L2 speakers to produce a syntactic structure that they have recently been exposed to or 'primed' by. It is unlikely, they argue, that the production of this structure is a simple repetition because it is often adapted by L2 speakers through the use of different content or function words. Moreover, it does not always appear immediately adjacent to the interlocutor's 'priming' structure. Authors therefore speculate that learners, through priming, may become sensitive to the underlying syntactic structure rather than to the surface form they have just heard or (indeed) have themselves recently produced. In this sense priming is a form of **implicit** learning. Cognitive explanations of the priming phenomenon are that the activation produced by hearing or speaking remains for some time after the speech event and/or that morpho-syntactic information is stored in long-term memory with a specific lexical item as a result of priming and this is then transferred to other similar lexical items which appear (to the learner) to be behaving in the same way in sentences. Other explanations (e.g., **individual differences** such as creativity) have yet to be explored. Moreover, longitudinal studies are still required in order to provide evidence that the priming effect is a powerful contributor to long-term acquisition.

Prior Knowledge see **Topic Familiarity**.

Private Speech see **Inner Speech**.

Procedural Knowledge see **Declarative Knowledge** see **ACT***.

Processability is a theoretical term coined by Piennemann (1998) and is a further development of his teachability hypothesis (1984). Processability theory links psychology and linguistics in a very direct way as it examines what we know about languages, through their description, with the mechanisms that the human brain has for dealing with linguistic information. In that sense it is a truly 'applied linguistics' theory. The theory posits that the human brain has a linguistic processor which has constraints in its ability to perform certain processing routines. These constraints and limitations are related to the nature of grammatical features of a given language. The combination of limitations on processing, and the features of the language, predict the route that acquisition of that language will follow. An example is provided by the complexity of linguistic elements in a sentence. In an English sentence involving subject-verb-object (the cat scratched the dog), no interference (or movement) of its elements is involved nor are other elements needed to intervene at different points in the sentence in order for the meaning behind the sentence to be conveyed. Although this requires relatively minimal computational effort, the relationships between 'the' and 'cat' will precede the relationship between 'cat' and 'scratched' and will need to be processed and acquired before the whole sentence can be produced. This requires knowledge of the semantic and grammatical categories of 'cat' and the function of the word in the head phrase. Nevertheless, typically, SVO structures are learnt early by L2 learners. If however the meaning requires a relative or subordinate clause(s) (the cat who scratched the dog quickly ran off down road), this requires more complex computational routines which cannot be put into effect until the earlier routines have been mastered. In that sense, processing is implicational. Later routines imply that earlier processing routines have been mastered.

Proficiency in language learning is a term normally used to describe the relative level(s) reached by an individual learner or user of a second language at any one moment in time in terms of their ability to perform in that language. Proficiency is not concerned with the length of time that an individual has taken to reach that level, nor the learning environment s/he has had experience of. The notion of proficiency is not one which is dependent on any particular syllabus or course content. Proficiency tests of English have been developed in order to provided information about an individual which may be usable across international contexts – for example for entrance to English-speaking universities. Typical proficiency tests are the Test of English as a Foreign Language, and the International English Language Testing System, both of which test the four skills of speaking, writing, listening and reading. Other terms are often used synonymously with proficiency, for example 'achievement', 'success' 'competence' 'ability' and 'skill' are all terms which have been used in studies which in fact were testing proficiency (see Macaro, this volume). Moreover, 'proficient' is sometimes used as synonymous, with high attainment, rather than as a relative measure, as in the Council of Europe's three levels of 'basic user', 'independent user' and 'proficient user'. Disagreement also exists as to what proficiency measures should be taking into account. For example, to what extent should a test of English proficiency take into account awareness of the target culture given that there are now so many world 'Englishes' and, as a corollary, whether there is an inherent test bias in relation to the cultural background of the test taker (see for example Verhoeven and de Jong 1992).

Prosodic Features see **Paralinguistic**.

Prototypicality in language is a term which applies to lexical items, phoneme recognition and grammar in terms of how typical are any examples from a sub-set. For example, we can say that a sparrow is a very good example of a bird, it reflects the essence of what it is to be a bird, and therefore it is highly prototypical. However, a penguin is considered to be a bird even though it has lost its power of flight and therefore is much less prototypical than a sparrow. Prototypicality can be applied by analogy to the rules of a language and their metalinguistic terms. Some sentences in a given language exemplify the rule really well, others do not. As a consequence prototypicality makes a difference as to whether learners find it difficult to acquire a grammar rule or not. Prototypicality has been found (Hu Guangwei 2002) to be a constraint which mediates other variables (such as time pressure and the amount of attention being given to form) during spoken production tasks.

Pyscholinguistics is an interdisciplinary field which brings together linguistics and psychology (both their theories and empirical methods) to understand the mental processes and psychological mechanisms which make it possible for humans to acquire, understand, produce and process language. The main themes in psycholinguistic research are how humans understand spoken and written language, and how we produce and acquire language. Unlike linguistics where the main focus is on understanding the structure of language and languages, in psycholinguistics, psychological techniques and methods are used to carry out studies aimed at understanding a range of issues which inform our understanding of the nature of the psychological mechanisms which allow us to acquire and use language. For example, neuroimaging techniques and methodologies allow the study of the relationship between the brain and linguistic behaviour, while experimental techniques with infants and young children enable the study of speech perception and early phonological, lexical and grammatical development. Within each area of interest under the broad umbrella term 'psycholinguistics', the general approach is data-driven where psychological methods are applied to address the questions in some form of investigation. This results in the production of psychological evidence which allows us to better understand the 'how' of language – how it is learnt, used and understood. As part of psycholinguistic research aims to draw upon both linguistics and psychology, much of psycholinguistic research aims to identify how language processes interact with known cognitive systems (such as memory systems, perception systems etc.). Much SLA research is informed by psycholinguistics theories and approaches, where the goal is on identifying the underlying nature of L2 learning mechanisms, L2 representation and knowledge etc. For example, Robinson (2001) presents a series of chapters illustrating how psycholinguistic issues (e.g., memory, attention, perception and processing) are understood within SLA research.

Questioning is a practical pedagogical technique used by teachers in order to achieve a number of objectives in SLA instructed environments and is central to much **classroom discourse**. One objective is to ascertain what the learner already knows or can say. Another is linked to the current learning objective, that is, encouraging the focused practice of specific linguistic forms or vocabulary groups new to the learner(s). Broadly, questions can be divided into 'genuine questions' which, although they may contain a target structure the teacher is interested in, nevertheless are conceptualized as wanting the learner to communicate some new information to the teacher (and/or other learners). These are sometimes referred to as referential questions. Display questions on the other hand are those where the teacher already knows what the answer will be. Take as an example: 'Sam, what time did you manage to get home last night?'. This may be a genuine question where the information that Sam gives might be followed by a genuinely interested response from the teacher: 'oh good, in spite of all that snow!'. Or it may be a question where the teacher has 'fed' the student the answer by, for instance, holding up a clock which says 8pm. Display questions can be further sub-divided into open and closed questions ('what's the time now?' and 'Is it 5.15 or 5.30?' respectively). It was generally accepted in the 1980s (e.g., Brock 1986; White and Lightbown 1984) that genuine questions elicit more complex and longer answers and are therefore more likely to result in pushed output (see **output hypothesis**) as well as being less likely to bore or de-motivate students. Surprisingly little research has been carried out on the effects of questioning types in more recent years (see also **turn-taking**).

Recasts are a type of oral feedback to learner errors and are usually thought to be the least disruptive to the on-going communicative activity (see **focus on form**). An example of a recast is:

Teacher: Yves, do you help with the cooking at home?
Yves: Yes I am helping at weekends.

95

Teacher: I help at weekends [*with downward intonation*] . . . only at weekends?

Thus a recast involves the teacher (or more advanced interlocutor) repeating the learner's utterance and changing only those elements needed to make it correct without changing any of the meaning, and allowing for the conversation or questioning sequence to immediately resume. A number of studies have reported that recasts are ineffective (e.g., Lyster 1998) in that learners may not regard them as corrections (being too involved with focusing on the message) and therefore defeat their very purpose which is to allow learners to notice the gap between their **interlanguage** and the correct form and, as a consequence, to **uptake** and **intake** the information. Interventions using recasts which appear to have been more successful have involved systematic recasting of the same grammatical element (e.g., Doughty and Varela 1998) or where the recast has been delivered with particular force or stress. Shorter recasts and ones where only one element is being recast also appear more likely to facilitate acquisition (Philp 2003).

Receptive vocabulary knowledge generally refers to the knowledge of a word that is perceived (form/meaning) during listening and reading, whereas *productive* knowledge is relevant for speaking and writing. This distinction is not entirely satisfactory because even during listening and reading tasks, a productive skill is required, namely to create meaning (Nation 2001). These terms are largely considered to be ends of a continuum as opposed to discrete categories. Some researchers interchange the terms *receptive* for *passive* and *productive* for *active*. However, others argue that *passive* vocabulary in particular is an inappropriate term as language users are engaged in active processes even during listening and reading tasks (Nation 2001). Nation states that for the most part, receptive vocabulary learning is considered easier than productive learning. Reasons underlying this observation include the fact that productive knowledge requires knowing something extra – all the knowledge involved in receptive vocabulary skills, plus the articulatory patterns.

Restructuring is a process that, in terms of language development, occurs gradually in long-term memory. Often associated with the work of the psychologist McLaughlin (1990), it refers to a qualitative change that takes place as a child learner moves from stage to stage in their development. Thus it is a process in which the building blocks or components of a current pattern in the brain are 'co-ordinated, integrated or reorganized into new units whereby the new units become more proficient' (p. 118) through two basic processes: automatization (no longer having to stop and think about what they are saying) and the principle of economy (discarding hypotheses that no longer match the new evidence).

One form of restructuring is the progression from more exemplar-based representations of language (e.g., formulaic language) to more rule-based representations (see also **U-shaped behaviour**) where its application to second language learning becomes more obvious. McLaughlin also gives the useful example of young children who may consider (advanced) age, appearance and behaviour to be fundamental to the meaning of 'uncle', whereas older children will focus on what they understand by kinship and family relations even if the uncle is only 15 years old. This could be said to mirror, in the L2 learning context, the transition from 'foreign' cultural conceptualizations to becoming familiar with those concepts.

Salience see **Frequency Effects**.

Scaffolding is a metaphor used both in SLA and general educational literature to refer to the assistance that a teacher or more proficient/experienced other learner can bring to an individual's process of learning. It is closely associated with Vygotsky's (1978: 86) concept of the *Zone of Proximal Development* which is 'the distance between the actual developmental level [of a child], as determined by independent problem solving, and the level of potential development' attainable through the guidance of others. The idea is that this 'other' provides the support as the learning edifice is being gradually constructed by the learner. It is not a question of simply transferring knowledge to the learner but of helping him/her progress up the different floors of the building by providing a process framework which guides the learner from floor level to floor level. Graham and Macaro (2008) used the terms 'high scaffolding' and 'low scaffolding' to describe the amount of teacher and researcher support and guidance provided to students during a listening strategies instruction programme. The emphasis was not on telling them *how* to listen but in *helping them to discover* their own best way of listening. In practical terms scaffolding can be provided by raising awareness of current knowledge and processes, teacher modelling, teacher feedback, providing reminders and clues during tasks. As students become more confident and proficient the scaffolding can be gradually removed leaving behind a more **autonomous** learner.

Schema theory, in educational contexts, is often associated with the work of the psychologist R. C. Anderson, although the term was probably introduced by Bartlett (1932) who proposed that knowledge is a gradually increasing network of mental structures involving propositions about the world. Basically schema (plural schemata) is what a person knows about the world through his/her interpretations of the experiences s/he has had. 'Topics', 'concepts' or units of schema are constantly being added to during one's lifetime. For example, one may have schematic knowledge linked to the word 'inferno' and, depending on one's life experience may only associate it with 'fire in a building' (from the film *Towering Inferno*) or, if the opportunity has arisen, further associate it with Dante's vision of hell. Schema information can thus be divided into universal properties (inferno always involves heat or fire); shared properties (as in the film, or Dante's poem); personal properties (a personal experience of a terrible fire which one has associated with the word 'inferno') as well as metaphorical properties.

Sometimes new information may contradict previous schematic information possibly throwing the learner into confusion until further information allows (accommodates) the new information to be linked to previous information. The understanding of new information is virtually impossible without some sort of prior knowledge. It is believed that concrete concepts lead to the gradual creation of abstract concepts and not the other way round. In SLA, schema theory is usually considered as a theoretical component of comprehension (see **top-down processes** and also **topic familiarity**). For an introductory discussion of its applicability to reading, see Carrell and Eisterhold (1983).

Self-determination see **Motivation**.

Self-regulation see **Motivation**.

Silent Period see **Natural Language Acquisition**.

(The) Silent way is an approach to language teaching and learning developed by Caleb Gattegno in the early 1970s. The focus of this approach is on the learner being autonomous and the teacher remaining silent for much of the time. Lessons are largely improvised with the aid of a standard set of materials which include phoneme, colour spelling, word and picture charts, a pointer and, most famously, a set of coloured 'Cuisenaire' rods (small coloured blocks of different sizes used in the teaching of mathematics), through which the teacher and learners create situations, referring to the various charts with the aid of the pointer.

Underpinning the Silent Way is the notion that language learners bring their own experience, language abilities and skills from their mother tongue which can be transferred to the language being learnt with minimal intervention from the teacher, while the teacher guides the learners in using the new language correctly in terms of sounds, prosody, vocabulary, grammar, etc., and its appropriateness to the situation. Gattegno stresses the difference between gaining knowledge of a language and developing 'know-how' in a language, which the learner can only gain through discovery, extensive practice, especially with physical objects, and solving problems.

Simultaneous (vs. Sequential) Bilingual L1 Acquisition. A child learning two languages from birth is considered an example of *simultaneous* bilingualism (also known as infant bilingualism or bilingual first language acquisition). A child learning a language after around the age of 3 years is considered a case of *sequential* bilingualism. However, it should be noted that the exact age at which bilingual L1 acquisition (the acquisition of two L1's simultaneously) becomes a case of sequential bilingualism (or L2 learning) is not yet clear from research (Baker 2006). One reasonably common pattern observed in simultaneous bilingualism is the case where one parent speaks one language to a child, while the other parent speaks a different language (known as *one parent, one language*). Sequential bilingualism can occur in contexts where the child speaks one language in the home environment, but upon starting pre-school or kindergarten is exposed to a second language. See Baker (2006) for a detailed review of different contexts and issues surrounding these different examples of bilingual language development.

Sociocultural theory springs from a realization in many authors that not all can be explained purely in terms of the internal cognitive processes of the individual. Drawing heavily on the work of the psychologist Vygotsky (1978), it argues that an explanation of learning has to reflect the totality of mental processes and those processes include the social milieu. Indeed the sociocultural setting may well be the determining variable in the development of higher orders of mental activity such as language. Just as humans use tools (both real and symbolic) to mediate between them and the physical world, so language is used as a mediating tool. SLA cannot stray from that fundamental principle. In SLA research (see the extensive work of Lantolf [Lantolf and Appell 1994] and of Kramsch 2002) socio-cultural theory has been used as a framework for analysing tasks and activities. Given the same task, not all students will interpret it in the same way and consequently their behaviour in relation to that task will vary with its interpretation (Couchlan and Duff 1994). It has also been used as a way to describe how learners regulate their learning behaviours through meta-comments about the language task and through interacting with others (Tarone and Swain 1995). See also **inner speech**: private speech.

Speech Rate see **Fluency.**

Strategies see **Language Learner Strategies**.

Sub-vocalizing see **Private Speech**.

Syllable stress in English is often difficult for learners as there are no absolute rules about which syllables to stress; a wrongly stressed syllable may lead to non-comprehension or misunderstanding (e.g., career vs carrier). There are some guidelines for learners, for example:

(1) Most two-syllable nouns and adjectives have their stress on the first syllable: table, bucket, present, lively (2) Most two-syllable verbs have their stress on the last syllable: suggest, present, begin. (3) Words ending in –ic, -sion and –tion have their stress on the penultimate syllable: telepathic, television, destination. (4) Words ending in cy-, -ty, -phy, -al have their stress on the ante-penultimate syllable (third from end): democracy, ability, geography. (5) For compound words, nouns tend to have their stress on the first part, as in 'blackbird'; adjectives on the second part, as in 'good-natured'; while for verbs, the stress is usually on the second part, as in 'overspend'.

Long compound words are sometimes said to have a secondary stress in addition to the main syllable stress, as, for example, in 'ammunition', where 'am' might be thought to have a stress in addition to 'ni'. However, it is probably best to think of English as having one level of word stress with some unstressed syllables being pronounced with vowel reduction.

Syllable stress in words should not be confused with sentence stress in which speech rhythms in English are maintained at roughly equal intervals (isochrony) through the tonic or stress on the main information word in a clause or sentence being spoken with more effort as in the sentence: I went to see the photographer, ^ but he wasn't there. This sentence contains three tonic or sentence stresses on main information words and also a so-called silent stress (a beat) before 'but' in order to maintain the rhythm and avoid stressing 'but', which, if it were stressed, would give the sentence an odd-sounding, nursery-rhyme rhythm.

Tandem learning takes its name from the idea that speakers of different languages may work closely together (i.e., 'in tandem') to learn one another's language and culture through a reciprocal exchange of language. Ideally, both partners should benefit equally from the exchange. Partners are responsible for establishing their own learning goals and deciding on methods and materials. Tandem learning may take place in face-to-face situations or by telephone or on-line, synchronously or asynchronously. Forms of tandem learning may also be called 'language exchange' or 'language buddies', or other terms which convey the reciprocal and autonomous nature of the learning.

Task-based learning (TBL) is a form of instruction situated at the extreme communicative end of a continuum of language teaching approaches and is generally associated with **communicative language teaching** (CLT). However, whereas teachers using a CLT approach usually plan for tasks at the end of a teaching sequence which might begin with presentation and practice, TBL starts with the task. A guiding principle of TBL is that there is a communication problem to be solved by the participants; therefore meaning is foregrounded. In TBL learners are not given the language with which to communicate as TBL is not concerned with displaying knowledge. However, because participants are forced to express meaning with the resources they have, they notice gaps in their linguistic competence which can be addressed in post-task 'language focus' activities. The whole procedure is then said to help drive development.

Research in TBL has centred on task-manipulation. For example, the extent to which allowing participants to plan a task in advance of performance results in greater fluency, complexity or accuracy (Ellis 2005). Another avenue of research has been whether different task-types produce more negotiation of meaning, again a source of possible development. Surprisingly two-way information exchange tasks appear to produce less quality negotiation than, say, one-way information exchange or 'consensus tasks'.

Criticisms of TBL have centred on the impression given that task X will produce universal student behaviour Y. For example Slimani-Rolls (2003) has demonstrated that different students interpret (and therefore perform) tasks differently according to the social and cultural situation they perceive themselves to be in. Critics have also argued that TBL is very difficult to use with low proficiency students, beginners or with large monolingual classrooms.

(The) Teachability hypothesis (usually associated with the early work of Pienemann 1984) is directly linked to a series of other theories: **acquisition orders, developmental sequences** and **learnability**. It recognizes that L2 learning is constrained in that stages cannot be skipped over but have to be sufficiently consolidated before the next stage can be learnt. As a consequence, it is fruitless for a teacher to attempt to teach without showing respect to established acquisition pathways. In Pienemann's study, German (L2) word order development was measured resulting from two weeks of instruction among Italian children in Germany. Results suggested that only the group that was 'ready' benefited from the instruction. In other words, once the appropriate stage has been reached then instruction can speed up progress to the next stage. An area of related research which has attracted considerable attention is whether teaching more marked (or 'more difficult') aspects of a grammatical feature automatically leads to the acquisition of less marked or easier aspects of the same feature.

Technology Mediated Language Learning see **Computer Assisted Language Learning**.

Topic familiarity in SLA is most often associated with research on listening and reading comprehension (see **top-down and bottom-up processes**). How familiar one is with a topic relates to **schema theory**, that is the complex set of mental structures in which information connected with a topic is stored. As the listener or reader of a text makes first contact with the meaning of that text through words or phrases it contains, the familiarity with the topic, triggered by those words and phrases, will be activated. The extent of activation, and the effectiveness of that activation, will depend on a number of factors which so far have been under-explored in the literature: the modality of the text (listening is more likely to involve initial levels of activation than reading); culturally linked familiarity, how the knowledge of the topic is structured; interest in the topic; learner characteristics and so on. A number of studies have suggested that, if one is familiar with a topic, comprehension is facilitated and this has led to a possible practitioner belief that all selected texts should be familiar to the learners. However, this approach may not necessarily develop comprehension skills when, 'in the real world' the topic is unfamiliar. Similarly, some authors have advocated the use of 'advance organizers' (see **graphic organizers**) where topic familiarity is stimulated by the teacher in order to facilitate comprehension. Again, this may or may not develop comprehension skills in the long term. Comprehension problems may arise when anomalies in the text are not detected by the learner, that is, when later in-text evidence, which is contradictory, is ignored and initial (imprecise) topic familiarity is not monitored and moderated (Tsui and Fullilove 1998).

Transfer see **Contrastive Analysis**.

T Unit. The T in T unit stands for 'minimal terminal unit' and was introduced as a term by Kellogg W. Hunt (1965) to measure the development of sentences in the writing of primary and secondary school children. According to Hunt (1970), each T unit contains one independent clause and its dependent clauses. In his terms, they are 'the shortest units into which a piece of discourses can be cut without leaving any sentence fragments as residue' (p. 189). Hunt found that the mean length of T unit (MLTU), obtained by dividing the number of T units into the total number of words in the writing sample, was a reliable measure of syntactic complexity and that gradual lengthening occurred from grade to grade . Examples of two types of T units are given below:

1. There was a little boy next door who had a red bicycle. [S (S)] = 1 T unit
2. There was a little boy next door, and he had a red bicycle. (S + S) = 2 T units

In example 1, a clause (in this case a relative clause) is embedded in an independent, main clause, giving the sentence one T unit. In example 2, two (it could be more) independent clauses (with subjects and finite verbs) are conjoined giving the sentences two T units.

T units have been widely used in SLA research to track the development of syntactic complexity and accuracy in second language learners, in both oral and written production. Measures include words per T unit (usually as mean), correct T units (and number of words) and clauses per T unit. T unit analysis has been criticized (e.g., by Kathleen Bardovi-Harlig 1992) for the artificial way in which it breaks up coordinated clauses and thereby ignores what might be sophisticated rhetorical structure in adult second language writers.

Turn-taking patterns in classrooms fall under the general heading of **classroom discourse** and are of interest to researchers because of what they reveal about levels of teacher control. Perhaps the best-known and researched turn-taking pattern is the Initiation, Response, Feedback (IRF) sequence. Take the following example:

Teacher: Who are the people in the picture . . . . euh . . . Massimo?
Massimo: A man and a woman.
Teacher: a man and a woman, yes, that's right, and where are they. . . .
Giorgia?
Giorgia: in front of a nightclub.
Teacher: Yeah, good, now let's think about the time of day in which this is set. . . .

Here the teacher 'Initiates' by asking a question about a picture that the whole class can see (**questioning: display**) and 'nominates' Massimo who 'Responds'. The teacher then provides 'Feedback' via the words 'a man and a woman, yes, that's right', before Initiating a second IRF sequence by nominating Giorgia.

A great deal of classroom discourse is structured around the IRF sequence. A negative consequence of this is that approximately two-thirds of classroom talk is produced by the teacher with the whole class sharing the other third. A further negative consequence is that it turns all talk into an evaluation of what learners know or can do.

Slightly less teacher-centred turn-taking patterns can be achieved by a teacher requiring one learner to Initiate and for another learner to Respond and withholding feedback unless absolutely necessary.

An introduction to the theme of turn-taking can be found in the early work of Allwright (1980). In L2 research there appears to have been relatively less interest in this theme in recent years, whereas a research effort has continued in L1 research.

Universal grammar (**UG**) is a linguistic theory proposed by Chomsky (1965) which attempts to account for the grammatical competence of every language user, regardless of which language s/he speaks. The basic notion underlying UG theory is that languages have a set of abstract underlying principles which govern the structures that languages can take. These principles, in addition to specific sets of parameters on which these principles can vary, constrain the problem of language acquisition and enable the developing child to learn their native language. A well-developed description of these principles and parameters is found in Chomsky's Government and Binding (GB) Theory (e.g., Chomsky 1990). The essence of UG then is to identify and describe these abstract principles underlying grammatical competence which enables a language learner to master their native language. With respect to SLA, White (1989) outlines the main issues of how UG relates to the questions of L2 learning. In particular, White discusses the evidence concerning the role of UG in L2 learning in older learners. The main issue is whether or not UG is available at all, or whether UG is an important aspect of language acquisition that is unavailable as a consequence of the offset of the **critical period hypothesis**. Cook and Newson (2007) also present a lucid description of UG and include a chapter on UG and SLA.

Uptake is a term used to describe a stage in a process of potential language acquisition and is a student 'move' during **interaction**. It is a signal, of whatever kind, that demonstrates to the teacher or the researcher that the student has **noticed** an element in the interaction. This element is usually some kind of negative feedback by the teacher or more advanced learner (e.g., a **recast** or more explicit form of **error correction**, see Ellis, Basturkmen and Loewen 2001). Examples of uptake, to a teacher correction (e.g., 'I went to the park'), of the student's incorrect formulation '*I goed to the park', could be any of the following:

1. nodding or other non-verbal signal
2. 'oh huh huh'
3. 'oh right ... went'
4. 'went to the park'
5. 'I went to the park'

Clearly, one of the problems with uptake is understanding or measuring the amount or depth of learning that is taking place. Examples 1 and 2 may just be signals that the learner has spotted a problem. Examples 3 and 4 show some evidence of focusing on the problematic area but no evidence of rule-based linking of function (describing a past event) with form. Example 5 could simply be a repetition with hardly any processing occurring. This has led some researchers to posit that only delayed measurements of learning are of value rather than immediate uptake moves and to other researchers arguing for stimulated recall techniques in order to better interpret uptake moves (Kim and Han 2007).

U-shaped behaviour refers to an observation that in development, learners often go through three distinct phases, where they can initially manifest accurate performance, then show a decrease in their performance, which in turn is followed by a progression in learning. Viewed on a graph, with time on the x axis, and accuracy on the y, this 'accurate, less accurate, accurate' pattern resembles a U shape, hence the term 'u-shaped function'. A classic example of this common developmental pattern can be found in children learning the inflection system of English verbs. Children go through a phase early on in learning where they are accurate on both regular and irregular English verbs, which is then followed by a phase where the child makes numerous errors on the irregular verbs and incorrectly adds regular inflection onto irregular forms (*wented* or *goed*). This period of relative ungrammaticality is then followed by a period where the child seems to have learnt to distinguish between the regular and irregular forms. Many developmental psychologists have argued that this U-shaped function illustrates learning. In the example used here, the child is 'learning' while in the trough of the U, that, while there might be a pattern that English verbs are inflected with the past tense morpheme [-ed], not all verbs take this morpheme. McLaughlin (1987) among others presents a view of SLA where learners are acquiring a complex skill, as in other domains of cognition, which requires constant **restructuring** where subskills for different tasks are integrated and become more automatic. This **restructuring** can often result in a u-shaped function on many features and aspects of L2 lexical and syntactic development.

Vocabulary see **Receptive Vocabulary**.

Washback effect refers to the practice of allowing an end to dictate the means. Most often it is applied to the practice of allowing language exams or tests to have an undue influence on how the language is taught. Some authors argue that a test's validity should include a measure of its positive effect on language teaching. Alderson and Hamp-Lyons (1996) compared exam and non-exam classes taught by the same teacher and concluded that a hypothesis which suggests a simple one-way relationship between test and prior teaching is much more complex than one would suppose.

Working memory is a temporary memory store within which information can be processed. The extent to which new information is processed in working memory can influence the likelihood that this new information will be committed to long-term memory and/or easily retrieved. The term working memory supplanted to a large extent the previously used term 'short term' memory, to underscore the importance of the level of processing which takes place within working memory – it is the temporary memory storage area where information is encoded and integrated. A widely considered model of working memory is found in Baddeley and Hitch (1974, and see Baddeley et al. 1998 for a description of how their working memory model is important in language learning). There are three main components to this model (but note Baddeley (2000) has argued for an additional component called the 'episodic buffer' which has received less attention). These components are the *Central Executive*, the *Phonological Loop* and the *Visuo-Spatial Sketchpad*. The Central Executive is the system which regulates and integrates information across the 'slave' systems (phonological loop and visuo-spatial sketchpad). The phonological loop consists of both an auditory store where auditory (phonological information) is stored temporarily, together with an articulatory rehearsal component in which this phonological information can be activated and processed. The visuo-spatial sketchpad is argued to hold visual information. This is a very influential model of working memory and the phonological loop in particular has been argued to be a critical component of word learning (Baddeley et al. 1998). Within SLA, researchers have shown that L2 learning can in part be predicted by working memory capacity and the ability to hold in working memory phonological representations of new (L2) input (e.g., Ellis 2001).

(A) Writing system is a finite set of visual symbols (and in the case of Braille tactile marks) which has been adopted by a given speech community to represent the spoken language. Clearly the purpose of adopting such a system is to enable communication via a visual medium. Writing systems can be divided broadly into alphabetic (e.g., Spanish), syllabaries (e.g., Arabic) and ideographic (e.g., Chinese). Additionally, and of particular interest to SLA, is the adoption for specific languages of a set of rules (e.g., type of script to be used, orthographic representations of words and utterances, punctuation) and conventions (appropriate use of certain written styles) according to the communicative writing situation (e.g., abbreviations, or symbols such as ☺). It is in the language specificity that lies the interest for SLA researchers (for an introduction see Cook and Bassetti 2005). English learners of Greek are required to learn a new set of letters whereas a French learner of English needs to learn no new letters. However, the latter may struggle with the **phoneme-grapheme** correspondence differences in the two languages. An Italian learner of Chinese will need to gradually overcome the fact that the written form of the target language is less reliant on the concept of the word than his/her first language. Learning to read and write across languages is a rapidly emerging area of SLA study and currently is particularly focused on young learners' literacy development (see for example Geva and Wang 2001).

Zone of Proximal Development see **Scaffolding**.

3 Research Methods in Second Language Acquisition

Andrew D. Cohen and Ernesto Macaro

Introduction

In the first chapter of this book Macaro provided a conceptualization of the 'landscape' of research into second language acquisition (SLA) that is, the kinds of themes that have been investigated in recent years and published in five of the most prominent international journals. This landscape, as he admits, is only one way, a very personal way, of conceptualizing the interests of SLA researchers.

In this chapter we provide a similarly personal conceptualization of the kinds of research methods and research instruments that have been used in order to further the research aims and traditions that were synthesized in Chapter 1. There are a number of very good volumes on second language acquisition research methods each with its own character and conceptualization. For example, Seliger and Shohamy (1989) take the reader through all the stages of a research project from understanding the epistemological basis for research to reporting and summarizing the results. Mackey and Gass (2005) innovate in their textbook by dealing early on and robustly with ethical guidelines for research, and by painstakingly describing in detail the kinds of measures that tend to accompany both quantitative and qualitative research studies. Dörnyei (2007) takes a similar approach to research methods in his more recent volume, though his volume is directed at more experienced researchers, looks more broadly at the full range of applied linguistics research and deals with the increasingly common phenomenon of mixed methods research. A very different approach to that of Mackey and Gass or Dörnyei is taken by Graeme Porte (2002) in his 'practical approach to critical analysis of quantitative research'. Here, principles and guidelines for carrying out research are presented as a series of questions that the reader of an article should ask themselves when reading it, and presumably, principles and guidelines they should then apply in their own work.

Given this fine set of textbooks on research methods, we asked ourselves what the most appropriate contribution that a single chapter on research methods could make. After some deliberation we decided that we would start by referring readers to the work of our colleagues and would limit ourselves to providing perspectives that we had not hitherto come across in SLA methodology discussions.

Therefore, we begin with a brief introduction to paradigms in educational research. We then provide an overview of research methods used in SLA in the first decade of the twenty-first century, before going on to focus on some specific research instruments and techniques, particularly on the tests and tasks that have been employed by researchers because these seem to be increasing in the more recent literature and to some extent overshadowing the use of more traditional instruments such as questionnaires, interviews and ethnographies.

Epistemological Basis for Research

It would appear that the split in applied linguistic and especially SLA research between more quantitative and qualitative approaches seems to draw from a distinction in educational research between positivist approaches and constructivist ones. The positivist approach relied on observation and reason as a means of understanding behaviour. It drew on scientific description and looked for verification of findings. The emphasis was on quantitative research, on empirical science and rational methods, with an emphasis on objectivity. Positivism was, in fact, the philosophical basis for most quantitative research in education (Shank 1993).

The constructivist view was that the human mind had a role to play in creating an understanding of behaviour and other phenomena. Constructivists contended that a mechanistic and reductionist view of nature excluded choice, freedom, individuality and life experiences. Moreover, it was considered dehumanizing to impose rules of behaviour and thought, reducing researchers into observers set on discovering general laws governing human behaviour. Constructivists argued that the capacity for subjectivity should be regained. Anti-positivist approaches included *phenomenology* – the study of direct experience taken at face value, where behaviour is determined by the phenomena of experience rather than by external, objective and physically described reality. It also included *ethnomethodology*, concerned with how people make sense of their everyday world: interactions in a social encounter (the assumptions they make, the conventions they use and the practices they adopt) (Cohen and Manion 1994, pp. 29–32).

This split in approaches to research methods really fronted the issue of just what the nature of enquiry was and how to conceptualize social reality. Is SLA a reality that is external to or independent of the collection of human learners or is it something that can only be understood through the lenses of human beings (i.e., with different people construing the world in different ways)? What it comes down to is researchers – whether fledgling students or experienced professionals in the field – determining for themselves the nature of knowledge before they even begin to select research methods for answering their questions of interest.

The traditional way to contrast qualitative and quantitative approaches to research is by providing descriptors for the two, such as the one by Larsen-Freeman and Long (1991, p. 12), and echoed in Lazaraton (2002):

Quantitative Research – controlled, experimental, objective, inferential, outcome-oriented, reliable, particularistic, hard/replicable data, generalizable, aggregate analysis;
Qualitative Research – naturalistic, observational, subjective, descriptive, process-oriented, valid, holistic, real, rich/deep data, ungeneralizable, single-case analysis.

In an effort to clarify this distinction, sociolinguist Barbara Johnstone (2000) noted that quantitative studies tend to ask the research questions in mechanical ways (e.g., counting instances, computing means, calculating statistics), while qualitative studies ask them in non-mechanical ways (e.g., by asking about, watching or listening to phenomena of interest). In other words, quantitative discourse analysts seek to determine *how often* something happens, while *why* and *how* things happen are the focus of qualitative discourse analyses.

While Brown (2004) would contend that it is preferable to view the distinction between quantitative and qualitative research as a matter of degrees or a continuum rather than a clear-cut dichotomy, Dörnyei (2007, p. 20) feels that making the dichotomous distinction is a useful starting place. Having said that,

Dörnyei does devote attention to what are referred to as *mixed methods research,* namely, hybrid studies that combine qualitative and quantitative methods. Such research is characterized by methodological triangulation, to help reduce the inherent weaknesses of individual methods. Dörnyei would see the variety of possible combinations of methods as rich depending on how the combining is carried out – e.g., not just sequentially. He provides the following arguments in favour of mixed methods (pp. 45–46):

1. Qualitative research is seen as too context-specific and involving unrepresentative samples. Thus, it may be wise to start with a robust sample. Yet a qualitative approach can complement a quantitative one which may be seen as overly simplistic, decontextualized and reductionist in terms of its generalizations, failing to capture the meanings that people attach to their lives and circumstances.
2. A mixed methods approach allows for a multi-level analysis of complex issues, where both numeric trends and verbal descriptions are included.
3. Using a mixed method can improve validity, through the convergence and corroboration of findings.
4. Such research can reach multiple audiences because of its potential interest to larger audiences of readers.

He then adds the following pitfalls of mixed methods:

1. There is a possibility that such research studies may become a substitute for sharp conceptual thinking and insightful analyses (Hesse-Biber and Leavy 2006, p. 334).
2. There is always the likelihood that the researcher does not have equal methodological skills for doing both kinds of research.
3. Mixing methods which are highly diverse may produce an 'anything goes' approach.

In any effort to determine just how often applied linguists were doing one or another kind of research – or at least getting it published – Lazaraton (2005) classified all the data-based, empirical research articles in *Language Learning, Modern Language Journal, Studies in Second Language Acquisition,* and the *TESOL Quarterly* during an 11-year period, 1991–2001. Her goal was to determine how many reported on quantitative vs. qualitative research, using as a criterion for quantitative that there was a rigorous statistical analysis of the data. She classified 86% of the 524 articles as reflecting quantitative research, only 13% as qualitative, and 1% as involving mixed approaches. She noted that at the time (namely, 6–7 years ago) the *TESOL Quarterly* would be the most likely of the four journals to publish a qualitative research report. Since Lazaraton's study was focusing primarily on the 1990s, we felt that it would be useful to take another look at the research picture a decade later.

Taking Stock of Current Research Practices

In this section, therefore, we will look at all the studies from five journals: *Modern Language Journal, Language Learning, Studies in Second Language Acquisition, Applied Linguistics* and *Language Teaching Research*. Given Lazaraton's analysis to 2001, we chose the dates between 2002 and 2007 and we here summarize the design types, their frequency and the frequency of the different instruments used. In essence, we first try to provide the reader with a brief compendium of current trends in research methods. Secondly, we conceptualize the aims of studies as potentially falling into four categories of investigation types:

1. investigations of linguistic knowledge
2. investigations of linguistic performance
3. investigations of attitudes and perceptions
4. investigations of learners' cognitive processing.

As Macaro began reporting in Chapter 1, a total of 419 empirical studies were examined from the five journals between the years 2002 and 2007 as follows: *Applied Linguistics* (N = 57), *Studies in Second Language Acquisition* (N = 75), *Language Teaching Research* (N = 77), *Modern Language Journal* (N = 103) and *Language Learning* (N = 107). We add a note of caution here. By 'examined' we mean that a small team of research assistants (acknowledgements made in Chapter 1) scanned the abstracts and main texts for the research questions, the overall design and the instruments used. The data reproduced here is as reported (and as could best be gleaned) in those sections of each study. It has to be said that the process of extracting the data we were interested in was not always easy. The reason is that research questions were not always stated under a clear heading, the type of study design had sometimes to be inferred, the instruments were not always clearly explained and, particularly, not always provided in the appendices. We return to this problem in our conclusions. In the meantime we should bear in mind that the data presented here may contain a few inaccuracies because the 'true' information we were looking for was buried in other sections of the article. We unfortunately did not have the resources to thoroughly read every single one of the 419 studies that we considered of an empirical nature and directly related to SLA.

Study Design Types

Of the 419 papers, as we can see from Table 1, a little under half were 'explorations of relationships', with 'descriptive studies' and 'experimental studies' taking up equally the remaining half.

We will now describe what we mean by this three-category system of study design.

In *descriptive studies*, the researchers (usually, or at least in theory) do not have a preconceived idea of the phenomenon under investigation. They intend to carry out an exploration of the phenomenon by simply observing, measuring it and/or describing it. Because they do not hold preconceived ideas about the nature of the phenomenon, they also do not hold beliefs about the independent variables which might affect the phenomenon. The term 'grounded approach' is often used to describe this type of study (because the data, as it were, emerge from the bottom up) and the over-arching methodologies used to describe the phenomenon are usually, ethnographic and/or qualitative in nature. 'Case studies' (see below) are good examples of descriptive studies, but descriptive studies are certainly not limited to descriptions of individual cases. Moreover descriptive studies can use quantitative instruments once the validity and suitability of these to answer the research questions have been established, usually after an initial qualitative phase. An example of a descriptive study is Hyland and Tse (2004). Here the researchers analysed 240 dissertations by students writing in their second language (L2) in order to arrive at an understanding of (1) the range of devices that writers deploy in order to organize the texts that they produce and (2) the ways in which they communicate with their readers. Another example of a descriptive study is that of Vickers (2007) who collected naturalistic data from seven team meetings of six university engineering students (one a non-native English speaker) in order to describe the interactional processes that defined who the expert, socialized participants were, and those interactional processes that worked to socialize novice participants.

Table 1 Study design types

Design type	Applied Linguistics %	Language Learning %	Language Teaching Research %	Modern Language Journal %	Studies in Second Language Acquisition %	Total %
Descriptive	42	19	45	29	4	28
Exploration of relationships	35	57	30	51	49	44
Experimental	23	24	25	19	47	28

Explorations of relationships studies look for relationships or associations among different variables. These are existing variables, occurring naturally in time and space, and the researcher does not change the nature of these variables nor add to them in any way. In these studies, however, researchers normally have some knowledge of the phenomenon under scrutiny or at least sufficient knowledge for them to ask questions such as 'what is the impact of phonological awareness on listening ability?', 'what is the relationship between learner motivation and teaching styles?'; 'what most affects success in L2 learning, length of residence in the target country or age of arrival in that country?'. In other words the relationship examined can be between dependent and independent variables or between two or more variables without specifying which one impacts on which. In effective studies exploring relationships, the 'face validity' of the relationship is high. For example, the relationship between assiduity of study and learning success has high face validity whereas the relationship between ownership of a washing machine and language learning success has less face validity – it makes less common sense.

An example of an exploration-of-relationships type of study is by Leeser (2004). In this study a number of variables were compared for their potential effect on students' comprehension of L2 texts, as well as their ability to process future tense morphology. So comprehension and ability to process morphology were the 'dependent variables', the outcome measures that Leeser was trying to investigate. The independent variables were 'mode' (the participants either read or listened to the text), 'topic familiarity' (whether the topic of the text was familiar to the students) and 'pausing' (whether short pauses were inserted in the text or not). In the Leeser study it is clear which are the independent and which the dependent variables. He was trying to test the effect of one variable on the other – to show causation. In fact, the majority of studies exploring relationships between variables attempt to show causation. A minority of studies take a correlational approach – in other words, investigating whether a higher value for X also means a higher value for Y. Such a study is Griffiths (2003) where 'strategy use', 'course level' and 'age' were correlated with one another to see which pair was most strongly linked.

Experimental studies investigate whether, by changing the world in some way (the independent variable), there is *an effect* on some other aspect of the world. In the case of SLA, the effect investigated is usually on language learning or on learner behaviour. In other words, the researcher manipulates the situation to see if the manipulation has an effect on the dependent variable. A typical researcher manipulation is an intervention of some kind. For example a researcher might investigate whether by exposing learners to a different kind of teaching method to what they are normally exposed to results in better learning. Or, a researcher may set up a situation where one group of learners is exposed to a particular technique and another group to a different technique.

113

For example one group might be exposed to a target syntactic structure by reading a short story and another group learns the same structure by having the rules explained to them by the teacher. Experimental studies should always have a 'control group' or 'comparison group', which does not get 'the treatment' or is not exposed to the change. The difference between 'control' and 'comparison' is usually explained by the procedure adopted for deciding which participants get the treatment and which do not. If the allocation is done through randomization of individuals to groups, the non-treatment group is usually called a 'control group'. If the allocation is done on the basis of non-randomization it is usually called a 'comparison group'. For example, using an intact class of learners that roughly matches the characteristics of the treatment class would be to use a comparison group.

The 'gold standard' for the experimental study is the randomized control trial where the participants are 'randomly allocated' to the different groups or 'conditions'. Experimental study designs in SLA are considered to be the most 'scientific' because they try to emulate the natural sciences' approach to research even though, in SLA, researchers are dealing with processes which ultimately occur in the brain but are investigated through means other than understanding the functions of the brain. In this type of study, the researcher usually formulates a hypothesis about what the outcomes are likely to be, based on the theory (or past evidence) that underpins the study. The intention is to test the theory, to see if it actually predicts what it claims to predict will happen if the right conditions are established and the situation is manipulated in a particular way.

Let us now look at how the five journals differ in their approaches and publication of different study types. Our intention is to provide information of use to authors who are looking for a good fit between the paper that they wish to submit and key journals in the field.

In *Applied Linguistics* there is a considerable focus on textual data and the journal *tends to* take a 'linguistics' rather than 'psychology' perspective. We should note again that this journal publishes articles on other aspects of applied linguistics not just SLA. Hence the total number of articles examined in this journal is considerably less than the other four. Because of its linguistic perspective, *Applied Linguistics* tends to have a predominance of 'descriptive studies' – ones where the language use or language development of a particular group is analysed in detail but with less reference to variables or to interventions.

In *Language Teaching Research*, classroom observation features strongly because much of the focus is, indeed, on teachers and teaching rather than learners and learning. Again, the tendency is towards descriptive studies but here it is behaviour that is being described rather than language in use.

The *Modern Language Journal* is probably the most eclectic of the journals both in terms of research designs and areas of research focus. We should note, nevertheless a predominance of exploration-of-relationships study designs with a considerable number of these employing survey or questionnaire type data (see below).

Language Learning is fairly experimental in character but also has a preponderance of explorations of relationships design types. A feature we have noted about *Language Learning* is the frequent use of triangulation and employment of mixed methods.

Studies in Second Language Acquisition is without doubt the most experimental of the five journals with many studies using randomization of groups to conditions. We should note that there is almost a total absence of purely descriptive studies and ethnography is rarely used by authors publishing in this journal.

We will now look in a little more detail at which were the most popular research instruments used.

Research Instruments in SLA

As we can see from Table 2, tests of various kinds or language tasks used for the purpose of measuring competence, performance or some other learner

Table 2 Types of research instruments

	Frequency of mention as 'used'	% of total number of studies
Tests and tasks to measure performance	338	80
Questionnaires/surveys (all types of structures) also e-mail and on-line	118	28
Observations (usually recorded) of a class, a teacher or a group of students	68	16
Interviews (including via telephone or e-mail) individually or in groups	53	13
Analysis of learners' L2 spoken corpus (naturally occurring, not elicited)	22	5
Stimulated recall	15	4
Think-aloud protocols and task-based verbal reports	14	3
Diaries/journals	10	2.3
Analysis of learners' L2 written corpus (naturally occurring, not elicited)	10	2.3
Case studies (as stated)	9	2.1
Ethnography (as stated)	6	1.4
Content analysis of, for example, teaching materials	3	< 1
Action research (as stated)	2	< 1
Autobiographies	1	< 1
Total	669	

Table 3 Different types of tests and tasks

	Number	%
Vocabulary tests (various)	62	20
Comprehension tests (various)	52	15
Oral production test (free and/or narratives)	32	9
Written production test (free and/or narratives)	25	7
Grammaticality judgement/acceptability test	23	7
Infogap/jigsaw task	19	6
Oral production test (controlled) (e.g., oral interviews)	18	5
Standardized and/or international and/or national tests of proficiency (IELTS, Michigan)	14	4
Written production test (controlled)	8	2
Cloze test	8	2
Role-play task	7	2
Working memory tests (various)	7	2
Word list reading test	5	1
Generalization test	4	1
Discourse completion task	3	1
Minimal pair reading	3	1
Oral imitation test	3	1
Sentence combination test	3	1
Inferencing (of words in text) task	3	1
Aptitude test	2	< 1
Interpretation task	2	< 1
C-Test	2	< 1
Summary completion task	2	< 1
Translation task	2	< 1
Semantic category judgement task (auditory)	2	< 1
Fragment (or word) completion task	2	< 1
Lexical judgement test	2	< 1
Lexical diversity measure	1	
Decision-making task	1	
Passage reconstruction task	1	
Input memory task	1	
Imitation test	1	
Form correction task	1	
Picture-word interference task	1	
Reading span test (computerized)	1	
Morphological awareness judgement task	1	
Contextualized preference task	1	
Translation (of word) recognition task	1	
Aural discrimination test	1	
Word associates test	1	
Sentence completion test	1	
Sentence conjunction judgement test	1	
Truth-value judgement test	1	
Sentence reading task	1	
Form recognition task	1	
Tense identification task	1	

Sentence recognition task	1
Sentence repetition task	1
Passage correction task	1
Cross-language similarity judgement	1

attribute, constituted the category most widely represented under 'research instruments'. Quite often a combination or 'battery' of tests were used and, as we have indicated above, often a combination of research types was also employed in order to gain multiple perspectives on a phenomenon.

We should pause here to note something about the use of questionnaires and surveys. Although the frequency of use is relatively high, our calculation does include Language Background Questionnaires or Language Contact Profiles. In other words these were instances where the instrument was used more as general background information, rather than as the vehicle for gathering data on the main variable. We would estimate that 70% of mentions of 'questionnaire use' were for this type of data and about 30% for actually eliciting the opinion, behaviour, perceptions or attitudes of the participants as part of the main research questions. However, this is only a rough impression.

Research Instruments and Their Purpose

In summary, our analysis of the measures that applied linguists have been utilizing in empirical research studies over the last six years in the five key journals described above, found that four fifths of the measures used represented tests or tasks to measure performance. However, the number of standardized tests used was very low and, as we shall see below, very little researcher attention seems to be devoted to ensuring the validity of these tests. Nor is there a stated concern with piloting of these tests and tasks. The overview does not provide us with an insight into the purposes that these instruments have been put to, and it is this to which we now turn.

Issues of Categorization

As noted above, some studies adopt a mixed-methods approach, where not only are quantitative and qualitative methods combined to fit the purpose, but also a broader range of instruments is being used to measure the variables of interest. Hence, it is increasingly important for researchers to have some familiarity with different types of measures, and how best to combine them to get the desired results. Depending on their research questions, researchers may find themselves needing measures that fall, for example, in all four of the areas listed below:

1. <u>linguistic knowledge</u> – including grammatical judgement tests, discourse completion tasks, verbal report data and reaction time measures.
2. <u>linguistic performance/skills</u> – anything from tests of receptive ability using a multiple-choice format to cloze and C-tests, to free-recall protocols or story narration, to role-play.
3. <u>attitudes and perceptions</u> – including questionnaire/surveys (on and off-line), interviews (varyingly structured), journals, or use of a 'repertory grid' (to get at people's perceptions, assumptions and concepts).
4. <u>cognitive processing</u> – mostly through verbal report measures such as think-alouds, introspective and retrospective self-observation (also referred to as *stimulated recalls*) and self-report.

While the categories of 'linguistic knowledge' and 'linguistic performance' above would appear to be relatively discrete, a study could be designed that would, say, use a role-play to ultimately get at someone's knowledge about the language, making use of retrospective self-observational data from the learners indicating what they knew about the various forms that they used. By the same token, it would also be possible to use a grammatical judgement test to determine someone's receptive skills, such as their knowledge of third-person singular –*s* in English, and then to follow it up with forced elicitation of the form to get at the performance side (Mackey and Gass 2005, pp. 49–50).

So, as suggested above, a way of arriving at a level of confidence that the instrument is doing the job of data gathering which it is intended to do is to use 'on-line' techniques, where the 'participants' voice' is heard regarding the task they are actually doing. We will therefore take a brief look at what we argue is a continuum of elicitation techniques stretching from think-aloud protocols to stimulated recall.

Verbal Report: From Think-Aloud Protocols to Stimulated Recall

We consider the two verbal report techniques, think aloud and stimulated recall, as representing two polarities on a continuum because they involve two variables: time and distance from the learning event.

In a think-aloud protocol, the participants are given a task to perform and during the performance of that task they are asked to verbalize (i.e., to articulate) what their thought processes are. The researcher's role is merely to encourage that verbalization through prompting the participants with utterances such as 'please keep telling me what you are thinking'; 'please keep thinking aloud if you can'. Think-aloud implies no direct inspection of the mental state, but merely reportage. There is considerable debate as to how feasible it is to reliably capture these inner thought processes and whether the process of thinking aloud might distort the way that the participants would normally go about doing the task (for discussions and research evidence see Bowles and Leow 2005; Ericsson and Simon 1993; Leow and Morgan-Short 2004).

Particularly of concern is the use of think-aloud with tasks which involve the processing of sound and use of phonological working memory. For example trying to think aloud while 'concurrently' listening to a tape recording is extremely difficult, and trying to think aloud when carrying out a speaking task is virtually impossible.

As a result, various time gaps from the actual processing of the task (the 'event') are either built in to the methodology or inevitably result from the trickiness of what the researcher is trying to do. For example, a researcher might stop the tape, during a listening task, and ask listeners to verbalize what they were doing in their heads during that segment of the text. This is the first step towards 'retrospective' verbalization, thinking back to what they were doing just a few seconds before. Or the researcher may allow the listener to decide for themselves where to stop the tape and to articulate what they had been doing to process the text. Both approaches have their disadvantages. The first because it assumes that the researcher knows the best place to stop in order to have the respondent give retrospective verbal report. This may not be the case and important data may be overlooked. The second because it is likely that the listener only stops at problematic moments and therefore does not report on processing which is relatively unproblematic.

A further move away from the time of the event is when the participants break away from the thinking aloud and start to report, or make a comparison with, what they were doing earlier in the task: 'earlier on I thought it meant this, now I'm wondering if it means this'. While this recursive processing may be legitimate evidence of monitoring one's understanding, it may also be methodology induced in that the participants may realize they have not told the researcher certain information that had occurred some time earlier.

A further move still away from the time of the event is when the participants declare that (and sometimes the researcher asks if) this is what they normally do in a similar task situation. Or the participants begin to summarize ('lump together') how they go about doing a task.

In order to avoid this undermining of the methodological intention, sometimes researchers quite simply admit defeat and opt for participants to think back, once the task is completed, on how they went about carrying it out. This can be carried out either in written form, or through researcher questioning. The main difference with this approach is that the processing is being filtered subjectively not only through the participant's (possibly inaccurate) perceptions of what they were doing at the time, but also with the knowledge of hindsight. In other words, the researcher may not be tapping into those true inner processes, and in addition, the summation of those processes may be affected by the participants' estimate of how well they did in the now completed task.

So far we have looked at techniques which vary in their distance from the event in terms of lapsed time. However, there are some situations where it is impossible (or unacceptable) to capture learners' thought processes in the space where the event was taking place. A typical example is during an actual language lesson, where for example a researcher may want to know what the learners' reaction was to a specific teacher behaviour. Or a researcher interested in investigating the theme of pragmatic competence sets up a role-play in a meeting between student and teacher. Here is where the technique of stimulated recall could be used.

With stimulated recall, the event is recorded in some way. In the above examples a teacher's behaviour or the role-play may be video-recorded. The event is then re-presented to the participants some time later and almost always *in a different place*, in order to stimulate what was going through their minds at the time of the event. Clearly here both time and location may have an impact on the accuracy with which what the participants now report reflects what their actual thoughts were at the time of the event. The more time that has elapsed the more they may have forgotten what they were thinking and/or the more they might be interpreting the event in the light of later events. Discussing in a small room face-to-face with one researcher may be a different experience for the participants than that of being in a classroom surrounded by their fellow learners. Moreover, stimulated recall is subject to the same methodological decision-making problems as in the think-aloud listening task example above. Should the researcher pre-select the episodes to be used as stimuli or should the participant be self-selecting them? Both have their advantages and disadvantages.

Despite the problems associated with the continuum we have described in this section from 'concurrent' reporting of participants' thoughts to stimulated recall, these participant-centred techniques continue to be very popular because of the rich data that they can elicit and researchers continue to refine the techniques as well as problematizing them. Further good coverage of issues relating to verbal report in L2 research can be found in Brown and Rodgers (2002, pp. 53–78), Cohen (1998, pp. 49–61), Green (1998) and Mackey and Gass (2005, pp. 75–85).

We now go on to consider in greater detail the most frequently adopted research instrument in second language acquisition, the test or the task.

A Focus on Instrumentation Involving Tests and Tasks

An important issue to consider is just what constitutes a *test* as opposed to a *task*. While there are measures that look more test-like and others that look more task-like, in the case of numerous instruments it is more their purpose that determines their nature. In part, the distinction is between measures intended to assess language proficiency as opposed to those intended for the purpose of exploring issues in second language acquisition (see Bachman and Cohen 1998). If a measure is referred to as a *test*, the implication is that there is a certain level of rigour, presumably established through piloting of the measure and establishing its reliability and validity. A test may also be expected to have norms for interpretation of results from its use in data collection, with the norms varying according to proficiency level, dialect of the language and other categories. A *task*, on the other hand, has not necessarily undergone the same rigorous scrutiny in terms of reliability and validity. Also, the results from its use would possibly have a different purpose than for a test. Having said this, in reality, the purpose for both tests and tasks may be identical. So there is a problem in the nomenclature.

In this brief description of measures, we will limit the discussion to measures of linguistic knowledge and linguistic performance. And given the fact that they overlap, let us keep the distinction in mind, but treat them as essentially a common set of measures where the focus may be more on knowledge or on performance.

Another caveat is that this section will not perform the traditional tallying of advantages, and disadvantages of each test or task. Such descriptions are also available elsewhere (e.g., Dörnyei 2007; Mackey and Gass 2005). Rather, we will describe a representative set of tests and tasks appearing in these leading research journals over the last six years, describe the rationale provided in the report and inform the reader of any limitations that either the authors provided or that we observed.

As indicated above (see Table 3), we actually found that well over 50 different types of tests and tasks were used in research studies since 2002. Twenty per cent consisted of vocabulary tests, 15% were comprehension tests, 9% were oral production tests, 7% were written production tests and grammaticality judgement tests respectively, 6% were information-gap tests, 5% were tests of oral production, 4% were standardized tests of proficiency, and then there were 28 different types of measures with a more limited frequency in the various studies (appearing in only 2% or fewer of the studies). In considering these instruments, we need to be somewhat wary of the labels attached to them, and for this reason it is best to consider their generic names, and to focus on their features or attributes, much as Cohen (1994) did in describing the item-elicitation and item-response formats for language assessment instruments some years ago. The advantage of doing a distinctive feature analysis of research measures is that instruments with dissimilar sounding labels may in fact be quite similar in nature and purpose except for one or another feature.

So let us now take a look at a representative sample of some of the measures that have been used recently to measure vocabulary, grammatical control, listening comprehension, oral discourse, reading and writing. An effort has been made to provide a relatively robust description of each measure, some of the theoretical underpinnings for using it, and observations about the instrument's possible limitations. The source is indicated for those who would like to obtain more details about a given instrument. This section, in summary, is intended to provide a sense of the kinds of tests and tasks that have found their way into the key journals at this point in time.

<u>Vocabulary knowledge through word association</u>: In this test, used by Greinadus, Beks and Wakely (2005), respondents were given a trigger word in the L2, in this case, French: for example, *jeune*. They then had to tick all the words in a provided list that they thought had a clear connection to the word:

- o *âge*
- o *blanc*
- o *fille*
- o *livre*
- o *oiseau*
- o *vieux*

They were given guidelines as to the meaning of 'clear connection':

1. The word may be synonymous or antonymous
2. One word may have a more general meaning than the other
3. One word may collocate with the other (*coup de soleil* = sun-stroke)
4. One word may be used to define the other
5. There may be a link in function or use between one word and another (pen = to write)
6. One word may refer to a part whereas the other word may refer to a whole (roof = house)

It could be argued that some respondents may be more creative than others and start using schema beyond clear connection (e.g., *jeune* = Jung = psychology). Greinadus et al. tried to solve this problem in one version of the test by telling the participants how many correct answers there were for each item. But this approach may create its own problems. Moreover, this is a test that could only be used with fairly well educated students who have a clear idea of the meaning of terms such as *antonymous, collocation* and *definition;* otherwise these words would need to be clearly explained and examples provided.

Inferencing vocabulary from a written context: This task, used by Paribakht (2005), involved the inferencing of L2 (English) words that represented concepts considered to be familiar to educated Farsi speakers but for which no lexical equivalents were found in their L1, Farsi (non-lexicalized words). Examples of concepts that could be paraphrased in Farsi, but for which single or compound lexical items do not exist in the language, were: *to elope, to indulge, proactive, prognosis, to stalk.* The selected target words were used in paragraphs on general interest and familiar topics (i.e., marriage, preserving the environment, the ice age, the world's forgotten poor, big city dreams and genetic engineering). A list of words for which L1 equivalents existed was also drawn up (lexicalized words).

Then texts were written so as to present a mix of lexicalized and non-lexicalized words in semantically unambiguous and frequently used contexts. The participants were asked first to read the text quickly for general comprehension and then to read it again trying to guess the meanings of the unfamiliar target words indicated in boldface. They were also instructed to verbalize what they were thinking and doing while carrying out the task, using Farsi, English or both languages, according to their preference.

Participants' inferred meanings for the unfamiliar target words were evaluated as a 'success' if an appropriate meaning or a synonym was provided, 'partial success' if an approximate meaning was given, or 'failure' if an inaccurate meaning or no meaning was inferred.

We found no mention of piloting of this test. In fact validity and reliability problems associated with this task are not discussed by the author. We would, however, suggest that a discussion of limitations might have been appropriate given that the task was linked to verbalization. For example, could it be that, verbalizing in the L2, may have produced different measures of success for the target words than verbalizing in L1, given that the concept-lexeme relationship in both languages was different?

Morphological judgement task: This task was used to assess morphological awareness in Hebrew (L1) and English (L2) by Schiff and Calif (2007). Separate task sheets were prepared for each language. All of the morphologically related task word pairs were a base and a linear derivational form.

Fifth-grade participants were presented with a printed sheet with 24 meaningful word pairs in L1 (Hebrew) and then a similar sheet in the L2 (English). Twelve of these word pairs were words that sound the same but had a different orthographic representation (heterographic homophones). The other 12 word pairs were words with phonological or orthographic similarities but that were not homophones. The task is not provided in the appendix to Schiff and Calif's study but examples of English word pairs given included 'no-know' and 'car-care'; examples of Hebrew word pairs given included *karish-karish* (the first with ◉ – IPA [k, x] and the second with ◉ – IPA [k]) 'a shark'–'a blood clot'; *mexir-makir* 'a price'–'he recognizes'. The word pairs were presented in two columns and a third column was reserved for the student's response. Half of these word pairs shared a morphologically based word family. The other half had shared letters but were not morphologically related. Participants were given both oral and written instructions for completing the third column: 'On the sheet in front of you are word pairs. Write "yes" after the word pairs where you think the meanings of the two words are related. Write "no" after the word pairs where you think the words are not related' (Schiff and Calif 2007, p. 281). The task sheet included two sample responses done for them.

The researchers, with regard to the validity of the task, point out that since word recognition is a receptive process and pronouncing words aloud is a productive process, it is possible that the participants might sometimes have recognized words accurately but nevertheless mispronounced them.

Translation task: The purpose of this task, used by Bruton (2007), was to investigate the acquisition of new (English L2) vocabulary from the act of writing. Using the justification that a translation task reduces the possibility of avoidance in writing, the researcher selected a translation task in order to 'push' the learners to use previously unknown vocabulary, in line with Swain's (1985) Output Hypothesis. He felt that such a task might induce learners to 'notice a gap in their own knowledge when they encounter a problem in trying to produce the L2' (p. 420).

The Spanish (source) text was adapted from student compositions on the same topic in English and then translated into Spanish (the students' L1). The text was about the Fair and Easter Week in Seville, which was assumed to be a familiar and relevant topic for the subjects. The text was in two paragraphs of 99 words each, making a total of 198 Spanish words. They were also provided with a glossary of bilingual entries using a pocket dictionary format. The students were also asked to underline any words they looked up.

No mention is made of whether the task was piloted first. With regard to the limitations of the task, Bruton (2007) admits that the technique needs to be employed judiciously, using translation tasks that are appropriate to the given subjects, hence making it feasible only with monolingual groups. Moreover, he observes that the students' look up behaviour may not be an accurate reflection of the words unknown to them in the translation task as they may simply have been checking known words. Finally, he notes that translation in these cases is a means, not an end, in the sense that students are not being trained to be translators.

Form-recognition task: This task, used by Leeser (2004), was intended to measure the extent to which learners notice L2 verb forms (in this case, the future tense in Spanish), either when they listen to a narrative passage recited to them orally or when they read the same text to themselves. In the study in which the form-recognition task was used, the oral recitation and the reading version each contained 60 items: 19 future tense forms from the passage, 5 nouns from the passage and 36 distracter items. In the recitation mode, the respondents ticked whether they remembered hearing a given word in the passage. In the reading mode, they ticked words if they remembered seeing them in the passage. The main finding was that they processed the passages for form more and better in the reading mode than in the recitation mode.

With regard to the limitations of this task, the researcher noted that since no online measure was used to determine what learners were actually comprehending or processing while they were reading and listening to the passages, there was no information as to what the learners were doing during comprehension. He suggested that online measures such as eye-tracking, reaction times and think-aloud could be used to investigate input processing, especially of the written texts. We would also venture an observation in relation to the validity of the form-recognition task. The readers, when they were ticking the list, were actually encountering the word a second time in written form, whereas the listeners were encountering the word in written form for the first time only. The task therefore may have favoured the readers both in the form-recognition task itself and when it came to the second task the participants did, a tense-identification task.

Grammaticality judgement tests: Grammaticality judgement tests (GJTs) have often been used in SLA research to tap into a learner's implicit knowledge. For an in-depth discussion of these tests and how they can be adapted to also test explicit knowledge see Ellis (2004).

A grammaticality judgement test, used by Cuervo (2007), was constructed to see the extent to which learners were aware of how the double-object construction in their (L2) Spanish differed from its English counterpart in its morphosyntactic properties (case, clitic doubling, word order) and its semantic properties (interpretation of arguments and restrictions on the construction). The test consisted of 13 conditions that belonged to one of three main components: a preposition construction with an indirect object interpreted as goal in the presence of the preposition (e.g., 'Mary sent a package to Peter'), a double object construction (e.g., 'Mary sent Peter a package') and a component involving the manipulation of morphosyntactic properties of the double object construction (testing knowledge agreement, clitic doubling, case and word order, the role of the particle *a* and *wh*-extraction of the dative phrase). The respondents were given a list of 38 grammatical sentences and 29 ungrammatical sentences plus 20 distracters, and were asked to judge their acceptability on a Likert scale from –2 for completely unacceptable to +2 for perfectly acceptable, according to their first impression.

This judgement of acceptability on a scale is a departure from the usual dichotomous 'correct' or 'incorrect'. Respondents were instructed that although

125

the option 0 was available for cases for which they could not make a decision, they should try to avoid that response but we are not told by the author the justification for that decision. A value of 1 or 2 was assigned to inaccurate responses and 3 or 4 to accurate responses. Participants completed the task in between 20 and 40 minutes. No limitations or even a discussion of the GJT (which is not offered to readers in the appendix) were provided despite the fact that this use of the measure departed from more traditional uses. Although piloting of the test is not mentioned the actual participants were given a practice task consisting of four sentences. It would have been interesting to have a discussion about (1) whether the scalar ranking was more appropriate than a dichotomous decision, (2) whether it is actually possible for participants to stick to their 'first impression' and (3) the extent to which the variability in the time it took for them to do the task might have affected whether overall the task was tapping in to implicit knowledge or whether explicit reasoning was involved.

Input memory task and generalization test: This investigation of the noticing of syntactic relationships (by Williams and Lovatt 2003) involved input of determiner-noun relationships in Italian (both oral and written), followed by respondents having to translate an English L1 phrase into Italian and having to generate new determiner-noun combinations. This combination of a task and a test was used in order to determine the extent to which morphological and phonological information contained in the input is processed in both short-term and long-term memory, such that the learner can then generate new morpheme combinations demonstrating acquisition of the underlying rules of a language system. Italian was used in this case as an 'experimental language' in that it was new to the participants. Italian has a very complex determiner-noun (D-N) system.

On the input memory task, determiner-noun (D-N) combinations were presented (in sets of three) as follows. After an English contextualizing sentence with a D-N combination in bold (e.g., 'Sally liked shopping with her best friend Jane. One Saturday they went shopping for **some shoes**'.), participants heard and saw *delle scarpe* (some shoes). This was repeated with two more sentences having different D-N combinations. Respondents were then presented with one of the English phrases (e.g.) 'some shoes'. Participants had to recall the Italian phrase. For the generalization test, respondents were required to translate an English phrase (one which they had not been exposed to in the input) into Italian, in order to determine the respondents' ability to produce *new* determiner-noun combinations. The authors do not discuss any problems, limitations or confounding variables that might be associated with these two tasks and the tasks themselves are not provided in the appendix although the Italian version of the items of the input memory task are provided in a table in the main text.

Sentence conjunction judgement task: This instrument is a measure of competence in tense and aspect that, as used by Montrul and Sablakova (2003), specifically tested the semantic implications of the preterite and imperfect tenses. The subjects received a list of sentences containing two coordinated clauses conjoined by *y* 'and' or *pero* 'but'. Some of the combinations were contradictory, while others made sense. The subjects had to indicate if the two clauses made sense together, making use of a scale ranging from –2 (illogical) to +2 (logical). They were to select 0 if they were not sure. In most cases, the first clause contained a verb in the imperfect tense which made the sentence logical, and the second clause had a preterite form which made it illogical. For example, the correct response to (a) is 2, and for (b) it is –2.

(a) *La clase era a las 10 pero empezó a las 10:30.* logical
'The class was-IMPF at 10 (i.e., "was scheduled for") but started at 10:30.'

(b) *La clase fue a las 10 pero empezó a las 10:30.* contradictory
'The class was-PRET at 10 (i.e., "took place at") but started at 10:30.'

There were 56 sentences (28 logical and 28 illogical) on the test – 14 with verbs of accomplishment, 14 with verbs of achievement and 14 with stative verbs. The instrument also had 14 sentences as distracters using other tenses, half logical and half illogical.

The researchers note that this task was not easy according to anecdotal accounts from the participants themselves and from empirical evidence. Respondents reported that they often felt unsure about their answers which may have led to them randomly opting for a point on the scale. These problems would have been picked up via a piloting phase.

Phonological awareness: In order to measure the phonological awareness of young Chinese children learning English, a team of researchers devised two measures, one focusing on awareness of initial sound and one on rhyming (Knell, Qiang, Pei, Chi, Siegel, Zhao and Zhao 2007). To get at awareness of the initial sound of a word (onset), each child first heard a stimulus word and afterwards three more words. The child was to indicate which of the three words had the same first sound as the first word. Accompanying pictures during the task served to reduce the memory load and to reduce the likelihood of memory being a confounder. So for example, if the stimulus word was 'ball', then the response items were 'bed', 'cake', and 'tree'. To get at rhyme detection, the child heard a stimulus word and then chose the word that rhymed with it or had the same ending sounds from a list of three words. So if the stimulus word as 'cat', the response items included 'fish', 'sun', and 'hat'. Possible issues relating to this kind of a measure could include a lack of concentration leading to guessing, or the child getting too involved at looking at the picture instead of listening.

Aural discrimination task: The task, used by Arteaga, Herschensohn and Gess (2003), consisted of an 18-item aural discrimination test with the items pre-recorded by a native French speaker. In the instructions for the test, the participants were told that French names often sound the same for both males and females, as for example, Claude, who may be a man or a woman. All items consisted of a proper name of this type, followed by the copular verb (in positive or negative form), followed by an adjective. The task was used to demonstrate the benefit of a context-based focus on phonological form for listening comprehension since it enhances auditory detection of morphological form in French, such as final consonant alternation in signalling gender agreement for adjectives.

In the task some names were used twice, but not necessarily with the opposite gender for each token presumably so as not to alert the participants to the underlying research objectives of the task. The following are sample stimulus sentences, which were all short and stripped of other cues. Note that although 'Emanuel' and 'Emanuelle' have different spellings, they are pronounced identically in French.

> *Fréderique n'est pas japonaise.* 'Frederique isn't Japanese' (f).
> *Emanuel est allemand.* 'Emanuel is German' (m).
> *Emanuelle est très petite.* 'Emanuelle is very short' (f).

Each item on the tape was repeated twice, and the participants marked one of three columns for 'masculine', 'feminine', and 'don't know'. The authors did not provide a discussion of any possible limitations associated with the use of this aural discrimination test in the write up of their study and we found no mention of any piloting stage for the task.

Reading span test of working memory: A test of working memory span was used to see if it was an important variable in L2 reading comprehension in general and specifically, in the processing of the Spanish future tense by beginning learners in particular. The researcher (Leeser 2007) used a computerized version of Waters and Caplan's (1996) *Reading Span Test* (RST) in English. The test contained 80 sentences, half of which were plausible and the other half were implausible. Participants read on a computer screen individual sentences that varied in length, syntactic complexity and plausibility (see Waters and Caplan for a discussion of sentence types). They were instructed to press the 'yes' or 'no' button on a button box depending on whether they thought the sentence was plausible or implausible. They were also instructed to remember the last word of each sentence. After reading and judging individual sentences in sets ranging between two and six sentences, the word 'RECALL' appeared on the screen. At that point, the participants wrote down as many of the sentence-final words as possible from the set. All participants were told that their reaction times, sentence plausibility judgements and recall of the sentence-final words were equally important.

According to the investigator, the theoretical underpinning for this test was that since working memory is limited, the central executive has to make decisions about where to focus attention and resources (comprehension, form, phonology, etc.). The idea behind this task is that reading the sentences aloud would tax the processing function of working memory, and attempting to remember the last word of each sentence would tax storage. In Waters and Caplan's (1996) computerized version of the RST, participants' working memory scores are based on three measures: (a) mean reaction times for correct responses on the acceptability of sentences, (b) the number of errors on the sentence judgements, and (c) the number of trials in which sentence-final words were incorrectly recalled. Their findings were that a number of respondents on the measure do trade speed for accuracy and speed for storage. Based on these results, Waters and Caplan questioned the reliability of working memory measures that only employ scores from the recall component of the RST.

A number of further observations could be made about this test. First it is unclear whether Leeser asked the respondents to read the sentences aloud, subvocalize them or read them silently. Each of these procedures may have theoretical implications. Reading aloud or subvocalizing encourages the utilization of phonological working memory. The sentence plausibility judgement requires the extraction of information from long-term memory and the fact that the sentences go off screen may also be testing the visual-spatial sketchpad – i.e., can the participant still 'see in his/her mind's eye' the last word(s). Given these complex demands on finite working memory capacity, the central executive has to make a decision about where, when and how to distribute processing capacity.

Timed sentence comprehension test: This measure was used to study the semantic and syntactic processing of an L2 German text appearing on a computer screen (Jackson 2007). In this measure, 24 target sentences were constructed consisting of a main clause followed by a subordinate clause. Each one was manipulated to create four different versions in German FL. The key portion of each sentence was in the subordinate clause, which contained a subject, identified by nominative case markings, and a direct object, identified by accusative case markings. The direct object in all sentences was an animate entity. Sentences varied according to animacy, specifically whether the subject was an animate (+ANIM) or inanimate (−ANIM) noun, and word order, namely, subject-first order (SO) or object-first order (OS). All animate nouns referred to human beings. The inanimate nouns were tangible objects, such as a photo, or intangible, but still clearly defined, objects or concepts, such as a law. The manipulation of these two variables led to four variations for each target sentence, as seen in the following example sentences taken from the comprehension task.

a. *Peter kann sehen, dass das Spiel den Trainer ärgert.* (subject-first; inanimate subject;

SO/–ANIM)
Peter can see, that [the game]NOM [the coach]ACC angers
'Peter can see that the game angers the coach.'
b. *Peter kann sehen, dass den Trainer das Spiel ärgert.* (object-first; inanimate subject;
OS/–ANIM)
Peter can see, that [the coach]ACC [the game]NOM angers
'Peter can see that the game angers the coach.'
c. *Peter kann sehen, dass das Kind den Trainer ärgert.* (subject-first; animate subject;
SO/∥ANIM)
Peter can see, that [the child]NOM [the coach]ACC angers
'Peter can see that the child angers the coach.'
d. *Peter kann sehen, dass den Trainer das Kind ärgert.* (object-first; animate subject;
OS/∥ANIM)
Peter can see, that [the coach]ACC [the child]NOM angers
'Peter can see that the child angers the coach.'

In the timed sentence comprehension task, the participants read the target and filler sentences one at a time on a computer screen. When they finished reading a sentence, they pressed the space bar. At this point, the target sentence disappeared, and two statements appeared. The participants were to choose the statement that best captured the meaning of the original target sentence. The investigator chose to measure L2 reading comprehension through the L1, so all of these summary statements appeared in English. Sample summary statements for the above target sentences are as follows:

a. The coach thinks the game is annoying.
b. The coach thinks the game is good.
c. The coach thinks the child is annoying.
d. The child thinks the coach is annoying.

The respondents were informed before beginning the task that they should read the sentences as quickly and accurately as possible, but that the task was nevertheless self-paced in that they controlled how long the target sentence and the subsequent comprehension statements remained on the screen.

Four-stage writing task: This task involved having EFL writers compare their output to native models in two revisions of a story that they wrote, with the focus being on what they noticed about their written production (Hanaoka 2007). According to the investigator, a task of this nature helps teachers understand the formulation problems of EFL writers, and what the students 'notice' – that is, the gap between the way that they write and the native models to which they compare themselves. The question that the researcher asks is whether 'noticing' later turns into better performance. The following are the four stages of the task:

Stage 1: The students were asked to write a story in response to a two-frame picture prompt (depicting a woman getting to class on time on a bicycle while a fellow student is stuck in traffic in his car). The pictures were intended to control the propositional content of the story that the students wrote. They were also asked to make notes on a separate sheet about whatever problems they noticed as they wrote. They were given specific examples (in Japanese) of notes that they might take: 'I don't know how to say X in English,' 'I wrote X, but I'm not sure if this is correct,' 'What is the past tense of X?' and 'I'm not sure whether the picture is describing X.'

Stage 2: The students were then immediately given two native-speaker models. For ease of reference, the two models were titled (A) and (B) respectively. The students were asked to write on a new sheet of paper whatever they noticed as they compared their original text with the models. Specific examples of note-taking were provided at the top of the sheet in Japanese: 'I couldn't say X, but (A) puts it Y,' '(A) says X, but (B) says Y,' 'I was impressed by (B)'s interpretation of one or the other picture.' Students were to compare their original to a native-speaker model and state what they 'noticed' in terms of differences between their interlanguage forms and target forms. At this point, the native models and Sheet 3 with comparisons were collected. Students retained their original Sheet 1 and the picture prompt.

Stage 3: Students then were to perform an immediate revision of their story on a new sheet based on what they remembered of what they had noticed.

Stage 4: Students performed another revision two months later. For this task, they received their first draft (Sheet 1) and were asked to rewrite it on a new sheet of paper.

The researcher speculated that having the respondents take notes while writing allowed them to engage in metalinguistic reflection and thereby enhanced the learning process. She felt it may have amplified the positive effects of what they noticed while writing and in turn may have improved retention of the noticed features.

We could observe that there is not a great deal of control going on in Stage 1 of the process. All sorts of avoidance strategies could have been used by the writers to avoid formulation problems. Specific requirements of what the writing should contain would perhaps have provided better control mechanisms.

In summary for this section, we have presented a range of tests and tasks which we believe reflect the kinds of tools used to measure competence and performance in more recent research in SLA. We have not only tried to describe the tests/tasks but have also provided what the authors' rationale was for choosing or designing that task. We have also reported the authors' own comments on the limitations or problems associated with the tests/tasks where these were available and, in some instances, have added a few comments of our own. We would suggest that all researchers, whether novice, experienced or experts, should be thinking about these three aspects (instrument, rationale for its use, and potential problems) and that they should be reported fully in a research publication.

Conclusions

It is clear that SLA research has moved on considerably from use of traditional instruments. As noted earlier, although questionnaires feature highly on the lists of instruments used, many of these were adopted for the purposes of providing very superficial background information on the participants, rather than constituting the main data being investigated. In fact we should note here that, although background information is collected in a number of studies, such information is rarely used to generate independent variables to use in analysing the data from the tasks described above.

The fact that more traditional instruments seem to be less used, suggests to us that SLA research is being conceptualized by the research community as quite different from general educational research, even though, in virtually all cases, SLA studies are concerned with the language education of students. SLA research has tried to develop a clearly distinctive set of tools specifically designed to be used with developing or actual bilinguals and yet those bilinguals are very often in formal educational contexts. To our mind this has both advantages and disadvantages. On the one hand we recognize and subscribe to the belief that the learning and use of a second language is an endeavour which sets it apart from other educational experiences. It is therefore appropriate that SLA researchers should seek the most appropriate discipline-specific tools to do the job. On the other hand, we can see dangers in fronting to this extent language tests and tasks without taking into account aspects of the learner as an individual, and as a socially situated and creative human being.

In some ways, it is not difficult to see why this has happened. First, the international nature of SLA research (compounded by the global status of English) almost demands that it be lifted and divorced from its original educational context. Why, for example, would a reader in Dalian (China) want to know how instructional practices in Nevada (USA) impact on the acquisition of morphemes? Yet it would seem to us (and as Macaro attempts to demonstrate in the last chapter of this volume), these are sometimes important questions that readers should be entitled to ask and that researchers should be required to report on. The second reason that this state of affairs may have developed is the lack of space available to authors when submitting work to top journals. Here too, though, we feel that creative solutions are now being offered by the internet and that these should be considered seriously.

There is a further and related issue. We have seen in this chapter that tests and tasks of many different kinds have been specifically designed to measure some aspect of participants' knowledge or performance. Because many of these tests and tasks are designed specifically for the research questions being asked, they have not been discussed (in our view) sufficiently in the methodological research literature of SLA, nor in many cases are they provided in the appendix to the study. There is perhaps an unwritten agreement that readers will accept measures used in an SLA study at face value without asking about their reliability and validity for the task at hand. Bachman and Cohen (1998) had raised this issue over a decade ago because it appeared that SLA tasks were (and probably still are) in need of more rigorous evaluation using the tools of language assessment. We speculate that measures currently used in SLA studies may vary in their reliability according to the L2 being tested and indeed the first language and culture of the participants. And this fluctuation in reliability would of course have serious implications for the validity of the measures as well.

We would like to have seen more of a critical analysis in the limitations sections of the studies regarding the design and use of these tests and tasks. In fact, in most of the studies reviewed, there was no formal 'Limitations Section' at all. Thus we recommend to researchers that they give critical consideration to the tasks and tests that have been used in the study and that journal editors require it. The analysis would include information concerning both the validity and reliability of the various measures used. The validation process could, in fact, include the use of verbal report, such as by means of online, learner-voice information.

Our primary aim in making the above points was not to criticize individual authors but to demonstrate our commitment to high-quality SLA research reflects our commitment to improving the teaching and learning that goes on in second language classrooms. Without a thorough examination of both the validity of the main tools being used, nor a situated explanation of the results obtained, future researchers working in different contexts cannot build on previous work, and practitioners will not be able to draw their own pedagogical implications from the findings.

Part 2

Issues and Relationships in Second Language Acquisition

4 The Relationship between First and Second Language Acquisition Revisited

Vivian Cook

The relationship between how people learn their first language (L1) and how they learn their second language (L2) and subsequent languages has concerned second language acquisition (SLA) research ever since it became an independent discipline (see Cook 1969, 1973; Ervin-Tripp 1974; Stern 1967 for a selection of early views). The relationship between the two languages is critical because it defines the very nature of L2 acquisition: if L2 acquisition did not differ in some way from L1 acquisition, SLA research would be only a sub-field of a general discipline of language acquisition research rather than a field of its own. It is a truism that the defining characteristic of L2 acquisition is the presence of a second language in the same mind as a first and that the crucial characteristic of an L2 community is the use of additional languages to the first language. A unique problem for SLA research is how this pre-existing language affects the L2 user's mind and the L2 user's community.

This chapter concentrates on the language of the individual rather than of the community. It shows how SLA research emerged out of the chrysalis of L1 acquisition research, looking particularly at the concept of stages of acquisition and at SLA research techniques. Then it links three contemporary approaches to L1 acquisition to SLA research. Next it looks at the differences and similarities that have been proposed between L1 and L2 acquisition. It concludes with a plea for the independence of SLA research from L1 acquisition research.

SLA Research Springing from First Language Acquisition

Early SLA research in the 1960s drew on L1 acquisition research not only for its ideas but also for its research techniques. The inherent dangers are using ideas and techniques that do not transfer to L2 acquisition for various reasons and employing them long after they have been abandoned in L1 acquisition research.

Using Ideas from L1 Acquisition Research

The mainspring that drove SLA research in the 1960s was the independent grammars assumption as applied to children's language by people such as Brown (1973) and McNeill (1966): children should be treated as children not as mini-adults. The child's language constitutes an independent system of its own rather than being a defective version of the adult system. Braine's work with two-word sentences set the trend (Braine 1963). Children's utterances like *more high* were not deformed adult sentences but reflected the unique pivot-open organization of early child grammar: to make a two-word utterance, combine a pivot word like *more* with a content word like *high*, yielding *more high*, a request to be lifted up. Children's sentences are proper sentences according to their own lights.

Taken into SLA research, the independent grammars assumption became known as the 'interlanguage' hypothesis: 'the existence of a separate linguistic system' (Selinker 1972). The learner's language system is a developing system in its own right, not a defective version of the native speaker's. This concept served to liberate SLA research from the dead hand of structural linguistics and Contrastive Analysis by starting from the learner rather than from a preset apparatus. The main focus became the detailed analysis of learners' speech, in principle independently of the language of native speakers. You no longer had to compare the total syntax and phonology of the two languages before you tackled L2 learning, as it were, but could start on what actual learners did and see what their syntax and phonology consisted of using their own speech or writing – in a sense a bottom-up data-led process rather than a top-down theory-based one.

Yet, despite paying it lip-service, the vast majority of SLA research never quite accepted the interlanguage assumption that learners have to be studied in their own right. In L1 acquisition research, researchers had indeed knuckled down to the task of looking at the child's own language development rather than searching for deviations from adult speech, as most introductions to L1 acquisition show to this day, (e.g., Bloom 2002; Clark 2003). L2 learners, however, were at every turn measured against the monolingual native speaker, both overtly as shown by remarks like 'Relative to native speaker's linguistic competence, learners' interlanguage is deficient by definition' (Kasper and Kellerman 1997: 5), and covertly through research techniques such as grammaticality judgements that implicitly use the native speaker as a touchstone.

The most influential concept borrowed from L1 acquisition research was undoubtedly that of developmental sequence. L1 children were believed to progress through distinct stages in language acquisition, just as their cognition developed through stages, whether those of Piaget (Piaget and Inhelder 1969) or Bruner (1966). Brown (1973) conducted the first major longitudinal study of the language of three children, followed by Gordon Wells' monumental attempt at recording 124 children (Wells 1981) and Bruner's observations of 120 children (Bruner 1983). In a sense such longitudinal projects aimed at establishing the stages of development; what does the child learn first, second, . . .? The explanations that were advanced for the sequence varied between the semantic explanations of Brown, the functional theories of Wells (1981) and the social interaction of Bruner (1983).

Dulay and Burt (1974) applied the Brown study techniques for investigating the sequence of so-called grammatical morphemes such as prepositions *to* and *in* and grammatical inflections such as *–ing* and *'s* to L2 development. They found evidence for an L2 sequence that was similar to, but nonetheless distinct from, the L1 sequence described in Brown (1973). Sequence of acquisition has dominated SLA research ever since this pioneering study; massive efforts have gone into investigating which sounds are learnt first (Major 1994), which syntactic structures (Zobl and Liceras 1994), and countless other areas of language. The most crucial piece of evidence for how people learn a second language has been taken to be the order in which they acquire the language; from this alone we can work out the learning processes involved. Few L2 studies have looked at overall development through longitudinal corpus studies like the L1 studies, apart perhaps from the work of the European Science Foundation (ESF) funded project with migrant workers (Klein and Perdue 1997) and Wode's study of his children (Wode 1981). But much of the SLA research has not been concerned with explanation at all, simply with the 'facts' of sequence. The explanations for the order of L2 development either deny the need for an explanation as it is just 'natural', as in the Natural Order Hypothesis (Krashen 1985), or are based on a single aspect of development, whether the social cognitive dimension of the ESF researchers (Klein and Perdue 1997) or the parameter setting/resetting of the Universal Grammar generativists (White 2003).

Hardly anybody seems to have taken heed of Chomsky's insistence that it is the acquired knowledge that is crucial, not the order in which it is acquired. He has often spoken of an idealized 'instantaneous' model of language acquisition that relates language input and competence as wholes without reference to chronological development (Chomsky 1986). Cook and Newson (2007) distinguish **acquisition** – the logical problem of how the mind acquires language independent of intervening stages – and **development** – the history of the intervening stages. As a car-driver, it does not matter to you in which order you learnt to steer, use the brake, change gear etc. It's what you can do that is important, not which component you learnt first, even if there is presumably a natural sequence for learning to drive. Developmental order in the first language is the product of factors other than language acquisition per se, such as frequency effects in the language input, the development of the child's working memory and so on. Teasing out language acquisition from these other factors is a major task for L1 acquisition research.

Nor is the concept of stage itself clearly defined. Ingram (1989) found several types of L1 'stage' – a 'continuous stage' referring to 'a point on a continuum', a 'plateau stage' where change halts for some time, a 'transition stage' before change takes off again, and an 'acceleration stage' where there is rapid acquisition before reaching a plateau. Most SLA research such as Dulay and Burt (1974) has used the continuum meaning; a stage has no coherent characteristics of its own other than its position on the continuum; one thing just comes after another. Processability theory (Pienemann 1998) is more like a plateau and transition stage theory with broad characteristics for each stage. Saying that language acquisition proceeds through stages of development is empty without defining what a stage is.

One question to be developed below is whether the L2 user's knowledge of the second language is the same as that of an L1 monolingual native speaker of that language. The main question for many researchers has been whether the stages and processes through which L2 learners develop are the same as those for L1 children. SLA researchers were impressed by the overall idea of sequence: the discovery of a common acquisition sequence for L2 learners is 'surely one of the most exciting and significant outcomes of the last decade of second language research' (Dulay and Burt 1980: 325). Experiments indeed showed that L2 learners acquired language in a sequence resembling L1 acquisition. Like L1 children (Cromer 1970), L2 users first confuse the difference between *John is easy to please* and *John is eager to please* and sort the two constructions out comparatively late (Cook 1973) – plateau stages with transitions – despite having no clear way of deriving the structure from the speech that they encounter. The importance of stagiation depends on whether you accept that the route is important rather than the process or the target. I can walk to work, or go by bicycle or by car, with slight variations according to one-way streets and pedestrianized areas etc., but does it matter what I do so long as I get there? SLA research often ran into the danger of reporting sequence with little or no explanation.

Research Techniques

As a new area of research, SLA research undoubtedly borrowed most of its research techniques from L1 acquisition and has continued to do so. After all, why not? Both disciplines are concerned with language acquisition; it would be surprising if techniques that worked in one area did not work in the other. It is the same human mind acquiring language in both cases after all. A useful practical survey of the main L1 research techniques is provided in McDaniel, McKee and Cairns (1996). For the most part it is not the sheer techniques themselves that are questionable in SLA research but the deductions and analyses that are based on them.

The techniques most obviously borrowed from L1 acquisition research are those for studying actual sentences that L2 learners produce, which we can call **natural data** (Cook 1986). The L1 corpus studies by Brown (1973) and Wells (1981) recorded children's speech over a period of years and analysed it in terms of mostly syntactic criteria. In SLA research the ESF project adopted a similar approach by recording large amounts of speech by migrants to five countries and producing an account of the learners' common basic grammar and semantic stages through which they progressed (Klein and Perdue 1997).

SLA research was also fond of a natural data technique called Error Analysis (EA) (Corder 1971). This looked first at the differences between the learners' speech and that of native speakers and then looked for explanations. However, EA fundamentally differed from the children's corpus analyses in that it looked for 'errors', defined as deviations from native speech – 'the methodology of description is, needless to say, fundamentally that of a bilingual comparison' (Corder 1971). EA in the main tried to find the origins of errors in the knowledge of the first language, an explanation that was clearly not possible for L1 researchers. Indeed the very concept of 'error' in L2 speech breaches the interlanguage assumption unless highly qualified; it could properly mean deviations from the learner's own interlanguage rules but it would be improper to mean deviations from monolingual native speech any more than the L1 child is measured against an idealized adult.

Another popular natural data technique was scoring obligatory occurrences of particular syntactic forms. Brown (1973) had defined 'obligatory' in terms of context; in some sentences the linguistic context makes you supply a demonstrative *that – that man –* or the prior context shows that you must say *the man*, not *a man* and so on. The continued use in SLA research from Dulay and Burt

(1974) to the Processability Model (Pienemann 1998), however, defines obligatory as what a native speaker would say – again the native speaker sneaking in by the back door. A proper use of obligatory would define it in terms of an ideal L2 speaker, not an L1 speaker; in either case it is measuring the learner's system against something it is not rather than treating it primarily as a system in its own right rather than a defective version of something else.

The second broad family of techniques borrowed from L1 research generated **controlled data** (Cook 1986) produced at the researcher's behest. One form this takes is getting learners to produce naturalistic speech. For example Slobin and Welsh (1973) devised the elicited imitation technique which asks L1 children to repeat sentences; the ways in which they change the sentence are believed to reveal properties of their underlying competence. Elicited imitation was used for L2 acquisition by Cook (1973) for testing the comprehension of relative clauses, and by many others. Eliciting sentences through picture description was also used by, for example, Bellugi and Brown (1964) for L1 plurals and by Dulay and Burt (1974) for L2 grammatical morphemes. Various ways of getting people to talk have been used ever since, for instance the well-known 'danger of death' question pioneered by Labov (1984), 'When did you come closest to dying?'. SLA research clearly is quite proper in using such techniques, which themselves have no necessary implication of a monolingual native speaker target.

An important additional source of information for SLA research is **introspection data** (Cook 1986). L2 learners are asked about their emotions, motivations and strategies, surveyed in, say, Dörnyei (2005) or McDonough (1981). Much of this data is unobtainable in L1 acquisition as the children's lack of maturity makes such testing virtually impossible. A key introspective technique in SLA research has been grammaticality judgements in which learners are asked whether they feel that certain sentences are grammatical or not and their answers compared with those of native speakers, explicitly or implicitly as in, say, Hawkins and Chen (1997). L1 research has mostly eschewed testing the grammaticality judgements of young children, partly because of doubts about what these judgements actually mean, partly because of the difficulty of administering them, though they are stoutly defended by McDaniel et al. (1996) provided they are carried out in a way that makes sense to the child. They are nevertheless popular in SLA research even with young L2 learning children (Hannan 2004). So by and large grammaticality judgements as an L2 research technique cannot be justified from L1 acquisition research, as they are simply not a primary source of data for L1 acquisition research – for good or for ill. They are particularly problematic for comparing L1 and L2 learning because one of the things that is known to change in L2 learners is precisely the ability to treat language metalinguistically (Bialystok 1993), on which they must rely.

L1 Acquisition Theories and L2 Acquisition

The views of L1 acquisition mentioned so far formed the historical basis for much SLA research. We now need to consider some current views of L1 acquisition before relating them to L2 acquisition.

Tomasello and Theory of Mind

Since the mid-1990s an influential psychology theory has been called usage-based linguistics, among other names. As described by Tomasello (2003), this has two important components: intention-reading and pattern finding, which reappear in different guises in other forms of cognitive psychology.

We will concentrate here on intention reading, which refers to the well-documented ability of young children to see the world from another's point of view. Trevarthen (1974) filmed mothers talking to babies face-to-face. When the mother started to look over the baby's shoulder, the baby would try to turn to see what the mother was looking at. Simple enough but a clear sign that the baby could see things from another's point of view: if I were my mother, moving my eyes would mean I was looking at something; therefore there is something to be seen if I turn round. Another example is the well-known false belief test, which has many variations. Typically two girls called Sally and Anne are in the same room with the experimenter. Sally hides a teddy bear under a chair; Anne goes out of the room; Sally picks up the bear and hides it under the table; the experimenter asks Sally 'Where does Anne think the bear is?'. If Sally says 'under the chair', she can see the other's point of view; if Sally says 'under the table', she cannot. Tomasello (1999) explores variations on this task, showing time and again that the child knows how other people see the world – a so-called theory of mind (TOM). The crucial thing for language acquisition is then being able to see the world from another point of view; lack of a theory of mind is one of the causes of autism (Baron-Cohen 1995). Hence the language interaction formats described by Bruner (1983) are a way of developing the child's theory of mind, of enabling him or her to see how an adult views the world.

Looked at from an SLA perspective, the L2 learner no longer needs to go through this process; L2 learners already have a theory of mind and do not need to develop it over again. Goetz (2003) has shown that young L2 learners pass such theory of mind tests earlier than monolinguals; learning a second language provides an initial impetus to getting a theory of mind. Children who were bilingual in pairs of spoken and sign languages such as Italian/Italian Sign Language and Estonian/Estonian Sign Language were better at TOM tasks than those raised with only a single language (Meristo et al. 2007). L2 learners may go a stage beyond a theory of mind to a theory of minds: monolingual children may get the impression that all other minds have a similar point of view; bilingual children or adults are soon convinced of the multiplicity of points of view.

This topic introduces a leit-motiv for this chapter: the L1 child's maturation is a transforming experience that does not need to be repeated by older learners in a second language, or indeed *cannot* be repeated. Stages of acquisition are non-reversible, if they depend on cognitive or social maturation; you don't lose TOM in a second language. Gleitman (1982) introduced the metaphor of frogs and tadpoles into language development: once a tadpole transforms into a frog, the process cannot be reversed. Language development and other cognitive processes are transformations of this kind; you can't change back into an earlier version of yourself, whatever beauty products may try to hint. Indeed I once conducted an experiment with hypnotic age regression that tried to demonstrate that adults could not speak like five-year-olds, alas abandoned for methodological and ethical reasons.

Halliday and Social Theories of Language

Language is for doing things and for relating to people. Halliday (1975) saw children's development in terms of the functions they want to express, initially starting with six distinct functions, gradually developing into the three simultaneous adult functions – the *interpersonal* (relating to people), the *ideational* (communicating ideas to other people) and the *textual* (relating one piece of language to another). The fundamental issue is 'learning how to mean' – discovering how to use the multiple simultaneous functions of language.

Social theories of language therefore imply the first language emerges through interaction between children and adults. In a sense this presupposes the TOM theory inasmuch as social interaction depends upon an awareness of others. Different social functions have been emphasized from time to time. Adults for example use a particular style of language when talking to children, altering the frequencies of the structures they use and employing baby-talk vocabulary like *bow-wow* (Snow and Ferguson 1977). Certain kinds of interaction are favoured; Bruner (1983) for instance documented the complex development of peekaboo games. Others have looked at characteristics of child-adult exchanges; Bellugi and Brown (1964) highlighted a process of 'imitation with expansion' in which the adult repeats back the child's sentence in a slightly different form,

Child: Baby highchair
Mother: Baby is in the highchair

These came subsequently to be called 'recasts'. These interactional devices clearly depend on the child having a theory of mind, as discussed above; nothing would be gained from recasts if the child reacted by thinking 'Why is this stupid person repeating what I say?'

SLA research has usually translated parent/child interaction into native speaker (NS) to non-native speaker (NNS) interaction. Recasts have featured highly in classroom interaction, defined as 'the teacher's reformulation of all or part of a student's utterance minus the error' (Lyster and Ranta 1997: 46). Han (2002) suggested that the success of recasts depends on intensity of instruction and developmental readiness. Often recasts have been linked to Vygotsky's 1930s theory of child development (Vygotsky 1934/1962, 1935/1978), a precursor to modern ideas. The main construct has been the ZPD (Zone of Proximal Development), in SLA research taken to be the gap between the learner's current stage and the next point on some developmental scale (Lantolf 2000). Yet this brings to light a distinct feature of L2 acquisition: whatever L2 learners need to learn it is *not* how to mean. They have learnt the functions of language itself along with their first language; they simply have to discover how second language exploits this. Their social interactions with others do not need to be directed towards acquiring knowledge of language functions and social interaction – except in so far as these differ from one language to another.

Chomsky and Knowledge of Language

Chomsky's Theory of Universal Grammar (UG) has primarily been concerned with the acquisition of syntax. It denies the premise common to two L1 theories described above that language arises from social contact by claiming that virtually all children learn human language regardless of their situations or the ways their parents talk. However much a theory of mind may be needed for social interaction, it is incidental to the acquisition of syntax. None of the modifications to speech or interaction of L1 parents can be shown to be necessary to language acquisition, even if they may provide a small assistance. However diverse the cultural pattern of interaction, children always manage to learn language; the dialogues with babies so often commended in Western societies are not found in many societies, say Samoa (Ochs and Schieffelin 1984). All you need to learn a first language is a normal human mind and exposure to language.

Chomskyan theory sees language acquisition as the child's language faculty creating language knowledge by reacting to language input. The child is said to possess inbuilt principles and parameters that are instantiated differently according to the properties of the lexical items the child learns. A lexical item like *faint* projects particular properties on to the sentence – it can't have an object, *he fainted her*, or an inanimate subject, *the house fainted*, its subject comes before it, i.e. *he fainted*, not after, *fainted he* and so on. According to Chomsky, acquisition is the process of acquiring the properties of thousands of lexical items like *faint*. Chomsky's more recent Minimalist Program (Chomsky 1995) has so far been too little applied to first language acquisition to say anything coherent here though SLA research on it has started to appear (Sorace 2004). Most work in developmental linguistics still uses the earlier Government and Binding Theory (Chomsky 1981), as shown in Guasti (2002), with the exception of a few mainstream syntacticians working in L1 acquisition, such as Rizzi (2004). Chomsky's theory remains a theory of knowledge of language to which both social relationships and general cognition are incidental.

The overall UG theory has led to 'generative' SLA research, a subfield with its own articles, conferences and journals, much concerned with the relationship between L1 and L2 acquisition. One controversy is whether L2 differs from L1 acquisition because L2 learners can no longer use the resources of UG in their minds. The initial debate concerned whether the L2 learner had 'access' to Universal Grammar: perhaps L2 learning differs from L1 acquisition because L2 learners can no longer apply the original principles of Universal Grammar or perhaps they use them differently. Mostly the answer seemed to be that L2 learners are still capable of learning aspects of language such as structure-dependency for which they do not have enough evidence in the language they hear, just like native children (Cook 2003a); hence there is exactly the same evidence for UG in their minds as there is for its existence in the monolingual child's.

The 1990s SLA generativists debated a number of 'hypotheses' about access to UG in L2 acquisition including Full Access, Full Transfer/Full Access and variations on partial access such as Minimal Trees, Valueless Features and Failed Functional Features, all attempts to pin down the syntactic configurations that may be available to the L2 learner. These hypothesis wars are detailed in Cook and Newson (2007) who conclude 'Rather than using the richness of the Universal Grammar theory, this area seems to have become the kind of discussion associated with the question, probably spuriously attributed to St Aquinas, of how many angels can dance on the head of a pin' (Cook and Newson 2007: 239).

In general, recent SLA research has drawn on L1 acquisition theories more for its own ends than to test the relationship between L1 and L2 acquisition. In particular it has not paid much attention to the massive descriptive work on L1 acquisition reflected in books such as Bloom (2002), Clark (2003) and O'Grady (2005), which summarize developmental studies of the past decade rather than sticking exclusively to a particular acquisition theory.

Differences and Similarities between First and Second Language Acquisition

Some of the differences between L1 and L2 acquisition are intrinsic and cannot be avoided; some are, so to speak, accidental in that they vary according to the circumstances in which L2 acquisition takes place, in particular inside or outside a classroom. Vanderplank (2008) for example considers that the proper comparison is between adult L2 learners and L1 children aged 5–9 rather than infants as these are closer to adults in memory processes and awareness of language. In the vast majority of cases L2 learners are older than L1 children; age inevitably brings with it a host of factors that have little to do with language acquisition itself. The discussion here excludes early childhood simultaneous bilingualism, considering this as 'bilingualism as a first language' (Swain 1972), i.e. a separate process in which first and second languages are not consecutive.

The Lack of Another Language in the L1 Child's Mind

It may seem to be labouring the obvious to say that the L1 child only knows a single language – that's what L1 acquisition means. L2 learners already have at least one other language in their minds; the initial language state of their minds is in principle different from the L1 child because of the first language they already know, however variously this may be interpreted.

This is implicitly denied if the acquisition of the second language is treated in complete isolation from the already present first language, assuming that L2 acquisition is a form of L1 acquisition undertaken later in life, a view that has chiefly come from language teachers rather than SLA researchers. Since the Reform Movement of the nineteenth century (Howatt 2004), mainstream teaching has advocated using the second language in the classroom as much as possible; 'The natural use of the target language for virtually all communication is a sure sign of a good modern language course' (DES 1990: 58). The argument is effectively that, since the L1 child cannot fall back on another language, neither should the L2 student.

The core of SLA research that distinguishes it from other areas is the relationship between two languages in the same mind, leading to the vast research area of transfer, whether from L1 to L2, L2 to L1 (reverse transfer) or one L2 to another L2 (lateral transfer) (Jarvis and Pavlenko 2008). L2 acquisition necessarily differs from L1 acquisition because everything the learner acquires and does potentially involves both a first and a second language. Weinreich (1953) suggested that two of the forms bilingualism may take are **coordinate bilingualism** in which the languages are effectively kept in separate compartments and

compound bilingualism in which they are in contact. The integrative continuum (Cook 2003b) sees a continuum from total separation to total integration of the two languages rather than discrete compartments; the point on the continuum varies for individual L2 learners, for different aspects of language and for different situations. That is to say, the L1/L2 mental relationship has many variations and cannot be stated in simple terms even for a particular individual, whose L1 and L2 vocabulary say may be closely linked, but whose L1 and L2 phonologies may be quite distinct. One doubts whether any L2 learner is actually at the extreme compound and coordinate poles of the continuum, given the persuasive evidence for influence of the second language on the first described in Cook (2003b).

The Comparative Maturity of the L2 Learner

L1 acquisition has seen continual controversy over the links between language development and social and cognitive development. At one extreme UG theorists attempt to isolate language from other cognitive systems, as has always been part of the Chomskyan tradition even if expressed in different ways (Chomsky 2000). For them the issue is whether the language faculty stays essentially the same from birth, just requiring language experience or exposure to be activated, called the Gradual Development Hypothesis (Deprez 1994) or whether the faculty itself matures – the Full Competence Hypothesis (Poeppel and Wexler 1993). How L1 relates to L2 acquisition in Universal Grammar theory depends on which of these hypotheses is correct, i.e. whether the same Universal Grammar is still present in the mind of the L2 learner as the native child starting to acquire language or UG has matured into some other form unlike the initial form in the native child.

At the opposite extreme from UG theories, language development has been directly tied into cognitive development. Piagetians have often traced particular aspects of language development back to cognition: the one-word stage depends for example on the sensorimotor abilities of object constancy and representational thinking; complex syntax requires the ability to conserve, acquired at the concrete operations stage (Sinclair de Zwart 1969). Rick Cromer claimed that *where* there was a link between language and cognition, language depended on cognition (Cromer 1974). The development of spatial concepts goes hand in hand with the development of L1 spatial terms, even if sorting out cause and effect is still uncertain (Bloom 2002).

Nor can it be coincidence that the child's development of vocabulary goes along with the expansion in the child's short-term phonological memory (Gathercole and Baddeley 1993). Social development too develops over the years the child is acquiring language. When children first attend playgroup for instance they prefer to speak to adults rather than to the other children present; they slowly develop the ability to talk to their peers (Cook 1979). Similarly they start with a poor awareness of how to switch speaking style; young children have no idea of when to whisper, often to the embarrassment of their parents (Weeks 1971). Many L1 acquisition researchers insist on connecting language development and other aspects of development, even if it should eventually transpire that the barrier between language and the rest of the mind in the UG theory is true.

L2 learners start from the position of having done all of this once already. They are usually older and more mature than the L1 child and so have whatever advantages that age confers in terms of working memory, conceptual and social development, command of speech styles and so on. The L2 learner does not start from the L1 tabula rasa of knowing nothing about language (apart from the built-in paraphernalia of Universal Grammar). More specifically, once children have learnt how to mean, they cannot regress to a point where they no longer know how to mean: language itself is there for the L2 learner, even if the specific second language is not.

Much maturation is then transformation. In Gleitman's terms, princes don't change back to frogs when they learn a second language. The aspects of language acquisition that are related to maturation are not reversible; the L2 learner starts with the attributes of maturation appropriate to their age, not those of the L1 child, whether emotional, conceptual or any other changes that growing up entails. One of the variables in L2 learning is that the L2 learner may be at any point on this developmental continuum, ranging say from a nearly adult-like working memory span to a nearly child-like memory and may be at any stage of Piagetian development from the infant's sensorimotor to the adult's formal operational. L1 children acquiring language are in step with normal development; L2 learners are out of step, to a greater or lesser degree – an extreme form of décalage between stages in Piagetian theory (Piaget and Inhelder 1969).

A major factor in many L2 learners' lives is literacy. Learning to read and write changes people's thinking (Luria 1976) and brain structures (Petersen et al. 2000). Most SLA research is, however, about literate L2 learners who have been transformed by literacy, as Bialystok (2007) points out. Specific types of writing systems differentially affect people's thinking (Cook and Bassetti 2005): Japanese children remember geometrical patterns better than English children (Mann 1986) because their writing system is more visual than phonological. English readers place images of events such as breakfast, going to school, going to bed etc. in a left-to-right order, while Hebrew and Arabic readers use right-to-left order, showing the directionality in the respective writing systems (Tversky et al. 1991).

Incidentally this undermines the view that L2 teaching should start with the spoken language; as Harmer (1998: 53) puts it, 'Because many people acquire languages by hearing them first, many teachers prefer to expose students to the spoken form first'. The reliance on spoken language is still very much at the heart of language teaching methods, which assume implicitly that speaking comes first and use writing as a prop for written tasks rather than as the main focus (Cook 2005). Literate adults rely on writing in all sorts of ways and organize their thinking differently.

Age has often been blamed for alleged deficiencies in L2 acquisition. L2 learners are typically older than children acquiring their first language. Perhaps there is a point of no return beyond which the second language can no longer be learnt in the same way or with the same efficiency that you learnt your first language. This is not the place to explore the vast literature on age differences as it is dealt with elsewhere in this volume. It might be for example that once Universal Grammar has been instantiated in one language it is no longer available for L2 acquisition. So a second language would have to be learnt in some way that did not involve Universal Grammar, as argued by, say, Clahsen and Muysken (1989). However it is not age per se that shuts the door but maturation on a particular scale: it's not being 30 that prevents you learning a new language but having the memory system, the cognitive abilities and the social situations etc. of a 30-year-old. The variable is not age itself but one of the inevitable companions of age.

Differences in Situation, Learner and Language Input

The vast majority of children acquire their first language in a primal family care-taking situation; the situations of human babies are rather similar, apart from cultural differences in child-rearing practices. Virtually all human children learn human language; nothing stops a child learning their first language other than the total absence of language. First language learning can be taken for granted: it's what human beings do to be human.

L2 learners, however, encounter the second language in a variety of situations, ranging from Palestinian prisoners in Israeli jails learning Hebrew to teenagers in the USA learning Chinese as a heritage language, from Vietnamese and Poles learning Italian in Toronto for their workplaces (Norton 2000) to footballers learning English to play in the English Championship League (Kellerman et al. 2005), and from Japanese children learning Spanish at school to married couples bridging the gap between their different first languages (Piller 2002). Cook (2009b) itemizes some of these L2 user groups as: people using an L2 within a larger community, people using an L2 internationally for specific functions, people using an L2 globally for a wide range of functions, people historically from a particular community (re-)acquiring its language as an L2, and people using an L2 with spouses, siblings or friends. Not to mention those learning the second language in schools just because it's a set subject on the curriculum.

One overall group of L2 situations can be called **natural**, i.e. picking the language up through encounters at work etc. Another group are **artificial**, i.e. learning it through instruction of one kind or another. In either case the people the learners speak to are not necessarily making concessions to their lower language knowledge, and are certainly not in charge of their lives in the way that an adult is in charge of a child. The perpetual dilemma for language teaching is whether it should deliberately stress the artificial in the classroom or should try and make it as natural as possible, captured in Krashen's well-known distinction between learning and acquisition (Krashen 1985).

Those who acquire a second language 'artificially' in a classroom may be exposed to teaching methods ranging from grammar-translation to task-based learning by teachers who may or may not be native speakers. Teaching practices vary round the world far more than child-rearing practices and they change rapidly according to the changing winds of language teaching. Neither the natural nor the artificial L2 situations come in a standard package, as L1 situations usually do.

Children barely differ in their acquisition of the first language so far as the main features of the spoken language are concerned. They all end up learning the phonology, vocabulary and grammar appropriate for their dialect, class, age, gender, etc. Individual differences in L2 acquisition, however, are extreme. You can't learn a second language, apparently, without having the right motivation, attitude, learning style, learning strategies, cognitive style, personality and all the other factors enumerated in books like Skehan (1989) and Dörnyei (2005), mostly concerned with artificial classroom learning. The majority of L2 students give up before they pass the threshold when the L2 becomes genuinely useful to them; allegedly 80% of all students of English in the world are beginners, implying only a small proportion go on to higher levels. Success in L2 learning is a matter of individual variation; success in L1 acquisition is not.

The language input that L1 children get from their caretakers differs dramatically from that provided to the L2 learner. In natural contact situations, the input is closest to that in L1 acquisition. Parents simplify what they say to children and how they interact with them, using what Bruner (1983) calls the LASS (Language Acquisition Support System); native speakers speaking to non-natives simplify their speech in ways known as foreigner talk but hardly simplify topics in the same way parents do to children (Freed 1980). In the artificial teaching situation, coursebooks and language teachers simplify the language in various ways, say the vocabulary limits put on graded readers (Nation, 2009). Practical language teaching is almost inconceivable without simplified language; approaches using authentic uncensored materials have usually either been used at a late stage or have used tiny amounts of speech (Cook 2008). The Interaction Hypothesis has however maintained since 1981 that what is necessary is simplified interaction, not just simplified language alone (Long 1981, 1996), undeterred by the lack of proof for its necessity in L1 acquisition; the simplified language is a by-product of the simplified interaction.

Language teaching has attempted to re-create the conditions of the L1 child in the L2 classroom mostly in terms of using only a single language and having a simple interaction between students and teachers or between students. The Interaction Approach holds recasts to be important for L2 acquisition (Long 1996). The Sociocultural Model too argues that, since L1 acquisition depends on bridging the ZPD gap between what the child can do unaided and what they can achieve with the help of others through 'scaffolding', then so should L2 acquisition (Lantolf 2000). But, however vital ZPD may be to an L1 child, an L2 learner in a different situation at a different developmental level may necessarily use scaffolding functions differently, for instance by using peer-to-peer scaffolding rather than the Vygotskyan expert-to-novice scaffolding .

The Alleged Lack of Success and Its Causes

The major difference between first and second language acquisition, according to many, is the success of L1 acquisition versus the failure of L2 acquisition, summed up by Bley-Vroman (1989):

> The lack of general guaranteed success is the most striking characteristic of adult foreign language learning. Normal children inevitably achieve perfect mastery of the language; adult foreign language learners do not . . . one has the impression of ineluctable success on the one hand and ineluctable failure on the other. (Bley-Vroman 1989, 42–44)

Undoubtedly this view has been shared by the majority of SLA researchers. Ellis (1994: 107) summarized nine differences between L1 acquisition and L2 acquisition, using Bley-Vroman (1988):

1. overall success (L2 learners don't achieve 'perfect mastery')
2. general failure (in L2 acquisition 'complete success is very rare')
3. variation ('L2 learners vary . . . in success . . .')
4. goals ('L2 learners may be content with less than target competence . . .')
5. fossilization ('L2 learners often cease to develop and also backslide . . .')
6. intuitions ('L2 learners are often unable to form clear grammaticality judgements . . .')
7. instruction ('there is a wide belief that instruction helps L2 learners')

8. negative evidence (in L2 'correction generally viewed as helpful . . .')
9. affective factors ('. . . play a major role in determining proficiency' in the L2)

Points (1)–(3) are directly concerned with the lack of success of L2 learners. (4) is about lack of 'target competence', presumably another form of failure. Success is implicitly measured in 1–6 as speaking like a native speaker – 'perfect mastery', 'complete success', 'target competence'; point (9) is about proficiency, ambiguous but likely to mean native proficiency. Five of the points boil down to the fact that L2 learners do not speak like native speakers. Incidentally, it is also moot whether the remaining categories actually represent sharp L1/L2 differences: L1 attrition also occurs in various circumstances (Schmid et al. 2004) , say when the L1 is no longer much used (point 5); L2 bilingual children are better at grammaticality judgements than monolingual children (point 6) (Bialystok 1993); instruction is only one stream of L2 learning (point 7); L2 inter-actional techniques such as recasts actually came out of L1 learning research (point 8).

The task of SLA research is then taken to be explaining why L2 acquisition is unsuccessful in comparison to L1 acquisition; 'why, in general, adults fail to achieve full native-speaker competence' (Felix 1987: 144). If an L1 child can master a language in a few years, why can an L2 learner not do the same over many years?

The explanations for this lack of success have drawn on many of the ideas presented earlier. Some are to do with the transformative power of maturation: in a nutshell, L2 learners are intrinsically not the same people as young mono-lingual children.

1. Universal Grammar may not be available in L2 acquisition (Clahsen and Muysken 1986)
2. adults rely more on explicit learning (DeKeyser and Larson-Hall 2005)
3. declarative memory declines physically (Birdsong 2005)
4. adults are in the formal operational stage of Piagetian development, which is a handicap to language acquisition (Tremaine 1975)

In a sense nothing can be done about these immutable differences between L1 and L2 learning, if they exist and are indeed language related.

Other explanations put the lack of success down to features of the environment

- the concentration on the here and now common in conversations with children is necessary for language acquisition but is lost in any adult con-versation (Hatch 1978), which is mostly concerned with topics unrelated to the participants' physical situation

- Adults are more likely to be learning in formal classrooms that are less conducive to natural acquisition (Krashen 1985)

These are in principle changeable: we could treat L2 learners like L1 children linguistically and socially, reducing them to child-like dependence etc. The most extreme suggestion from McNeill (1965) was that L2 learners should memorize the two-word sentences of young L1 children like *more up*, to provide them with the 'deep structure' missing in L2 learning.

However the issue of success is a red herring. The child is learning their first language and has no other: the L2 learner is learning a second language when they already have a first. Why should the mastery of a second language be measured against the mastery of a first? L2 learners are only failures if they are measured against something they are not and never can be – monolingual native speakers. Does an apple make a good pear? A classic demonstration of this bias was the Bitch 100 test, which proved white Americans were failures at speaking Black American English (Williams 1975); my own *Can you talk Black?* test attempts to make the same point (Cook, 2009c). Clearly, if we test monolingual native speakers on knowledge of another language they would score zero. The success of L2 users is not necessarily the same as that of monolingual native speakers; they are doing different things with language with different people and have a range of other abilities for code-switching and translation unavailable to monolingual native speakers. To call what the vast majority of L2 users achieve 'failure' is to accept that the only valid view of the world is that of the monolingual: knowing only one language is normal, knowing two is unusual. Only in a monolingual universe is a multi-competent person a failure for not speaking like a monolingual.

The lack of success has haunted the discussion of L1 and L2 acquisition. If you expect L2 knowledge and processing to be identical to that of a monolingual speaker of the language, you're going to be disappointed. The L2 user has a more complex overall language system that includes two languages; neither the first nor the second language in a bilingual is isomorphic with the first language in a monolingual of either language. In recent years researchers have made a nod in the direction of abandoning the monolingual native speaker as the model of L2 acquisition – and then go on to use a research methodology which precisely compares the L2 user with native speakers to their disadvantage – grammaticality judgements, obligatory occurrences and the rest. SLA research methods need to get rid of the ghost in the machine, namely the monolingual native speaker, and use techniques that can stand on their own two feet, regardless of whether they originally came from L1 acquisition research or from elsewhere.

So, whatever the differences between L2 learners and L1 children, they are not a matter of success but of difference. L2 users are successful with regard to L2 use, not L1 use. The measurement of success is relative to the goal, not absolute. The rationale for comparing them with the monolingual native speaker is convenience; as we saw at the beginning, L1 acquisition research has a range of discoveries and techniques that SLA research can draw on. But, unless used carefully, they only measure L1 success, not L2 success. Many L2 learners indeed 'fail' to reach successful levels of L2 use but this has little to do with the levels reached by monolingual native speakers. If there are indeed differences between L1 and L2 acquisition, relying on L1 measures of success for L2 users will prevent any unique features of L2 acquisition such as differences in metalinguistic ability (Bialystok 1993) or cognition (Cook et al. 2006) from manifesting themselves and categorize any differences as failure.

Conclusions

To sum up, the discussion has presented the main points of the relationship between L1 and L2 acquisition that have been raised in SLA research. The relationship has been symbiotic for SLA research in terms of underlying theories and of specific research techniques. It has been largely one-way in that L1 acquisition research does not seem to have been influenced by SLA research. The relationship is complex and has to be handled with caution, avoiding oversimplistic claims: in some respects the two processes are similar, in some respects different, and this depends partly upon factors that have nothing to do with acquisition per se. There are many ways of understanding L1 acquisition with no single unifying model, even more ways of looking at L2 acquisition. Arbitrarily deciding on one L1 theory, say generative L1 acquisition, or picking out one L1 acquisition factor, say Subject-Object-Verb word order, hardly allows one to assert L2 learning is fundamentally different from L1 acquisition, as in say Clahsen and Muysken (1986).

I have also hinted throughout that asking if L2 acquisition is like L1 acquisition may not be a proper question. Like has to be compared with like; if the processes were quite different, this would not be revealed by measuring one of them by the standards of the other. There are pear-shaped apples called Worcester Pearmains but this says little about apples as a fruit, just about some of their non-prototypical forms. L1 acquisition theory and L1 acquisition research methods are a convenient source that SLA research can draw on, just as Teflon frying pans were allegedly a spin-off from the NASA space program. They are a source of ideas for looking at L2 acquisition itself, like ideas borrowed from reading research or from connectionism and so on. Using them does not force SLA research into a junior role in the research; they're being used for different purposes.

The shark lurking beneath the surface is the assumption that there is only one true form of language knowledge, the native speaker's, and only one true form of language acquisition, L1 acquisition. If exploiting the L1/L2 relationship goes beyond borrowing methods, the ideas of L1 acquisition confine SLA research and inevitably lead to seeing L2 acquisition as a pale imitation of L1 acquisition. If one accepts the multi-competence hypothesis that knowing and using two languages is a distinct state of human minds, the L1/L2 comparison becomes problematic: L2 acquisition is necessarily different because it involves the constant presence of a second language in the same mind as a first.

Going beyond this is the argument that the overall theory of language acquisition has to accommodate the human potential for learning more than one language from the outset, not as a footnote to the acquisition of the first language (Cook 2009; Satterfield 2003). Looked at through the looking-glass of multi-competence, language acquisition is acquiring two or more languages; monolingual L1 acquisition is a historical accident that stops the child reaching the normal human multi-competence state. The monolingual native speaker is language-deprived; they would have acquired multi-competence in more than one language if their caretakers had not deprived them of a second language, a standard Chomskyan argument about the environment translated to L2 acquisition (Cook 2009a).

The same applies to the relationship of the L1 and L2 communities (Cook, 2009b), which we have not tackled here. SLA and bilingualism research have assumed a dominant L1 community; the L2 user petitions to belong to another community: 'An individual's use of two languages supposes the existence of two different language communities; it does not suppose the existence of a bilingual community' (Mackey 1972: 554). Many parts of the world like India and Central Africa are, however, genuinely multilingual communities where languages function alongside each other in diverse roles. It is meaningless to say that the L2 user joins a monolingual community as an outsider rather than belonging to a community that uses many languages, called 'the multi-competence of the community' by Brutt-Griffler (2002). The comparison of L1 and L2 in the community is interesting but it may conceal the distinctive nature of the truly multilingual community.

One sub-theme here has been language teaching. Most language teaching methods have prejudged the relationship of L2 to L1 acquisition by assuming that 'natural' L1 acquisition is the basis for all acquisition, however much they differ in what they understand by 'natural'. For example Total Physical Response 'simulates at a speeded up pace the stages an infant experiences in acquiring its first language' (Asher 1986: 17). From the Direct Method to Task-based Learning, language teaching has insisted on a mock target language situation, in which the first language plays a minimal part. Students are required to speak the second language from the moment they step inside the classroom and should not be allowed to revert to the first language; the teacher should make the classroom a monolingual target language situation, not a bilingual situation. While the first language necessarily exists in the L2 learner's mind, the accepted view is that it should be forcibly prevented from manifesting itself in the classroom. The implications of the multi-competence approach for language teaching have been spelled out elsewhere (Cook 2007). But, to take a more neutral position, one should say that teachers at least should be wary of accepting advice about language teaching goals and methods based on the comparison of L1 and L2 learning rather than on the independent study of second language acquisition.

5 The Relationship between Age of Learning and Type of Linguistic Exposure in Children Learning a Second Language

Victoria A. Murphy

Introduction

There have been many informative books, chapters in books and articles written about the relationship between age and language learning in both first language (L1) and second language (L2) contexts. Many of these previous discussions have focussed on the issue of the *Critical Period Hypothesis (CPH)* – the idea that humans are biologically pre-disposed to learn language in their early childhood more successfully than later on in their lives. Hence, the main focus of much of the literature on age has been concerned with identifying the extent to which the CPH is validated by examining literature within both the L1 and L2 domains. This chapter is not one of those. The focus of this chapter is *not* whether or not we can find sufficient evidence to either accept or refute the CPH in L2 learning. As Bialystok and Miller (1999) and Singleton (2005) have noted, there is so much variability in terms of how the CPH is defined and the types of learner and task types that have been researched in empirical investigations of the CPH that it is hardly surprising that the evidence for the CPH, to put it mildly, is mixed. Rather, the focus of this chapter is on examining the interaction between the age of a language learner and the context in which the second language (L2) is being learnt within child L2 acquisition. This latter issue of course does relate to the notions embodied within the CPH, and as a result there is a brief introductory section below on some of the essential issues surrounding this discussion in the L1 and L2 literature. The question posed in this chapter is more specific and is motivated by a growing phenomenon around the world, namely early L2 learning at school.

Increasingly, primary (elementary) school-aged children around the world are being given some form of L2 instruction, motivated in part by the research supporting the CPH and which argues for a 'younger is better' approach to L2 learning (e.g., Johnson and Newport 1989). What is less well understood, however, is the more specific relationship between the age of the child, the type of L2 provision being offered and the general success the child has at learning the L2. Within the UK context, for example, L2 instruction in the primary school years will be mandatory by the year 2010 (DCSF 2002). Surprisingly, however, very little research has been carried out in the UK concerning the optimum age at which children should receive L2 instruction. Indeed, little research focusing on these issues in the UK has been carried out since Burstall (1975) who showed that without the appropriate L2 provision, younger can be less effective for L2 at primary level. It is not just the UK either that is developing educational policy without a wealth of empirical evidence to support it. L2 programmes around the world are being offered to children at primary level, but again, without the empirically driven understanding of what constitutes the *best* L2 provision for different linguistic contexts. These issues are of course important because not everyone comes to learn their L2 in the same way and in the same kind of educational and linguistic community. It is reasonable to assume that the influence of age might be different depending on both the way in which the language is learnt (e.g., is it the medium of instruction or is it the subject matter itself?) and both the amount and type of exposure the L2 learner has to the language (e.g., naturalistic input in the language majority environment or restricted mostly to classroom interaction and L2 teaching materials?). This chapter therefore will review some of the evidence which speaks to these issues in child L2 acquisition. While this chapter will not be able to provide an answer to the questions of 'what is the best age' for learning an L2 and 'what is the best L2 provision' questions, hopefully it will serve to present a summary of some of the main findings regarding school-based L2 learning in children, in different educational contexts, which could become a first step towards an answer to the important 'what age' and 'what type' questions.

The first educational context examined below is the 'language minority' context where children come to school from a home language environment that is not the majority language in the community. For many children learning their L2 in this context, entering school presents them with their first significant exposure to the L2, and often children are in a position of having to learn academic subject matter through the medium of the L2 (without much L2 instruction per se). The second context discussed is one where the L2 is a foreign language and is taught, as a subject, in school as part of the school curriculum. This kind of L2 instruction, particularly where the L2 is English, is becoming increasingly prevalent around the world. The final L2 section examines the relative differences between early and late immersion, where language majority children are learning an L2 mostly through content-based instruction, with comparatively little focus on linguistic form(s). First, however, a brief discussion of issues surrounding the CPH is necessary to contextualize the child L2 acquisition discussion.

Age and First Language Development

As mentioned above, the Critical Period Hypothesis (CPH) has been invoked to explain the observation that children seem to be able to 'soak up language like a sponge' whereas adult older learners seem to have much more difficulty. The claim is that we get progressively less sponge-like as we age, at least with respect to our abilities to 'soak up' language. The origins of the CPH are usually traced back to Lenneberg (1967) who was among the first researchers to propose a biological explanation for language acquisition, noting as he did that young children seem to have a heightened sensitivity to language acquisition. Lenneberg (1967) based some of his conclusions on the findings of Penfield and Roberts (1959) who demonstrated that the human brain is considerably more 'plastic' or flexible in early development, allowing for specific areas in the brain to become associated with specific cognitive functions, language being one of them. What was less clear in these early discussions was the exact onset and offset of the CPH. Lenneberg, for example, originally proposed that the onset of CPH was 2 years, with the offset around 12 years (corresponding to the approximate onset of puberty). These claims initiated a tremendous amount of research that aimed to systematically examine the strength of these ideas (see Herschensohn 2007 for a detailed review). As Herschensohn (2007) has shown, almost all of Lenneberg's original claims have been refuted (see also Snow 1987). For example, we know now that the onset of a putative CPH must be at birth, not 2 years, and many proponents of a CPH have argued that the offset is much earlier than puberty, perhaps around 5–6 years of age when typical L1 development is nearly complete (Herschensohn 2007). However, despite this lack of support for some of the details of the original claims concerning the CPH, the question of whether or not language acquisition is subject to some kind of critical, or rather 'sensitive' period (sensitive implying there are no exact cut-off points) is still hotly debated.

Singleton and Ryan (2004) and Herschensohn (2007), among others, catalogue and review the evidence from the L1 literature in support of the CPH for L1 acquisition. This evidence ranges from neurological studies regarding the lateralization of brain function (e.g., Penfield and Roberts 1959), to research with deaf children showing that deaf children born into deaf families benefit from having early exposure to sign language over children who are exposed to sign language later on in their development (e.g., Emmorey 2002; Newport 1990) to examples of children developing in extreme isolation and who then go on to fail to develop a native-like linguistic competence (e.g., Curtiss 1977; Curtiss et al. 2004). Evidence of this sort has served to convince some researchers of the notion that 'younger is better' when it comes to L1 acquisition. However, as Herschensohn (2007) has illustrated, despite research showing an advantage to L1 acquisition in the early vs. later years of childhood, a number of researchers have argued this evidence to be inconclusive and do not support the claims of the CPH (e.g., Bortfeld and Whitehurst 2001; Hakuta 2001; Snow 2002).

In summary, within the L1 literature there has been considerable debate concerning how the CPH should be defined and considered, both in terms of defining the onset and offset of the CPH, in considering whether the CPH is indeed a *critical* period or rather a *sensitive* one, and the extent to which the evidence showing an advantage of younger over older L1 learners is indicative of critical or sensitive periods. Needless to say this is a rather unsatisfactory situation since there are as of yet no definitive answers that all can agree on concerning the CPH, despite the fact it is much studied and often discussed.

The situation in the L2 literature is equally mixed with respect to whether and to what extent the CPH can explain the relative success (or lack thereof) of older learners acquiring an L2. As identified above, it is not the focus of this chapter to review this evidence in any detail or to try to reach a definite conclusion. There are numerous texts devoted to just this endeavour (e.g., Birdsong 1999; DeKeyser and Larson-Hall 2005; Hyltenstam and Abrahamsson 2003; Moyer 2004; Scovel 2000; Singleton and Ryan 2004). As Moyer stated, 'Clearly age of exposure is but one factor in ultimate attainment, and not an especially informative one . . .' (Moyer 2004: 138). She argues for the importance of 'Putting age effects in Context' and while for her context means either the *psychological*, *social* or *cognitive* context (which undoubtedly are important contexts to consider in relation to age and L2 learning) another perhaps more obvious form of context considered below is the linguistic environment and nature of experience the L2 learner has with the L2. Below I consider 3 different kinds of contexts that are relevant for millions of children around the world: Bilingual education programmes for language minority children, children learning the L2 as a foreign language and finally immersion contexts.

Minority Language Learners in a Majority Language Community

Minority language children are those who come from a linguistic background which is different (and less represented) than the language spoken and used in the larger community/society. Often language minority children are from immigrant families, but there are examples around the world of children who live in communities where the 'heritage language' or L1 is spoken in their community within the larger context (e.g., Spanish-speaking communities in California). For many of these children, where the L1 is supported in the home community, entry into school can be the first significant point of contact with the majority L2. Language minority children are found worldwide, and some educational authorities around the world have developed different forms of educational policies and programmes to try to assist children to access curricula which is being delivered in what is effectively a relatively unknown L2. Arguably the majority of research on language minority children has come from the USA and therefore, for illustrative purposes only, the issues relating to programmes which introduce children to the L2 in different types of programmes from within the USA context will be discussed below.[1]

Language minority children in the USA (most commonly children who speak Spanish as an L1 in the home and home community) often have access to different types of educational programmes within primary school to help them develop their L2 linguistic skills and to ultimately help them access the curriculum (for a review of different bilingual education programs in the USA for language minority students see Genesee 1999). There are different kinds of programmes, some of which reflect some of the issues discussed above – namely, the notion that 'younger is better' and that children from language minority contexts might benefit most from maximal exposure to the L2 (English in the USA) from the moment they enter school at kindergarten (aged 3/5) or grade 1 (aged 5/6). Traditional L2-only programmes exemplify this ideal, opting for the language minority child having complete instruction in English, with (perhaps) some ESL instruction 'on the side'. This is a common format in the UK for English as an Additional Language (EAL) children as well. For example, EAL children in the UK typically begin school in entirely L2-only provision alongside their native-speaking peers. EAL children do, however, receive some remedial support, but the nature of this support varies across different districts. Contrasted to these more traditional programmes are *bilingual education programmes* where *both* English (L2) and the child's native L1 is used in the classroom, and within these bilingual programmes there are some which carry on the use of both the L1 and L2 throughout primary and some into the secondary years (developmental bilingual programmes). Other bilingual programmes are *two-way immersion programmes* where both language minority and language majority children are educated together with half the time spent in the minority L1, and the other half in the majority L2. Another type of bilingual programme is the *transitional* programme where the language of instruction at the very beginning stages of primary is the child's L1 but is used as a sort of scaffold, with a transition into L2 only after the first 3 years of primary education (Genesee 1999).

One obvious feature of these programmes reflects an interaction between the amount of exposure to the L2 and the age at which the child experiences the L2. In the traditional L2-only programmes, the L2 is the sole medium of instruction from the beginning of the child's experience at the school. The L2 for most of the school day for these children is the medium of instruction, with relatively minimal amounts of time being devoted to L2 instruction per se. An assumption underlying this kind of programme is that maximum exposure to the L2, from the very earliest age, is most effective.

The two-way immersion and developmental programmes reflect a somewhat different assumption, namely that instruction in the L1 in conjunction with the L2, is most effective. In terms of age, as in the L2-only programmes the child is exposed to the L2 as a medium of instruction from the earliest levels at primary. However, not all of the school day is spent in the L2 (and the amount of time spent in the L2 can range from 10% to 50%). Finally, the transitional bilingual programmes seem to reflect an assumption that 100% L2 exposure from the earliest experience at primary level is less effective, and therefore the child is *transitioned* from having the L1 as the medium of instruction in the first 3 years of primary to having the L2 as the medium of instruction after 3 years.

The age at which the child receives initial exposure to the L2 is similar in each of these examples, namely, the child is exposed to the L2 as a medium of instruction, and sometimes as the subject matter itself (as in the L2-only programmes with ESL support) from the beginning of primary school (which amounts to 5/6 years of age). The one exception is of course in the transitional programmes where the L2 would be gradually introduced and, by the end of the child's third year (8/9 years old), all instruction will be in the L2. However, given these are language minority children one can also assume with confidence that even children in transitional programmes will have a degree of exposure to the L2 in the wider community. What differs more significantly, however, is the nature and amount of exposure the children receive. Maximum L2 exposure is found in the L2-only programmes (100% of the day in L2), with the developmental and two-way programmes overall providing the least amount of L2 exposure since a significant proportion of the school day is devoted to the L1 as well across the primary years. In these programmes, as little as 10% of the day to as much as 50% of the day might be spent in the L2. These programmes therefore, present us with a comparison where the age of the L2 learner is held reasonably constant but the exposure varies. If 'younger is better' and maximum exposure to the L2 input is best, then children in

L2-only programmes should have the most sophisticated L2 skills by the end of primary years. Lower L2 performance should be found in the other types of bilingual programmes, with the least proficient L2 performance in the developmental and two-way immersion programmes. If 'younger is better' no matter what the L2 exposure, then there should be little difference across these different programmes for these language minority children. If it is better to immerse the child in the L2 when they are older, then children in the transitional programmes, who do not have full L2 exposure until the end of Year 3, should have the most well-developed linguistic skills. So what does the evidence tell us?

In answering this question it is first important to consider the notion that there are different types of language proficiency, and in particular, different types of communicative situations which draw more or less on different aspects of proficiency. For example, Cummins (2000) presents a framework illustrating that communication which differs in terms of contextual support requires different degrees of linguistic proficiency. Cummins argues that communication that is *context-embedded* and thus receives a lot of support from the context requires a different sort of proficiency than *context-reduced* and more *cognitively demanding* communication. It is the context-reduced forms of communication that are more cognitively demanding and often more relevant to language minority children in certain aspects of academic development (for e.g., reporting on a science experiment in school). Unfortunately it is beyond the scope of this chapter to delve into this issue to the extent that it deserves. However, for a more detailed review see Genesee, Paradis and Crago (2004). Cummins and others note that context-embedded and cognitively undemanding communication is much faster to develop in language minority children. Importantly too, Cummins (1980, 1981) and Cummins and Swain (1986) have argued that it is *older* L2 learners who show a higher mastery of features of the L2 related to literacy (e.g., syntax, morphology and vocabulary) since these are the features that are more cognitively demanding and context-reduced forms of communication benefit from a degree of cognitive maturity.

In terms of language minority children developing their overall L2 proficiency, a number of different sources have argued that it can take as long as 5 to 7 years for a language minority child to develop L2 proficiency that is comparable to their native language peers (e.g., Lindholm-Leary and Borsato 2007; Thomas and Collier 1997). This finding alone suggests that learning an L2 in childhood must amount to more than 'soaking it up like a sponge'. What is more pertinent to the focus of this chapter concerns whether there are any differences across the different kinds of bilingual programmes in terms of L2 learning. The relevant evidence for this question has been summarized nicely in Genesee, Paradis and Crago (2004) where they ask two important questions: (1) Does schooling in a bilingual programme enhance or retard the acquisition of the majority language and (2) What is the relationship between the amount of exposure to the *minority* language in school and the development of that language?

With respect to the question about whether being in a bilingual programme enhances or retards the acquisition of the majority language, Genesee et al. (2004) review evidence from a range of studies and present two patterns of findings. The first pattern illustrates an advantage for children who are in developmental or two-way bilingual programmes (e.g., Lindholm-Leary and Borsato 2007; Thomas and Collier 1997). The finding is that students in these developmental bilingual programmes demonstrate *higher* levels of proficiency in English relative to language minority children who are in L2-only or transitional bilingual programmes. In other words, despite the fact that *less* time is spent in English, given that a proportion of time is spent on developing the L1 in these developmental programmes, these children end up with a higher level of L2 proficiency. The second pattern that has emerged from some studies is that there is no *disadvantage* (without a comparable advantage) to language minority children in bilingual programmes (e.g., see Lindholm-Leary and Borsato 2007). Taking these two patterns together, it seems that developing the L1 in conjunction with the L2 in bilingual programmes is (a) minimally not harmful to the developing L2 and (b) potentially advantageous to the developing L2. What these findings clearly show is that the educational context can play a significant role in the developing L2.

Genesee et al. (2004) also address the exposure question in their review, asking whether there is a linear relationship between the amount of exposure to the L2 (the majority language) and the level of L2 proficiency developed by language minority children. Based on the synthesis of research presented in Lindholm-Leary and Borsato (2007), Genesee et al. argue that perhaps somewhat surprisingly there is no linear relationship between the *amount* of exposure to the L2 and the L2 proficiency gained by the language minority students. They argue that language minority students who have a greater exposure to English (those in bilingual programmes where 50% of time is spent in the L2) show an initial advantage over those students who receive less exposure to the L2 (e.g., those who spend 10% of the time in the L2). Interestingly, however, Genesee et al. claim that by the end of Grade 3 (i.e., after 3 years of being in the bilingual programme) students in programmes with more exposure to English (50%) no longer show an advantage over those students who spend less time in school in the majority L2 (10%). Genesee et al. (2004) also show that this is the same pattern found in children in L2-only programmes compared to those in bilingual programmes; there is an *initial* advantage to the children in 100% L2 programmes, but by the end of the primary years, the advantage is gone with, in some cases, the advantage being transferred to those children who participated in the bilingual programme (i.e., who effectively had *less* exposure to the majority L2 in school) (Lindholm-Leary and Borsato 2007). Genesee et al. (2004)

and Lindholm-Leary and Borsato (2007) argue that this rather unexpected relationship stems from the fact that these language minority students would have a relatively high degree of exposure to the L2 in the wider language majority community outside the school. There is also a wealth of evidence to show that supporting the L1, and specifically L1 literacy skills, has a facilitative effect on the developing L2 (see August and Shanahan 2008; Genesee et al. 2006). These two factors together, the language majority context outside the school, and the developing L1 literacy skills, presumably have a considerable influence over the effectiveness of different L2 learning programmes for language minority children.[2]

Summary of Language Minority Context

The research of Cummins (2000) and others (e.g., Genesee et al. 2007) has shown that even in young child L2 learners, it can take many years for a child to gain sufficient mastery of the L2 so as to be linguistically comparable to their native-language peers. In this respect then it seems that L2 learning, even in children, takes time. But importantly, the research examining the relative effectiveness of these different bilingual programmes shows that 100% exposure in school to the L2 does not guarantee the greatest success in the long run.[3] Having greater exposure to the L2 for these children seems to have a positive impact early on in their L2 learning. However, measures at the end of the primary years show that programmes which consistently promote the L1 (even if that means less time spent on the L2) can result in higher L2 skills than those children who are in either L2-only programmes or bilingual programmes with less L1 instruction and support. 100% exposure to L2 in the early years helps with initial *rate* of learning, but in the long run, supporting the L1 seems to yield higher L2 proficiency, as well as comparable academic outcomes (Genesee et al. 2006).

Clearly, these findings demonstrate that there is indeed an interaction between success at learning the L2 and the kind of programme/context the child is in. All the children in the research cited above were language minority children, this means then that they were exposed to their L2 not just within schools, but also in the broader community. Being a language minority child means being educated in part, or wholly through the L2, and in many cases can often mean little use of the L2 in the home. There are clearly a host of variables, not just the ones mentioned above, that influence the success of L2 learning for language minority children around the world. Genesee et al. (2007) present a detailed and comprehensive review. For the purposes of this chapter, however, this research illustrates importantly that exposure to the L2, and the context in which the L2 is being learnt can have a significant impact on both the success and rate with which the child learns his/her L2. What is useful now for the focus of this chapter, is to compare the relative success of these language minority children, to other children learning an L2 in different kinds of educational contexts.

Age and Second (Foreign) Language Instruction

The research described above focused on children who are learning the L2 of the wider community. Of course, this is not the only context in which children are expected or required to learn an L2. In contrast to language minority children, children learning an L2 as a foreign language are likely to have minimal to no exposure to the L2 outside of the L2 classroom. As mentioned above, increasingly around the world children are required to learn a second (foreign) language at primary school. For example in Europe, EFL teaching and learning at primary school has increased significantly in the last 15 years, partly as a response to the European Union's 1995 white paper 'Teaching and Learning: Towards the learning society' in which the importance of L2 learning at primary level is emphasized. One of the assumptions underlying directives such as these is that 'younger is better'. However, as the focus of this chapter indicates, it is critical to understand the extent to which 'younger is better' in all different L2 situations in order to best understand the most effective ways to support L2 learning in children. A fair amount of research has been carried out in the last decade or so asking this specific question, namely, what is the effect of age in foreign language acquisition. As English is the international *lingua franca*, most of the research that has focused on this issue has investigated English as a Foreign Language (EFL).

Answers to these questions can be found in a number of volumes, one of which is García Mayo and García Lecumberri (2003). In this volume a number of different research studies are presented which examined the question of age and EFL learning from a variety of different perspectives and focusing on different aspects of L2 learning and performance. Cenoz (2003) for example, reports on findings of research examining the affect of age on EFL in terms of the children's proficiency, code-mixing and attitudes to learning. The context for this study, and indeed many of the studies in this volume, is actually a third language acquisition (L3) context since the study focuses on children who are Basque/Spanish bilinguals learning English as a foreign language at school. All of the children in Cenoz's study had received 600 hours of English instruction but importantly for comparative purposes, they had started learning English at different ages; 4 years, 8 years or 11 years old. The children in Cenoz's sample were tested on measures of English oral production, listening comprehension measures and a cloze test based on 'Little Red Riding Hood'. They were also given a reading comprehension and grammar test as well as a questionnaire to measure their attitudes and motivation towards English, Basque and Spanish. All the children were tested after 600 hours of English instruction, either at the end of Year 5 at Primary (the youngest learners), Year 2 of Secondary School (middle age group learners) or Year 5 at Secondary School (oldest learners). The results showed a clear advantage for the older learners on all the measures of proficiency (oral production, listening and reading comprehension and grammar/cloze test). However, the results of the questionnaire data indicated that the youngest learners had the highest scores for both attitude and motivation towards language. The code-mixing data came from the oral production data and were based on utterances which had been transferred from Basque or Spanish into English. The results of this analysis indicated that learners who started learning English at the youngest age (age 4) did not mix the languages more than the older learners who started learning English at age 8 or 11. In other words, Cenoz (2003) reports no clear patterns in code-mixing in relation to age. In summary, Cenoz (2003) presents an interesting study which shows a clear interaction between age and task type. Older is in fact better if considering measures of English proficiency since the older children scored higher on all the proficiency measures. On the attitude/motivation measure, however, younger does seem to be better as this age group produced the highest (most positive) attitudes and motivation. On the code-mixing measure, no evidence was found which indicated any relationship between age and code-mixing.

García Mayo (2003) asked a slightly different set of questions, focusing on whether length of exposure to EFL influences performance on grammaticality judgement tasks – that is, on language competence rather than performance. As in Cenoz (2003) the participants in García Mayo's study were bilingual Basque/Spanish students learning EFL. Two groups of children were tested on a grammaticality judgement (GJ) task who were matched on number of hours of exposure and type of instruction but who differed in terms of their age of first exposure to English (either 8/9 years or 11/12 years). Children were tested after 396 hours, and then again after 594 hours of English instruction. The results indicated that perhaps unsurprisingly length of exposure seems to lead to greater target-like performance on the GJ task (i.e., the longer the exposure, the more target-like the responses). In terms of the age effect, however, the results indicated that the older learners (those who were first exposed to English at age 11/12 years) produced statistically more target-like responses on the GJ task than children who were first exposed to English at a younger age. Similar results were found in looking at metalinguistic awareness data, whereby the older learners were more able to identify the source of ungrammaticality in the sentences on the GJ task and identify what needed to be corrected to render the sentence grammatical. As with Cenoz (2003) then, García Mayo (2003) finds an advantage for older, not younger learners in an EFL setting.

García Lecumberri and Gallardo (2003) report on a study which examines the relationship between age in EFL and English pronunciation. The study is contextualized with a discussion highlighting the fact that of all the levels of linguistic analysis, phonology is one area that many researchers concede is the most likely to be subject to some form of sensitive period, or at least, is an area in which the younger the learner, the more native-like the learner will sound in their language production. As in the other two studies described above, the context of this study is Basque/Spanish bilinguals learning EFL at different ages. In this study, however, García Lecumberri and Gallardo examine EFL students' perceptual and production skills in English in the L2. For the perception skills the students were required to discriminate between minimal pairs differing in either a consonant and vowel sound. In the production aspect of their study, the EFL students' English production on *The Frog Story* (where a story is presented in pictures and the child has to describe what's happening) were recorded and presented to native speakers of English to rate in terms of Degree of Foreign Accent (DFA) and intelligibility. In terms of the perception task, the youngest learners (the learners who began learning English at 4) showed the worst results in discriminating minimal pairs on the basis of both vowels and consonants, while the oldest learners (who began learning English at 11 years) had the highest results. In terms of the production measures, the oldest learners were rated as having the smallest DFA, namely they had less pronounced foreign accents in their production of English relative to the two younger groups (who began learning English at 4 and 8 years respectively). García Lecumberri and Gallardo (2003) conclude by arguing that the age at which a learner starts EFL learning is not a factor that facilitates foreign language sound acquisition. This finding is particularly interesting in light of the significant amount of research which has suggested that if there is a CPH it is for phonology. They speculate that perhaps it is due to the foreign language setting which requires a greater length of exposure (than what their participants had had) for early starters to show their expected and characteristic advantage on this aspect of L2 knowledge, although the foreign accent of the primary teachers involved in this study was not controlled for and could have been an influencing variable.

Other contributors to the García Mayo and García Lecumberri (2003) volume show a similar pattern of 'older is better' in EFL settings. For example, Lasagabaster and Doiz (2003) show that in FL written production older learners outperform younger learners on holistic and quantitative measures of students' English written production. Similarly Victori and Tragant (2003) demonstrate that learners who started learning EFL at an older age report using both a larger range of language learning strategies and strategies that are more cognitively demanding.

A very clear picture emerges then from the García Mayo and García Lecumberri (2003) volume that the notion of 'younger is better' does not seem to be substantiated in a context where the language being learnt is being instructed as a subject matter in a school context where the majority of exposure the learners have to the L2 is wholly within the school context. Interestingly, this 'older is better' message in EFL seems to be confirmed across a range of different linguistic skills (oral production, written production, proficiency measures (reading and listening), strategies and even foreign language accent).

A similar volume with a similar message can be found in Muñoz (2006a) where a number of different studies are presented investigating the effect of age on EFL in Catalan/Spanish bilingual children learning English in school. Systematic comparisons across children who learnt English at different ages are made in a number of studies in this volume investigating a wide range of linguistic skills such as: foreign language perception and production, vocabulary, morphosyntax, learner strategies and writing development. A specific focus of a number of the contributions to the volume are on the question of age and rate of acquisition. For example, Muñoz (2006b) reports on a study comparing 4 different groups of subjects who differed in terms of their Age of Onset (AO) of learning English as a Foreign Language. The specific AOs included were 8, 11, 14 and 18+ years. The students in this study were compared after 200 hours, 416 hours and 726 hours of English instruction respectively. The measures used included dictation tests, cloze tests, listening comprehension, grammar, written composition, oral tasks and phonetic imitation and discrimination. The general pattern found in this study were that there are age-related effects in terms of rate of learning EFL. The 18+ learners in the study had the highest scores after 200 hours of instruction, but their learning slowed between 200 and 416 hours of English relative to the other groups. Students who began learning at age 14 had statistically higher scores and a more rapid rate of learning than the younger learners (8 and 11). Those whose AO was 11 years also had statistically higher scores than the youngest group at time 2 (after 416 hours of English instruction).

Muñoz (2006b) also wanted to know whether or not the younger learners could catch up to the older learners, as this had been shown in previous studies that older is better for initial rate, but younger is better for ultimate attainment (see Snow and Hoefnagel-Höhle 1978). Muñoz (2006b) reports that in the time span covered in her study, overall the younger learners did not surpass the older learners in terms of their scores on the measures used in her research, however, on some measures the younger learners did seem to catch up to the older learners (e.g., aural perception). Therefore, there seems to be an interesting interaction here between rate, age and task type/linguistic skill. Muñoz concludes her discussion by suggesting that it is the interaction between the learners' stage of cognitive development and the kind (i.e., instructed) and amount of exposure they receive that will determine the point at which the younger learners catch up to the older ones.

The general conclusions reached in both the García Mayo and García Lecumberri (2003) and the Muñoz (2006a) volumes is that in an EFL setting, younger is not better, though it is important to remember that this research is limited to one national/educational context and may not be generalizable across other educational and linguistic contexts. Nonetheless, a consistent and overall pattern (with relatively few exceptions) is that older is better across the range of studies presented and the different levels of linguistic knowledge and task types tested. There are interesting interactions between a number of different variables but the general pattern is quite clear. Muñoz (2006b) and others suggest that the reason for this older advantage relates to the cognitive development of the learner, namely that older learners are able to draw upon more advanced and well-developed general cognitive learning mechanisms in order to take the fullest advantage of the minimal input that they receive in the EFL settings. This suggestion is reinforced by the findings of Victori and Tragant (2003) and Tragant and Victori (2006) who showed that older EFL learners use more, and more cognitively developed, language learning strategies.

Nonetheless, the results and conclusions reported in the García Mayo and García Lecumberri (2003) and Muñoz (2006a) volumes have not gone without criticism. For example, Larson-Hall (2008) has suggested that one important confound present in the work cited in these two volumes is that of the age of the learner at the time of testing. Larson-Hall predicts that given research in the psychological literature has shown an advantage in older over younger learners in different kinds of test situations (e.g., IQ) the fact that the learners not only were older when they began learning EFL but also when they were tested could be an explanation for their superior performance across a range of tasks. To try and tackle this question Larson-Hall (2008) carried out a study which attempted to examine the relationship between the age at starting studying English as a foreign language and scores on a phonological and morphological task. The participants in Larson-Hall's study were Japanese learners of English as a second language who were students at a university in Japan a proportion of which reported learning English before junior high school and were considered 'early starters'. The participants took part in a GJ task, a phonemic discrimination task and an aptitude test which was used to factor out the possible contribution that aptitude could make on the participants' responses on the GJ and phonemic discrimination tasks. They were also given a comprehensive language background questionnaire which was used to identify variables such as how many hours of exposure to English the students had per week, and the nature of the interaction the students had with English outside (and inside) the English classroom. Larson-Hall (2008) used careful statistical analyses using partial correlation techniques to factor out relative contributions of potentially confounding variables from her data. She reports that there were 'modest' effects for an early starting age in both grammatical and receptive phonological

171

abilities as measured by the GJ task and phonemic discrimination task. Early starters seemed to have an advantage over later starters on the GJ task, a relationship which accounted for 14% of the variance when controlling for total hours of input to English. Larson-Hall further reports that while morphosyntactic skills can be enhanced by an early start, this advantage requires a substantial amount of input since results from analysis of co-variance indicated that total hours of input helped explain the scores on the GJ task. Larson-Hall suggests that the fact that her data indicated some (albeit modest) advantage for early starters in an foreign language context can be attributed to the fact that the learners in her study had significantly higher levels of input to English than those reported in previous studies (e.g., García Mayo and García Lecumberri 2003). She goes on to conclude from her research that starting young can have some advantages in a foreign language context and that the amount of input seems to be a critical factor. This conclusion seems to echo that of Muñoz (2006b) who argued that the role of input was a significant factor in determining the extent to which the younger learners would eventually catch up to the older learners in her study.

Summary of EFL Context

Even with Larson-Hall's (2008) findings, the picture is remarkably consistent that 'older seems to be better' in a foreign language setting. We should consider carefully, however, the specific relationships between starting age, levels of linguistic knowledge, task types and amount of input since Larson-Hall (2008) and indeed other studies (e.g., Cenoz 2003) did not report a uniform advantage of starting older in an EFL context. What these findings clearly demonstrate, however, is that the 'best' age at which to start learning an L2 really does seem to depend on a number of other factors, the quality and amount of input being two critical variables.

There are some interesting differences across the language minority context described above and the EFL contexts. The language minority research showed that when the learners have wider exposure to the language in the community, spending *less* time on the L2 in the classroom and more time on developing L1 literacy skills seems to result in the most well-developed L2 performance. In the EFL context the L2 is *not* supported in the wider community and the learners more or less only have access to the L2 in the classroom. In this context we find a reasonably clear picture that starting EFL learning at the earliest years in primary school (which is what happens to the language minority students) is unlikely to be the most effective course of action, unless as Larson-Hall (2008) suggests significant amounts of input are available to the L2 learning child.

Age and Immersion

Children who come to school who speak a majority societal language (e.g., English in Canada or Japanese in Japan) yet who are schooled in another language (e.g., French in Canada or English in Japan) are considered to be receiving a form of bilingual education called *immersion*. This term originated with the seminal work of Lambert and Tucker (1972) focused on French immersion for English-speaking (majority language) students in Canada. Genesee (2004) outlines a number of different reasons students might be educated through immersion programmes such as to promote national policies of bilingualism (e.g., French immersion in Canada), to promote proficiency in important world languages (e.g., English immersion in Japan) among others. Different kinds of immersion programmes can be found around the world (see Johnson and Swain 1997). One of the ways in which immersion programmes can differ is with respect to the age at which the child begins immersion education. For example, *early immersion* is offered to children at the beginning of primary school (kindergarten or grade 1), *delayed* or *middle immersion* starts at the beginning of grade 4 or 5, and *late immersion* starts at the beginning of grade 7, the beginning of secondary school. These differences allow us to examine the relative effectiveness of starting early or late, in immersion, on L2 proficiency.

There have been a number of studies which have carefully examined the effectiveness of immersion programmes with different starting grades. Unlike the research in the EFL context described above, the results are not so systematic and consistent across the different studies. Two general patterns seem to emerge which will be discussed below.

A first general finding in studies comparing early vs. late immersion programmes is that older learners can achieve comparable levels of L2 proficiency as students who start immersion in earlier grades. For example, Genesee (1981) and Adiv (1980; see Genesee 1987) investigated the relative effects of starting immersion at different grades in French immersion programmes in Montréal, Canada. Students who were in early immersion programmes (beginning in kindergarten) were compared against students in two-year late immersion programmes where students engage in immersion in grades 7 and 8 only. Children in these two-year programmes would have already received instruction in French as an L2 as a part of the normal academic curriculum in Canada, so these children would start immersion in grade 7 and 8 already having had 6/7 years of French as a subject in school. Children in Genesee's (1981) and Adiv's (1980) studies were tested on listening comprehension, oral production, reading comprehension, dictation and writing. In both studies, there were no significant differences across the two types of immersion programme on these measures. The children in the two-year immersion programme would have had significantly less exposure to French than the children in the early immersion programmes (1,400 hours for the late immersion students compared to 5,000 hours for the early immersion students). However, even when the amount of exposure to French was equated (Genesee 1987) the older learners were either similar to, or in some cases outperformed the early immersion students. Genesee (1981, 1987) suggests that the fact that these older students are not different from the early immersion students implies faster learning on the part of the older students. These findings are compatible with the findings described above in the EFL context of faster rates of learning for older learners. Genesee (1987) suggests that the advantage for these older learners may also stem from the fact that learning an L2 in school often requires the more cognitively demanding and context-reduced forms of communication Cummins (1980) has referred to (discussed above) and which are more manageable in older learners due to their relative cognitive maturity.

The second pattern of findings from studies comparing immersion programmes with different starting grades suggests that early starters in immersion programmes do have an advantage over later starters. Genesee (1981) compared early immersion, and late immersion students (after one year of immersion in grade 7) on tests of listening, speaking, reading and writing and found that the early immersion students' performance was significantly higher than the late immersion students. This finding is particularly interesting because after two years of late immersion (after grades 7 and 8), research (see above) has shown that there are no longer differences between the two groups of students. Genesee (2004) argues that the relative advantage of starting late (or early) is therefore, linked with the amount of exposure. After only one year of exposure to immersion instruction the late starters do not show an advantage over the early immersion students, however after two years, the late immersion students are comparable to the early immersion students.

In other studies and reviews the picture seems to generally favour early immersion students. For example, in Wesche, Toews-Janzen and MacFarlane (1996) which presents a comprehensive review of evaluations of early, middle and late immersion programmes, the authors conclude that 'Early French immersion students consistently out-perform middle French immersion and late French immersion students overall . . .' (Wesche et al. 1996: ii). Wesche et al. go on to note however, that the differences between these different groups of immersion students tend to diminish towards the end of secondary school suggesting that even with less overall input, the older immersion students are capable of catching up with the younger ones.

Genesee (2004) argues that success of early immersion programmes over later ones can be due to a range of factors such as students' natural language learning aptitude, positive attitudes towards learning and increased exposure. It is worth noting that Cenoz (2003) found younger learners in EFL had more positive attitudes and higher motivation and thus this fits in with Genesee's

(2004) discussion. Furthermore, Larson-Hall (2008) argued that with significant amounts of input early starters can benefit over later ones in an EFL setting, which also is compatible with Genesee's comment that extended exposure results in an advantage for early learners.

Genesee (2004) also identifies factors invoked to account for those studies which report an advantage of late immersion learners over early ones. These include having a well-developed L1, in particular, well-developed L1 literacy skills which can facilitate L2 development (Cummins 2000; Genesee et al. 2006). Genesee also notes that self-selection can be a factor in contributing to late immersion success. Immersion programmes (those studied in the research reviewed above) are voluntary and thus those students/families who opt for the immersion option tend to have high degrees of self-motivation. Academically advantaged children may also self-select for immersion programmes which could lead to immersion classes made up of students who are both academically strong and highly motivated, which in turn could account for their relative success.

Other factors relating to the quality of the provision are raised in Stevens (1983). In her study, late immersion students who differed in terms of the amount of exposure they had to the L2 (French) were compared on a range of L2 measures. Somewhat surprisingly, the students who received 80% of their school day in French did not consistently score higher on these measures than other late immersion students who only spent 40% of their school day in French. Stevens suggested that this somewhat surprising result was due to the pedagogical approach of the programme for the 40% input students which allowed for a higher degree of choice and individual interaction with the language tasks relative to the students in the 80% French day. This finding is somewhat reminiscent of the results from the developmental bilingual programmes in language minority context whereby it isn't just the overall amount of exposure to the L2 that counts, but other variables matter as well (e.g., pedagogical approach in Stevens (1983) work and support for the L1 in the developmental bilingual programmes).

Summary of Immersion Context

The results, then, are somewhat mixed concerning the relative effectiveness of starting immersion at a younger than an older age. Genesee (2004) argues that what the research *does* show unequivocally is that *both* primary and secondary level students can benefit from immersion education 'provided effective and appropriate pedagogy is implemented' (p. 13). He goes on to suggest that other factors (apart from the age of the student) should be considered in tackling the question of which is the best age to begin immersion education. So for example,

175

in communities such as Québec (Canada) and Belgium, where two languages are spoken with a relatively high degree of frequency in everyday life, early immersion might be best so that the child can get used to using both languages and take advantage of language learning opportunities outside of school.

Discussion and Conclusions

The focus of this chapter has been to examine the over-arching research findings from different L2 learning contexts for primary children in educational settings. The context of this review stems from the often invoked idea that 'younger is better' in L2 learning. Indeed, many educational directives crying out for the need to start L2 learning early in school seem to stem from the research investigating the CPH in more naturalistic contexts arguing for advantages for early over late L2 learning. However, Genesee (2004) notes that this work on age in naturalistic language learning contexts is largely uninformative in considering L2 learning at primary school since there are so many other factors relating to pedagogy, materials and student-led variables (e.g., attitudes, motivation etc.) that can influence the effectiveness of L2 learning in school-based contexts. Nonetheless, given that there has been such an increase in L2 learning programmes at primary level, the focus of this chapter was on the effects of different L2 educational contexts on children (of different ages) in L2 learning which is a related yet somewhat differentially focused question than asking what is the best age to begin learning an L2.

The research described above demonstrates clearly that young children are eminently capable of learning an L2 in different types of educational contexts. Importantly, however, the research across the three educational contexts described above (bilingual education for language minority students, foreign language instruction, immersion programmes) all reveal that a complex constellation of variables interact together to result in successful L2 learning in these programmes.

In the work on bilingual education for language minority children we see from the work of Cummins (1980, 1981, 2000) that the type of communication task itself is an important dimension since it can take these L2 children a number of years (e.g., up to 7) to gain sufficient mastery of the L2 to be able to adequately tackle the more context-reduced and cognitively demanding communication tasks found in school-based settings. Additionally, the degree of L1 support seems to be a critical variable in determining the ultimate success of L2 learners in these programmes. The research discussed above demonstrates an initial but rather short-lived advantage for children in English-only L2 programmes, while the children in developmental bilingual programmes who have a considerable and consistent amount of L1 literacy support seem to go on to ultimately have the most advanced L2 (and academic) ability. Additionally, other variables not discussed in this chapter, but considered in other more comprehensive reviews (e.g., August and Shanahan 2008; Genesee et al. 2006) indicate that variables such as socio-economic status, home language use and mother's level of education can have powerful influences over the ultimate success of language and academic learning in these children.

In the foreign language context we saw that a large body of research consistently demonstrates that older learners seem to have an advantage over younger ones when the L2 is taught as a subject in school settings. The research described above mostly stemmed from large-scale projects in Spain where bilingual children (Basque/Spanish or Catalan/Spanish) children are taught English as an L2. Across a range of different linguistic tasks children who start learning the L2 at an older age seem to have an advantage over those who start earlier on. While this pattern is consistent, there are a few exceptions such as Cenoz (2003) who found advantages for younger learners on attitude and motivation measures and Larson-Hall (2008) who argued that early learners can be at an advantage over later learners given sufficient input. Indeed, the question of the input seems to be a critical variable here as evidenced by Larson-Hall's discussion that her results most likely differ from previous studies due to the significantly larger amounts of input her participants had received relative to other studies. A number of researchers have argued that this advantage for older learners in EFL settings is likely to stem from the fact that as they are more cognitively mature, they have a wider range and more well-developed cognitive mechanisms at their disposal to enable them to make the most of their L2 learning. This notion is consistent with evidence stemming from research on the nature of communication tasks within the language minority context.

In the immersion context, where language majority students are taught academic content through an L2, we saw a more mixed picture. On the one hand, there is some evidence to support the idea that, like the foreign language context, older learners can benefit from immersion programmes as much as, if not more than, younger learners. However, other reviews have argued that overall, the consistent pattern is that early starters in immersion end up with higher levels of L2 proficiency on a range of different measures than later starters (Wesche et al. 1996). As in the foreign language context, the nature and quantity of the input seems to be a critical factor in the relative success of immersion programmes.

So is younger better in L2 learning within school? Well the answer must be 'it depends'. It clearly depends on the kind of exposure to the L2, both in terms of amount and in terms of the kinds of interactions the child can have with the L2, in and outside of the classroom. Indeed, it must also depend on a range of other pedagogical and student-led variables which make this issue highly complex. Clearly the answer to this important question is not best served by a 'one solution fits all' approach to child L2 instruction and certainly any approach to L2 instruction for children which has not carefully considered these variables and their relative contribution to ultimate L2 success is careless and likely to be ineffective. The more we begin to ask these important questions *in context*, the more confident we will be in our ability to make informed decisions regarding the most effective forms of L2 instruction for children around the world.

Notes

1. One should note, however, that the USA is just one context and different linguistic contexts might present different patterns of results. More research on language minority children being schooled in an L2 needs to be carried out in other countries and systematically compared.
2. It should be noted that there are area numbers of other variables that contribute to successful L2 learning in these contexts, such as socio-economic status and use of the L1 and L2 in the home. It is beyond the scope of this chapter to discuss these issues in detail but see Genesee et al. (2006), and August and Shanahan (2008) for comprehensive reviews.
3. As noted in Genesee (2004) and Genesee et al. (2004) the success of bilingual programmes depends on day-to-day issues such as quality of instruction (including materials) programme delivery, competence of instructors etc. Genesee (2004) also points out that often the results of successful programs are the ones that get published, therefore there is likely to be a degree of bias in the literature.

6 The Relationship between L2 Vocabulary Knowledge and L2 Vocabulary Use

Paul Meara

Chapter Overview	

At first glance, the relationship between vocabulary knowledge and vocabulary use looks as though it should be a very straightforward one. However, as with many things involving vocabulary, what ought to be simple turns out to be much more complex than we might have expected.

The Vocabulary Knowledge Framework

The main problem we face when we try to address this issue involves what we mean by 'vocabulary knowledge'. A number of scholars have attempted to catalogue the essential aspects of what knowing a word means. Richards (1976), for example, provided a set of eight features which are listed in Table 1, and argued that fully knowing a word involved learners knowing the value of all these features for any single word. For a long time, this list of features was the standard way of characterizing vocabulary knowledge in L2 speakers, and it informed much of the research on vocabulary knowledge which took place in the 1980s and 1990s (e.g., Kang and Golden 1994; Wikberg 1979). An important development of this idea is Nation's (2001) characterization of knowing a word as encompassing sixteen different aspects of word knowledge.

Table 1 Richards' eight assumptions about vocabulary knowledge (1976)

1. The native speaker continues to expand his vocabulary in adulthood, whereas there is little development of syntax in adult life.
2. Knowing a word means knowing the degree of probability of encountering that word in speech or print. For many words, we also know the sort of words most likely to be found associated with the word.
3. Knowing a word implies knowing the limitations imposed on the use of the word according to variations of function and situation.
4. Knowing a word means knowing the syntactic behaviour associated with that word.
5. Knowing a word entails knowledge of the underlying form of the word and the derivatives that can be from it.
6. Knowing a word entails knowledge of the network of associations between that word and the other words in language (sic.)
7. Knowing a word means knowing the semantic value of the word.
8. Knowing a word means knowing many of the different meanings associated with the word (p. 83).

Actually, Richards' characterization of vocabulary knowledge, and the later work that built on it, is not as helpful as it appears at first sight. There are a number of reasons for this. First, Richards' work was taken out of context by some writers, and treated as a comprehensive account of vocabulary knowledge, whereas in fact, this does not seem to have been the main intention behind Richards' paper. In the 1970s, Applied Linguistics was very much about the application of *linguistics* to language teaching, and Richards' paper needs to be seen in this historical light. All the features of vocabulary knowledge that he lists in this paper had been the focus of some fairly intense linguistic research in the previous decade, and Richards' intent here seems to have been an attempt to explore the relevance of this work for second language acquisition in general, and for vocabulary teaching in particular. That is, Richards' framework is a pedagogic framework, rather than a psycholinguistic one. This focus explains why Richards' account of vocabulary knowledge contains just these eight features, while it conspicuously omits other features which might have been thought relevant to a theory of vocabulary knowledge, why the eight features are listed in what most people would consider an odd order, and why Richards refers to his features as 'assumptions' about vocabulary knowledge. The answers to these questions are all to be found in the research which had been published in the previous decade, and the list of features will be familiar to anybody who has a copy of one of many anthologies of linguistic research which were published around the time Richards was writing. Lyons (1971), for instance, contains papers that touch on all eight of the assumptions in Richards' list.

The second problem with Richards' approach is that although it looks like a comprehensive account of vocabulary knowledge, each of the eight assumptions actually masks a lot more complexity than is apparent on the surface. We can illustrate this by looking in more detail at Richards' assumption 6:

knowing a word entails knowledge of the network of associations between that word and other words in the language.

There are a number of hidden assumptions in this statement:

a. each word in a language enters into a network of associations with other words in the language;
b. the resulting network is broadly similar for all speakers of a language;
c. it is possible for us to specify what this network is;
d. a speaker of the language 'knows' the network (the use of *know* is problematical here);
e. the network is fixed and stable;
f. the network of associations is a primary feature of a lexicon – rather than a secondary phenomenon which derives from some other, deeper structural property;
g. bilingual lexicons are not significantly different from the lexicons of monolingual speakers.

And so on. It is clear from the short account, that assumption six is not nearly as straightforward as it looks at first glance. Specifying exactly what we mean when we assert that 'learner L knows the network of associations that word X has with other words in the language' is by no means a simple task, and many of the key assumptions that underlie it are nowhere near fully specified.

The third problem with Richards' approach to vocabulary knowledge is that it is essentially a word-centred approach. At first sight, a word-centred model of lexical knowledge might not seem to be a bad thing. Obviously, one might argue, learners acquire a great deal of knowledge about individual words, and this knowledge needs to be codified and catalogued if we are to give a proper account of what it is the learners learn when they develop L2 lexical competence. Unfortunately, this approach runs into the problem that one of the defining characteristics of vocabularies is that they are typically very large, and even a modest vocabulary will contain several thousand words. This makes Richards' approach to describing vocabulary knowledge impractical simply on logistical grounds.

Let us imagine that we *could* identify a set of eight features which characterized learners' knowledge of vocabulary items. In order to describe the status of a learner's vocabulary, we would need to describe the current status of each of the words that make it up. It seems very unlikely that we could design simple tests that would work with any word, and that implies that we would need to design specific tests for each word in the vocabulary. Designing tests of this sort would be a massive job. Implementing and administering a set of tests of this sort would be a logistical nightmare. Unfortunately, the unavoidable logic of using Richards' framework as a description of vocabulary knowledge is that it forces us to look more and more closely at knowledge of individual words, and in the end the level of detail which we are forced to handle becomes overwhelming.

Consider, for instance, a simple question like 'Does X know FISH?' The Vocabulary Knowledge Framework turns this into a much more complex set of questions:

Does X know the probability of encountering FISH in print?
Does X know the probability of encountering FISH in speech?
Does X know the limitations on the use of FISH?
Does X know the syntactic behaviour associated with FISH?
Does X know the derivations of FISH?
Does X know the network of associations linked to FISH?
Does X know the semantic value of FISH?
Does X know the different meanings of FISH?
And so on.

I suppose that in an extreme case it might be possible to devise a set of tests which could, in principle, provide appropriate answers to these questions. Note, though, that if we are dealing with a word which has many different meanings, then the number of basic questions gets very large very quickly. FISH, for example, has at least four different meanings: the living animal, the flesh of the animal, the verb *to fish*, a children's card game and so on. There is also a range of metaphorical extensions of these basic meanings, *fishing for compliments*, for instance or *fishing for personal information* on the internet. Add to this the derivatives of FISH such as *fishing, fishery, fisherman* and so on, and the task of describing what it means 'to know FISH' rapidly assumes humungous proportions. Testing all of these various aspects of 'knowing FISH' would require us to develop and administer a battery of 40 or 50 tests, just to describe knowledge of a single vocabulary item. This is clearly out of the question for most practical purposes, and definitely out of the question for more than a handful of words. Furthermore, even if we could devise a battery of tests of this sort, we would inevitably find that many L1 speakers and an even larger number of L2 speakers failed on some parts of the test battery. Partial knowledge of words seems to be the norm in L1 as well as in L2, but it is not obvious how that partial knowledge can be succinctly analysed and described.

These problems clearly make things very difficult for the framework approach. If we extend the framework approach to a vocabulary of any size, say 10,000 words, then the sheer size of the measurement task makes the approach unworkable in real-life situations. If we work with smaller target vocabularies, then it is difficult to produce generalizations about vocabulary knowledge as a larger concept. In the end, the framework approach ends up by disappearing up its own assumptions, as it were: it is difficult to see how it can avoid making more and more detailed statements about fewer and fewer words.

Some Alternatives to the Word Knowledge Framework

How can we avoid this impasse? The solution to this problem appears to be for vocabulary researchers to develop measures which apply to whole vocabularies, rather than to individual words. Ironically, measures of this sort, in the guise of vocabulary size tests, began to appear shortly after the publication of Richards' Framework paper (e.g., Nation's Vocabulary Levels Test (Nation 1990) and Meara's Yes/No tests (Meara 1994; Meara and Buxton 1987)). At the time, these tests were seen as a way of assessing basic recognition vocabulary skills. That is, they addressed Richards' assumption 7 and assumption 8, while ignoring other features that were included in the vocabulary knowledge framework. Gradually, however, this work changed its focus and developed into an attempt to measure vocabulary size, rather than knowledge of individual words. Initially, this shift may not appear to be a significant one, but measuring vocabulary size – how big a person's vocabulary is – turns out to be a much more interesting and tractable way of looking at vocabulary. Although we measure vocabulary size by testing learners' knowledge of individual words, vocabulary size is not actually a property of these individual words. Rather it is a property of the vocabulary as a whole. This is an important distinction which is often overlooked in the literature. More importantly, perhaps, because vocabulary size is a global property, rather than a word-specific one, we can estimate the overall size of learners' vocabularies without testing every single word that their vocabularies contain – a small sample of well-chosen words should be sufficient to allow us to estimate how big a person's vocabulary is. It turns out that this single global property of vocabularies is a very useful one for researchers, since it correlates with other aspects of linguistic performance. Vocabulary size is a good indicator of overall linguistic performance (e.g., Meara and Jones 1988).

There are two standard measures of vocabulary size which have been adopted by the research community. The 'industry standard' test is Paul Nation's Vocabulary Levels Test (Nation 1990). This test was originally developed in the 1980s as part of a wider programme of research into reading in a second

**Table 2 The Vocabulary Levels Test:
a sample item from the 2K level**

1: original		
2: private	_____	complete
3: royal	_____	first
4: slow	_____	not public
5: sorry		
6: total		

language, but it seems to have much wider implications than this narrow focus implies. The test has a slightly unusual format, which is illustrated in Table 2:
In this test, each test item consists of a set of six words combined with three definitions. The test-takers' task is to show that they understand the meanings of the target words by matching up the definitions to three of the target words in each item. This format is relatively easy for learners to handle, and the test does not require any special equipment, so it is easy to administer. Nation's original tests consisted of six items of this sort grouped into five Levels based on the frequency of the items being tested – a 2K level, a 3K level, a 5K level and a 10K level, and an additional level comprising words from the *University Word List*, a list of words with a high frequency of occurrence in academic texts. Subsequent revisions (e.g., Beglar and Hunt 1999; Schmitt et al., 2001) have preserved the original format, but improved the actual items to make them more reliable. The result is a very solid test, backed up by a great deal of detailed background research (e.g., Cobb 2000; Shiotsu 2001). The Levels Test is often treated as a direct indicator of vocabulary size – basically, if a test-taker scores X percent on the Levels Test, this is often taken as an indicator that they know X per cent of the words at that particular frequency level. There are some problems with this approach, especially when the revised versions of the test are used in this way, but in practice the Levels Test has proved itself to be a remarkably robust and reliable instrument.

Meara's Yes/No tests take a rather different approach to measuring vocabulary size. In the Yes/No tests, test-takers are presented with a list of items consisting of single words. Some of these words are genuine words, while other items are non-existent pseudo-words which look like words in the target language, but actually are not. Test-takers are asked to indicate whether they know the meaning of each item or not. See Table 3, which illustrates the general approach. In this table, the first set of real words come from a high-frequency word list: it is a straightforward matter for fluent speakers to distinguish between the real words and the non-words. In the second set of items, the real words are low-frequency items, and in this case it is difficult even for fluent native speakers to identify the real words reliably. Meara's tests are considerably longer than the

Table 3 Sample items in a Yes/No test

set 1	adviser	ghastly	contord	implore
	morlorn	patiful	profess	stourge
	moisten	discard	disdain	gleanse
	weekend	boyralty	partine	indoors
	storage	vibrade	dostage	refusal
	sarsage	bariner	mertion	smother
set 2	mascule	palangane	bezel	maparotomy
	peneplain	rangue	aliver	orduad
	leat	prunella	gamelkind	masquinade
	ablegate	mittimus	rickwall	quoddity
	algorism	myosote	killick	windlestraw

Levels Tests, but because Yes/No format is easier for test-takers, these tests can still be completed very quickly, and this makes it easy for the Yes/No tests to sample very large numbers of vocabulary items. One computerized version of the test format tests 120 words in about 10 minutes, and scores itself automatically (Meara and Milton 2003).

In theory, this should make the Yes/No format more reliable than the Level Test format, but in practice this advantage has been outweighed by some difficulties with the treatment of non-word responses (cf. Beeckmans et al., 2001; Huibregtse et al., 2002; Mochida and Harrington 2006), and some complicated interactions between scores on the test and the L1 of the test-takers.

Deep Word Knowledge

A number of people, notably Read (e.g., Read 1997), criticized both of the basic vocabulary size tests on the grounds that they were only assessing passive recognition knowledge of vocabulary and it soon became common to make a distinction between vocabulary breadth (how many words you know) and vocabulary depth (how well you know them). Several researchers attempted to develop measures of depth, the most widely used approach being the Vocabulary Knowledge Scale developed by Wesche and Paribakht (Paribakht and Wesche 1993; Wesche and Paribakht 1996). This scale has been widely adopted and adapted by other researchers, (e.g., Rott 2005 and Folse 2006). The test format requires testees to rate how well they know a word by using a scale like the one in Table 4. Marks are awarded for each level of self-assessment.

The test seems to be good at picking up small increments in knowledge of individual words which come about as the result of reading exposure, but it has a number of unavoidable disadvantages. The main disadvantages are that it needs to be administered individually and there is no obvious way of

Table 4 Wesche and Paribakht's Vocabulary Knowledge Scale

1: I do not know this word
2: I recognize this word, but I do not know what it means
3: This word means _____.
4: I can use this word in a sentence, e.g. _____.

A fifth point is usually included on this scale:
5: The word is used with appropriacy and correct grammar in the sentence.

Table 5 An example item from Read's Word Associates test

edit			
arithmetic	film	pole	publishing
revise	risk	surface	text

automating some of the assessments and checking that testees' self-assessments are accurate, and this inevitably limits the number of words that can be assessed. There are also some problems with interpreting the testees' scores when the marks from a number of items are aggregated into a single figure.

Read's own suggestion for assessing depth of vocabulary knowledge is the Word Associates format (e.g., Read 1993, 1995, 1998). This test format has gone through a number of variants, but in its simplest format each item consists of a single test word and a set of eight other words, four of which have an associational link with the test word. Table 5 provides an example:

In this example, *film, text, publishing* and *revise* all have associational links with *edit*. The first two are examples of syntagmatic associates, *revise* is an example of a paradigmatic association and *publishing* is an example of an associate that shares some of the meaning of edit but is not a precise synonym. Read suggests that this format is an economical way of assessing learners' knowledge of high-frequency content words.

It seems to me, however, that both these attempts to measure vocabulary depth mark a return to the word-based approach that is implicit in Richards' Vocabulary Framework. They focus once again on the individual words that a vocabulary is comprised of, and test learners' knowledge of these words in some detail. In this respect, they illustrate the problems that we have already identified with Richards' Vocabulary Knowledge framework: they probe learners' knowledge of individual words in some detail, but it is difficult to see how we can generalize from this level of detail. The tests described seem to allow us to make interesting statements about learners' knowledge of individual words, but they don't allow us to step back from the individual words, and look at the vocabulary as a whole.

Two approaches buck this general trend of focusing on individual words in more and more detail and have tried instead to work with vocabulary depth as a characteristic of an entire vocabulary, rather than as a feature of individual words. My own work (e.g., Meara 2008) has focused on the idea that it might be possible to develop a measure of lexical organization based on the number of associational connections between words in an L2 lexicon. It has become a widely accepted convention to talk about vocabularies as if they are networks of connections between words (e.g., Aitchison 2003) and to represent vocabularies as formal graphs – collections of nodes and links which connect these nodes together. An example of this sort of thinking is shown in Figure 1, which illustrates a cluster of fifteen words that most native speakers of English would consider to be loosely associated with each other. It is easy to imagine that a non-native speaker of English might not have all these connections as part of their lexical repertoire. For instance, the link between 'banana' and 'split' or the link between 'yellow' and 'submarine', both of which are complex cultural references might be absent. If this were the case, then this cluster of words would not link up to the rest of the vocabulary through the words 'split' and 'submarine'.

Extending this idea to a much larger set of words looks as though it ought to be reasonably straightforward. It also looks as though we ought to be able to develop a simple measure that could quantify the differences between L2 learners and native speakers in respect of the organization of their lexicons. This would allow us to talk about vocabulary depth in a way which does not require us to ask lots of detailed questions about individual words, and this would resolve some of the logistical problems which I highlighted earlier in

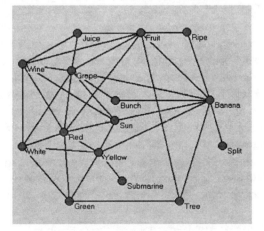

Figure 1 A small association network: 15 words

this section. More importantly, a tool of this sort might allow us to develop models about the rate at which vocabulary organization changes, and whether vocabulary organization is independent of vocabulary size. My current view is that vocabulary organization is not entirely independent of vocabulary size, but the relationship between them changes as vocabulary size increases. In the early stages of learning an L2, vocabulary size seems to be a critical factor which affects the way speakers perform in their L2. Once a basic vocabulary has been acquired, however, size becomes less important in the sense that further increases in vocabulary size do not appear to make much difference to a learner's performance. At this level, what does seem to be important is the way learners can exploit lexical structure to improve their performance.

It has turned out to be surprisingly difficult to develop a reliable testing tool which would enable us to evaluate these ideas. There are two reasons for this. The first reason is that although the idea of connections between words looks straightforward, it is in fact difficult to pin down in practice. A lot of the work we have done in this area has tended to operationalize a 'connection' as a word association link between two words. Thus, *sleep* has a close connection with *wake* and *dream*, while *eat* has a close connection with *food* and *chocolate*. But what about *line* and *worm* or *scale* and *tone*, or *potato* and *profit*? Most people would probably say that these pairs were not strongly linked, but anyone who goes fishing would immediately recognize a connection between *line* and *worm*, while any musician would recognize that *scale* and *tone* go together, and some farmers make large *profits* on *potatoes*. This means that individual test items often work in unpredictable ways with different populations, or even within the same population. The second reason why it has proved difficult to develop a good testing methodology is that even a small vocabulary contains an enormous number of potential links. In a 1,000-word vocabulary, each word can potentially link to 999 other words. This means that we are looking at 1000*999 = 999,000 potential links, and clearly if we are dealing with larger vocabularies, then this problem gets exponentially worse. It is certainly not the case that all these possible links will actually exist, but even if we assume conservatively that each word only connects with 20 other words, we are still looking at 20,000 possible connections in a relatively small vocabulary. Obviously, we cannot possibly test all of these links, and some sort of sampling method is needed. We have tried to get round these problems by developing test formats which ignore the actual associations people make, and focus instead on the number of associations that they find in sets of randomly selected words. We can then extrapolate from these data to an estimate of the total number of association links among the words in the target vocabulary (Meara 2008; Meara and Wolter 2004).

The second approach which uses a dimensional approach to vocabulary depth has been developed by Henriksen. She suggested (e.g., Henriksen 1999) that lexical competence could be specified using three dimensions: a partial~precise dimension, a depth of knowledge dimension and a receptive~productive dimension, but she argues that most research on vocabulary knowledge has actually focused on the first of these dimensions, and has not paid much attention to the development of lexical networks. In a series of sorting tasks carried out repeatedly in longitudinal studies with individual subjects (e.g., Haastrup and Henriksen 1998), Henriksen has attempted to show how small lexical networks develop over time. The data from these sorting tasks suggests that networks in an L2 develop rather slowly, and do not show much change over time, but it is possible that this finding is a result of the small networks that Henriksen investigates – her largest network (Haastrup and Henriksen 2000) contains only 31 words, and most of the work reported uses networks which are smaller than this. Scaling up from these small networks to much larger ones is not straightforward.

Vocabulary Use

It will be obvious from this brief overview that characterizing learners' vocabulary *knowledge* in an L2 is complicated. It will come as no surprise, then, that similar problems emerge when we come to characterize learners' vocabulary *use*. Again, the main problem here is that even vocabularies that we would think of as 'small' can often contain many thousands of words. This makes it difficult in practice to test whether learners know how to use each word they can recognize. A systematic test of this sort would just be too long to be practicable. Despite these problems, some people have tried to develop tests of productive vocabulary which attempt to assess potential productive vocabulary from a small number of items actually used in a production task. The best-known of these methods is Laufer and Nation's Productive Levels Test (Laufer and Nation 1999). This test piggybacks on Nation's Levels Tests in the sense that it uses the same target words as the Levels Test, but it is very different in format. Basically, the Productive Levels Test is a gap-filling format, in which test-takers get a series of sentences with one word partially blanked out. For instance in the example below, the target word is *counsel*, and the letters COUN serve to ensure that this specific word is selected, rather than other words (**advice**, perhaps) which might fit the gap if it were not constrained in this way.

The lawyer gave some wise coun_____ to his client.

Laufer and Nation claim that this test format is reliable and valid, and that it distinguishes clearly between learners at different levels of proficiency. The fact

189

that two parallel forms of the test are available has led to it being widely used in studies of productive vocabulary knowledge.

Most attempts to measure vocabulary in use have taken a different approach, however. Because learners typically do not use all the vocabulary they know in a single output session, a lot of effort has gone into developing surrogate measures which are believed to vary with productive vocabulary size. The most important of these surrogates is a series of measures based on Type-Token ratios in the kind of texts that learners can be persuaded to produce. The assumption here is that a person with a large vocabulary will typically use more different words in a text than will a person with a smaller vocabulary, and this difference will manifest itself in fewer repetitions of words that have already been used. This idea is formalized in the Type-Token ratio for the text – i.e. the number of different word types in the text divided by the total number of word tokens it contains. Type-Token ratios can vary between 1 (all the words in the text are different) to a value that approximates zero (many words occur more than once). High TTRs are taken as a sign that the person who generated the text has a larger use vocabulary available to them.

There are a number of problems with this approach. One problem is that it assumes that people do not consciously manipulate the TTRs of the texts they generate, by deliberately recycling words for stylistic reasons. For instance, if I write:

'Ha'! said the wolf. 'That pig! I hate that pig. That pig will be my supper, tonight.'

the Type-Token ratio is low because of the deliberate repetition of 'that pig', and is not a direct reflection of the total vocabulary I have at my disposal. A second problem is that Type-Token ratios only look at whether the words in the text are repeated, and they do not take into account whether the words are common or more difficult items. For instance, all three sentences below have the same Type-Token ratio

the wolf ate the pig.
the wolf devoured the pig.
the wolf consumed his tormentor.

despite the fact that the second and third sentences use words which we would normally consider to be signalling that the writer has a very large use of vocabulary.

These problems have largely been ignored by the research. Instead, this research has focused on another problem, namely the fact that TTRs tend to get smaller as the texts they are based on get longer. This is basically an unavoidable

Table 6 The principle measures of vocabulary richness

Type Token Ratio	V/N
Herdan's Index	log V / log N
Guiraud's Index	V / √N
Carroll's Index	V / √(2N)
Dugast's Uber Index	log 2 N /log(N/V)

where V = the number of different word types in the text, and N = the number of word tokens in the text.

mathematical problem, which makes it difficult to interpret TTR values in the abstract. A number of authors have tried to solve this problem by using variants of the Type-Token ratio, instead of a raw TTR figure, and some of the main variants are listed in Table 6.

Until recently, there was a consensus that Guiraud's index is the best of these variants for L2 work, especially for spoken texts (see Broeder et al. (1988), Daller et al. (2003)). However, as a result of work by Malvern and Richards (e.g., Malvern and Richards 1997; Malvern et al., 2004) simple TTR measures have now largely been replaced by an index which they refer to as D. D is a complex statistic which is derived by repeatedly sampling a text at random, and computing TTRs for a set of samples of different lengths. A typical computation of this kind involves the calculation of 750 TTR figures for the text which are then summarized into a single value. Malvern and Richards claim that D is not affected by the length of the text being analysed.

There is some evidence that D-values do increase as vocabularies get bigger, and D has been widely adopted by the research community as the standard measure of lexical richness for L2 learners (e.g., Jarvis 2002; Marsden and David 2008; Miralpeix 2008; Richards and Malvern 2000). By default it has come to be taken as an index of productive vocabulary size in L2 learners. My own view, however, is that the link between the D-value of a particular text and the productive vocabulary size of the text's author is more complex than this equation allows for.

Given the complex computations that underlie D, it is not surprising that other ways of looking at vocabulary use have also been explored. The most widely used methodology here is the Lexical Frequency Profile (LFP), first developed by Nation, and further explored in some detail by Laufer. Like D, Lexical Frequency Profiles are also generated by a computer program, usually Heaton and Nation's RANGE program, but here the underlying approach is considerably more intuitive, and the indices produced by the program are easier to interpret. RANGE takes a text as input and compares the words the text contains to a series of base word lists. The base word lists are largely, but

Table 7 A Lexical Frequency Profile for the preceding paragraph

	Wd families	*Wd types*	*Wd tokens*	%
1K	58	66	116	69.88
2K	6	6	13	7.83
Acdmc wd list	14	17	22	13.25
Not in the lists	?	10	15	9.04

not entirely, built from frequency lists, and the reports that RANGE produces tell us what proportion of the text is made up of 1K words, 2K words and so on. Plotting these proportions out provides us with a profile of the vocabulary contained in the text. The profile for this paragraph is shown in Table 7.

Points to note here include the very large proportion of 1K words that the text contains, and the number of words that are not found among the most frequent words of English. Both figures are typical of a certain style of academic writing. We would expect learners with smaller vocabularies to produce profiles which look rather different, and specifically we would expect low-level learners with very small vocabularies to produce texts which consist mostly of high-frequency words. Laufer (1994), Laufer (2005) and Laufer and Nation (1995) make a number of interesting claims about these profiles. Specifically they suggest that the profiles of texts produced by L2 writers are fairly stable over moderate time intervals, and that two texts generated in quick succession by the same writer will tend to have similar profiles. They further suggest that the profiles are sensitive enough to pick up increases in vocabulary size resulting from exposure to input in the L2.

One problem with the LFP approach is that profiles do not behave like the scores we get from ordinary vocabulary tests, and this sometimes makes LFP data difficult to interpret. It is, for example, not obvious how a profile should be reported, or how it can be succinctly summarized. However, Collins and Edwards have suggested that typical LFP profiles are actually tightly constrained by some linguistic frequency patterns first identified by Zipf (1935), and this significantly reduces the range of different profiles we might expect to find if the profiles were not constrained in this way. In particular, Zipf's model implies that the proportion of 2K words we would expect to find in a profile is a function of the proportion of 1K words in the text being analysed. This work provides a solid theoretical justification for Laufer's observation that the critical feature of the vocabulary profiles is simply the number of low-frequency words a text contains – her *Beyond 2000* measure (Laufer 2005). This work opens up the possibility that it might be feasible to summarize a profile in a single score, and it is further possible that this score might be related to the size of writer's productive vocabulary. Some exploratory work along these lines can be found in Meara and Miralpeix (2008). Their work suggests that the paragraph earlier analysed using LFP (see Table 7) has an underlying vocabulary of around 19,400 words.

Conclusions

Clearly, finding convincing measures of vocabulary use is a lot more problematic than finding plausible measures which can account for the words we know. To put that another way, the relationship between passive, receptive vocabulary knowledge and active, productive vocabulary has proved to be a lot more difficult to tease out than we might have expected, some interesting preliminary work in this area notwithstanding (Laufer 1998, 2001; Webb 2008).

Not very long ago (e.g., Palmberg 1987) it was assumed that this relationship was basically straightforward. The words learners acquired were seen as positioned along a kind of cline – often called the Passive Active Continuum. Newly acquired words started off at the passive end of the continuum, and gradually moved towards the active end of the continuum as a result of practice and exposure. Getting to know a word better nudged it along the continuum, and made it more likely to be used. With hindsight, of course, this view now looks to be amazingly naïve, and a lot more serious research on the relationship between vocabulary knowledge and vocabulary use will need to be undertaken before this deceptively simple relationship is properly understood.

7 The Relationship between L2 Input and L2 Output

Susan Gass

Linking L2 Input and L2 Output

This chapter deals with the relationship between input and output. More often than not, these concepts have been dealt with as separate constructs, primarily because the relationship is not often seen as a direct one. In this chapter, I will first describe what is meant by input, with brief illustrations of characteristics of input to learners. I will then focus on output and the role that output is hypothesized to play in second language acquisition (SLA). This will be followed by a discussion of the link between the two, both from an historical perspective and a perspective that takes current thinking into account.

Input

Input is without a doubt the *sine qua non* of acquisition. No acquisition (child or second) can take place without some regular and consistent input to *feed* the growing language system. This is not disputable; what is disputable is the function that input serves and this depends in large part on the theoretical perspective that individual researchers take. As Carroll (2001: 2) notes, 'there is no agreement on what kind or how much exposure a learner needs. Indeed, we know very little still about the kinds of linguistic exposure learners actually get.'

Definition and Description

Input, in its simplest definition, is the language that a learner is exposed to. In the definition pursued in this chapter, input refers to the ambient linguistic information, that is, the linguistic information that is available for grammar construction. This can come in written form (reading) or from the spoken language, or, in the case of sign language, from the visual mode. Hatch (1983: 81), in talking about input and intake, sees the latter as a subset of the former. '. . . we might say that input is what the learner hears and attempts to process. That part that learners process only partially is still input, though traces of it may remain and help in building the internal representation of the language. The part the learner actually successfully and completely processed is a subset called intake.'

The distinction between input and intake originated in SLA with Corder (1967). As noted above, input is the language that is available, whereas intake refers to what is actually internalized (or in Corder's terms, 'taken in') by the learner. When learning a second or foreign language, one is often confronted with a rapid stream of speech which, at times, is not comprehensible and often not even segmentable into meaningful units. This is input even though the learner may not be able to do anything with it at the time of hearing. It can only be deemed intake once there is some processing and the language from the input becomes integrated into a learner's developing system.

An important part of understanding what happens to input is an understanding of the nature of that input. One thing that is clear is that language addressed to non-proficient speakers is often different from language addressed to native speakers of a language. This modified speech, known as *foreigner talk*[1] was initially documented by Ferguson (1971). His study was aimed more generally at issues of linguistic simplicity, including not only foreigner talk but, in general, language directed towards linguistically deficient individuals (young children, non-native speakers of a language) with the ultimate aim of showing the similarities among these speech varieties. Through his research, he documented that native speakers (or fluent individuals) make numerous adjustments to their speech, most notably, in the areas of pronunciation, grammar and lexicon.

Generally speaking, foreigner talk adjustments reveal speech patterns that would not ordinarily be used in conversations with native speakers. Some of the most salient features of foreigner talk include: slow speech rate, loud speech, long pauses, exaggerated (stretched out) speech, simple vocabulary (e.g., few idioms, high frequency words), repetitions and elaborations, and paucity of slang. Native speakers who have considerable experience speaking with learners are often able to fine-tune their speech to the level of their interlocutor (see Gass and Selinker 2008 for examples).

Adjustments to one's speech often occur during the course of a conversation, particularly when a native speaker recognizes that there is a communication problem. Example 1 illustrates this. This example comes from a survey on food and nutrition that non-native speakers (NNS) conducted over the telephone with native speakers (NS).

Example 1: From Gass and Varonis 1985: 48.
NNS: How have increasing food costs changed your eating habits?
NS: Well, we don't eat as much beef as we used to. We eat more chicken, and uh, pork, and uh, fish, things like that.
NNS: Pardon me?
NS: We don't eat as much beef as we used to. We eat more chicken and uh, uh pork and fish. . . .We don't eat beef very often. We don't have steak like we used to.

In the initial response (*Well, we don't eat as much beef as we used to. We eat more chicken, and uh, pork, and uh, fish, things like that.*), there was little indication of modified speech. One reason for the lack of immediate modification is that the initial statement was scripted and was read quite fluently (albeit with an accent). Uttering *Pardon me?* undoubtedly made the NS responder aware of the fact that this was not a smooth conversation, and she made adjustments which were not of the variety normally described as part of foreigner talk, but which involved restating, repeating and amplifying the original response. One can imagine that the NS believed that this type of elaboration would make it easier for the NNS to understand.

In sum, these data suggest that when addressing NNSs or non-proficient speakers of a language, modifications occur. These modifications are not static, but rather change as perceptions of the need to modify change during the course of a conversational interaction. Thus, while there are standard features that one can describe, there are others that result from the on-going assessment of one's interlocutor's language ability. Second language learners are exposed to both modified and unmodified speech; the range of possible input makes it difficult to establish a direct link with output.

Function of Input

Historical

Early views of second language learning were based on a behaviourist perspective within which speaking was viewed as consisting of mimicking and then analogizing. We say or hear something and analogize from it. Basic to this view is the concept of habits. We establish a set of habits as children and continue our linguistic growth by analogizing from what we already know or by mimicking the speech of others. It is the input that is crucial for mimicking and analogizing and eventually creating habits. In Bloomfield's words (1933, pp. 29–30):

> Under various stimuli the child utters and repeats vocal sounds. This seems to be an inherited trait. Suppose he makes a noise which we may represent as *da*, although, of course, the actual movements and the resultant sounds differ from any that are used in conventional English speech. The sound vibrations strike the child's ear-drums while he keeps repeating the movements. This results in a habit: whenever a similar sound strikes his ear, he is likely to make these same mouth-movements, repeating the sound *da*. This babbling trains him to reproduce vocal sounds which strike his ear.

Thus, it is the input that is essential for acquisition, at least for children where learning involves mimicking that input. These behaviourist views were challenged in the child language literature of the 1950s and 1960s and in the early phases of SLA research in the 1960s and 1970s. Researchers moved away from an input-output model such as that exhibited in the behaviourist stimulus-response framework, recognizing that between the input and the output, there was a significant amount of cognitive activity. Along with a paradigm shift away from behaviourism, in which, as noted, the major driving force of language learning was the language to which learners were exposed (the input), research interest in the nature and function of input also waned. Because of the focus in the 1960s and 1970s on innateness and the nature of the innate system that a learner brings to the second language learning situation and given that language learning is constrained by that innate system and input is only needed to trigger that system, the significance of the input was minimized, or in the case of the Input Hypothesis to which we turn next, it was redirected and refined.

Input Hypothesis

What did remain, however, from this early emphasis on input is The Input Hypothesis, developed by Krashen (cf. Krashen 1985), as part of his overall Monitor Model which he argued was a way of understanding of how second languages were learnt. The Input Hypothesis was intended to supplement the

Natural Order Hypothesis which in its simplest form argues that elements of a second language (L2) are learnt in a specific order regardless of the first language (L1). The issue that arises relates to the transition from one point to another. If there is a natural order of acquisition, how is it that learners move from one point to another? The Input Hypothesis was intended to provide the answer. Second languages are acquired 'by understanding messages, or by receiving "comprehensible input"' (Krashen 1985: 2), where comprehensible input is that bit of language that is heard/read/seen and that is slightly ahead of a learner's current state of grammatical knowledge. Language containing structures a learner already knows essentially serves no purpose in acquisition. Similarly, language containing structures way ahead of a learner's current knowledge is also not useful. Krashen defined a learner's current state of knowledge as i and the next stage as $i + 1$. Thus, the input a learner is exposed to must be at the $i + 1$ level in order for it to be of use in terms of acquisition. 'We move from i, our current level to $i + 1$, the next level along the natural order, by understanding input containing $i + 1$' (1985: 2).

So, in this view, we still see the important role for input, but it has now been narrowed down to a specific type of input. Its role is different from that of the behaviourist role to provide language for imitation. In Krashen's view, input activates an innate structure and, furthermore, it is not all input that is relevant – only input that is a step ahead of a learner's current grammar. One ancillary point is the role that this conceptualization of acquisition has for the classroom. If this theoretical stance were substantiated, the teacher would only have to provide appropriate input (in Krashen's terms, $i + 1$); specific teaching of a structure would not be necessary to trigger grammar change.

There were a number of arguments against the conceptualization of learning and the role for input outlined by Krashen (see Gass and Selinker 2008 for an overview), but the important point is that Krashen attempted to maintain a central role for input refining that role within the context of cognitive approaches to SLA.

SLA as a discipline is replete with ways of conceptualizing the process of acquisition and its outcomes. We turn now to some of the dominant views in current SLA thinking in an attempt to understand perceptions and conceptualizations of input. As will be seen later in this chapter, not each of these sees output as a factor that contributes to learning.

Current SLA Approaches

Universal Grammar (UG)
This chapter is not the place for an overview of the generative perspective on language and language acquisition (see White 2003, 2007). However, in

order to appreciate the role input plays within this theoretical perspective, it is necessary to understand its basic tenets. Generative linguistics seeks to determine the nature of linguistic knowledge (known as competence) that speakers have of their native language. An important part of this understanding is the determination of how children acquire that knowledge. When we use language, for example, in speaking, reading, writing, signing and/or comprehending language, we rely on an abstract linguistic system, a system that we do not have conscious knowledge of. When children learn a first language, much of this knowledge is innate and does not have to be learnt; it is derived from Universal Grammar. The assumption of innate universal language properties is motivated by the need to explain the uniformly successful and speedy acquisition of language by children in spite of insufficient input. For second language learning, the goals are similar: what is learnt and how does this knowledge come about?

Linguistic knowledge, also referred to as the mental representation of language, is derived in part by universal principles and input has a limited albeit not insignificant role. When considering the outcomes of acquisition including the well-recognized fact that we learn more than what we are exposed to and, particularly for second language learning, what is learnt is not identical to the input (if it were identical, we would never hear a sentence such as 'Where I go now?' for 'Where do I go now?'). In generative terms, it is often said that our linguistic knowledge is underdetermined by the input. If the outcome of acquisition is a complex abstract system that underlies native speaker knowledge, then there must be something in addition to the input to enable this system to develop. Universal Grammar (UG) is posited as that something. UG is an innate faculty that limits the extent to which languages can vary. The task for learning is greatly reduced if one is equipped with an innate mechanism that constrains possible grammar formation.

A central question relates to the *evidence* that learners (first and second) use to construct a mental representation. One type of evidence that is postulated is known as positive evidence and is composed of a limited set of well-formed utterances of the language being learnt (input). It is on the basis of positive evidence that linguistic hypotheses can be made. We will turn to another type of evidence, negative evidence, below in our discussion of interaction.

So, what, then, is the role of input? How far can it take us? A basic assumption, as noted above, is that learners (particularly children – the role of UG for second language learners is less agreed upon) come with an innate faculty (UG) that forms the basis of what they know about language. Knowledge of UG is part of the human endowment and, as such, is present with or without input. This is not to say that input is not crucial to acquisition for aspects of UG are triggered by the input. In particular, there are certain linguistic features that vary across languages. These are known as linguistic parameters and different languages have different values. A parameter may have a set of properties associated with it. Input is needed for a learner to determine which parametric choice is represented in the language she or he is learning. For example, some languages have movement out of a clause (English) and others do not (Chinese). A learner of Chinese will be exposed (input) to the following sentence.

> Example 2: (From White 2007: 40).
> Ni xihuan shei?
> You like who
> 'Whom do you like?'

This is sufficient to trigger the [–] value of the *wh*-movement parameter without necessary exposure to more complex structures as in example 3 as a learner will recognize that Chinese does not allow movement as exemplified above.

> Example 3: (From White 2007: 41).
> Nanhai shenmoshihou shuo ta zenyang nong qing
> Boy   when   say   he how   got bruise
> 'When did the boy say how he got a bruise?'

On the other hand, as White explains, an individual learning English would be exposed to a sentence like example 4

> Example 4
> 'Whom do you like?'

and the [+] value of the same parameter will be triggered, allowing sentences like example 5

> Example 5
> 'When did the boy say how he got a bruise?'

but not

> *The boy say when how he got a bruise.

A theoretical perspective such as this allows for the essential role of input, although not as extensive a role as was seen with behaviourism or other approaches which we discuss below. A learner, then, has an easier task than would be necessary if properties were not linked because in such an instance, each structure would require appropriate input. With regard to second language acquisition, there is the additional problem of first language influence;

nonetheless, the theory remains the same, with significant debate centring around the starting point of acquisition (i.e., is UG available and if so in what form?).

Autonomous Induction Theory

Autonomous Induction Theory (AIT) (see Carroll 2001) has similarities to UG-based research in that the same general question is being asked: What is the nature of the linguistic competence of second language learners? A psychological mechanism for language learning, the Language Acquisition Device (LAD) interacts with various modules (sound, morphosyntax, semantic systems) and, in fact, is constrained by the processing systems of those modules. The role of input in this theory is complex in that it serves multiple purposes. First are the actual data that serve as stimuli for learning. A second type of data is what Carroll (2007) refers to as *input-to-processing mechanisms*. AIT is heavily reliant on processing mechanisms that are responsible for creating novel structures and/or novel correspondences across representational levels (semantics, morphosyntax, sound). AIT is based on Jackendoff (2002) who argues that there are processing components that build representations. Carroll (2007) describes the input to the processing components as follows:

> . . . the phonetic processor takes the speech signal as input and creates some sort of prelexical phonetic representation, encoding sequences of pitch, rhythm, and duration. The phonological processor takes such phonetic representations and other aspects of the segmented signal as input and creates a structured prosodic representation as output (= *a sound form or prosodic word*). This representation activates a lexical entry of the word in the mental lexicon. This activation process makes available the word's morphosyntactic features and its transitivity and argument structure, as well as its semantic features. The morphosyntactic processor takes the morphosyntactic information contained in the activated lexical entry and uses it to integrate that word into a morphosyntactic structure of the sentence. A distinct semantic processor will take the semantic information in the activated lexical entry and attempt to build a conceptual structure containing the relevant meaning of the word. (p. 160)

A third type of input is *input-to-the-LAD*. Input in this category feeds into the LAD and helps the LAD restructure the L2 system to incorporate some new feature. For example, if a language has a category of classifiers for nouns and the native language (e.g., English) does not, there has to be some information to the LAD to allow it to restructure the representation of nouns so that this feature is part of that representation. Thus, for AIT there are multiple functions of input, each one of which plays a unique role in acquisition.

Connectionism

A very different approach is seen in Connectionism (e.g., N. C. Ellis 2003, 2008). Unlike the role of input in UG, which only serves to trigger certain grammatical patterns, Connectionism relies heavily on input frequency as learners make associations among elements. Also referred to as constructivist approaches, the emphasis is on usage. Rather than starting with something innate that prespecifies parts of one's grammar, the task for a learner is to determine regularities as they are presented in the input. Not only is it a matter of simple extraction of patterns or regularities, but one also needs confirmation that these extractions are correct. This comes from repeated exposure. Frequency accounts (N. Ellis 2002) of second language acquisition rely on the assumption that '[h]umans are sensitive to the frequencies of events in their experience' (p. 145). The approach is also referred to as an exemplar-based approach; the input provides examples and learners use those examples to create complex linguistic patterns. According to N. Ellis (2002: 144), 'comprehension is determined by the listeners' vast amount of statistical information about the behavior of lexical items in their language.' Thus, the abstraction of regularities is the main task for learning. Language representations of learners are not all of the same strength; rather, variable strengths reflect the frequency of the input and the connections that learners are able to make. In this approach, learning is seen as simple instance learning which proceeds based on input alone; the resultant knowledge is conceptualized as a network of interconnected exemplars and patterns, rather than abstract rules. In sum, the significance of input is quite distant from the role input has in a generative approach to SLA.

Input Processing

Input processing (see VanPatten 2007) makes the assumption that comprehension is essential to acquisition. That is, if language is not comprehended at some level (see also Gass 1997 who refers to comprehended rather than comprehensible input), learning will not take place. Input processing is concerned with comprehension and what happens as a learner is faced with a stream of speech or words on a piece of paper or manual signs in the case of sign language. Hence, to relate this to the topic of this section, it is concerned with the input that a learner is exposed to and how the learner processes the input. The main issue is to determine how learners make form-meaning connections and under what conditions these connections are made and under what conditions they are not.

There are a number of principles involved in input processing, focusing on what aspects of language are processed first (e.g., lexical items before grammatical markers, non-redundant material before redundant materials). What is noteworthy with regard to this discussion of input is that it relies on processing of input as the mainstay of what has to be explained with regard to acquisition.

Socio-Cultural Theory

Socio-cultural theory relies on language use in context, with learning being anchored in the social practices that a learner engages in with the assumption that human activity is mediated by artifacts, language being one of them. Language enables humans to connect to their environment (both physical and social) and to go beyond the immediate environment and to think about and talk about events and objects that are far-removed both physically and temporally. An in-depth discussion of socio-cultural theory is beyond the scope of this paper (see Lantolf 2007; Lantolf and Thorne 2006). However, important to note is that because language emerges from the experiences that we have, the interactions that learners are engaged in and the input to which they are exposed are crucial in linguistic development.

Interaction

The interaction approach accounts for learning through input (exposure to language), production of language (output) and feedback that comes as a result of interaction (see summary by Gass and Mackey 2006, 2007). There is a robust literature that confirms the positive relationship between interaction and learning (see Gass 1997; Gass and Varonis 1994; Kuiken and Vedder 2002; Mackey 1999; Mackey 2007; Pawlak 2008 among many others). These studies deal with both lexis and features of grammar.

As Gass (2003) notes, this approach to research:

> takes as its starting point the assumption that language learning is stimulated by communicative pressure and examines the relationship between communication and acquisition and the mechanisms (e.g., noticing, attention) that mediate between them. (p. 224)

Interaction simply refers to conversations and with regard to second language learning, conversations in which learners are engaged. The following conversations illustrate important aspects of interaction. The first snippet from a conversation between two learners of English (one a native speaker of Japanese and the other a native speaker of Spanish) shows the two individuals in a significant amount of negotiation. They are in the midst of a conversation when the Spanish speaker says that her father is retired. This word is apparently not understood by her conversational partner and triggers a lengthy negotiation until the problem is finally resolved. There is a constant give and take between the input and output which is referred to as negotiation of meaning. Essentially, negotiation involves those instances in conversation when participants need to interrupt the flow of the conversation in order for both parties to understand what the conversation is about,

Example 6: (From Varonis and Gass 1985, pp. 78–79)
J =   NS of Japanese; S = NS of Spanish
J: And your what is your mm father's job?
S: My father now is retire.
J: Retire?
S: Yes.
J: Oh yeah.
S: But he work with uh uh institution.
J: Institution.
S: Do you know that? The name is . . . some thin like eh control of the state.
J: Aaaaaaaah.
S: Do you understand more or less?
J: State is uh . . . what what kind of state?
S: It is uhm.
J: Michigan State?
S: No, the all nation.
J: No, government?
S: All the nation, all the nation. Do you know for example is a the the institution mmm of the state mm of Venezuela.
J: Ah ah.
S: Had to declare declare? her ingress.
J: English?
S: No. English no (laugh) . . . ingress, her ingress.
J: Ingress?
S: Ingress. Yes. I N G R E S S more or less.
J: Ingless.
S: Yes. If for example, if you, when you work you had an ingress, you know?
J: Uh huh an ingless?
S: Yes.
J: Uh huh OK.
S: Yes, if for example, your homna, husband works, when finish, when end the month his job, his boss pay – mm – him something
J: Aaaah.
S: And your family have some ingress.
J: *Yes ah,* OK OK.

> S: More or less OK? And in this in this institution take care of all
>   ingress of the company and review the accounts.
> J: OK I got, I see.
> S: OK my father work there, but now he is old.

A second aspect of interaction is what is known as recasts. Recasts are reformulations of an incorrect utterance that maintain the original meaning of the
utterance. Two examples are given below (both from Sheen 2007: 306) and relate
to grammatical form:

Example 7: (S = student; T = teacher).
> S: He has car.
> T: He has a car.

Example 8:
> S: Why did he hitted the baby?
> T: hit the baby.

In example 7 an incorrect utterance is fully recast, whereas in example 8, only
the erroneous part is repeated with a correction. There are many issues that
need to be considered with regard to recasts; we return to this topic below.

A construct related to the attention that interaction brings to language forms
is the concept of input enhancement. Polio (2007), in her review of input
enhancement, points out the nebulous nature of this term. It can be defined
quite narrowly referring to highlighting some text (as when a teacher might
make a certain part of a text bold or coloured). Or, it can be broadly defined
to incorporate the notion of drawing a learner's attention to form. As Polio
concluded (p. 14), 'The input has to be enhanced . . . the learner's attention
needs to be directed to features of the language through a variety of techniques,
regardless of what such techniques are called.'

Earlier in this chapter, we discussed the concept of positive evidence. Within
the context of interaction, there is another related concept that is particularly
relevant—negative evidence. Recall that positive evidence is essentially the input
and is the basis on which new grammars are formed (coupled with information
based on UG within some theoretical frameworks). Negative evidence, on the
other hand, is composed of information to a learner that his or her utterance is
deviant with regard to the norms of the language being learnt. Negative evidence
can come in many different forms. For example, there can be direct correction,
such as *That's not right* or indirect questions, such as *What did you say?*[2] or any of
the numerous exchanges that happen in a negotiation sequence. Perhaps the
most indirect form of correction comes from recasts which we turn to next.

We defined recasts earlier in this chapter. What is important is that recasts are positive evidence because they provide an example of a correct form and negative evidence because they provide a correction to an erroneous form. The definition, however, belies the complexity of recasts. For example, is it a partial recast? A full recast? A response to a single error or to multiple errors (how many changes are made)? Additional examples of recasts are given in examples 9–12. In the first, there is a word order change. In the second, there is a change of the verb form but no rising intonation and the verbal morphology is changed from future to subjunctive (required after *avant que*). Other differences in recasts relate to the opportunity that a learner has to respond (see Oliver 1995 for a more in-depth treatment of this topic). In example 11, the learner has an opportunity to respond, but in example 12, she does not.

Example 9: (From Philp 2003: 108)
    NNS: Why he is very unhappy?
    NS: Why is he very unhappy?

Example 10: (From Lyster 1998: 58)
    S =   student; T = teacher
    S: Avant que quelqu'un le prendra.
          before someone it will take
          'Before someone will take it.'
    T: Avant que quelqu'un le prenne.
          before someone it takes
          'Before someone takes it.'

Example 11: Recast with opportunity to respond (From McDonough and Mackey 2006: 702)
    Learner: Why he must say it like that?
    NS: Why did he say that?
    Learner: Yeah

Example 12: Recast with no opportunity to respond. From McDonough and Mackey 2006, p. 702.
    Learner: How many sister you have?
    NS: How many sisters do I have? I have one sister.

There have been a number of recent reviews of recasts in the second language literature, focusing on experimental as well as theoretical concerns (Ellis and Sheen 2006; Long 2007; Mackey and Goo 2007; Nicholas et al. 2001). Because recasts are an indirect form of correction, it is not clear to what extent they are relevant to acquisition. Empirical studies have focused specifically on the effectiveness of recasts (e.g., Ammar and Spada 2006; Ellis, R. 2007; Ellis, R. , Loewen, and Erlam 2006; Ishida 2004; Leeman 2003; Lyster 2004; Lyster and Ranta 1997; Mackey and Philp 1998; McDonough 2007; McDonough and Mackey 2006). The results from these studies are mixed.

Even though a number of studies have suggested that there is a positive effect for recasts on later learning (see Mackey and Goo 2007 and Nicholas et al. 2001), there are problems with the interpretation of effectiveness. A primary problem is the concept of uptake which refers to an indication by the learner that she or he has understood the corrective function of recasts, as in example 13 below.

Example 13: Uptake (From McDonough and Mackey 2006: 705)
    NNS: when it happen?
    NS: when did it happen?
    NNS: when did it happen?

While the learner indicates that the comment has been heard, there is no indication of incorporating this fact into her grammar, as would be the case were she to use the form later, as in example 14 below.

Example 14: (From Gass and Varonis 1989: 81)
   1. Shizuka: When will you get married?
   2. Akihito: When? I don't know. Maybe . . . uh . . . after thirty.
   3. Shizuka: Thirty?
   4. Akihito: Yeah, after thirty I'll get marriage—I'll get married . . .
              (3 turns)
   5. Akihito: . . . then if I fall in lover with her, I'll get marriage with
              her. (11 turns)
   6. Akihito: And . . . uh . . . when I saw her. I liked to get married with
              a Chinese girl because she's so beautiful.

In example 14 Akihito hears (line 1) the correct form *get married*. In lines 4 and 5, he still seems to be struggling between the two forms, *get married* and *get marriage*. One can assume that the form he initially provided (*get marriage*) was his learner-language form and that the correct modelling by Shizuka resulted in the confusion seen in Akihito's second utterance. One can further assume that he struggled with these alternate forms for the duration of this conversation (16 exchanges). At the end, he finally used, apparently without hesitation, the appropriate form, which may, in turn, suggest that he has learnt the correct form. Of course, this latter claim would have to be verified with further data which are not available here.

A difficulty arises in the interpretation of the effectiveness of recasts. When there is no uptake as sometimes occurs when there is no opportunity for response (see Oliver 1995), it is difficult to interpret the immediate effect, although one can determine a later effect through production. And, even when there is uptake, it is not clear if a response is anything more than a repetition with minimal processing.

From the child language literature, we are provided with an explanation of how recasts might work to promote learning. We will discuss this in the final section when we deal with linking input and output because it is in the context of recasts that there is unquestionably both input and output.

Output

Definition

Simply put, output is what a language learner spontaneously produces without an experimental prompt or without repeating the utterance of another individual. This could be signing in the case of sign language or speech in the case of spoken language or writing. Importantly, it is not isomorphic with knowledge, one reason being that learner speech is not always a direct reflection of what the learner actually knows (e.g., slips of the tongue or fear of making a mistake). Certainly, output is based on knowledge which originally came from input. What is intended is that it may not always reflect the mental representation of learner-language. For example, if an educated NS of English says 'I walks to the store', even without a self-correction, one would probably recognize that this utterance did not reflect what she 'knows' about English, but might attribute this to a 'slip.'

Function of Output

Historical
Earlier versions of language teaching philosophies suggested that producing language was a way of practising what had been taught/learnt in a previous part of a lesson. So, for example, there might have been a lesson on a particular grammatical structure followed by an exercise in which use of this structure was a way of practising and ultimately learning.

Current Approaches
In the 1980s Krashen's notion of comprehensible input, as the main ingredient for learning, became dominant. However, it became apparent, primarily based

on research in Canada, that input alone was not sufficient for learning. Children in immersion programmes were, after years in the school system, not as proficient as native speakers. One difference that was noted was that they used language less frequently than their native speaking counterparts (Swain 1985).

Why should use be important? The processes involved in understanding language are quite different than those involved in producing language. For example, in understanding language, it is often the case that you don't have to understand all of the grammatical indicators or all of the function words. If learners were to hear the following sentences: *Yes, he was surprised, wasn't he? Little boys don't drink,* they could relatively easily extract meaning; they do not have to know the form of tag questions, or the form of the negative marker in English. It is possible to extract the appropriate meaning solely from understanding the main content words of *surprise, little, boy, drink.* However, if those same learners were to produce those sentences, much more language information is required. And, when accurate or meaningful language is not used, correction is likely to follow, as exemplified in the conversation in example 15.

> Example 15: (From Johnson 1995: 23).
> T: Vin, have you ever been to the movies? What is your favorite movie?
> L: Big.
> T: Big. Ok, that's a good movie, that was about a little boy inside a big man, wasn't it?
> L: Yeah, boy get surprise all the time.
> T: Yes, he was surprised, wasn't he? Usually little boys don't do the things that men do, do they?
> L: No, little boy no drink.
> T: That's right, little boys don't drink.

In the situation exemplified above, even though the learner could presumably understand the sentences, he couldn't produce it. The NS's interventions served as indicators to the learner that there were problems with his speech. The main point, however, is that comprehension requires a different amount of linguistic knowledge than does production, or output, where one is forced to use grammatical markers, to have full meaning of words, and to put words into some order. As Swain noted, production 'may force the learner to move from semantic processing to syntactic processing' (1985: 249).

Given this role of output, research turned to an attempt to understand how output might actually contribute to learning. In her 1985 paper, Swain introduced the notion of comprehensible output or 'pushed' output. What is meant by this concept is that learners are 'pushed' or 'stretched' in their production as a necessary part of making themselves understood. As they are pushing their language, there are learning consequences. As learners modify a previous utterance (as in example 15 above) or they try out forms that they had not used before, there is often rejection by the NS which can come from an indication of non-understanding or confirmation which can come from an indication of understanding.

Comprehensible output refers to the need for a learner to be 'pushed toward the delivery of a message that is not only conveyed, but that is conveyed precisely, coherently, and appropriately' (Swain 1985: 249). In a more recent explication of the concept, Swain claimed that 'output may stimulate learners to move from the semantic, open-ended, nondeterministic, strategic processing prevalent in comprehension to the complete grammatical processing needed for accurate production. Output, thus, would seem to have a potentially significant role in the development of syntax and morphology' (1995: 128).

Mackey (2002) conducted a study in which learners reflected on a previous interaction through a stimulated recall procedure (see Gass and Mackey 2000). Example 16 followed by recall comments provides an interesting example of what the learner was thinking as she was engaged in an exchange that involved negotiation and recasts as the learner struggled to find the appropriate word.

> Example 16: Example of pushed output (From Mackey 2002, pp. 389–390).
> NNS: And in hand in hand have a bigger glass to see.
> NS: It's err. You mean, something in his hand?
> NNS: Like spectacle. For older person.
> NS: Mmmm, sorry I don't follow, it's what?
> NNS: In hand have he have has a glass for looking through for make the print bigger to see, to see the print, for magnify.
> NS: He has some glasses?
> NNS: Magnify glasses he has magnifying glass.
> NS: Oh aha I see a magnifying glass, right that's a good one, ok.

Particularly noteworthy are the recall comments following this episode:

> In this example I see I have to manage my err err expression because he does not understand me and I cannot think of exact word right then. I am thinking thinking it is nearly in my mind, thinking bigger and magnificate and eventually magnify. I know I see this word before but so I am sort of talking around around this word but he is *forcing* me to think harder, think harder for the correct word to give him so he can understand and so I was trying. I carry on talking until finally I get it, and when I say it, then he understand it, me. (emphasis mine)

As can be seen, the learner was pushed (note the word *force*) through the negotiation sequences to make her language clearer.[3]

So, the question becomes: How does output play a role in learning?[4] Gass (1997) and Swain (2005) considered a number of ways that output may provide learners with a forum for important language-learning functions: (a) testing hypotheses about the structures and meanings of the target language; (b) receiving crucial feedback for the verification of these hypotheses; (c) developing automaticity in interlanguage production; (d) forcing a shift from more meaning-based processing of the second language to a more syntactic mode; and (e) noticing.

Testing a hypothesis can be seen in the following example. Mackcy, Gass and McDonough (2000) video-taped interactive tasks and immediately following the interactive task replayed the video asking learners what they were thinking about at the time of the interaction. Example 17 (from their study, but not published therein) below illustrates the notion of hypothesis-testing.

Example 17: Hypothesis testing (INT = interviewer).

NNS:	*poi un bicchiere*
	then a glass
INT:	*un che, come?*
	a what, what?
NNS:	*bicchiere*
	glass
Recall by NNS:	'I was drawing a blank. Then I thought of a vase but then I thought that since there was no flowers, maybe it was just a big glass. So, then I thought I'll say it and see. Then, when she said "*come*" (what?), I knew that it was completely wrong.'

'I'll say it and see' suggests that she was using the conversation as a way to see if a hypothesis was correct or incorrect.

With regard to the language learning function of receiving feedback, the interviewer's response *come* (what?) was her indication that her hypotheses about word choice was not correct. In recent work by Kim (2008), we see an interesting example (18) where a student, in a writing task, recognized a problem, waited for feedback and utilized feedback.

Example 18: The role of feedback
  (a) Student acknowledging the gap in her second language knowledge
  ((Reads: in severe political circumstances . . . or in *the* severe)) . . .
  Oh, I think I have problems with ar- with using articles. I'm not sure about the change that I made here.

211

(b) expressing anticipation of feedback

I think that most of the changes I made into my essay just was about articles, you know, I deleted the or I added the or I just, you know, I I I just I just replaced this or that. I don't know. Hmm . . . I'm soooooooo curious to know what changes the teacher made in my essay to know more about these articles and where to use them and where not to use them.

(c) while comparing her revisions to the teacher's reformulations: ((Reads: in *the* severe political circumstances)) Mm. Oh, nice, because that's that's that's what I was saying I don't know if I made the right change or not.

The third function, automaticity, takes us back to earlier notions of practice. Using language provides us with repeated opportunities to map grammatical knowledge to output. The more we do something, the more it becomes automatic and the less deliberation is needed for each movement (e.g., riding a bike) or for each word (speaking). For example, English speakers learn that the response to 'Hi, how are you?' is 'Fine, you?' We do this without thinking and are somewhat puzzled when this automatic exchange is deviated from (as when one takes the initial question as a true question about one's health or well-being). The fourth function, moving to a more syntactic processing, has been discussed earlier. The fifth function, noticing, is crucial to the learning process and will be discussed further below. Izumi, Bigelow, Fujiwara and Fearnow (1999) specifically investigated the noticing function of output, finding partial support for this hypothesis and pointing out the need to balance cognitive and linguistic demands. McDonough (2005) tested the output hypothesis directly in her study of Thai learners of English. In a study investigating the acquisition of English questions, four groups carried out communicative tasks. The four groups focused on salience (enhancement) and opportunity to modify following feedback. Her detailed study provides evidence that the best predictor of acquisition, in this case operationalized by the acquisition of more advanced questions, is the opportunity to modify one's speech.

Input/Output – Possible Links

As we attempt to make links between input and output, it is necessary to reiterate two important initial points. First, even though we have described the type of input that learners are often exposed to, apart from recording all language input, there is little way of knowing[5] the extent of a particular learner's exposure to language. Secondly, actual output may not be a reflection of the totality of one's knowledge. There are a number of factors that might interfere with the translation of knowledge into production, among them, personality (fearful of making a mistake), confidence in one's knowledge and the willingness to try things out depending on the context, and strength of knowledge representation.

An example of the disparity between knowledge and actual production is provided by Swain (1985: 248), who quoted from an eighth grade immersion student: 'I can hear in my head how I should sound when I talk, but it never comes out that way.' Thus, there appear to be limitations on the translation of knowledge into output.

Historical Perspective

From an historical perspective, the idea of a mismatch between input and output was not seriously considered. For example, the behaviourist position was one in which the input determined knowledge. Errors (or output that did not match the input) was a consequence of faulty imitation; correction was what allowed a learner/child to get back on track to make the output match the input. With second language learning, another source of mismatch was the native language which serves as input/starting point in some models of learning.

Beginning with research in the 1960s and 1970s, the recognition that a stimulus-response model of learning was not sufficient enabled researchers to consider cognitive aspects of learning and to look more closely at what a learner was producing as well as the source of that production. During this period, however, the role of input was not considered seriously because, at least for some, it reflected earlier periods of stimulus response research. Krashen, as noted earlier, maintained a focus on input while at the same time linking it to cognitive approaches to language learning.

Current Perspectives

Earlier in this chapter, we focused on different perspectives to acquisition emphasizing the different functions that each attributed to input. In this section we deal in greater depth with the interactionist perspective as a way of linking input and output. With some other approaches, the emphasis is on language knowledge (e.g., UG and AIT), with little said about output. How does this knowledge of an L2 come about? The input to the L2 linguistic system comes from many sources, among them in some views is the innate system available to children as well as the native language. The extent to which the native language plays a role differs depending on individual research positions (see White 2007 for a review). And, because the focus is on linguistic knowledge, the concept of output is of little importance. Data gathering comes from a variety of sources only some of which are based on actual language output, others of which attempt to determine a linguistic system through indirect means (e.g., judgements of grammaticality). Even when output is used as a basis for understanding L2 knowledge, there is rarely an attempt to link that knowledge to input with the exception of linking it to native language input.

In a psycholinguistic approach such as connectionism or input processing, similarly the emphasis is on processing, leaving little room to examine the input-output connection. Interesting work on the processing of formulaic sequences (e.g., Conklin and Schmitt 2008) suggests a processing advantage of formulaic sequences over matched non-formulaic sequences. What is not known, but is an interesting question, is the extent to which this processing advantage which stems from repeated exposure from the input (necessary for the understanding that certain sequences exist) has an effect on output. Within a socio-cultural framework, the attempt is to understand language as it is situated in a particular context although there is not an emphasis on linking precise input with precise output.

In what follows, we turn our attention to conversational interactions in which learners engage. In this regard, the input is a very specific input and the output can be seen as a response to that input.

The interactionist approach, as noted above, takes the constructs of input, output and feedback as primes. There are numerous factors that are involved in learning through interaction. For example, what are the individual characteristics that allow some individuals to learn more from feedback than others? What is it that mediates between input and output?

Long (1996) describes the relationship between input and output as being mediated through negotiation of meaning:

> . . . *negotiation for meaning*, and especially negotiation work that triggers *interactional* adjustments by the NS or more competent interlocutor, facilitates acquisition because it connects input, internal learner capacities, particularly selective attention, and output in productive ways. (pp. 451–452)

He further notes that environmental contributions to acquisition (which we may view as input)

> . . . are mediated by selective attention and the learner's developing L2 processing capacity, and that these resources are brought together most usefully, although not exclusively, during *negotiation for meaning*. Negative feedback obtained during negotiation work or elsewhere may be facilitative

of L2 development, at least for vocabulary, morphology, and language-specific syntax, and essential for learning certain specifiable L1-L2 contrasts. (p. 414)

It is through interaction and particularly through feedback that a learner's attentional resources (selective attention) are directed to a 'gap' in knowledge. This occurs when the learner is able to focus on the difference between what she says and what she hears her conversational partner say. Attention (see Schmidt 1990, 2001) in an interactional setting mediates between input, learning processes and potentially output and is often considered to be the mechanism that allows learners to sort through the input they receive. Further details are beyond the scope of this paper, but it is important to understand that attention is a complex construct and different scholars have differing perspectives on the nature of attention, its function and particularly its relationship to awareness and working memory (see Posner 1988, 1992; Posner and Petersen 1990; Robinson 1995, 2001, 2002; Tomlin and Villa 1994).

As noted, the path from input to output is a long and arduous one that needs to take into account numerous factors. Gass (1988) outlined five stages in this process which will only be mentioned here: (a) apperceived input, (b) comprehended input, (c) intake, (d) integration and (e) output. The interested reader is referred to the original work. The main point is that in whatever way the relationship between input and output is viewed, it is unlikely that the link is a direct one.

Figure 1 is intended to illustrate the relationship between input and output and the variables that may intervene in that relationship. Input takes many forms including one's L1 or other languages known, UG, which in some views is the starting point of acquisition, and actual speech/reading. There is little doubt as to the fact that the native language provides some input into the developing system. The role of UG, however, is somewhat more controversial. All of these feed into a learner's developing grammar with focused attention and internal capabilities such as aptitude being intervening variables. From there, there are additional variables that determine output, primary among them are learner internal variables (e.g., personality, willingness to talk).

Perhaps the most crucial aspect of the relationship is found in the construct of feedback because it is through feedback, both negotiated and recasted, that the link between input and output is clearly discernible with exchanges going back and forth with output leading to feedback (i.e., input) to output (corrected) to more feedback (confirmatory/corrective) to more output and so forth.[6]

In fact, Saxton (1997, 2000, 2005), based on child language acquisition has proposed the Direct Contrast Hypothesis (see also e.g., Chouinard and Clark 2003; Otomo 2001; Saxton, Backley and Gallaway 2005; Saxton et al. 1998; Strapp 1999; Strapp and Federico 2000). This hypothesis claims that a contrast,

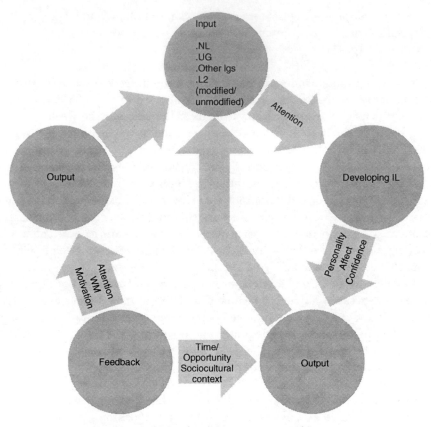

Figure 1 Relationship between input and output

particularly one that comes from adjacent utterances, highlights an erroneous form and affords an opportunity for a learner to understand that his/her utterance is incorrect. However, even acknowledging that recasts serve a learning purpose because of the juxtaposition of incorrect and correct forms, it must also be noted that the juxtaposition and consequent recognition of a language problem may only be an initial step in learning. Through a recast, learners' attention is drawn to a problem (negative evidence) while simultaneously being presented with a correct form (positive evidence). A learner still needs to extract the correct pattern from the recasted element and determine ways in which his/her grammar needs to be modified. The mere fact of doing this work may mean that the result is meaningful and lasting. Having said this, it is important to recognize the myriad problems with recasts (see Ellis and Sheen 2006). For example, uptake that follows a recast may only be a communicative moment rather than a learning moment. The complexity of the situation is deepened when one considers other elements such as proficiency level (e.g., Ammar and Spada 2006; Philp 2003) and other learner characteristics such as inhibitory control (see Gass, Behney and Uzum, in preparation). For example, Philp found that recall of recasts was affected by the proficiency of level of the learner, with higher proficiency learners having greater recall than lower proficiency learners. In the Gass et al. study on learning from interaction (not specifically focused on recasts), learners who are better able to inhibit information (based on a Stroop test) showed greater learning gains following an interactive task.

Similar comments can be made about negotiation even though there is frequently greater participation on the part of the learner and consequently greater involvement. Although both types of feedback, recasts and negotiation, reflect a direct relationship, at least on the surface, between input and output, it belies the complexity involved and ignores the vast amount of learner processing that may be going on during the event or which is stimulated by the event.

One reason that feedback may not be as successful in directly modifying a learner's grammar – which if it were, would argue for a direct relationship between input and output – has to do with a learner's perception of what the feedback is about. This is particularly the case for recasts which can be interpreted by the learner as a source of negative evidence or as a stylistic alternative to what she or he uttered. Furthermore, there is often a mismatch between intent of the feedback (e.g., a correction of grammar) and the understanding of that intent. An example from (Mackey, Gass and McDonough 2000) illustrates this.

Example 19: Morphosyntactic feedback (perceived as lexical feedback).
NNS: C'è due tazzi.
'There is two cups (m. pl.).'
INT: Due tazz-come?
'Two cup – what?'
NNS: Tazzi, dove si può mettere té, come se dice questo?
'Cups (m. pl.), where one can put tea, how do you say this?'
INT: tazze?
'Cups (f. pl.)?'
NNS: ok, tazze.
'Ok, cups (f. pl).'
Recall: I wasn't sure if I learned the proper word at the beginning.

In this example, the interviewer was attempting to correct the learners' erroneous ending on the word *tazza* (which is feminine in Italian). The learner was using a masculine plural form. In a recall session following the interaction, the learner had not noticed at all that the attempt at correction was about the morphological ending. Rather, she thought it was about word choice.

Language instruction, in a very simplistic sense, attempts to link input (explicit instruction or naturally occurring input) with learning, as demonstrated by output of some sort. Here, too, difficulties abound. Macaro and Masterman (2006) explored a relationship between intensive grammatical instruction (input) and later production (output). They did not find great improvement following an intensive course in French grammar on production (for other measures there was improvement). What this further suggests is a non-linear relationship between input and output and the relationship may be mediated by other factors such as working memory or even analytical abilities.

A final point to make relates to prefabricated patterns, for this is an area where a direct link can be made. A detailed discussion of this phenomenon is beyond the scope of this paper. However, one can see from the following example how a learner takes a form from the input, erroneously interprets it and erroneously produces it. Hakuta (1974) in a study of child second language investigated the acquisition of English by a 5-year-old Japanese child. Early in her learning history, she produced the following:

Example 20: (From Hakuta 1974, pp. 293–294).
How do you do it?
Do you have coffee?
Do you want this one?
What do you doing, this boy?
What do you do it, this, froggie?

What do you doing?
Do you bought too?
Do you put it?
How do you put it?

To explain these data (both correct and incorrect uses of *do you*) Hakuta proposes that this fixed phrase functions as a chunk which the learner took directly from the input as adults engaged her in conversations in which they asked questions using *do you*. These chunks allowed the child to engage in interactions until she reached the point where she recognized the two separate parts of the phrase. This was evidenced from additional data with the use of *did* and pronouns other than *you*. Thus, the direct almost mindless link between input and output provided the child with linguistic tools necessary for conversation which in turn allowed her to be the recipient of additional input necessary to her success in sorting out the relevant facts of English.

In sum, feedback, broadly construed, and responses to that feedback are a direct means of determining the input-output relationship. However, as has been mentioned throughout, there are other means as well which would shed light on the relationship. These are psycholinguistic in nature that would control input and examine output. Nonetheless, one would still need to examine the final step and determine if experimental responses are the same as/similar to naturalistic learning.

Conclusions

As has become clear throughout this chapter, output is complex and the input-output relationship is even more complex. In some instances, output may be a reflection of interlanguage knowledge which, in turn, is based on prior input; in others it represents a holding pattern (e.g., prefabricated patterns) while learners sort out the appropriate linguistic patterns and incorporate them into their interlanguage, and in still others, it may be a mindless repetition representative only of the need to be an active participant in a conversation. This being the case, we can expect the input-output relationship to be nothing but indirect with curves and detours along the way.

Notes

1. Teacher talk (the way teachers talk to students) can in some sense be considered a subset of foreigner talk. Despite the fact that some examples in this chapter are from classrooms, the specific discussion is limited to the more general area of foreigner talk.
2. A phrase such as *What did you say?* may not always be a reflection that an error has occurred. For example, with fluent speakers and a passing train, it may truly indicate that something has not been heard. However, with non-proficient learners and no external noise, it is likely that it is an indication of some sort of non-accurate speech.
3. It is not clear from the description in the original article whether the learner had actually seen the word 'magnifying glass' as part of the input (although she does say that she had seen the word before) and was trying to recall it or if she was generating it from what she had heard in the exchange. Regardless, it is through the interaction that this learner was able to come up with the correct word.
4. One should not be surprised to learn that output plays a role in learning. As with other kinds of learning, one must put one's knowledge to use. One cannot imagine learning how to play a sport by watching, observing and understanding the motions involved. Parts of any sport can be learnt that way (e.g., knowledge of the rules of the game, strategies), but actual implementation cannot.
5. This clearly excludes specific experimental contexts in which input is controlled through limited exposure to a target language or through the learning of an artificial language.
6. Macaro (personal communication) makes the interesting and correct point that feedback appears to be crucial because the gap between input and output is reduced to a minimum given the adjacency of the utterances. This allows a learner's attention to be easily activated. However, change takes time (see also Gass 1997) and it may be that the more significant link is one that takes place as a result of a gradual process of restructuring.

8 The Relationship between Pedagogical Focus and Interaction in L2 Lessons

Paul Seedhouse

Introduction

This chapter focuses on the relationship between pedagogical focus and interaction in second language (L2) lessons. It deals, therefore, specifically with the processes of instructed Second Language Acquisition (SLA) in classroom settings. The chapter proposes that there is a reflexive relationship between pedagogy and interaction, and that this relationship is the foundation of the organization of interaction in the L2 classroom setting. In order to understand the processes of instructed SLA, it is vital to analyse the fine detail of this relationship as it unfolds in classroom talk. The general methodological framework adopted in this chapter is that of Conversation Analysis (CA). CA is a multi-disciplinary methodology for the analysis of naturally occurring spoken interaction which is now applied in a very wide range of professional and academic areas; it has become increasingly applied to SLA over the last decade or so.

The chapter considers how intended pedagogy becomes converted into actual pedagogy and how the pedagogical focus of a lesson may be determined. The discussion then moves to interaction and a review of the different methodologies which have been employed to describe and analyse language classroom interaction. I then provide a detailed elaboration of the complex, non-linear and reflexive relationship between pedagogy and interaction, which is illustrated by means of classroom transcripts. Finally I suggest that the phenomena described can be understood from a complex systems perspective.

Pedagogy in Language Teaching

There are a number of possible definitions of pedagogy in the field of L2 teaching/SLA and the boundaries of pedagogy are somewhat fuzzy. The Oxford English Dictionary defines pedagogy as the art, occupation or practice of teaching. In this chapter, L2 pedagogy is defined as the teacher's planning and implementation of activities for teaching and learning languages. However, as we will see in the next section, planning and implementing activities are not necessarily the same thing.

In 1983 Stern (p. 452) wrote that 'for over a century, language educators have attempted to solve the problems of language teaching by focusing attention almost exclusively on teaching method.' Methods such as the Direct Method and the Audiolingual Method were presented in terms of a series of classroom procedures. There was considerable variation across methods in the amount of attention paid to promoting spoken interaction in the L2. In the Grammar-Translation Method, 'little or no systematic attention is paid to speaking or listening' (Richards and Rodgers 1986: 3). In the Audiolingual Method, by contrast, 'speech had a priority in language teaching' (Richards and Rodgers 1986: 49). Stern (1983) points out that towards the end of the twentieth century, there was a break with the method concept. Communicative Language Teaching (CLT) was seen as a comprehensive approach rather than a method (Richards and Rodgers 1986: 66). At the start of the new millennium, there are two approaches which inform L2 pedagogy and which have descended in some ways from CLT. These are Task-Based Learning and Teaching (Ellis 2003) and Sociocultural Theory (Lantolf 2000). These approaches have a number of aspects in common. They are comprehensive frameworks which attempt to integrate classroom procedures with theory and research in relation to language, language use, psychology, language learning, material and course design and testing. Moreover, these approaches have developed a perspective on classroom interaction with two aspects. First, it is vital to learning processes. Secondly, it is problematic and

221

needs to be researched, in that a linear relationship cannot be assumed between what is intended to happen and what actually happens. As Ellis (2003: 187) puts it, '. . . tasks of the kind commonly used in SLA research are not just performed but rather are interpreted, resulting in activity that is "constructed" by the participants in accordance with their particular motives and goals.'

Intended Pedagogy and Actual Pedagogy

A recent development in the study of language pedagogy, therefore, is that of how intended pedagogy becomes converted into actual pedagogy; the realization has been that learners actively interpret and transform the teacher's intended pedagogical focus. Of course language teachers have always been aware that there is sometimes a sizeable difference between what they intended to happen and what actually happens. However, it was only with the advent of recording technology that it became possible to investigate the fine interactional detail of the development of lessons. A variety of terminology has been used in the literature to refer to this gap between intended and actual pedagogy. This study employs the terms 'task-as-workplan' and 'task-in-process' (Breen 1989). The task-as-workplan is the intended pedagogy, the plan made prior to classroom implementation of what the teachers and learners will do.[1] The task-in-process is the actual pedagogy or what actually happens in the classroom.

In practice, there is sometimes a significant difference between what is supposed to happen and what actually happens. There is now ample evidence in the literature (Coughlan and Duff 1994; Donato 2000; Foster 1998; Mori 2002; Ohta 2001; Platt and Brooks 1994; Roebuck 2000) of tasks-as-workplan resulting in different and unexpected tasks-in-process. For example, Coughlan and Duff (1994) demonstrate that the same task-as-workplan does not yield comparable results in terms of task-in-process when performed by several individuals, or even when performed by the same individual on two different occasions. It is important to understand which factors may be involved when there is a gap between task-as-workplan and task-in-process. This is because the factors identified may all have a bearing on the relationship between pedagogy and interaction. In this section I examine extracts which uncover some of these factors.

In pair or group work, learners may introduce topics of talk which are more interesting to them in some way than the task-as-workplan. Markee (2005) demonstrates how learners recorded working on a pairwork task can switch instantly from on-task institutional talk to off-task social talk:

Extract 1
1 L9: this writer has a ra[ther- com- pli-] this is [co-] writer has a
2 L11:   [I slept five ho-]   [huh]

3 L9:   complicated uh,
4 L11: yea:h [(h)] ((L11 looks left, lifts his left hand to his mouth
5   and looks down))
6 L9:   [h] heh heh .hhh
7 L11: (what'd I say.)
8   (1.0) ((L9 scratches his forehead with his right hand.
9   Simultaneously, L11 drops his hand back to his lap.
10   As L11's hand reaches his lap, he begins his turn at line 11))
11 L11: I'm so tired I slept five hours ((L11 looks at his watch))
12 L11: that night ((L11 drops his hand back to his lap))
13   (0.6)
14 L9:   a:::h. ((L9 uses a tone of mock sympathy))

(Markee 2005: 202)

In lines 1 and 3, L9 tries to continue the official task-as-workplan topic of discussion of the writer Günter Grass' position in the debate on German reunification. But as L9 harks back to this previous topic, L11 overlaps L9 at line 2 with the announcement that he only slept five hours and introduces off-task social talk. L11 later (after this extract) invites L9 to a party that night where free beer is available! The social chat is in L2 English as the two learners have different L1s. Markee demonstrates how the learners in the extract carefully disguise their social talk from the teacher and are able to instantly switch back on-task when required. So learners can simply disengage from the intended pedagogical focus and produce whatever off-task talk interests them.[2]

The social dynamics of the classroom can radically alter the focus of the interaction. In Seedhouse (1996) I recorded four separate groups of Norwegian learners, aged 17–18 in a state school. All groups were working on the same task and I found that the interaction and enactment of the task-as-workplan was radically affected by group dynamics. The task-as-workplan was group discussion of statements about immigration to the USA. In the groupwork below, the group dynamics become the focus of the interaction as the discussion becomes somewhat heated, with the extract 2 characterized by competition for the floor, interruptions and disagreement.

Extract 2
1 L2:   aha. so how can you believe just like you said that everyone is like that when=
2 L3:   =I don't say everyone.
3 L2:   you just said the Italians doesn't want to=
4 L1:   =yeah. and the Mexicans.
5 L2:   so what so what do you suggest=
6 L3:   =angry you get just angry=
7 L1:   = no this was about=

8 L3: = just angry. you can twist and turn the words as much as you like but you
9   can't change my attitude.
10 L2: no but=
11 L1: = no but this is about education.
12 L3: stop twisting my words so fucking much.
13 L1: (laughs)
14 L3: you're twisting my words =

(Seedhouse 1996: 400)

In a different grouping within the same class and lesson, L3 assumed the inter-actional role of teacher and allocated turns to the other students. Resentment at L3's presumption and refusal to co-operate sometimes surfaced:

Extract 3
L3: do you have anything to e:r (2.0) say about that?
L5: no (4.0) I don't think white dominance is threatened in the USA.
L3: why not?
L5: I don't think so?
LL: (laugh)
L3: you don't think so OK? and you Jon?
L6: e:m I don't really care.
L3: you don't really care.
L6: I don't live in the US.
L3: OK. e:m and you Tone?
L4: e:m I don't know. e:r
L3: OK.

(Seedhouse 1996: 380)

Learners may try to nominate their own pedagogical focus instead of the task-as-workplan nominated by the teacher. A common scenario in the data is for learners to try to express personal meanings or issues which interest them, as in extract 4.

Extract 4
(L2 is male and L6 is female)
1 T: okay do <u>you</u> have any questions about using these words? okay?
2 L: okay
3 L6: yeah
4 T: what
5 L6: how many - girlfriends do you have here? (to L2)
6 L2: o::h

(Van Lier 1988: 160)

According to Van Lier (1988: 160) the above extract shows learners attempting to change a specific interaction type into another one because they prefer just talking to other, more regimented activities. In line 1, the teacher indicates that the questions should be about using specified words in a vocabulary exercise. L6 takes up the invitation to ask a question in line 3, but the question is not within the allocated area (the use of specified words) and it shifts the pedagogical focus to classroom relationships.

The task-as-workplan can also be affected by learner misunderstanding of participation requirements, as in extract 5.

Extract 5
1 T: now again (1.0) listen to me (1.0) <u>I've got a lamp</u>
2 LL: [I've] got a lamp
3 T: [wha-]
4 T: don't repeat now, don't say after me now. Alright I say it and you and you just
5   listen. I've got a lamp. what have you got? (1.0) raise your hands.

(Seedhouse 1996: 472)

In line 2, the learners display an understanding that they should repeat what the teacher says, but in line 4 the teacher conducts repair.

Students can also misunderstand the nature of the pedagogical focus.

Extract 6
1 T: I'm fine thanks and you? can you say that? I'm fine thanks and you?
2 L: e:r I'm fine too
3 T: okay can you just repeat that sentence, I'm fine thanks and you?

(Van Lier 1988: 200)

Here we find the teacher posing a display question in line 1, intending a form and accuracy focus, but the learner answering in line 2 as if it were a referential question within a meaning and fluency focus. Tension between focuses on form and accuracy and meaning and fluency can often cause confusion and communication problems.

Sometimes teachers (particularly inexperienced ones) fail to establish their intended pedagogical focus, i.e. the task-as-workplan is not enacted. The data below are from an English lesson in a British language school, and the teacher is a trainee. It should be noted that the lesson as a whole is fairly successful and that the trainee is having a little local difficulty in this episode of the lesson.

Extract 7
1 T: OK right (0.5) this time let's just think (looks at textbook)
2   about these children of courage we've got Mark Tinker? (0.5)

3   who's aged 12 comes from London (0.5) Jackie Martin 14 comes from
4   Manchester (0.5) and Daniel Clay who's 13 and comes from Newcastle.
5   (0.5) right can you see the pictures? (0.5) can you see them Malta?
6 LL: ( )
7 T: right children of courage what do you think (0.5) children of courage will
8   do? (2.0) what do children of courage do. (1.0) or what did they do rather
9   what did they do? (2.0) what does courage mean? what's this idea if I am
10   courageous (2.0) how would you describe me? (2.5)

(Seedhouse 1996: 306)

The students have a textbook open in front of them; the text is entitled 'Children of Courage' and has various photographs of children with stories of their courageous acts. The teacher attempts to create a text-based focus by shifting her gaze towards the textbook simultaneously with starting to read information from the textbook concerning the characters. However, the precise pedagogical focus is unclear, as we shall see. The intended task-as-workplan is for learners to give examples of courageous acts performed by these children. At first (lines 7–9) the teacher appears to want the learners to predict the content of the story ('what do you think children of courage will do?'), and then to describe the content of the story which they have not yet read ('what did they do?'). Then the teacher tries to elicit the meaning of a single lexical item (line 9), and then asks the learners to supply a description of herself (line 10). So although the learners can be fairly clear that there is now a text-based focus in that they are apparently being required to look at the text and supply an answer from the text, they have been given four contradictory sets of pedagogical focuses by the teacher.

Extract 7 (continued)
11 L2: I describe one person?
12 T: yes well anybody if you (0.5) were (0.5) one of these children of
13   courage (6.0)
14 L3: don't understand
15 T: you don't understand. OK people of courage. what would they have
16   done? what do you think they do? (0.5)
17 L4: he is on holiday?

(Seedhouse 1996: 306)

In line 11, L2 has latched onto the teacher's last instruction (line 10) and tries to clarify whether the required aim is to describe the characters in the text. T's utterance in line 12 does nothing to clarify the issue. L3 also indicates non-comprehension in line 14, but rather than clarifying which of the four sets of aims which have already been introduced the learners should focus on, the teacher actually takes a previous question (from line 7), changes the subject from 'children' to 'people', and changes the tense of the question twice (into the rather difficult conditional perfect and conditional forms), thus confusing the learners further. L4 assumes that the required aim is to describe what the characters in the text are doing and provides an answer from the textbook in line 17. At this stage it is clear that the students have no idea what the intended pedagogical focus is. The task-as-workplan, then, has not been established in any way so far.

So there is very clear evidence that we cannot take for granted that intended pedagogy will bear close resemblance to actual pedagogy; it is essential to track how the task-in-process evolves. It is difficult to predict in advance which factors will impact on interpretations of a particular task-as-workplan by particular students. However, it is possible to identify some of the factors involved, as in the discussion above. In this section we have seen that the relationship between pedagogy and interaction is not a linear one. It is a complex relationship which may be affected by a number of factors on a number of levels.

How Can Pedagogical Focus Be Determined?

In order to understand how the relationship between pedagogy and interaction develops, it is important to be able to determine the pedagogical focus at any stage of a lesson. Pedagogical focus is defined as the language teaching and learning activity which is in force at any given time. How can we know, upon observing a lesson or upon looking at lesson transcripts, what the pedagogical focus is at any given point? This is problematic since, as we have seen above, we cannot assume that what the teacher intends and plans to happen in terms of pedagogical activity will be what actually happens. In practice, however, we can determine the pedagogical focus at any particular point in a lesson using three types of evidence,[3] as follows.

Type 1. In many lessons there is a text-internal statement by the teacher of the intended pedagogical focus. In many cases this is stated explicitly by the teacher, e.g.: 'Today's class is going to be about describing objects and we're going to look at 3 different types of description' (Seedhouse 1996: 272). This type of text-internal evidence is often (but certainly not always) available in the data in that it is generally accepted to be good pedagogical practice for teachers to state the intended aims of the classroom activity both at the outset of the lesson and before each activity. Type 1 evidence provides us with clear evidence of the intended pedagogical focus, although in practice the task-in-process may differ from the task-as-workplan.

Type 2. There are now increasing amounts of classroom data available (e.g., Carr 2006; Lubelska and Matthews 1997) which provide, in addition to the video and transcript lesson data, a detailed description of lesson aims and other text-external or ethnographic evidence of intended pedagogical focus. So, for example, in Seedhouse (2004) I analyse an extract and use as evidence of intended pedagogical focus a statement made by the teacher in a video interview after the lesson. The advantage of type 2 evidence is that it does provide text-external, independent evidence of the type which would tend to be convincing to applied linguists. By contrast, it is likely that CA practitioners would have reservations about this kind of background evidence as it is external to the talk and does not originate in an emic perspective as understood by CA (Seedhouse 2004). There is doubt that type 2 evidence provides us with clear proof of the actual pedagogical focus, since the task-in-process may differ from the task-as-workplan.

Type 3. Evidence of pedagogical focus may also be available in the details of the interaction. In their turns, participants display their analyses of the evolving relationship between the pedagogical focus and the organization of the interaction. So for example in extract 8 below the analysis of and orientation to pedagogical focus by the participants is manifest and available to us in the details of the interaction.

Extract 8
1 T: now again (1.0) listen to me (1.0) <<u>I've got a lamp</u>>
2 LL: [I've got] a lamp
3 T: [wha-]
4 T: don't repeat now, don't say after me now. Alright I say it and you and you just
5   listen. I've got a lamp. what have you got? (1.0) raise your hands.
6   what have you got Eirik?
7 L1: e:r I've=
8 T: =can you say=
9 L1: =I've got a book.=
10 T: =alright, fine. I've got a telephone. what have you got? (2.5) Trygve.
11 L2: I've got a hammer.

(Seedhouse 1996: 472)

In line 1 T introduces a new pedagogical focus, which is for T to say what he has got and then to nominate one learner to say what s/he has got. However, we see in line 2 that the learners display their analyses of the pedagogical focus as being to repeat whatever T says. In lines 4–6 T displays his analysis of LL's turn in relation to the pedagogical focus as being a mismatch and T restates the pedagogical focus. In line 9 we see that L1 re-analyses the pedagogical focus as being for him to say what he has got and we see in line 10 that 10 analyses L1's turn as matching the pedagogical focus and so T is able to continue with the same pedagogical focus. Now we should note that all of the evidence for the evolving pedagogical focus is endogenous to the details of the talk; the participants are displaying their analyses of and orientations to the pedagogical focus in their turns at talk.

Type 3 evidence of pedagogical focus may be subject to a criticism of circularity by applied linguists as the evidence for the pedagogical focus comes from the interaction itself. However, this text-internal type of evidence is most convincing to CA practitioners precisely because it is endogenous to the talk and derives from an emic perspective – the evidence relating to the participants' concerns inhabits the details of the talk. Moreover, the CA objection to evidence of Types 1 and 2 would be that they are merely statements of *intended* pedagogical focus or task-as-workplan; as we saw in several extracts above, the actual pedagogical focus or task-in-process can turn out rather differently to the way anticipated; indeed, this happens in line 2 of extract 8 above. Furthermore, the pedagogical focus can be switched from one turn to another by learners as well as by teachers, and the interdependent relationship between pedagogy and interaction means that the evolving patterns of interactions affect the pedagogical focus. Explicit statements of intended pedagogical focus (evidence of Types 1 and 2) do not necessarily reflect the reality of how the participants actually analyse and orient to the pedagogical focus. The task of CA analysts is to match the evolving pedagogical focus with the evolving patterns of interaction in the same way as the participants do and using the same evidence that they do, i.e. each other's turns at talk.

So we should be aware that identification of the pedagogical focus in interaction is a complex undertaking; it can never be taken for granted as it may be transformed from one turn to the next. There are 3 different types of evidence of pedagogical focus. Different methodological approaches will find some types of evidence more convincing than others and each has its inherent advantages and disadvantages. An ideal situation would be one in which all 3 types of evidence were available for analysis.

Interaction in Language Teaching

Language teaching pedagogy has a long history; Stern (1983: 452) reports that the question of how to teach languages has been debated for over 25 centuries! By contrast, the detailed, intensive study of interaction in L2 classrooms only took off in the 1960s with the advent of audio and, later, video recording technology. This is not to suggest that there was no interest in interaction before that. Sauveur's account of a 'natural method' lesson in the nineteenth century, for example, contains a 'transcription of a typical lesson' (Howatt and Widdowson 2004: 219). However, developments in technology meant that classroom interaction could more easily yield data for serious, intensive research. To some extent, the analytical methodology which is employed to research human spoken interaction will influence the findings, and so in this section we try to tease out how different research methodologies have produced different portrayals of L2 classroom interaction.

The first wave of development in the description and analysis of L2 classroom interaction was observation or coding schemes from the 1960s. The basis of classroom coding schemes is that an interactant is making one move on one level at a time. The move the teacher is making can be specified and coded as a pedagogic move, for example *initiates or replies*. An influential early scheme was FLINT (Moskowitz 1976) and the 1980s saw the development of extensive, detailed coding schemes which are still in use today: the COLT instrument (Froehlich, Spada and Allen 1985) and TALOS (Ullman and Geva 1984). Many observation schemes have been developed for the L2 classroom and a list of observation instruments is available in Chaudron (1988: 18). The overall picture of interaction which emerges from use of coding schemes is that it consists of a series of discrete pedagogical moves by the teacher and response moves by the learner. The observer may select in advance which of these moves are of interest to the research and are to be counted. These may then be linked in some way to achievement, an example being Moskowitz's (1976) study of the behaviour of outstanding teachers.

A second major development was the use of discourse analysis (DA) from the 1970s. DA uses principles and methodology typical of linguistics to analyse classroom discourse in structural-functional linguistic terms (Chaudron 1988: 14). For example, 'Could I borrow your pencil?' could be mapped as 'request'. Once sequences of speech acts or moves have been plotted, a set of rules can then (in theory) be written which show how the units fit together to form coherent discourse. Then, hierarchical systems which depict the overall organization of classroom discourse could in principle be developed. It should be noted, however, that a full-scale and explicit DA model of the organization of L2 classroom interaction has never been published. The outstanding study of (L1) classroom interaction which takes this DA approach is Sinclair and Coulthard (1975). Their most significant finding as far as the teaching profession is concerned is their identification of the three-part sequence typical of classroom interaction. This sequence is generally known as Teacher Initiation, Learner Response and Teacher Follow-Up or Feedback (IRF). There does seem to be general agreement that IRF patterns are found in many different types of classroom around the world and in many different pedagogical approaches. It seems impossible, then, to link the IRF pattern exclusively to a specific pedagogical approach, but there is evidence that it occurs in some varieties of classroom interaction but not in others (Seedhouse 2004).

The DA system of analysing classroom interaction proved highly appealing to the language teaching profession (particularly as it uses a linguistic approach) to the extent that a majority of studies of classroom interaction during the 1980s and 1990s were based more or less explicitly on it. The DA approach has been subject to considerable criticism on a theoretical level, most notably by Levinson (1983: 289), who suggests that there are strong reasons to believe that such models are fundamentally inappropriate to the subject matter, and thus irremediably inadequate. Seedhouse (2004) suggested that DA cannot portray the flow of the interaction because it is essentially a static approach which portrays interaction as consisting of fixed and unidimensional coordinates on a conceptual map. Since the DA approach was developed for L1 classrooms and transferred for use in L2 classrooms, it has difficulty in portraying the extra dimension which distinguishes L2 classroom interaction from L1 classroom interaction. As Willis (1992: 162) puts it, 'Language is used for two purposes; it serves both as the subject matter of the lesson, and as the medium of instruction. It is precisely this dual role that makes language lessons difficult to describe.' A central argument of this chapter is that in the L2 classroom, pedagogy and interaction are intertwined in a mutually dependent relationship and that we must examine the minute detail of the interaction to gain a full understanding of the instructed L2 learning process. In DA, interaction is 'translated' into functions and this diverts attention from the minute linguistic detail in which the complex, reflexive relationship between pedagogy and interaction is manifest. However, DA does have several advantages as a methodology. It is relatively quick and easy for practitioners to learn, it fits well into a linguistic paradigm and language teachers are used to teaching the functions of language and so are familiar with DA constructs. The overall picture of L2 classroom interaction which emerges from use of a DA methodology is that it consists of successions of sequences like the IRF pattern. This has a tendency to conceal the complexity of the interaction and to homogenize it.

With the development of coding schemes and DA studies, from the 1980s, the importance of interaction as a vital element in the instructed second language learning process became clearer. During this period, ethnography was introduced as an approach to studying L2 classroom interaction, notably by Van Lier (1988). Ethnographic studies continue to be popular, (e.g., Creese 2006) and have contributed greatly to our understanding of the context and culture of L2 classrooms. Allwright (1984: 159) sums up this new perspective on interaction:

> Bluntly, classroom interaction is important because interaction is the sine qua non of classroom pedagogy. interaction is the process whereby lessons

are 'accomplished', to use Mehan's very apt term. . . . We are not talking about interaction in terms of 'communication practice' for example, but in terms of pedagogy itself, in the most general sense that all classroom pedagogy proceeds, necessarily, via a process of interaction, and can only proceed in this way. . . . The above arguments point to the conclusion that successful pedagogy, in any subject, necessarily involves the successful management of classroom interaction.

Towards the end of the last century, strong interest emerged in applying a new methodology to the description and analysis of L2 classroom interaction. Conversation Analysis (CA) is a multi-disciplinary methodology which is now applied in a very wide range of professional and academic areas; see, for example, Drew and Heritage (1992a); Richards and Seedhouse (2005). There have been a number of different conceptions of the relationship between CA and the broad field of language learning and teaching and CA has indeed been applied in research in this field in many different ways. CA only emerged in the 1960s, had no obvious connection with learning and in its genesis dealt exclusively with monolingual English data. It is only in the period 1995–2005 that publications have started to address the relationship between CA and instructed second language learning. Space precludes an introduction to CA methodology here, but these are available in Ten Have (1999); Heritage (1984); Hutchby and Wooffitt (1998); Levinson (1983); Seedhouse (2004). Of particular interest was CA's highly detailed system of transcription and its ability to portray the multi-layered complexity of interaction. CA asks the questions 'Why that, in that way, right now?' This encapsulates the perspective of interaction as action (why that) which is expressed by means of linguistic forms (in that way) in a developing sequence (right now). This seemed to promise a more holistic, multi-layered perspective on interaction than had previously been possible. The final section of this chapter provides an exposition of the relationship between pedagogy and interaction using a CA methodology. The overall picture of the L2 classroom which emerges from the application of a CA methodology is that it is a very complex, dynamic and fluid interactional environment. In general, CA tends to reveal complexity.

A significant strand of psycholinguistic SLA research has focused on interactional phenomena which are thought to be of pedagogical significance. These phenomena are at the point of intersection of pedagogy and interaction and are therefore of particular significance to this chapter. This approach can be termed 'linear', in that a direct connection is made between constructs and their occurrence in interaction; these can be extracted from their interactional environment for quantification without in-depth analysis. To some extent this 'linear' approach is at variance with the approach I present in this chapter. However, this approach is important in linking interaction to cognitive processes and in the conclusion below (and in Seedhouse 2004, 2005) I suggest that it is possible to combine the two approaches productively. The first major wave of such studies was associated with Long's (1985, 1996) interaction hypothesis. The features which were selected for quantitative treatment are clarification requests, confirmation checks, comprehension checks and self-repetitions, which are all characteristic of 'modified interaction' or negotiation for meaning. A second wave of studies focused on recasts (e.g., Nicholas et al. 2002). A recent collection (Mackey 2007) combines the above constructs under the heading of 'implicit feedback' and also examines explicit or metalinguistic feedback. The overall picture of L2 classroom interaction which emerges from use of this 'linear' approach is that the interaction contains specific phenomena which are of special interest from a learning perspective. These can be extracted from their interactional environment for quantification and it can thereby be demonstrated that these phenomena are associated with more effective acquisition.

In this section, we have seen that a number of different methodologies have been employed, each of which tends to generate a different perspective on interaction. At the time of writing, journals of applied linguistics and SLA contain articles using a variety of methodologies to analyse interaction in L2 classrooms. The Modern Language Journal, for instance, is a journal which contains a number of studies of classroom interaction. During 2007, one study was published in the journal using an ethnographic approach, two using CA, one using a socio-cognitive approach, one using a socio-cultural approach and one using Bakhtinian analysis. A special issue of the Modern Language Journal was devoted to classroom interaction (2004) and it has become common practice for articles to include discussion of classroom transcripts. Other methodologies which have also been employed (but are not reviewed here) include Critical Discourse Analysis (e.g., Hammond 2006) and systemic-functional linguistics (e.g., Leung and Mohan 2004).

The Relationship between Pedagogy and Interaction

It may be argued that the relationship between pedagogy and interaction has always been central to the learning process, and that in the writings of Plato it was evident that learning processes were inextricably linked to the interactional structure of Socratic dialogue. Nonetheless, in the field of applied linguistics and SLA, very little has been written specifically on the nature of the relationship between pedagogy and interaction in the instructed language learning process.

The Pedagogical Landing-Ground Perspective

According to Seedhouse (2004), the implicit, default perspective which has dominated the language teaching literature has been the 'pedagogical landing-ground perspective'. This consists of the linear view that intended pedagogical aims and ideas translate directly into actual classroom practice as if the L2 classroom had no intervening level of interactional organization. In other words, the task-as-workplan or intended pedagogy translates directly into the task-in-process or actual pedagogy. The pedagogical landing-ground perspective has, to the best of my knowledge, never been stated explicitly by anyone and has no methodological basis. Nonetheless, it is by far the most pervasive perspective and indeed is the implicit or 'default' perspective if none other is stated. If one opens any L2 teaching magazine or journal or course book at random, one will most often find that this perspective is implicit, in that there is no consideration of how the proposed pedagogy will interface with the interactional organization of the L2 classroom or of how the task-as-workplan will translate into the task-in-process. In other words, the conceptualization in the literature is overwhelmingly in terms of the task-as-workplan or intended pedagogy. The pedagogical landing-ground perspective, then, is the default perspective if no consideration is given to how pedagogy is translated into interaction.

How Intended Pedagogy is Transformed

The perspective on the relationship between pedagogy and interaction developed by Seedhouse (2004) was intended to replace the pedagogical landing-ground perspective. Seedhouse employs a CA methodology and argues that L2 classroom interaction has a specifiable organization, which is outlined briefly below and in detail in Seedhouse (2004). Pedagogy and interaction are entwined in a reflexive relationship which is the basis of the organization of L2 classroom interaction. It is argued that it is important to take the interactional architecture of the language classroom into account when planning activities because it transforms task-as-workplan into task-in-process, intended pedagogy into actual pedagogy. The pedagogical vision of the task-as-workplan interacts with the interactional organization of the L2 classroom to produce an interactional sequence, which combines the pedagogical focus *as analysed by the participants* with an organization of the interaction appropriate to that focus. To illustrate how this transformation occurs, I will examine extract 9 below, involving Turkish university students learning English. The task-as-workplan is for L8 to ask L11 a question with the present perfect followed by a question with the simple past. This sounds fairly unproblematic in terms of task-as-workplan, especially as the teacher has just drilled the learners in the infinitive, past simple and past participle forms of the verbs involved.

Extract 9
```
 1  T:     °have you ever° (whispers)
 2  L8:    (.) you ever: (.) gone to (.)
 3  T:     gone to?
 4  L8:    er: gone to Sümela Manastır? Sümela attraction?
 5  L11:   (1.0) hmm yes=
 6  T:     =YES [(laughs )]
 7  LL:          [(laughter)]
 8  T:     yes okay ask him now when? when?
 9  L1:    when?
10  LL:    (laughter)
11  T:     (uses body language) make a sentence (laughs)
12  L1:    when uhm-
13  L11:   last summer
14  TLL:   (laughter)
15  T:     when last summer okay (laughter) okay now someone else (.) ask
16         him with who with who
```
(Üstünel 2003: 75)

A problem arises with the task-in-process precisely because the task-as-workplan interacts with the interactional organization of the L2 classroom to produce a particular sequence organization and because the learners interpret the pedagogical focus in a different way to that intended by the teacher. There is a question-answer adjacency pair in the present perfect in lines 2, 4 and 5. The consequence is that the follow-up question in lines 9 and 12 needs only the single word *when*? to form a complete turn-constructional unit precisely by virtue of its sequential location. So, although we can see in line 11 that T wants a full sentence with the past simple, she accepts the sequence produced (line 15). The sequence which the learners have produced is a very 'natural' and understandable one and in fact their analysis of the task demonstrates a good understanding of sequential organization. So the mismatch between task-as-workplan and task-in-process, between intended and actual pedagogy, is due to the way in which the pedagogical focus has interacted with the interactional organization of the L2 classroom and the way in which the learners have re-interpreted the task in the light of this.

How is L2 Classroom Interaction Organized?

Seedhouse (2004) applies CA methodology to an extensive and varied database of language lessons from around the world and attempts to answer the question 'How is L2 classroom interaction organized?' The operational definition employed is that L2 classroom interaction is interaction which is produced in the L2 by teachers and/or learners in normative orientation to a pedagogical focus. Many other varieties of interaction can occur in the physical setting of an L2 classroom, but the above is the sole focus of this section. This means that the description provided in this section does not apply to, for example, grammar-translation lessons conducted in L1.

The main thesis developed, as stated earlier, is that there is a reflexive relationship between pedagogy and interaction in the L2 classroom, and that this relationship is the foundation of its context-free architecture. The omnipresent and unique feature of the L2 classroom is this interdependent relationship between pedagogy and interaction. So whoever is taking part in L2 classroom interaction and whatever the particular activity during which the interactants are speaking the L2, they are always displaying to one another their analyses of the current state of the evolving relationship between pedagogy and interaction and acting on the basis of these analyses. So interaction in the L2 classroom is based on the relationship between pedagogy and interaction. Interactants are constantly analysing this relationship and displaying their analyses in their talk.

CA attempts to understand the organization of institutional interaction as being rationally derived from the core institutional goal. Therefore, the first step towards describing the interactional architecture of L2 classroom interaction is to identify the institutional core goal, which is that *the teacher will teach the learners the L2*. This core institutional goal remains the same wherever the L2 lesson takes place and whatever pedagogical framework the teacher is working in. This is a most important point. In many kinds of institutions, e.g. businesses, the institutional goal may vary considerably even between businesses in the same town. However, in L2 teaching the institutional goal of the teacher teaching the L2 to the learners remains constant whatever the teaching methods, whatever the L1 and L2 and wherever in the world the L2 is taught. It remains the same if the teacher delegates some responsibility to learners in a learner-centred or learner autonomy approach. From this core goal a number of consequences issue both rationally and inevitably which affect the way in which L2 classroom interaction is accomplished. Drew and Heritage (1992b: 26) suggest that each institutional form of interaction may have its own unique *fingerprint*, 'comprised of a set of interactional practices differentiating (it) both from other institutional forms and from the baseline of mundane conversational interaction itself'.

Three Interactional Properties

There are three interactional properties which derive directly from the core goal, and these properties in turn necessarily shape the interaction. The three properties follow in rational sequence from each other and constitute part of the unique fingerprint of L2 classroom interaction and part of its context-free machinery.

1. Language is both the vehicle and object of instruction.
2. There is a reflexive relationship between pedagogy and interaction and interactants constantly display their analyses of the evolving relationship between pedagogy and interaction.
3. The linguistic forms and patterns of interaction which the learners produce in the L2 are potentially subject to evaluation by the teacher in some way.

Property One
Language is 'Both the vehicle and object of instruction' (Long 1983: 9). This property springs rationally and inevitably from the core goal. The core goal dictates that the L2 is the object, goal and focus of instruction. It must be taught, and it can only be taught through the medium or vehicle of language. Therefore language has a unique dual role in L2 classroom interaction in that it is both the vehicle and object, both the process and product of the instruction; see *Seedhouse* (2004) for exemplification of this point. In other forms of classroom education (history, engineering) language is only the vehicle of the teaching. This property creates an extra layer of complexity in the interaction which needs to be portrayed in our analyses. As Appel (2007: 282) puts it, 'verbal interaction in the language classroom can be seen as a reflexive mode of communication which uses some of the resources characteristic of performance to make language its special focus.'

Property Two
Property one generates a mutually dependent relationship between pedagogy and interaction. This means that as the pedagogical focus varies, so the organization of the interaction varies. This point is illustrated through the analyses in Seedhouse (2004). However, this relationship also means that the L2 classroom has its own interactional organization which transforms the pedagogical focus (task-as-workplan) into interaction (task-in-process); see extract 9 for an example of this. The omnipresent and unique feature of the L2 classroom is this reflexive relationship between pedagogy and interaction. So whoever is taking part in L2 classroom interaction and whatever the particular activity during which the interactants are speaking the L2, they are always displaying to one

another their analyses of the current state of the evolving relationship between pedagogy and interaction and acting on the basis of these analyses. We can see how this works even in the first exchange a Chinese L1 beginner makes in his first English class in extract 10.

Extract 10
1 T: OK my name's,
2 LL: my name's,
3 T: OK, (.) er, hello, (addresses L1) my name's John Fry.
4 L1: (.) my name's John Fry,
5 T: oh!
6 LL: (laugh)
7 L1: my name's Ping. Ping.
8 T: Ping? yes hello, °you say° (whispers) hello.
9 L1: hello my name is my name's Ping.

(British Council 1985 volume 1: 15)

We can see in line 4 that L1 displays an analysis of the current relationship between pedagogy and interaction as being that he must repeat whatever the teacher says. T, however, displays in lines 5 and 8 that his analysis is that this is not the required relationship and that L1 should instead produce a specific string of forms including L1's own name. L1 then changes his analysis of the relationship between pedagogy and interaction so that in line 9 it finally conforms to that required by T.

Property Three

The linguistic forms and patterns of interaction which the learners produce in the L2 are potentially subject to evaluation by the teacher in some way. As Van Lier (1988: 32) puts it, 'Everyone involved in language teaching and learning will readily agree that evaluation and feedback are central to the process and progress of language learning.' This property does *not* imply that all learner utterances in the L2 are followed by a direct and overt verbalized evaluation by the teacher, as the data show this clearly not to be the case. It means that all learner utterances are *potentially* subject to evaluation by the teacher.[4] This third property derives rationally from the second property; since the linguistic forms and patterns of interaction which the learners produce in the L2 are normatively linked in some way to the pedagogical focus which is introduced, it follows that the teacher will need to be able to evaluate the learners' utterances in the L2 in order to match the reality to the expectation. Seedhouse (2004) proposes that these three properties are universal, i.e., they apply to all L2 classroom interaction and they are inescapable in that they are a rational consequence of the core institutional goal and the nature of the activity. Furthermore, the data from many different countries, types of institutions and types of lesson which are analysed in Seedhouse (2004) demonstrate the universality of these properties. These properties, then, form the foundation of the rational architecture and of the unique institutional 'fingerprint' of the L2 classroom.

A Basic Sequence Organization

Whoever is taking part in L2 classroom interaction and whatever the particular activity during which the interactants are speaking the L2, they are always displaying to one another their analyses of the current state of the evolving relationship between pedagogy and interaction and acting on the basis of these analyses. So although L2 classroom interaction is extremely diverse and fluid, it is nonetheless possible to state a basic sequence organization which applies to all L2 classroom interaction, as follows.

1. A pedagogical focus is introduced. Overwhelmingly in the data this is introduced by the teacher but it may be nominated by learners.
2. At least two persons (including the teacher) speak in the L2 in normative orientation to the pedagogical focus.
3. In all instances, the interaction involves participants analysing this pedagogical focus and performing turns in the L2 which display their analysis of and normative orientation to this focus in relation to the interaction. Other participants analyse these turns in relation to the pedagogical focus and produce further turns in the L2 which display this analysis. Therefore, participants constantly display to each other their analyses of the evolving relationship between pedagogy and interaction.

Through this sequence the institution of the L2 classroom is 'talked into being'. This is the case because introducing the pedagogical focus is directly implicative of the institutional goal, i.e. to teach the learners the L2.

An Analytical Methodology

The above properties and sequence organization provide us with a ready-made methodology for analysing L2 classroom interaction. The idea that an analytical procedure or methodology can emerge from the structure of interaction is a familiar one in CA. Our task as analysts is to explicate how L2 classroom interactants analyse each others' turns and make responsive moves in relation to the pedagogical focus. The description of the interactional architecture of the L2 classroom above, specifically the properties and basic sequence organization, provides the analyst with a ready-made emic analytical procedure. The participants display in their turns their analyses of the evolving relationship between pedagogy and interaction, i.e. how the pedagogical focus relates to the turns produced in L2. Therefore, the methodology can be stated in this way: *The analyst follows exactly the same procedure as the participants and traces the evolving relationship between pedagogy and interaction, using as evidence the analyses of this relationship which the participants display to each other in their own turns.*

So the methodology which is used for the analysis of L2 classroom interaction is the next-turn proof procedure in relation to the pedagogical focus. In the vast majority of cases in the database we can state the procedure more specifically as follows. The classroom teacher compares the linguistic forms and patterns of interaction which the learner produces with the pedagogical focus which s/he originally introduced and performs an analysis and evaluation on that basis. The analyst can do exactly the same thing, comparing the teacher's intended pedagogical focus with the linguistic forms and patterns of interaction which the learner produces, and then analysing the interaction on the basis of the match or mismatch. This methodology is exemplified in the analyses in this chapter and in Seedhouse (2004).

The Complexity of the Relationship between Pedagogy and Interaction

In this section I intend to uncover some of the complexity of the relationship between pedagogy and interaction by analysing the detail of some extracts of L2 classroom interaction. An additional level of complexity (which has not been mentioned so far) is frequently added to the relationship between pedagogy and interaction by the use of multiple languages in the classroom (see Cook, this volume, on the relationship between L1 and L2). It is possible to understand and analyse code-switching in L2 classrooms by tracing how language choice relates to developments in sequence and the shifting pedagogical focus. Üstünel and Seedhouse (2005) applied an adapted version of the classic CA questions to interaction involving code-switching, namely *why that, in that language, right now*? The study suggests that code-switching in L2 classrooms is orderly and related to the evolution of pedagogical focus and sequence. Through their language choice, learners may display their alignment or misalignment with the teacher's pedagogical focus. This therefore creates an additional level of complexity which needs to be accounted for in our portrayal of the relationship between pedagogy and interaction.

Extract 11

1	T:	Ayvalık here
2		(0.5)
3		so twenty
4		(0.5)
5		twenty
6		(0.5)
7		twenty <u>good</u> persuaders
8	L5:	Thank you
9	T:	persuade?
10		(0.5)
11		What was persuade?
12	L5: →	*ikna =etmek*
		[tr: to persuade]
13	T:	=/ /good* sell of people okay, wonderful .hh this
14		time go back to your original partner
15		(0.5)
16		original?
17	L2:	=/ /*gerçek*
		[tr: real]
18	L5:	=/ /*ilk*
		[tr: the first]
19	L7:	=*orjinal*
		[tr: original]
20	T: →	yeah *ilk partnerinize geri dönüyorsunuz* (.) *beraber yazdığınız*
21		[tr: return to your first partner with whom you have written]
		((LL talk in English in groups))

(Üstünel and Seedhouse 2005: 315)

Extract 11 above is taken from a post-task activity. In lines 1 and 7, the teacher comments on the task results. In lines 9, 11 and 16 the teacher initiates question turns that 'induce' the learners to code-switch, but she does not code-switch to Turkish herself. In line 12, S5 switches to the L1 to provide a translation of the L2 word and in lines 17, 18 and 19 three learners provide translations in the L1 of the L2 word 'original'. These learner turns display the learners' analysis of the teacher's pedagogical focus as being for them to code-switch to the L1. The teacher's follow-up turn in lines 13 and 20 provides positive feedback, which confirms that the learners had complied with the pedagogical focus. The data contain many such examples. In extract 11 the teacher's utterance in the L2 has the pedagogical aim of the learners producing an utterance in the L1. The learners display affiliation to the teacher's pedagogical focus precisely by replying in the L1 and the teacher recognizes them as affiliative responses. Üstünel and Seedhouse (2005) suggest that it is only possible to understand and analyse code-switching in L2 classrooms by tracing how language choice relates to developments in sequence and the shifting pedagogical focus. In other words, language choice becomes entwined in the relationship between pedagogy and interaction, creating a third strand.

The following extract illustrates a number of the themes explored in this chapter. The class are looking at a picture of people in a building.

Extract 12
```
 1 T:    where is the man?
 2 L1:   (2.5) <in the: se:cond floor>
 3 T:    in the second floor? ((T's face shows disapproval))
 4 L2:   on the second [floor.
 5 TLL:                 [on the second floor.
 6 T:    what's he wearing?
 7 L1:   (1.9) er::: the: shirt eh yellow? (1.0) and the trousers green?
 8 T:    okay. (.) °shirt yellow?°
 9 LL:   (.) orange orange
10 L1:   orange
11 T:    yellow
12 L1:   orange
13 T:    a yellow shirt ((T's hands move to show word order))
14 L1:   yah
15 T:    he's wearing a yellow shirt (1.5) >everybody< a yellow shirt.
16 LL:   a yellow shirt.
17 T:    he's wearing a yellow shirt.
18 LL:   he's wearing a yellow shirt.
19 T:    good
```
                                                              (Carr 2006 dvd 14)

In line 2, L1 produces an answer whose meaning is clear, but in which the incorrect preposition is used. In this L2 classroom context T is focusing on form and accuracy and the aim is for learners to produce specific strings of linguistic form accurately, and T initiates repair until these are performed. In line 3 T therefore uses a specific repair initiator, providing vocal emphasis on the incorrect preposition and indicating disapproval with his face. In line 4 L2 provides the correct string of linguistic forms and this is approved by T and chorused by other learners in line 5. In line 7, L1 produces an answer whose meaning is clear, but in which the incorrect word order is used. In line 8, T again employs a specific repair initiator, repeating the two words which constitute trouble.

This time, however, the repair initiation is unsuccessful as the learners (in lines 9, 10 and 12) identify the trouble as being the colour of the shirt; they therefore correct the colour to 'orange'. At least 3 different learners all identify the same trouble source. T is therefore obliged to conduct other-repair in line 13, using his hands to indicate that word order is the trouble. Finally in line 18 T has got the learners to practise the targeted string of linguistic forms. In lines 3 and 8 T employs the same basic repair initiation technique (other-initiated self-repair). This works well in the first instance but not in the second instance. The reasons why this does not work well in the second instance include the following. 'Shirt yellow' in line 8 can easily be heard as 'Is the shirt yellow?', which appears to be identifying the colour as the trouble source. Also, the repair initiation in line 8 does not give any indication that word order is the nature of the trouble. Neither word in line 8 is stressed by T and the default assumption in such cases is that it is the final word of the utterance which is the trouble item.

In the video it is clear that at least 3 learners provide the response 'orange', so the learners appear to be following a default route here in interpreting the colour as the trouble item. The teacher has been caught in a bind here, with pedagogy and interaction working in different directions. From the pedagogical perspective, the teacher initiates repair so the learners themselves can correct the error, which is the positioning of the two words in relation to each other. The teacher cannot stress either word (unlike in line 3) as this would indicate that a single word were the trouble source. However, form and accuracy contexts have their own organization of repair (Seedhouse 2004) which means that, if no single word is stressed in this type of repair initiation, the final word is taken to be the trouble source. In L2 classrooms, then, pedagogy and interaction can work in opposition to each other and create trouble for the participants.

Extract 12 illustrates a number of themes included in the discussion above. On the surface this seems like a very simple, workaday exercise, a teacher question/learner answer sequence in which learners are required to produce simple sentences based on a picture prompt. However, the workings of the relationship between pedagogy and interaction complicate matters. The problem in L2 classroom interaction is that learners may make errors in their L2 production on numerous levels – phonological, lexical, grammatical, discoursal, content/meaning – and each of these categories can be broken down further. Having perceived one or more errors (often a number of errors on a number of levels) in the learner's utterance, the teacher needs to take an instant decision on whether to initiate repair or not. If so, the teacher needs to decide which type of repair trajectory is most appropriate for which type of error. A repair initiation technique which works well with one type of linguistic error may not work with a different type, as we have seen above.

I would now like to demonstrate that the teacher is balancing multiple and sometimes conflicting demands. As Edmondson (1985: 162) puts it, 'The complexity of the classroom is such that several things may be going on publicly through talk at the same time.' The teacher is orienting to four separate (though related) concerns simultaneously.

1) The teacher has to orient to an overall pedagogical plan. In this particular lesson (Carr 2006 book 14) the overall aim is to revise a number of prepositions of place. In this particular episode of the lesson, the teacher is asking questions to prepare students to undertake a communication activity (they must spot 10 differences between 2 pictures) which will be done in pairs.
2) The teacher also responds to linguistic incorrectness in the individual learner's utterances and initiates repair on them.
3) The teacher must also orient to the other learners in the class. One problem faced by teachers is that individual learners often produce responses which are inaudible or incomprehensible to the other students in the class. So in lines 5 and 17 of extract 12 the teacher is simultaneously displaying approved versions of learner utterances so that the other learners are able to follow the flow of the interaction and are also able to receive correctly formed linguistic input. The learners are then asked to repeat the target string of forms so the teacher is able to evaluate their production.
4) As noted above, language has a unique dual role in the L2 classroom in that it is both the vehicle and object, both the process and product of interaction. Students may respond to language as vehicle or as object, to the linguistic form or the propositional content of what the teacher says. In the above extract, the teacher is attempting to repair the linguistic form (word order) of what L1 says, whereas the learners believe the problem to be related to propositional content (colour of shirt).

The above extract is a simple and straightforward classroom exercise. However, the turns that learners produce are often unpredictable and the teacher needs to analyse them instantly and respond to them on a number of levels. Even in very simple exercises, then, the pedagogical and interactional work which a teacher is involved in, on a turn-to-turn basis, can be very unpredictable, demanding and complex. Since L2 classroom interaction is organized around the relationship between pedagogy and interaction, it sometimes becomes difficult to separate pedagogy and interaction in analysis. They are in effect inextricably intertwined in a reflexive relationship, which is why it is argued that our analytical methodology needs to portray this relationship in full detail.

Conclusions

This chapter suggests that an understanding of the complex relationship between pedagogy and interaction is vital to an understanding of the process of instructed SLA, for two reasons. First, because the interactional architecture of the language classroom is based on this relationship. Secondly, because whatever teachers and learners say in L2 classroom interaction displays an analysis of the current state of the relationship between pedagogy and interaction.

A further conclusion of this chapter is that the relationship between pedagogy and interaction is a non-linear one. Any pedagogical phenomena (e.g., recasts) which occur in L2 classroom interaction are inextricably entwined in a complex and mutually dependent relationship with many other phenomena on a number of different levels. This has strong implications for SLA research involving interaction. An implicit assumption is often made that a linear connection can be made between pedagogical constructs (e.g., recasts) and their occurrence in interaction and that these can be extracted from their interactional environment for quantification without analysis. This chapter suggests that there are fundamental problems with such assumptions.

However, a solution would be to adopt a multi-strategy research approach with research processes in two stages. The first stage would involve conducting a CA microanalysis of each extract as an instance of discourse in its own right. Any definitions and categorizations used in the study would have to be generated inductively, bottom-up from the data. In the second stage the analysed interactional data (e.g., recasts) could be used for quantitative treatment with their construct validity assured. There is therefore a clear role or 'vacant slot' which CA can play in that part of the SLA project which relates to classroom interactional data. Such a preliminary stage is particularly necessary with phenomena like recasts, which occur 'incidentally' as and when errors occur, are therefore bound to be unique and heterogenous and would certainly have to be analysed as individual instances before quantification.

The study of the relationship between pedagogy and interaction in L2 classrooms is very much in its infancy and there are many issues which need to be explored. Even in its infancy, however, there are indications that this emergent field needs to be located within the broader field of complexity theory (Larsen-Freeman and Cameron 2008). Complexity theory is an interdisciplinary methodology to explain the non-linear interactions of microscopic elements in complex systems (Mainzer 1997). A defining characteristic of a complex system is that its behaviour emerges from the interactions of its components (Larsen-Freeman and Cameron 2008: 9–10) and so complexity theory is always looking for a holistic or ecological perspective rather than a reductionist or atomistic one (Gleick 1993: 7). The phenomena I have described in this chapter are non-linear, complex and emergent in this sense. They relate to a number of areas which have been studied in complexity theory and can be integrated under its umbrella, namely society, culture, learning, the mind and language.

Notes

1. Coughlan and Duff (1994) use the terms 'task' and 'activity' to express the same distinction.
2. Off-task talk is any talk taking place during the task-in-process which is not related to the task-as-workplan.
3. Stimulated recall would be another possibility.
4. Of course, not all learner utterances are heard by a teacher.

9 The Relationship between Language Aptitude and Language Learning Motivation: Individual Differences from a Dynamic Systems Perspective

Zoltán Dörnyei

Language aptitude and language learning motivation have traditionally been seen as the primary individual difference (ID) variables in the study of a second/foreign language (L2), that is, the learner characteristics that have been found to exert the greatest amount of consistent influence on the SLA process. Although other ID factors such as cognitive/learning styles or learner beliefs have also received attention in the literature (see Dörnyei 2005), their impact on SLA has been negligible compared to that of the aptitude-motivation dyad. The magnitude of the influence exerted by aptitude and motivation depends on how these constructs are assessed and what the criterion measures are, but correlations between aptitude and L2 attainment indices are often as high as 0.50 and meaningful correlations with motivation have usually been reported within the range of 0.30–0.40. However, regarding the assessment of motivation, if (a) the criterion measure is related to learner behaviours rather than holistic proficiency measures (e.g., the extent of learners' participation in a task rather than, say, TOEFL scores); (b) the motivation measure is situated (i.e., it focuses on aspects of the learners' classroom experience); and (c) the co-construction of motivation by the participants is taken into account (i.e., by pooling the motivation of both learners in a task performed by dyads), then correlations with motivational factors can exceed 0.50 and multiple correlations involving all the assessed motives together can reach 0.70 (Dörnyei 2002; Kormos and Dörnyei 2004).

A common conception of aptitude and motivation has been that the former is the most important *cognitive* variable, while motivation is the primary *affective* factor shaping second language acquisition/learning (see, e.g., Gardner and MacIntyre 1992, 1993). As a result, including both an aptitude and a motivation measure in a research paradigm has typically been seen as a fairly comprehensive characterization of the learner's contribution to the SLA process. Thus, the current task of addressing the relationship between aptitude and motivation in this chapter goes beyond merely looking at two specific ID factors – it concerns, in effect, the broader examination of how individual difference variables in general are related to each other and how they exert their cumulative impact. As we will see below, answering these questions will lead us to the re-analysis of the overall nature of learner characteristics within the learner-environment-learning complex.

In the following discussion I first provide a brief outline of the history of L2 research on aptitude and motivation, highlighting emerging problems about the traditional conceptualization of the concepts. I then present a novel approach to understanding learner characteristics which replaces the modular view of individual differences involving multiple discrete ID factors with a tripartite system of the human mind that comprises *cognition, affect* and *motivation* within a dynamic systems framework. I will argue that from this perspective identifying 'pure' individual difference factors has only limited value; instead, a potentially more fruitful approach is to focus on certain higher-order combinations of different attributes – or trait complexes – that act as integrated wholes. I conclude this chapter by introducing three attribute complex candidates for the new approach, *aptitude/trait complexes, interests* conceptualized in a broad sense and *possible selves*.

A Brief History of Language Aptitude Research

Following the success of intelligence research in educational psychology at the beginning of the twentieth century, language aptitude research was initiated in the USA in the 1920s (for a historical overview, see Spolsky 1995). The main objective of the pioneering language aptitude tests was, similar to the first intelligence test developed by Binet and Simon in France in 1905, to increase the cost-effectiveness of language education in the public school system by identifying slow L2 learners. This prognosis aspect of aptitude tests also motivated the second wave of aptitude test development 30 years later, in the 1950s and 1960s, which produced the two best-known language aptitude batteries, the *Modern Language Aptitude Test* (MLAT; Carroll and Sapon 1959), and the *Pimsleur Language Aptitude Battery* (PLAB; Pimsleur 1966). These batteries became so widespread both in research and in various educational practices that the L2 research community developed the tacit understanding that language aptitude is simply what language aptitude tests measure. From a theoretical point of view this has been somewhat problematic given that both the MLAT and the PLAB had been developed without any well-established underlying theoretical construct, largely through a trial-and-error process that involved administering a great number of different tasks to learners and selecting those that discriminated best between good language learners and their slower peers (Dörnyei 2005).

So, what exactly is 'language aptitude'? Most scholars would agree that the concept covers a range of different cognitive factors making up a composite measure that can, in turn, be referred to as the learner's overall capacity to master a foreign language. In other words, foreign language aptitude is not a unitary factor but rather a complex of 'basic abilities that are essential to facilitate foreign language learning' (Carroll and Sapon 1959: 14). In one of the best-known taxonomies, Carroll (1981: 105) proposed that the language aptitude construct comprised four constituent abilities:

1. *Phonetic coding ability*, which is considered the most important component and is defined as 'an ability to identify distinct sounds, to form associations between these sounds and symbols representing them, and to retain these associations'.
2. *Grammatical sensitivity*, which is 'the ability to recognize the grammatical functions of words (or other linguistic entities) in sentence structures'.
3. *Rote learning ability*, which is the 'ability to learn associations between sounds and meaning rapidly and efficiently, and to retain these associations'.
4. *Inductive language learning ability*, which is 'the ability to infer or induce the rules governing a set of language materials, given samples of language materials that permit such inferences'.

Carroll's (1981) taxonomy was derived from extensive *post hoc* analyses of MLAT scores and was, therefore, inevitably determined by the composition of the actual MLAT tasks – indeed, other scholars who derived their taxonomies from using other aptitude tests produced different theoretical constructs (e.g., Pimsleur 1966). As a result, even though the composite measures yielded by language aptitude batteries consistently explained a significant amount of variance in learning achievement, simply equating these composite test scores with 'language aptitude' was seen as increasingly unsatisfactory because the notion of language aptitude defined in this way was too broad an umbrella term, referring to an unspecified mixture of cognitive variables (Dörnyei 2009b). Therefore, scholars investigating specific cognitive abilities such as working memory (e.g., Miyake and Friedman 1998) or word recognition (e.g., Dufva and Voeten 1999) started to avoid using the term altogether. Indeed, the common theme in the various post-Carroll research directions has been the examination of the SLA-specific impact of specific cognitive factors and subprocesses, thus going beyond the use of the language aptitude metaphor (see Dörnyei 2005). For recent reviews of language aptitude research, see Ranta (2008) and Robinson (in press).

A Brief History of L2 Learning Motivation Research

Many overviews exist to describe the history of L2 motivation research from its genesis at the end of the 1950s in Canada by the work of Robert Gardner and Wallace Lambert (1959) to the most contemporary process-oriented or self-based approaches (see e.g., Clément and Gardner 2001; Dörnyei 2005; Dörnyei and Ushioda in press; MacIntyre 2002; MacIntyre et al. 2009; Ushioda and Dörnyei 2009). These reviews vary somewhat in their emphases, because the scope of the various approaches of understanding what motivates language learners to initiate and sustain the lengthy process of mastering an L2 encompasses a wide range of different theoretical perspectives. Gardner and his colleagues' initial stance involved a social-psychological perspective and the motivation construct they developed was centred around language attitudinal variables. The key component of Gardner's (1985) theory was the *integrative motive*, which concerns a positive interpersonal/affective disposition towards the L2 group and the desire to interact with and even become similar to valued members of that community. It implies an openness to and respect for other cultural groups and ways of life; in the extreme, it might involve complete identification with the community and possibly even withdrawal from one's original group.

In the 1990s there was a broadening of perspectives in L2 motivational research, exploring a number of different motivational dimensions originally introduced in educational psychology (for a review, see Dörnyei 2001). This 'cross-fertilisation' led to an unprecedented boom in L2 motivation studies and a variety of new models and approaches were put forward in the literature, resulting in what Gardner and Tremblay (1994) called a 'motivational renaissance'. A common feature of these new research attempts was the move towards a more *situated approach* to the study of motivation, examining how the immediate learning context influences the learners' overall disposition and how motivation, in turn, effects concrete learning processes within a classroom context. It was argued that the classroom environment had a much stronger motivational impact than had been proposed before, highlighting the significance of motives associated with the L2 course, the L2 teacher and the learner group.

Thus, by the end of the 1990s motivation research was characterized by a colourful spectrum of diverse theoretical strands and constructs, and in the absence of a 'gravitational centre' scholars often followed a 'pick-and-mix' method in conceptualizing motivation for their particular research purposes. This eclectic background provided fertile ground for theoretical developments, giving rise to a number of salient research programmes: Kim Noels and her colleagues (e.g., Noels 2003, 2009; Noels et al. 1999, 2001) implemented Deci and Ryan's (1985) well-known *self-determination theory* for the purpose of studying SLA, examining how the various intrinsic/extrinsic components were related to orientations developed in L2 research, and how the learners' level of self-determination (i.e., autonomous self-regulation) was affected by various classroom practices. MacIntyre and his colleagues (e.g., MacIntyre et al. 1998, 2003) adapted McCroskey's notion of L1 *willingness to communicate* (WTC) to the study of L2 communication. Other researchers such as Dörnyei (2000, 2001; Dörnyei and Ottó 1998) Ushioda (2001) and Williams and Burden (1997) adopted a *process-oriented perspective*, highlighting the fact that an individual's motivation is never stable but continuously shows a certain degree of fluctuation. Still others linked motivation with various aspects of the learner's *identity*, either by adopting a postmodern, poststructuralist approach (e.g., Norton 2000, 2001; Pavlenko 2002; Ushioda 2007) or by drawing on social psychological research on the self (e.g., Higgins 1987, 1998; Markus and Nurius 1986) in conceptualizing *motivational self-guides* (e.g., Dörnyei 2005, 2009a) – I will come back to this latter strand below when discussing motivation-cognition overlaps and again later when describing higher-order amalgams of learner characteristics.

Problems with the Modular View of Individual Difference Variables

As the previous sections illustrated, the conceptualizations of language aptitude and motivation have been diverse over the years, and in fact, in a book-length overview of individual differences I have concluded that 'all the variables described in this book are either in the process of, or in desperate need of, theoretical "restructuring"' (Dörnyei 2005: 218). Yet, at that stage I did not question the general concept of modular ID variables being the core building blocks of learner characteristics. Indeed, the notion of ID factors appeared to be solid and the ID concept had been well established in SLA research in a relatively straightforward manner: IDs were usually seen as background learner variables that modified and personalized the overall trajectory of the language acquisition processes, accounting for *why, how long and how hard* (motivation), *how well* (aptitude), *how proactively* (learning strategies) and *in what way* (learning styles) the learner engaged in the learning process.

Recently, however, I have come to a new understanding of individual differences and argued (Dörnyei 2009b) that the seemingly comprehensive and straightforward picture of IDs being stable and monolithic learner traits that concern distinct learner characteristics is part of an idealized 'individual differences myth' that may not hold up against scientific scrutiny. As far as I can see, the basic problem is that if we take a situated and process-oriented perspective of SLA – which I think we ought to – we simply cannot fail to realize that the various learner attributes are neither stable nor context-independent, but display a considerable amount of variation from time to time and from situation to situation. Furthermore, and what is particularly relevant to the current chapter, a closer look at both language aptitude and motivation reveals that neither construct is monolithic but is, instead, made up of a number of constituent components.

Kosslyn and Smith (2000) explain that cognitive abilities in general can be divided into 'lower' and 'higher' brain functions: Lower functions such as early perception and motor control rely on a relatively small collection of processes that display straightforward interactions. In contrast, higher functions are made up of the integrated operation of a relatively large numbers of processes, which may themselves have complex internal structures. It is clear that the ID variables that SLA research has been interested in – such as language aptitude and motivation – are complex, higher-order attributes, which was already recognized in the literature by the fact that – as shown above – neither language aptitude, nor L2 motivation has been seen as uniform, heterogeneous factors but rather composite measures. This is in line with Kosslyn and Smith's (2000) argument that higher-order learner characteristics comprise a selection of hierarchically organized and dynamically interacting sub-components.

Once we take such a multicomponential view of L2 ID factors, however, we are forced to move even further in our thinking because a closer look reveals that many (if not most) learner characteristics mentioned in the literature involve at one level or another the cooperation of components whose nature is very different from that of the main attribute in question – for example, motivational factors may involve cognitive constituents – resulting in 'hybrid' attributes. This means that not only is the stable and context-independent nature of ID variables highly doubtful, but there are also serious questions about the whole theoretical foundation of the traditional view of individual differences as a modular collective of distinct ID factors. As a result, over the past two years I have come to conclude that the traditional conception of learner characteristics fuelled by the 'individual differences myth' does not do justice to the dynamic, fluid and continuously fluctuating nature of learner factors and neither does it account for the complex internal and external interactions that we can observe in higher-order intellectual functions (for specific illustrations of such interactions within SLA, see the next section below). The following description of motivation by Ellis and Larsen-Freeman (2006: 563) is, I believe, characteristic of ID variables in general: 'Motivation is less a trait than fluid play, an ever-changing one that emerges from the processes of interaction of many agents, internal and external, in the ever-changing complex world of the learner.'

As a result of these considerations, I have recently proposed the adoption of a new dynamic systems perspective on individual differences (Dörnyei 2009b), according to which individual variation in performance is not so much a function of the strength of any individual determinant (e.g., aptitude or motivation) as of the way by which the complex system of all the relevant factors works together. I will describe this dynamic view in more detail below, but before doing so let us have a specific look at the interaction and overlap of the two key learner characteristics in focus in this chapter, language aptitude – or more generally, cognition – and motivation.

Cognition-Motivation Interaction and Overlap in SLA Research

As mentioned in the introduction, a common conception of aptitude and motivation has been that the former is the most important *cognitive* variable, while motivation is the primary *affective* factor shaping SLA. They have traditionally been seen as distinct from each other with no interaction or overlap, and this view was formalized in Robert Gardner's socio-educational model of second language learning (Gardner 1985, 2005; Gardner and MacIntyre 1992, 1993), according to which 'there are two primary individual difference variables involved in language learning, viz., ability and motivation. These two factors are expected to be relatively independent because some students high in ability may be high or low in motivation for any host of reasons, and vice versa' (Gardner 2005: 5).

This traditional view has been questioned recently on a number of accounts. To start with, strictly speaking there is no such thing as 'language aptitude' or 'motivation', because we have seen above that both constructs are umbrella terms subsuming a rather diverse range of factors. Therefore, proposing that aptitude and motivation are the two lynchpins of individual differences is problematic in itself. Furthermore, there is an obvious second concern with the cognitive/affective dichotomy of aptitude and motivation, namely that almost all influential contemporary motivation theories in psychology are cognitive in nature and affective (i.e., emotional) issues hardly ever feature on motivation research agendas. As Schumann (2004: 3) has concluded, 'motivation is not independent of cognition (as it is frequently treated in SLA research), but instead it is part of cognition, and therefore, there can be no "cognitive" approaches to SLA that do not include motivation.' If this is so, however, in what way is motivation different from language aptitude, which – as we have seen above – is the collective term used to refer to a mixture of cognitive factors?

The aptitude-motivation distinction becomes even more untenable if we look at the details of specific motivation constructs. What we find is that at one level or another certain established cognitive constructs play a salient role in determining the motivational outcome. Let me describe three examples of this motivation-cognition interplay: 'flow' (Csikszentmihalyi 2000; Egbert 2003), 'motivational task processing' (Dörnyei 2003; Dörnyei and Tseng 2009) and the 'ideal L2 self' (Dörnyei 2005, 2009a).

Flow

The experience of 'flow' is a theoretically intriguing and intuitively appealing phenomenon, making its chief advocate, Mihaly Csikszentmihalyi (1990), both a bestselling author and a leading international psychologist. The popularity of the concept is due to the fact that it concerns a highly valued experience that many of us have had in the past: Flow entails a state of intensive involvement in and focused concentration on a task that feels so absorbing that people often compare it to being outside everyday reality. This state is, however, not the kind of passive spiritual experience that some people can evoke through meditation; to the contrary, flow is experienced while people are at their most active or creative, being engaged in completing an absorbing task. Thus, flow can be seen as a heightened level of motivated task engagement; in many ways it is the optimal task experience. It happens when, faced with a challenging activity, people are fully aware of what needs to be done and how, and at the same time they are confident that the task is doable and their skills are sufficient to succeed. An often mentioned feature of a fully fledged flow experience is that the extent of absorption can be such that people even lose self-consciousness and a track of time. While this may sound like a science-fiction fantasy, all we need to do is observe children (and even adults) playing computer games to realize that flow is a very real phenomenon.

In a pioneering study on the role of flow in SLA, Egbert (2003) found that the task conditions under which flow occurs can be organized along four dimensions: (1) there is a perceived balance of task challenge and participant skills during the task, (2) the task offers opportunities for intense concentration and the participants' attention is focused on the pursuit of clear task goals, (3) the participants find the task intrinsically interesting or authentic and (4) the participants perceive a sense of control over the task process and outcomes. These underlying dimensions display a balanced mixture of cognitive and motivational constituents (see also Guastello et al. 1999): While flow is usually discussed under the motivation rubric as a specific type of intrinsic motivation (explained by the experience of enjoyment that is one of the key features of flow), it is fundamentally determined by cognitive factors such as the appraisal of the challenge of the activity; the self-appraisal of the level of the individual's skills and competence involved in the activity; a firm sense of control over the completion of the task; clarity about the task goals, and focused attention. The reason why flow is a particularly good example for the integrated operation of motivational and cognitive aspects is that the flow experience can only occur if all these conditions are met; that is, the cognitive factors are prerequisites rather than mere modifiers of the motivational phenomenon.

Motivational Task Processing

In a recent study, Dörnyei and Tseng (2009) examined the validity of a theoretical construct that I proposed in 2003 concerning motivational task processing (Dörnyei 2003). As I argued then, the motivational dynamics of learning tasks are dependent on how the participating learners process the various motivational stimuli they encounter and, as a result, how they activate certain necessary motivational strategies. The construct suggests that L2 learners are engaged in an ongoing appraisal and response process, involving their continuous monitoring and evaluating how well they are doing in a task, and then making possible amendments if something seems to be going amiss. This process can be represented through a dynamic *task processing system* that consists of three interrelated mechanisms: *task execution, appraisal* and *action control* (see Figure 1).

Task execution refers to the learners' engagement in task-supportive learning behaviours in accordance with the task goals and the action plan that were either provided by the teacher (through the task instructions) or drawn up by the student or the task team. In other words, this is the level of actual 'learning'. *Task appraisal* refers to the learner's continuous processing of the multitude of stimuli coming from the environment regarding the progress made towards the action outcome, comparing the actual performance with the predicted or hoped-for ones or with the likely performance that alternative action sequences would

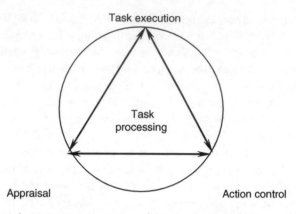

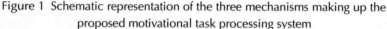

Figure 1 Schematic representation of the three mechanisms making up the
proposed motivational task processing system

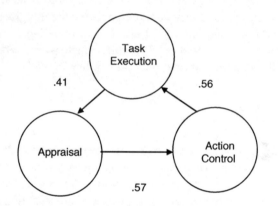

Figure 2 Structural equation diagram of motivational task processing
(Dörnyei and Tseng 2009)

offer. *Action control* processes denote self-regulatory mechanisms that are called
into force in order to enhance, scaffold or protect learning-specific action; active
use of such mechanisms may 'save' the action when ongoing monitoring reveals
that progress is slowing, halting or backsliding.

Dörnyei and Tseng's (2009) validation study has involved a structural equation modelling (SEM) analysis of the proposed construct, and has confirmed the
circular relationship of the three components (see Figure 2): Signals from the
appraisal system concerning task execution trigger the need to activate relevant
action control strategies, which in turn further facilitate the execution process.
Thus, a process that is primarily motivational in nature relies heavily on a cognitive appraisal component. Interestingly, the inclusion of appraisal in broader
non-cognitive constructs is not unique to this example because, for example,

most theoretical conceptualizations of emotion contain a cognitive appraisal component that is responsible for the evaluation of the situation that evokes an emotional response (Lewis 2005).

The Ideal L2 Self

The *ideal L2 self* is the central component of a new conceptualization of L2 motivation, the 'L2 Motivational Self System', which I proposed in 2005 (Dörnyei 2005). The main objective of developing the new construct had been to synthesize a number of influential approaches in the field (e.g., Gardner 1985; Noels 2003; Ushioda 2001) and at the same time also to broaden the scope of L2 motivation theory to make it applicable in diverse language learning environments in the current, increasingly globalized world (for a detailed description, see Dörnyei 2009a). The ideal L2 self is the L2-specific facet of one's *ideal self*, which refers to the representation of the attributes that someone would ideally like to possess (i.e., representation of hopes, aspirations or wishes) (see Higgins 1987, 1998; Markus and Nurius 1986). The theory suggests that if the person we would like to become speaks an L2, the ideal L2 self is a powerful motivator to learn the L2 because of the desire to reduce the discrepancy between our actual and ideal selves. This is expressed in everyday speech when we talk about someone following, or living up to, their dreams.

Thus, the ideal L2 self acts as a future self-guide, providing incentive, direction and impetus for action. However, past research has shown that the motivational capacity of this self-guide is not automatic but depends on a number of conditions; accordingly, the ideal L2 self is an effective motivator only if:

1. the learner *has* a desired future self-image;
2. which is elaborate and vivid;
3. which is perceived as *plausible* and is in harmony – or at least does not clash – with the expectations of the learner's family, peers and other elements of the social environment;
4. which is *regularly activated* in his/her working self-concept;
5. which is accompanied by relevant and effective *procedural strategies* that act as a *roadmap* towards the goal;
6. which also contains elaborate information about the *negative consequences* of *not* achieving the desired end-state.

What is important from our perspective is that the effective functioning of the ideal L2 self is dependent on the operation of several underlying cognitive components, most notably on the learners' self-appraisal of their capabilities and evaluation of the affordances of their personal circumstances in order to anchor their vision in a sense of realistic expectations. As Pizzolato (2006: 59) puts it, 'The relation between what students want to become and what students actually become may be mediated by what students feel they are able to become'. In addition, learners also need a repertoire of task-related strategies that are activated by the priming of the ideal L2 self: Effective future self-guides need to come as part of a 'package', consisting of an imagery/vision component and a repertoire of appropriate plans, scripts and self-regulatory strategies (Dörnyei 2009a). In a study examining the relationship between motivation, cognition and action, Locke (2000) calls the knowledge of such strategies 'task knowledge' and he also argues that this knowledge illustrates the interdependence of cognition and motivation. This integrated operation of cognition and motivation is expressed clearly by Cross and Markus (1994: 434–435):

> A possible self may serve as a node in an associative network of
> experiences, strategies and self-knowledge. In this way, the possible self
> may link effective steps and strategies . . . with beliefs about one's ability
> and competence in the domain.

Cognition-Motivation Overlap in Cognitive Psychology

The three examples described above offer specific illustrations of the interplay and cooperation of cognition and motivation in SLA, but this overlap is not restricted to L2 research. In the psychological literature we find many examples for motivation-cognition interfaces, and in a study specifically focusing on the integration of motivation and cognition, Bickhard (2003) argues that the common view of modelling motivation and cognition as distinct processes – 'motivation as some form of initiating and directing – pushing and pulling – behaviour, and cognition as the manipulation of encoded representations in memory' (p. 41) – is inaccurate and counterproductive because it makes it difficult to understand interrelationships between them or their interactions in behaviour and development. This claim was further substantiated in a high-profile volume edited by Dai and Sternberg (2004) on *'Motivation, Emotion, and Cognition: Integrative Perspectives on Intellectual Functioning and Development'*. As the title suggests, the contributors of this book – some of the best-known contemporary cognitive and educational psychologists – set out to present a powerful case for the need to view cognition and motivation as two interlocked facets of an integrated mental system, with emotion being a third constituent. In the Introduction, the editors summarize this objective as follows:

> In this introduction chapter, we attempt to make a case that intellectual
> functioning and development never occur as solely cognitive events but

involve motivation and emotion, or the whole person vis-à-vis adaptive pressures and challenges. Going beyond cognitivism does not imply that motivational and emotional issues are more important than or as important as cognitive processes and mechanisms. Rather, our point is that without taking into consideration the motivational and emotional aspects of intellectual functioning and development, we cannot even properly understand cognitive processes involved. Reducing intellectual functioning and development to merely cognitive matters is simply no longer tenable both on theoretical grounds and in light of empirical evidence. (Dai and Sternberg 2004: 29)

Following the Introduction, the volume contains 12 further chapters on various cognition-motivation-emotion interfaces, ranging from motivational effects on attention, cognition and performance (Dweck et al. 2004) to the role of interest in combining affective and cognitive functioning (Hidi et al. 2004). Thus, this volume opens up a whole range of new perspectives and research agendas, providing support for Linnenbrink and Pintrich's (2004: 83) conclusion that the 'relation between affect and engagement as well as cognitive processing suggests that there may be a complex interplay among affect, cognition, and motivation that needs to be further investigated'. Although looking at cognition and motivation (and affect) in such a blended manner is still a very recent research orientation, it can potentially offer substantial gains because the evidence presented in the above volume and elsewhere in the literature leaves no doubt that the availability/allocation of cognitive resources is very closely linked to the direction, intensity and persistence of action, that is, with the traditionally conceived central motivational domains.

A Dynamic Systems Approach to Understanding Learner Characteristics in SLA

Having illustrated the reality of the cognition/motivation interface in SLA and having shown that the separation of cognition and motivation has been increasingly seen as an outdated and inaccurate conceptualization in cognitive and educational psychology, let us return to the question of adopting a new, dynamic systems perspective on individual differences as suggested earlier in this chapter. As I have argued (Dörnyei 2009b), the 'individual differences myth' claims that while the main trajectory of SLA is determined by language acquisitional processes, relatively stable and monolithic learner attributes – called individual differences – cause systematic deviations from the overall trend. However, when we look at them more closely, individual learner characteristics appear to be rather different from the meaning we tend to assign to them in everyday parlance or in traditional professional discourse: They are not at all stable but show salient temporal and situational variation, and they are not monolithic either but constitute complex constellations that are made up of different parts that interact with each other and the environment synchronically and diachronically. As a result, simple cause-effect relationships are unable to do justice to these multi-level interactions and temporal changes. Instead, I would suggest, individual learner variation can be better accounted for in terms of the operation of a complex dynamic system in the sense that high-level mental attributes and functions are determined by an intricate set of interconnected components that continuously evolve over time and which also interact with the environment in an ongoing manner. The value of each constituent keeps changing depending on the overall state of the system and in response to external influences, making ID factors dynamic system variables. Therefore, the logical next step of conceptualizing individual differences is to attempt to reframe them within a dynamic systems perspective.

Although describing the nature and the operation of dynamic systems goes beyond the scope of this chapter (for L2-related overviews, see e.g., de Bot, Lowie and Verspoor 2007; Dörnyei 2009b; Ellis and Larsen-Freeman 2006; Larsen-Freeman and Cameron 2008; van Geert 2008), we can conclude that, broadly speaking, a system can be considered dynamic if it has two or more elements that are interlinked with each other and which also change in time. In such systems the complex interferences between the multiple system components' developmental trajectories make the system's behaviour unpredictable as it follows non-linear changes. In the social sciences, dynamic systems have been discussed by four interrelated theories: *dynamic systems theory, complexity theory, chaos theory* and *emergentism,* which can be seen as overlapping strands within the same broad theoretical family, each examining complex, dynamic, non-linear systems. While the four theories are associated with somewhat different research traditions and priorities, the labels describing them have not been used consistently across disciplines and in most cases the four theories converge in the same general non-linear systems approach.

Dynamic systems display – by definition – continuous fluctuation, yet a very important point from the perspective of this chapter is the fact that there are also times of seeming stability in most systems, when the system behaviour seems to be predictable. How can we explain these non-dynamic, settled states within a dynamic systems framework? The answer is provided by the concept of *attractors* and *attractor states*. These refer to preferred patterns to which the system is attracted (hence the name) and in which the elements are coherent and resist change. Not every system reaches such settled attractor states, but if there are strong attractors in place, a relatively wide range of starting points will eventually converge on a much smaller set of states because the process unfolds in the direction of the attractor (Nowak et al. 2005). In contrast, unstable phases in the development of the system are characterized by weak or changing attractors. In the light of these considerations, it is not unreasonable to suggest that higher-order ID variables can be seen as powerful attractors that act as stabilizing forces; for example, a strong goal, incentive, talent or interest can definitely bring stability to the system of learner characteristics/behaviour, and this stability, in turn, translates into consistency and predictability (see Dörnyei 2009b).

A Tripartite Framework of Learner Characteristics

Given the dynamics of learner characteristics and the complex and interlocking nature of higher-order cognitive human functioning described above, is there any justification for proposing any macro-structuring principles to individual variation in human mental functions such as separating certain cognitive and motivational functions? In other words, if we look at the tapestry of human mental characteristics as an interwoven and fluid system, does it make any sense to keep speaking about any subsets of these characteristics (such as motivational or cognitive factors) as distinct entities? I believe that the answer is yes, because there is one perspective from which such a separation is justifiable: the *phenomenological* (i.e., experiential) perspective. Motivation and cognition can be differentiated from each other because they 'feel' different: If we want something, we have the distinct experience of 'wanting' it and we can even grade this experience in terms of its strength (e.g., *I can hardly wait . . .* or *I really-really-really want it!*); and similarly, cognition/thoughts also have their distinct experiential feel, which is revealed in phrases such as 'cold intellect', capturing a key feature of cognition, namely that it has no valence (i.e., it is not gradable in terms of intensity either in the positive or negative directions).

It is important to note here that in addition to these two basic types of mental functions (i.e., cognition and motivation), we can also identify a third salient phenomenological category, *emotions* or *affect* (e.g., fear, anger, distress or joy), that is clearly distinguishable from the previous two. Thus, although this chapter does not cover affective issues (for a review, see Dörnyei 2009b), it needs to be pointed out that emotions constitute the third main dimension of learner-based characteristics, adding up to a comprehensive, tripartite framework. Each of the three mental dimensions can be viewed as dynamic subsystems that have continuous and complex interaction with each other and which cannot exist in isolation from one another. As Buck (2005: 198) put it, 'In their fully articulated forms, emotions imply cognitions imply motives imply emotions, and so on'.

Interestingly, scholars have traditionally divided mental processes along this tripartite structure. Scherer (1995) explains that already Plato proposed that the human soul contained three components: *cognition* (corresponding to thought and reason and associated with the ruling class of philosophers, kings and statesmen), *emotion/passion* (corresponding to anger or spirited higher ideal emotions and associated with the warrior class) and *conation/motivation* (associated with impulses, cravings, desires and associated with the lower classes). This division into 'an appetitive part that produces various irrational desires, a spirited part that produces anger and other feelings, and a reasoning part that permits reflection and rationality' (Parrott 2004: 7) has traditionally been referred to as the 'trilogy of mind', reflecting three interrelated but conceptually distinct mental systems.

In conclusion, I have been arguing above that the complex of learner characteristics can be best understood at the interface of two somewhat conflicting perspectives: On the one hand, given the integrated nature of mental functions, the modular view of individual differences – consisting of stable and monolithic personality traits – is untenable. This would suggest that there is not much point in examining factors such as language aptitude or motivation independently of each other. On the other hand, I believe that it is worth maintaining a broad, phenomenologically validated organizing framework of cognition, motivation and affect, as long as we recognize that these dimensions are best seen as interlocking complex subsystems.

Higher-Order Amalgams of Learner Characteristics

Where do all the above considerations leave us? What is the main advantage of introducing a dynamic systems perspective in the study of learner differences? It certainly won't make life easier for us, since thinking of the human mind in such an integrated way is admittedly rather difficult (for a discussion of this difficulty, see Dörnyei in press). Indeed, our natural tendency is to isolate the most relevant subsystem or factor and try to establish its impact on the phenomenon in focus (which is why we have so many studies on 'motivation and SLA' or 'language aptitude and SLA'). However, the problem with such a discrete treatment of dispositional attributes, as Lubinski and Webb (2003) conclude, is that examining them individually is often challenging and unfruitful, because the manner in which each operates depends on the full constellation of personal characteristics. As these authors conclude, even people with outwardly similar ID patterns can travel very different paths as a result of some difference in a personality constituent that is seemingly irrelevant or of secondary importance – this is exactly what dynamic systems theory would expect. This would imply, then, that trying to isolate discrete ID factors such as various aptitude or motivational components or cognitive styles is unlikely to take us too far. Instead, it is my belief that the best way forward is to identify higher-level amalgams or constellations of cognition, motivation and affect that are relatively stable (i.e., are governed by a strong attractor) and which act as 'wholes'. In other words, and related to the specific topic of this chapter, if we can identify optimal combinations of cognitive and motivational (and emotional) factors, these can have the potential to work as powerful attractors, which would make the system of learner characteristics/behaviour predictable and therefore researchable.

Do we know of any such ID complexes from the literature? We do, and it is in fact a strong validity argument for the theoretical considerations described above that ID complexes of this sort constitute some of the most promising cutting-edge findings in the study of learner characteristics both in educational psychology and in SLA research. In the following I describe three such constructs: *aptitude/trait complexes*, the broad notion of *interests* and *possible selves*.

Aptitude/Trait Complexes

A central issue in ID research over the past decade, and one that has emerged in aptitude research in particular, has been the suggestion that although isolated ID factors and personality traits are often shown to have a substantial impact on learning outcomes, certain optimal combinations of such traits are likely to have more predictive power than traits in isolation. One researcher in particular, Richard Snow, was influential in highlighting the potential importance of such ID constellations, or as he called them, *aptitude complexes* (for an overview of the legacy of Richard Snow written by his former students and associates, see Corno et al. 2002). His initiative has been taken up by several of his followers because, 'Although isolated traits often have . . . substantial impact on learning outcomes, it may be that combinations of traits have more predictive power than traits in isolation' (Ackerman 2003, p. 92).

The best-known work to date along these lines has been Phillip Ackerman and his colleagues' conceptualization of 'trait complexes' (e.g., Ackerman 2003, 2005; Ackerman and Heggestad 1997; Ackerman and Kanfer 2004). These scholars have identified four broad trait complexes, called 'social', 'clerical/conventional', 'science/math', and 'intellectual/cultural'. They are made up of various combinations of cognitive abilities, personality dimensions and interests, and they function as 'wholes' in affecting the direction and intensity of the investment of cognitive effort and the type of knowledge/expertise acquired during adulthood. Interestingly, Ackerman (2005) stresses that these complexes are only the beginning, because they represent 'only a small sampling of underlying cognitive, affective, and conative communalities' (p. 104). Future, more principled research might be able to extend the current conceptualizations and may add new ability trait operationalizations; Ackerman mentions 'emotional intelligence' as a likely candidate for the latter (for more information on emotional intelligence, see Dewaele et al. 2008).

In SLA, the notion of trait complexes has been addressed by Peter Robinson's (e.g., 2001, 2002, 2007) research programme on language aptitude-treatment interaction. He conceptualized language aptitude as the sum of lower-level abilities, grouped into cognitive factors, which differentially support learning in various learning situations/conditions. A particularly interesting feature of Robinson's proposal is his attempt to describe concrete sets of cognitive demands that can be associated with some basic learning types/tasks, and then to identify specific aptitude complexes to match these cognitive processing conditions. Robinson distinguished three conditions of exposure to input – implicit, incidental and explicit learning – and then discussed a number of *cognitive resources* (e.g., attentional or working memory capacity) and *primary abilities* (e.g., pattern recognition or processing speed) that combine to define sets of *higher-order abilities* directly involved in carrying out learning tasks (e.g., noticing the gap, or metalinguistic rule rehearsal). These second-order abilities can then be grouped into aptitude complexes that exert an optimal influence on learning in specific learning conditions, such as focus on form via recasts; incidental learning via oral or written content (by means of orally or typographically salient 'input floods'); and explicit rule learning.

Interest

The term 'interest' in the psychological literature is often used more broadly than, for example, the 'interest in foreign languages' category in Gardner's (1985) integrative motivation construct. It refers to a broad orientational dimension that has been found to be defined by six general interest themes: 'realistic' (working with things and tools), 'investigative' (scientific pursuits), 'artistic' (aesthetic pursuits and self-expression), 'social' (contact with and helping people), 'enterprising' (buying, marketing and selling), and 'conventional' (office practices and well-structured tasks) (Lubinski and Webb 2003). Some scholars have reduced these themes to two broad dimensions, 'people' versus 'things' and 'data' versus 'ideas', and the strength of the people/thing factor is evidenced by the fact that, as Lubinski and Webb (2003) describe, it displays some of the largest sex differences discovered by psychological science on a continuous dimension (with women towards the 'people' end of the cline, and men towards the 'things' end). Interests are heritable, are predictive of a broad spectrum of criteria in areas ranging from educational and vocational settings to activities in everyday life (hobbies and pastimes), and the concept appears to be theoretically more straightforward and temporarily more stable than several other ID factors.

Lubinski and Webb (2003) report an interesting longitudinal study in which they compared, over a period of 10 years, the developmental trajectory of three different types of profoundly gifted individuals. The three groups consisted of students who were (a) high on mathematical reasoning and relatively low on verbal reasoning; (b) high on verbal reasoning and relatively low on mathematical reasoning; and (c) high on both abilities. As could be expected, the abilities acted as strong attractors for long-term development, and differential interests were apparent in the three groups in their choice of favourite courses in high school and college, as well as in the awards and other accomplishments they achieved: high-math individuals tended to succeed in areas of science and technology, whereas high-verbal individuals tended to succeed in the humanities and arts. This study provides a clear illustration of how long-term interests are made up of a combination of cognitive and motivational factors.

Possible Selves

Possible selves represent the individuals' ideas of what they *might* become, what they *would like* to become and what they are *afraid of* becoming (Markus and Nurius 1986). The novelty of the possible self concept lies in the fact that it concerns how people conceptualize their as-yet unrealized potential and as such, it also draws on hopes, wishes and fantasies. In this sense, possible selves act as 'self-guides', reflecting a dynamic, forward-pointing conception that can explain how someone is moved from the present towards the future. From an educational perspective the most important possible self is the 'ideal self', which has already been described earlier when illustrating the cognition-motivation interaction in the L2 field. It was pointed out there that the ideal L2 self is a powerful motivator to learn the L2 because of the desire to reduce the discrepancy between our actual and ideal selves.

Although in my 'L2 Motivational Self System' (Dörnyei 2005) I emphasized the motivational capacity of the ideal L2 self, possible selves present broad, overarching constellations that blend together motivational, cognitive and affective areas. Already the originator of the concept, Hazel Markus (2006), pointed out that the possible self-structure could be seen as a 'dynamic interpretive matrix for thought, feeling and action' (p. xi), and I have demonstrated earlier that the ideal self does indeed have a salient cognitive component. In addition to this, MacIntyre et al. (2009) also highlight the emotional aspect of possible selves, because without a strong tie to the learner's emotional system, possible selves exist as 'cold cognition, and therefore lack motivational potency'

(p. 47). As the authors explain, 'When emotion is a prominent feature of a possible self, including a strong sense of fear, hope, or even obligation, a clear path exists by which to influence motivation and action' (p. 47).

Finally, this cognition-emotion-motivation amalgam features a further significant dimension, a salient *imagery* component: Markus and Nurius (1986) emphasize that possible selves involve tangible *images* and *senses*, as they are represented in the same imaginary and semantic way as the here-and-now self; that is, they are a *reality* for the individual: people can 'see' and 'hear' a possible self. In this sense, possible selves are not unlike visions – an Olympic athlete's ideal self is not merely an intellectual goal but a vision of him/herself walking into the Olympic Stadium, completing the race and then stepping onto the top of the podium. As Markus and Ruvolo (1989: 213) summarize, 'imaging one's own actions through the construction of elaborated possible selves achieving the desired goal may thus directly facilitate the translation of goals into intentions and instrumental actions', and a similar idea has been expressed by Wenger (1998: 176) when he described the concept of 'imagination':

> My use of the concept of imagination refers to a process of expanding
> our self by transcending our time and space and creating new images
> of the world and ourselves. Imagination in this sense is looking at an apple
> seed and seeing a tree. It is playing scales on a piano, and envisioning a
> concert hall.

Thus, in many ways it is the integration of fantasy with the self-concept construct that marks Markus and Nurius's (1986) work as truly innovative (Segal 2006). This is certainly the aspect that grasped my own attention when I first encountered this work, and this is, I believe, what makes the concept of possible selves a particularly powerful ID constellation that encompasses the whole spectrum of the human mind, from our thoughts and feelings to our senses.

Conclusions

I pointed out in the introduction of this chapter that the task of addressing the relationship between aptitude and motivation goes beyond merely looking at two specific ID factors, as it concerns, in effect, the broader examination of how individual difference variables in general are related to each other and how they exert their cumulative impact. I further argued that the traditional notion of individual difference factors conceived as stable and monolithic learner characteristics that act as modifying filters in the SLA process (i.e., the 'individual differences myth'), is untenable because it ignores the multicomponential nature of these higher-order attributes and because the constituent components continuously interact with each other and the environment, thereby changing and causing change, and subsequently displaying highly complex developmental patterns. The study of such complex constellations of factors requires a dynamic systems approach, and this perspective would suggest that identifying 'pure' individual difference factors has only limited value both from a theoretical and a practical point of view; instead, a potentially more fruitful approach is to focus on certain higher-order combinations of different attributes that act as integrated wholes.

In the light of this theoretical backdrop, specifying the relationship between language aptitude and motivation – which has been the specific theme of this chapter – requires a new, integrated approach whereby we focus on the blended operation of cognition and motivation rather than the discrete treatment of the two ID variables. Thus, I do not believe that it is a particularly worthwhile scientific endeavour to examine the impact of isolated areas of L2 aptitude or motivation; instead, we should try and identify viable constellations whereby the cognitive and the motivational (and also the emotional) subsystems of the human mind cooperate in a constructive manner. This chapter presented several concrete illustrations of the reality and validity of such an integrated approach and I do hope that these have convinced the readers that this admittedly difficult agenda is worth pursuing.

10 The Relationship between Strategic Behaviour and Language Learning Success

Ernesto Macaro

Some people are more successful (however this is defined) than others at learning a second language

Joan Rubin (1975: 41)

It is important to emphasize that in characterizing some students as less successful we are implying no judgement of their potential as learners, but are merely referring to the fact that at the time of our study they had not been successful learners of English, for any of a number of possible reasons

Green and Oxford (1995: 269)

Introduction

This chapter is about the relationship between independent and dependent variables in research in language learner strategies (LLS). It attempts to put forward an argument that, in this field of published work, researchers have not paid enough attention to one of the variables. The dependent variable in LLS research has to be, in the long run, success at second language learning. That is why we look at individual (and for that matter group) differences in terms of strategic behaviour. We wish to explore whether these differences are the underlying causes, as is often asserted, of the fact that unlike first language acquirers, second language learners vary enormously in terms of the success of their learning enterprise. However, as in the above comment by Joan Rubin in the mid-seventies suggests, there are many ways of defining success.

The LLS research field is marked by countless attempts at theorizing, defining and categorizing strategies and then with exploring their relationship to other variables such as motivation, aptitude, situated experiences, field-independence and language learning success. These relationships have been researched and analysed through factor analysis, cluster analysis, T-test, ANOVA, regression, questionnaire, interview, think-aloud protocols, case studies and combinations of these. However, very few researchers, it seems to me, devote any time to defining language learning success or to thinking deeply about how to measure it.

In problematizing language learning success in this chapter I am not referring to the socio-cultural and philosophical discussion about what the ultimate goal of second language learning should be. In other words, I am not entering into the issue of whether a language learner should be trying to emulate a native speaker or aiming to become a competent user of two or more languages. I agree that there is still a very important discussion to be had about that issue but it is not my purpose in this chapter to add to it. Rather I am making an assumption that the participants, in the studies I review below, wanted to keep on improving their language learning at whatever point their competence or performance was being measured.

In this chapter, therefore, I will first of all propose that (what should be) the dependent variable 'success', in LLS research, has been under-theorized. I will attempt to demonstrate that researchers have used a variety of terms to describe successful learning without providing justifications for using these different terms nor justification for the instruments used in measuring their conceptualization of success. As a consequence I will propose that this practice presents a problem when used in relation to LLS research. Secondly, I will try to show that there is often considerable confusion as to which are the dependent and which the independent variables in studies on strategies, leading to insufficient evidence that strategy use leads to success. Thirdly, and linked to the previous two points, I want to reappraise the notion of what a 'Good Language Learner' is, given that it has persisted as a notion in the literature for more than 30 years, and argue that this reappraisal needs to be at the heart of strategy instruction. I will then offer some solutions to the problems identified.

Defining Success in Studies of Strategic Behaviour

The first aspect of the problem that I have already alluded to in the Introduction is the definition of 'success' at second language (L2) learning. Table 1, summarizes 48 studies that I have reviewed which either directly or indirectly investigated LLS in relation to other variables. The distinction between directly and indirectly investigating strategies will become apparent as my argument progresses. For now we should note that measures of successful learning in one guise or another, whether as the dependent or the independent variable, feature in virtually every study reviewed. However, this measure of success is described variously using the terms 'proficiency', 'ability', 'expertise', 'achievement', 'effectiveness', 'skilled' as well as the term 'success' itself. A further alternative has been to define success through the use of 'course placement', that is, the practice of grouping students by some kind of measure of proficiency so that intra-group levels do not vary excessively. Let us therefore examine if there are clear differences between these terms used to define success at language learning. In other words, is the use of different terms for 'success' justifiable?

'Proficiency' is the term used by many of the authors in the studies reviewed. These can be divided into two groups, those that measured proficiency in a particular skill (e.g., Block 1986; Cumming 1989; Hosenfeld 1977; Khaldieh 2000; Taillefer 1996) and those that measured proficiency more generally (e.g., Gan et al. 2004; Nisbet et al. 2005; Park 1997; Wharton 2000). Studies in the first group are the more numerous. Hosenfeld's large sample of students took the MLA-cooperative test of reading proficiency and she used this outcome measure to describe her 'successful' and 'unsuccessful' readers. Cumming, in his smaller scale study of writing expertise, assessed L2 writing proficiency via three different writing tasks during which students articulated (using think-aloud protocol) their strategies. By contrast, in her investigation into the reading strategies of non-native speakers (and compared to 'poor' native readers), Block used two outcome measures after the students had articulated their strategies: a 'retelling' task (a recalling of the content without access to the text) and a multiple choice task. Khaldieh evaluated holistically the essays produced by the participants and used this measure to compare with self-reported writing strategy use. Although Taillefer used the term 'ability' in the title of her investigation of whether L1 reading ability predicted L2 reading success, the outcome

Table 1 Studies examining relationships between strategic behaviour and 'success' at L2 learning

Year of publication	Reference and number of participants	Dependent variable(s) (stated or implied)	Independent variable(s) (stated or implied)	Causation: strategy use leads to success[1]
1. 1977	Hosenfeld 1977 (N = 210)	Standardized reading 'proficiency' test ('successful')	Strategies	Implied
2. 1978	Bialystock and Frohlich 1978 (N = 157)	'Achievement': grammar tests and receptive tests	Aptitude strategies motivation field independence	Stated
3. 1981	Wesche 1981 (N = 37)	'Success' by improvement in speaking and listening	Observable characteristics; strategies	Implied
4. 1983	Politzer 1983 (N = 90)	'Achievement' by course level and student grades	Learning 'behaviours'	Implied
5. 1985	Paribakht 1985 (N = 25)	Communication strategies	Proficiency	No
6. 1986	Block 1986 (N = 9)	Reading comprehension	L1 reading 'ability' strategies in L2	No
7. 1986	Nation and McLaughlin 1986 (N = 42)	Test of artificial grammar learning	'Expertise': multilinguals, bilinguals, monolinguals	Implied
8. 1989	Cumming 1989 (N = 29)	L2 writing 'expertise'	L1 writing 'expertise' L2 proficiency	Implied
9. 1989	O'Malley et al. 1989 (N = 11)	'Listening strategies'	Effective/ineffective listeners (by) teacher designation	Implied

(Continued)

Table 1 (Cont'd)

Year of publication	Reference and number of participants	Dependent variable(s) (stated or implied)	Independent variable(s) (stated or implied)	Causation: strategy use leads to success[1]
10. 1989	Oxford and Nyikos 1989 (N = 1200)	Strategies (general) factored	Proficiency sex motivation class type	Stated
11. 1989	Poulisse and Schils 1989 (N, not given)	Compensation strategies	Proficiency tasks	Stated
12. 1990	Vann and Abraham 1990 (N = 2)	'Unsuccessful' by rate of progress	Strategies related to specific tasks	Stated
13. 1991	Anderson 1991 (N = 28)	Reading comprehension	Proficiency (by placement test) strategy use	No
14. 1993	Oxford et al. 1993 (N = 107)	Teacher created 'achievement' test (proficiency)	Strategies motivation styles	Stated
15. 1995	Erhman and Oxford 1995 (N = 855)	proficiency (end of course) in speaking and reading	Strategies + many others	No
16. 1995	Sanaoui 1995 (N = 50)	'Success' [at vocab learning] by vocab test	Strategies ('approaches/ study habits')	Stated
17. 1996	Taillefer 1996 (N = 53)	Reading comprehension	L1 reading ability L2 proficiency	No
18. 1997	Christianson 1997 (N = 51)	'Successful' written productions from dictionary look-ups	Strategies	Stated
19. 1997	Goh and Foong (1997) (N = 175)	Strategy use	Proficiency (standardized test) gender	Implied

			Strategies (SILL)	Implied
20. 1997	Park 1997 (N = 332)	Proficiency (TOEFL)	Strategies (SILL)	Implied
21. 1997	Lee and Shallert 1997 (N = 809)	L2 reading comprehension	L1 reading comprehension (and strategies by inference) L2 vocabulary and grammar knowledge ('proficiency')	No
22. 1997	Porte 1997 (N = 71)	Revision strategies	Students' opinions/beliefs teachers' expectations	No
23. 1998	Chien and Wei 1998 (N = 15)	'Listening strategies' (reported in interview) 'listening comprehension' scores	Linguistic knowledge (vocabulary and grammar test)	Implied
24. 1999	Bremner 1999 (N = 149)	Analysis 1: strategies (SILL) Analysis 2: proficiency (tests)	Analysis 1: proficiency (tests) Analysis 2: three levels of strategy frequency	No
25. 1999	Chamot and El-Dinary 1999 (N, not given)	Effectiveness in reading and writing (by) teacher rated proficiency	Strategies	Implied
26. 1999	Kojic-Sabo and Lightbown 1999 (N = 90)	'Success' vocab test cloze test	Strategic approach	Stated
27. 2000	Bonk 2000 (N = 59)	Lexical knowledge (and strategies by implication)	Listening proficiency	No
28. 2000	Goh 2000 (N = 16)	Strategies	Higher/lower ability listeners	No
29. 2000	Khaldieh 2000 (N = 43)	Writing 'proficiency'	Strategies	No
30. 2000	Manchón et al. 2000 (N = 30)	'Backtracking strategies' in written compositions	Language they backtracked in (L1 or L2) task type	No

(Continued)

Table 1 (Cont'd)

Year of publication	Reference and number of participants	Dependent variable(s) (stated or implied)	Independent variable(s) (stated or implied)	Causation: strategy use leads to success[1]
31. 2000	Wharton 2000 (N = 678)	Strategies (using the SILL)	Self-rated proficiency motivation gender language studied	Implied
32. 2001	Norton and Toohey 2001 (N = 2)	'Success/proficiency' (the Good Language Learner)	Human agency in social-environmental circumstances	Implied
33. 2001	Osada 2001 (N = 91)	'Listening strategies' top-down/bottom-up; local/global	Listening proficiency	Yes
34. 2002	Olivares-Cuhat 2002 (N = 11)	'Achievement' on written compositions	Strategies (SILL)	Implied
35. 2003	Gu 2003 (N = 27)	'Success' college proficiency test	Vocab strategies	Stated
36. 2003	Nassaj 2003 (N = 21)	'Success' at inferencing new words	Knowledge sources strategies	Stated
37. 2003	Victori and Tragrant 2003 (N = 766)	Strategies	Age proficiency	No
38. 2003	Vandergrift 2003 (N = 36)	'Skilled/less skilled listeners' (by) listening comprehension test	Listening strategies	Implied
39. 2003	Wang 2003 (N = 8)	Language switching as a strategy during written composition	General proficiency level task type	No
40. 2004	Gan et al. 2004 (N = 16)	'Success' by: entrance test classroom performance (teacher perception)	Strategies motivation	Implied
41. 2005	Nisbet et al. 2005 (N = 168)	Proficiency (TOEFL)	Strategy use (SILL)	No

		Dependent and independent variables		
42. 2006	Nikolov 2006 (N = 52)	Strategies in reading and writing	Success at (researcher created) task (but confounded with 'good and poor learners').	No
43. 2007	Kemp 2007 (N = 144)	Grammar strategies (range and frequency)	Number of languages learnt	Stated
44. 2008	Graham Santos and Vanderplank 2008 (N = 2)	Listening proficiency	Strategy use	Implied

Dependent and independent variables

Green and Oxford 1995 (N = 374)	Neither stated nor implied: general strategy use (SILL) proficiency level (course placement) gender
Griffiths 2003 (N = 348)	Neither stated nor implied: strategy use; course level; age; sex; nationality
Raimes 1987 (N = 8)	Neither stated nor implied: language proficiency writing performance writing strategies
Vandergrift 1998 (N = 7)	Neither stated nor implied: 'Proficiency' by oral proficiency test 'listening success' 'listening strategies'

[1] By 'implied' is meant that the current author assumes that this is the case from the conclusions drawn.

measures were two reading proficiency tasks tapping into either specific item or holistic understanding of text: a scanning task and a reading for meaning task.

An unadapted version of the TOEFL was used to measure proficiency in the studies by Park (1997) and by Nisbet et al. (2005). On the other hand, Gan et al. (2004) measured success by a college entrance exam together with the teacher's perceptions of performance in class. Using a teacher's judgement would suggest tapping into something in addition to proficiency. However, it is possible that the teachers made their subjective judgements in the knowledge of the entrance exam grades. Thus whether this expands the construct of proficiency in any way is debatable. Wharton (2000) used participants' self-estimates of general proficiency (poor, fair and good) and this, as the author acknowledges, may have also been tapping into the learner's 'self-concepts' of themselves. Politzer (1983) used course level (elementary, intermediate, advanced), together with course grades and teacher evaluations, but since these are not reported it is difficult to consider this study other than as a study about proficiency and learning behaviour (although the actual term that Politzer uses in the title is 'achievement').

Thus far, then, the language performance measures used in studies about strategy use appear to be measures of proficiency. My definition of proficiency, and one which I believe to be the generally accepted definition, is a snapshot in time of the performance of a learner regardless of any factors in their language background. Proficiency tests are blind to 'rate of progress' and to 'ultimate attainment'. They do not describe (because they are not designed to) a student's learning trajectory, the fluctuations in their learning, nor whether they go on to be interpreters at the United Nations. They do not provide information about the number of years of language learning nor the number of hours spent reaching that particular level of proficiency. Proficiency measures are not interested in the intensity of the effort expended, nor the amount of financial investment by the learner or the learner's family. They simply tell us what that student can do against pre-established graded criteria at that particular moment in time.

If proficiency is a snapshot of what a language learner can do at one moment in time, is there a different construct intended by the use of the word 'achievement'? This was a term used by Bialystok and Fröhlich in their 1978 study of four different variables which might predict success, of which one was strategies (specifically, 'practising', 'monitoring' and 'inferencing'). To measure achievement they gave the students an aural grammaticality judgement test, a fill the gap grammar test and listening and reading comprehension tests. In other words these measured both 'formal' aspects of their learning and performance and 'functional' aspects. By contrast, Oxford et al. (1993), who also used the word 'achievement' to describe their outcome measure used a final examination described simply as a Japanese Language Achievement Test which was 'teacher created' and of a 'multiple choice variety' (p. 39), and Olivares-Cuhat (2002) used 'achievement' to describe the best compositions of her students in a Spanish writing class.

So, does 'achievement' advance our understanding of the measure of 'success', beyond what is offered by 'proficiency'? I believe not. Although Bialystok and Fröhlich appear to use a more comprehensive measure, tapping in to both competence and performance, it does not, in any way, describe the learning trajectory of an individual student. Both the interpretations of proficiency and achievement are measures of a *product* of learning. Although Olivares-Cuhat's (2002) study of Spanish (L2) writing was carried out over a six-week period, this slightly more longitudinal approach does not compensate for the fact that the age range in the small sample was enormous, no baseline proficiency test was reported and learners came from a variety of language backgrounds including heritage Spanish. In any case, although the study appears to be longitudinal, strategy use was only measured via two writing tasks in that six-week period.

One way in which achievement might be interpreted differently is in seeing it as a product *in context* and *over time* (see Figure 1). In educational research authors talk about high-achieving learners where possible confounding variables have been controlled for or where progress is measured longitudinally. They tend to study learners who have received the same educational experience, the same number of years of learning, with often the same teacher as their peers. They sometimes study learners who come from the same socio-economic background, and yet seem to be doing better than others. Here we are still looking at a product of learning but we are taking many more factors into account and/or factoring them out. We can begin to detect, in the learning trajectory, the notion of 'achievement against the odds', something which a proficiency test cannot provide insights about. It is this achievement against the odds that I want to put forward as the language measure that needs to be used in relation to LLS research.

Of course some might argue that where students are at a particular moment in time is all we should be interested in anyway. Why would we want to know their language learning past? Teachers may simply want to know proficiency level information in order to decide in which class to place the students or, in the

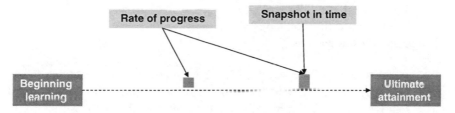

Figure 1 Achievement versus proficiency

case of mixed proficiency classes, how to differentiate their language teaching objectives and materials. However, I want to argue that this goes to the heart of the pedagogical problem that strategy research is trying to redress. In order to make that argument clear to the reader we will need to consider LLS theory in some detail before returning to other terms used in the literature such as 'expert learners', 'successful learners', 'skilled learners' and 'effective learners'.

Defining Strategic Behaviour

There is a lack of consensus as to the definition of a strategy in the literature (see Cohen 2007; Dörnyei 2005; Macaro 2006; Tseng et al. 2006), particularly as to whether strategies are learner-internal or learner-external, small or large, abstract or concrete, individual or inextricably linked. There is, nevertheless, a general consensus that they are what learners 'do' with the linguistic resources available to them at various levels of consciousness. Some would argue that strategies are deployed by learners in order to compensate for deficiencies in their linguistic competence (Field 2004). Others would argue that they are the very stuff of conscious processing in working memory (Macaro 2006) in that they are used for retaining, retrieving or manipulating all linguistic information (O'Malley and Chamot 1990). Some propose that they are behaviours or techniques learners use to *improve* their language development (Ehrman and Oxford 1995), others propose that they are quite simply 'behaviours that learners engage in to learn a second/foreign language' (Vann and Abraham 1990: 177).

Strategic behaviour formed part of Canale and Swain's (1980) notion of communicative competence and Bachman's (1990) model of communicative language ability. Although concerned primarily with communication strategies rather than general strategies, in these models, too, there is an underlying proposition that strategic behaviour is what L2 learners deploy in order to maximize their L2 linguistic knowledge resources (henceforth LKR) available to them at any one time. By linguistic resources I mean the following:

1. lexical-semantic knowledge
2. phonological-graphological knowledge
3. morpho-syntactic knowledge
4. pragmatic knowledge

Note that in defining a notion of LKR, I am not including strategic competence. I am suggesting that (what I call) strategic behaviour is the valued-added factor that L2 learners bring to LKR and that this, together with variability in LKR leads to variability in performance.

Where do L2 learners get their strategic behaviour from? Much strategic behaviour is already present in first language use. Communication strategies (confirmations signals, hesitations, fillers, circumlocutions) are all part of L1 speech when for some reason the going gets tough. 'Inferencing', 'examining affixes', 'monitoring understanding' are all strategies that L1 readers use when confronted with unknown words in a difficult text. The difference with L2 strategic behaviour is first that 'the going' is usually tougher than it is in L1. Secondly, L2 strategic behaviour *can take into consideration* L1 strategic behaviour. In other words, L2 learners can say to themselves: 'what would I do if this was an L1 task? Would I approach it in the same way? If not, in what way should I approach it differently and for what reasons?'. This difference between L1 strategic behaviour and L2 strategic behaviour is central to a number of the studies I review later in this chapter and which I have labelled as 'indirectly' related to strategies research. These are studies which examine whether, to what extent and at which level of LKR, L1 strategic behaviour can be transferred to an L2 activity. However, the important notion to keep in mind for the moment is that strategic behaviour is present in both L1 and L2 processing but usually occurs with greater intensity in the latter.

The balance between LKR and strategic behaviour can best be illustrated by considering language tasks. From Figure 2 we can see that, as the mismatch between LKR and the demands of a task increases, so the amount of strategic behaviour has to increase. For example, if an L2 reading task contains only

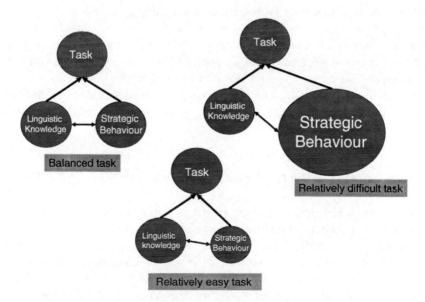

Figure 2   Relationship of strategic behaviour to linguistic knowledge and task

words that the reader knows well, then (unless the writer is being particularly obscurantist or poetic) the reader will have to deploy relatively low levels of strategic behaviour. The processing of the text will be relatively automatic; the reader will not have to stop and think about it. Put in the same text 10% of words unfamiliar to the reader, and s/he will have to deploy considerable levels of strategic behaviour in order to infer their individual meaning and their impact on the whole text.

Therefore, one of the things that researchers into LLS attempt to do is to understand language learning as a *process*, not simply as a product. We want to know what it is in the learner's processing of language that leads to variability in success. Central in that investigation is (or should be) understanding two things. First, we need to understand how strategic behaviour moderates between LKR and success with a language task. That is one reason that there has been a gradual decline in use, for research purposes, of large-scale questionnaires exploring general and somewhat abstract learning processes, in favour of adopting concurrent and retrospective verbal reports by students while engaged in specific learning- or skills-based tasks. Secondly, we need to understand how strategic behaviour moderates between LKR and success *over time*. In other words, how do the strategic choices that a learner makes at one time point in relation to a particular task inform the learner as to the efficacy of those choices for future and similar tasks? How will their evaluation of those choices affect their strategic behaviour in the future?

So what has all this LLS theory to do with the dependent variable 'success'? Well, my central argument is that success, resulting from effective strategic behaviour in relation to a given LKR, has to be measured at a number of time points in order to demonstrate a consistent link between what a learner does with their current LKR and what they achieve. These measurements will help to explain the 'learning trajectory' idea I introduced earlier.

We now return to our various definitions of terms used. However, now we do so in the context of (hopefully) a more shared understanding of strategy theory.

Defining Success in the Context of Strategy Theory

Another term which has been used in the literature associated with LLS is 'expertise'. This reflects an interest more widely in what experts have in common as they go about all kinds of cognitively demanding tasks (for a thorough discussion, see Johnson 2005, chapter 1). The general consensus is that experts are able to do things more quickly and at a greater depth than novices, partly because they are able to carry out some processes automatically thus freeing up capacity to process details.

One study which considered the difference between novices and experts in language learning was by Nation and McLaughlin (1986) who compared the performance at learning an artificial grammar by monolinguals, by bilinguals and by multilinguals and found that the multilinguals (the 'experts') outperformed both the other two groups in the implicit version of the learning task. The researchers infer that the better performance might be due to the experts' greater ability to abstract structural information from stimuli in the input and to their past experience of deploying greater processing effort in making sense of such stimuli. However, a possibility which the authors did not consider was the different learning trajectories of the bilinguals and monolinguals. The former had learnt their second language (English) in naturalistic settings, either at home 'between the ages of 6 and 11' (p. 44), or had been exposed to the language from birth. These would appear to be very different learner types from the multilinguals, of whom we are told very little except that at least two thirds were not Americans, and we can only assume had learnt their four or five languages in instructed contexts.

The study of experts, as McDonough (2005) quite rightly points out, does not solve the chicken and egg problem, that is, the relationship between proficiency and strategy use. Is the expert someone who is able to deploy a more complex or effective range of strategies by virtue of having studied more languages? Or is it that their effective use of strategies has led them to be successful at language learning and therefore encouraged them to learn more languages? Although the answer may well be both (or either) it does not help with LLS research which tries to establish characteristics of the good language learner for other learners to emulate. We shall be returning to this theme later in the chapter.

Let us now consider the use of the terms 'skilled' or 'effective' learner in LLS literature. Clearly if the terms are used synonymously with 'highly proficient', meaning 'having reached a high level in a particular language skill such as reading', then there is no advance on the insights provided by the proficiency studies outlined above. We are still dealing with a snap-shot measurement of the product of learning. However, what begins to creep into the concept of the skilled learner is a process dimension. Vandergrift (2003) investigated the types of strategies used by more skilled and less skilled listeners not as revealed simply by their performance in a listening comprehension test but as revealed, *in addition*, by thinking aloud their strategic behaviour. In his study skilled listeners adopted more questioning strategies and world knowledge strategies than less skilled listeners who, in turn, had a compulsion for translating individual words or short phrases. So skilled listeners, by this reckoning, can be characterized as proficiency *plus* certain strategic behaviour.

The same applies to the term 'effective learner'. Once again, if an effective learner is simply one who does well in a proficiency test, then we are talking about a product measure. Chamot and El-Dinary (1999) use the term 'effective learners' when they state that their sample of children in primary school was sub-divided into two groups: highly effective; less effective. The way this was done was as follows:

> Teachers were asked to rate the target language proficiency of students as high (exceeds expectations) average (meets expectations) or low (fails to meet expectations). Teachers were advised to make their rating for each student independently of the ratings of other students in the class. Thus in a high achieving class, half or more students might be rated high, and the reverse could occur for a low-achieving class. (p. 321)

In other words (at least if I have understood correctly) teachers were asked to avoid norm-referencing but rather were encouraged to use a somewhat vague criterion reference 'expectations' in order to arrive at a measure akin to 'proficiency'. Even if we let this somewhat confusing selection procedure pass without further comment, we still begin to detect the slow creep of the process dimension when we learn that 'Effective learners [were] more flexible with their repertoire of strategies and more effective at monitoring and adapting their strategies' (p. 332). So once again we seem to have the formula: proficiency + certain strategic behaviour = effectiveness.

There is a problem with this conceptualization of success. In any measure of proficiency there is already *built in*, a strategic behaviour component. Proficiency, as I have argued, is a product measurement and the measurement that the researcher was using in the listening performance of Vandergrift's (2003) participants, or that the teachers were using in any of their skill-related proficiency judgements (in Chamot and El-Dinary 1999), must have *included* strategic behaviour. In other words, the task they used for measuring demanded of the participants both LKR and strategic behaviour. Therefore to include the same construct twice in the same measurement is problematic. It does not unpack the relationship between LKR and the value-added that strategic behaviour brings to LKR.

Now, I have to stress that the above is my interpretation of what was being proposed in these studies of skilled and effective learners. It is merely what I understand the authors to be saying. On the other hand, if what they are saying is that certain strategic behaviour simply *correlates* with proficiency then my argument is not valid. However, if this is all they are saying, then it is a much weaker claim than what they appear to be claiming and it undermines the model for the 'skilled listener' (Vandergrift 2003). We will return to correlation versus causality in the next section. For now let us look finally at the use of the term 'successful' itself in the LLS literature.

It is interesting that the term 'success' is more often than not used as an out-come term in studies which measure very specific aspects of learner perfor-mance rather than one of the four skills, or indeed general proficiency. Gu (2004) and Sanaoui (1995) use the term to describe the effect of strategy use on vocabu-lary learning tasks; Christianson (1997) uses 'success' to describe correct written productions resulting from strategies used while looking words up in a diction-ary, and Nassaji (2003) uses 'success' as a term to describe the correct inferenc-ing of new words. It is interesting because with specific aspects of learning it is easier, at least in the short term, to make a causal relationship between strategic behaviour and success. This reflects my argument earlier that the link between LKR, strategic behaviour and success has to be measured longitudinally not at one point in time. Moreover, we can more easily detect situational circum-stances and levels of LKR difference which might mediate between strategic behaviour and success. For example in the Gu study two Chinese EFL learners (used as case studies from a much larger sample), varied considerably in their strategic approaches to learning vocabulary, but both were successful vocabu-lary learners. In the Sanaoui study, with ESL learners in Canada on the other hand, it was the students described as 'organizers' who outperformed the 'non-organizers'.

One of the few studies to use the term 'success' more broadly than above was by Wesche (1981). Here a sample of adult learners was selected on the basis of high aptitude scores and their 'learning behaviours' observed by the researcher. What is also fairly unique about this study was that it was longitu-dinal, measuring end of nine-week course achievement via standardized test and by teacher ratings. Probably the most notable finding of this study was that more successful students were willing to take part in role-play tasks in which they adopted appropriate prosodic and paralinguistic features. There appear to be some problems with this study however. First, the observable behaviours were very broad and seem to equate more with general effort and enthusiasm than with appropriate cognitive and metacognitive activity (see Macaro 2006 for further discussion of these different conceptualizations of strategies). Sec-ondly, although this was supposed to be a 'beginning level training programme (for civil servants)' (p. 416), 'initial placement level was entered to control for pre-training French knowledge' (p. 421) which seems contradictory without further explanation. Lastly, selecting the sample on the basis of high aptitude scores and then examining their learning behaviours may well be confounding the results. Was the key variable that made them successful the learning behav-iours observed (which are theoretically amenable to change or treatment) or was it their language aptitude (which theoretically is less amenable to change or treatment)? Nevertheless, there are some key features (longitudinal, use of triangulation) in this early study which might have helped enlighten the success-strategies relationship if subsequent researchers in the field had adopted them and refined them.

One further study using 'success' as an outcome measure merits mention here. Vann and Abraham (1990) is an often cited study because it made a number of departures from our (at the time) understandings of strategy theory. First, it was an in-depth study of two *unsuccessful* (Saudi) learners, and not just by self-report, but by relating their observed strategic behaviour against specific tasks comprising both LKR and performance. Secondly, it measured not proficiency but *rate of progress* through 'weekly gains' (p. 179) on an intensive English programme. Thirdly, the case study data included background information in which the respondents told the researchers about their past experiences in learning languages. Vann and Abraham concluded that these two unsuccessful learners were using the same strategies as successful learners but inappropriately against the demands of the task and that this mismatch was evidently occurring over time.

In summary for this section, *I have begun* to argue that:

1. different authors use different terms to describe 'success' in language learning. Most, however, simply mean some kind of test of proficiency, a snap-shot in time, the product of learning, not the process;
2. proficiency cannot be used to define successful learning in the context of strategy research because it does not provide sufficient evidence (the learning trajectory) that strategic behaviour has produced that level of proficiency;
3. proficiency should not be used as a correlate of strategic behaviour because proficiency tasks already include strategic behaviour;
4. LLS research claims that good learners maximize their LKR through strategic behaviour of some kind;
5. the interrelationship between LKR and strategic behaviour has to go beyond correlation in order to show that appropriate strategic behaviour is a key ingredient, a value-added factor, in successful language learning;
6. the claim for a causal relationship in the direction LKR + appropriate strategic behaviour = achievement, is strengthened by two factors: observing its effect over time, and through the control of possible confounding variables.

I will now try to deepen my argument by discussing correlation and causality in greater detail. I will attempt to demonstrate that the relationship between LKR and strategic behaviour, controlling for confounding variables and using appropriate outcome measures are all aspects of the problem of demonstrating the direction of causality.

Correlation and Causality in Strategy Research

Nation and McLaughlin (1986) list, among the problems which beset individual differences, the fact that there remains

> the question of causal direction. There may in fact be instances where the direction of causality is from learning to personality factors rather than the other way round (p. 42)

Of the 48 studies reviewed for this chapter (see Table 1) 17 either clearly stated that successful learning was the dependent variable (DV) being investigated or made it sufficiently obvious, through their argumentation, research questions and discussions, that this was the case. Of the other 31 studies, in four (Green and Oxford 1995; Griffiths 2003; Raimes 1987; Vandergrift 1998) I could not detect which were the dependent and which the independent variables (IV) and therefore concluded that they were exploratory correlational studies. Theirs seems a perfectly acceptable approach to take even though I would have thought that to be still researching simple correlations after nearly thirty years of LLS research endeavour might become a little frustrating. Moreover, I should point out that, in the Griffiths (2003) study, if one takes in the general tone of the discussion, it seems there is a fairly strong implication that strategy use *leads to* students being placed in higher course levels.

In the remaining studies, the DV appears to be strategic behaviour not 'success'. At least that is the impression that I believe most readers would get. However, the situation is by no means clear in all of these studies. Certainly in Paribakht's (1985) study of communication strategies used by adult Persian ESL learners, the author makes clear that a key IV was linguistic knowledge and that lack of linguistic knowledge might preclude (type) and reduce (frequency) of certain communication strategies which *require* that knowledge. Additionally, the author suggests that language distance may have a significant effect on communication strategy use. Therefore the direction of causality appears to be linguistic factors causing different strategic behaviour to be adopted.

A similar study investigating the influence of task and proficiency on oral communication (compensation) strategies, considered more cognate languages (Dutch and English). Here the researchers Poulisse and Schils (1989) observed the strategic behaviour of advanced, intermediate and beginner learners in three tasks: they had to 'communicate' an object, the L2 word of which was unknown to them; retell a story in L1 they had heard in L2; take part in a 20-minute interview. As might be predicted, lower proficiency groups used more compensation strategies simply because they knew fewer words. Interestingly, however, they found a bigger effect for task difference than for proficiency level, suggesting that the recent interest in linking LLS investigations more directly to tasks is a good idea. In this study too, then, there is no suggestion of causation in the direction that strategy use leads to higher proficiency.

In another group of studies the underlying claim being made is that strategy use leads to successful learning yet, at first, the DV appears to be strategic behaviour. For example in the often cited O'Malley et al. (1989) study, 11 Hispanic ESL learners at intermediate level of English proficiency were designated as 'effective' and 'ineffective listeners' by teachers according to the following criteria:

1. attentiveness in class;
2. ability to follow directions
3. ability and willingness to comprehend the general meaning of a difficult listening passage
4. ability to respond appropriately in conversation
5. ability and willingness to guess at meaning

The authors found that the principal characteristics of effective listeners were: 'self monitoring' 'elaboration' and 'inferencing'. These strategies 'differentiated effective from ineffective listeners' (p. 434) and 'less effective students can learn to use learning strategies and apply them' (p. 435). In other words, although the DV appears to be strategy use, the opposite direction of causality (strategy use leads to effective listening) even if not stated explicitly, is certainly strongly implied in the discussion.

Many other studies where strategies appear to be the DV being researched follow the same path of argument. Goh and Foong (1997) report in their study of 175 Chinese EFL learners that participants' strategies were 'significantly influenced' by proficiency levels. Yet the authors imply in their recommendations, that strategies, if taught, may influence proficiency. We should observe, however, in a more recent study (Goh 2000), that the author's conclusion seems to be that lower proficiency students are *unable* to deploy the same strategies as higher proficiency students. Anderson (1991) appears to arrive at the same conclusion with regard to reading strategies: 'beginning level learners may know what strategies to use but because of lack of vocabulary, or other schema related information, they may not have a strong enough language foundation to build on' (p. 469).

The conclusion that the direction of causality is more likely to be 'proficiency affects strategy use' is also arrived at by Osada (2001) whose lower listening proficiency students 'could not help' using less cognitively demanding, text-based (bottom-up) strategies, and by Khaldieh (2000: 530) who demonstrated that all students appeared to be using 'the right tools, that is, strategies and techniques; however, not all of them seem to possess the right substance – linguistic knowledge'. On the other hand, Nikolov (2006), investigating the test-taking strategies of young Hungarian good- and bad-performers in reading and writing, appears to arrive at no conclusion whatsoever as to the relationship between performance and strategic behaviour.

There is clearly some confusion in the LLS literature as to what causes what, and I would argue once again that this stems from a reluctance to sufficiently theorize successful learning as an outcome measure and to control for variables which would clearly show the effect of strategic behaviour on that outcome measure. One of the variables that has to be controlled for is LKR, as a number of the studies reviewed above would suggest, but do not themselves put into their procedures.

Two studies that did attempt to control for LKR are Chien and Wei (1998), and Graham, Santos and Vanderplank (2008) who, in addition to listening proficiency tests, gave students tests of vocabulary and grammar. In the Chien and Wei study once again the direction of causality seemed to be that listening proficiency differences lead to differentiated strategic behaviour in that the authors report that 'The highest ranking group *were able* [my emphasis] to exercise a greater number of strategies . . . simultaneously' (p. 76). Presumably this ability was because greater LKR freed up working memory processing capacity. However, they also make the tantalizing assertion that students at the same level of grammar and vocabulary knowledge did not necessarily perform as well in their listening comprehension. Unfortunately this latter assertion is not elaborated on by the authors nor statistical tests reported of vocabulary and grammar in relation to proficiency. The reason that I say 'unfortunate' is that, as I have posited earlier, if we control for LKR and find that learners of similar LKR levels are performing differently on tests of proficiency (as the authors appear to be claiming), then we can deduce that this must be due in large measure to their strategic behaviour. If we can also elicit that behaviour and show variability in it then we can be pretty confident that we have a direction of causality: appropriate strategic behaviour leads to better performance on profi-ciency measures.

A number of methodological features make the Graham et al. (2008) case study research stand out from previous studies and it may be these differences which produced a different set of findings from some of the others we have looked at, and more strongly suggest a direction of causality: appropriate strategic behaviour leads to success. First, the strategic behaviour of two stu-dents, who performed differently in a listening comprehension test, was assessed at two time points some seven months apart. Secondly, and crucially, the two students were given vocabulary and grammar tests (measures of LKR) and found to 'display similar levels' of linguistic knowledge. Thirdly, the authors provide an item by item analysis (the elicitation task was multiple choice) of the strategic reactions of the two students to the particular problems posed by each item. They found that the less successful listener used many strategies associated with successful listeners but used them badly on both occasions. For example she listened out for particular words (selective attention); asked herself if she had understood (comprehension monitoring); used 'deduction' (mostly based on what she had *not* heard). However she deployed these strategies (claimed by some authors to be the marks of the good listener) repeatedly, in isolation, and with no follow-up. On the other hand, the stronger listener acknowledged the provisional nature of his interpretations and double-checked against later in-text evidence, combining strategies into more effective clusters.

A somewhat different attempt to control for confounding variables is a very interesting study by Victori and Tragrant (2003). Noting that age as a variable had rarely been explored in strategy research, the authors collected both cross-sectional and longitudinal data of adolescent learners of English in Spain. They found that older students reported using more and different strategy types (particularly more complex strategy combinations). The direction of causality seemed to be that the older and more proficient students are enabled to use different strategies. In other words age and proficiency level affect strategy use. The authors also propose that there may be a threshold point during the learning trajectory where strategies undergo a more noticeable development. Unfortunately, from their data, it is not possible to detect which is the stronger predictor of that development, increasing maturity or increasing LKR.

The idea of the existence of a threshold of LKR below which a full range of strategies cannot be deployed has been examined in studies which earlier I indicated as being 'indirectly' involved in investigating strategic behaviour and success. These are studies which do not explicitly investigate strategies but adopt, in my view, the same objective from a different angle. In these studies, however, the assumption is that strategic behaviour is universal in nature, irrespective of whether it is being deployed in L1 or L2. For example in Lee and Shallert's (1997) study a hypothesis being tested was whether the contribution of general L2 proficiency was greater than the contribution of L1 reading ability in predicting L2 reading ability. Now, given that the level of linguistic knowledge is necessarily different in a learner's L1, the common factor between L1 reading ability and L2 reading ability that is being measured is what readers do with their respective LKR. In other words, I would argue (and I think Lee and Shallert would agree) that L1 reading ability must be L1 LKR + strategic behaviour. The researchers operationalized the L2 proficiency of a large sample of Korean high school students (age 14–17 controlled for) through a word meaning test and a grammaticality judgement test (what I would call aspects of LKR rather than proficiency). They found that performance on these tests of LKR explained 56% of the variance in L2 reading while L1 reading ability explained only 30% of the variance. Therefore a learner in a low L2 proficiency group was less likely to use L1 type reading strategies than a learner in a high L2 proficiency group. This is an interesting study as it indirectly suggests a balance of influence of successful reading between LKR and strategic behaviour. Three things might improve a future study of this kind in my view: a test of participants' L1 LKR, a more reliable L1 reading ability test (reported reliability was .68), and some indication of where that threshold of L2 LKR actually lies.

Similar results were obtained in a 'threshold' study carried out by Taillefer (1996). L1 reading ability and L2 proficiency were both significant predictors of L2 reading comprehension but varied according to the reading tasks demanded of the students. In tasks of high cognitive complexity, L2 proficiency was a significant predictor whereas in a low cognitive task (scanning for words in a text) it was not. Both these studies of the threshold hypothesis, through their methodology, attempt to arrive at a direction of causality.

This issue of causality is tackled head-on by Bremner's highly insightful (1999) study. Using the SILL (Oxford 1990) as a measure of frequency of strategy use and a series of proficiency measures, he challenged the lack of clarity in previous LLS literature by analysing his data via ANOVA *twice*: First with proficiency as the IV and strategy use as the DV, and then with strategy use as IV and proficiency as the DV. He found that when proficiency was the IV, there were significant differences in the frequency of a number of cognitive strategies reported. When students were then grouped as high, medium or low strategy users and entered as the IV there were also significant differences by proficiency and that many of the cognitive strategies could have been 'either contributors to the acquisition of proficiency or, alternatively, be made more possible by increased proficiency' (p. 502). He concluded that:

> if strategies are not causes but features of proficiency, then they are not worth investigating- they are simply outcomes of increased proficiency, an increase that has to be accounted for in other ways. (p. 507)

As we have seen, then, there appears to be considerable confusion as to the direction of causality and which are the IVs and DVs being examined. One further problem that readers might encounter when reading (the more 'direct') studies of relationships between variables is the nuanced language used in this regard. Authors rarely pin their colours to the mast as to whether they are reporting correlation or causality. When a whiff of causality appears to be in the air, the direction of that causality is still unclear and sometimes there are even claims to causal direction and correlation in the same article. I can understand that researchers are trying to be cautious in their conclusions, but this nuanced approach does not further our development of strategy theory.

289

Here are some typical examples, in chronological order, of concluding moves by LLS authors:

> the higher the student's self-perceived proficiency in each of these three skills, the more frequently the student chose to use learning strategies. . . . greater strategy use accompanied perceptions of higher proficiency, and a causal relationship actually existed between proficiency self-ratings and strategy use (Oxford and Nyikos 1989: 294–295)

> 'motivation and strategy use made a great difference' . . . 'played a very important role in language achievement' . . . 'the more motivated the students were and the more they used learning strategies, the better their Japanese achievement was' (Oxford et al. 1993: 46)

> The significant difference in the strategy use [of different proficiencies] provides evidence for the relationship between the strategies used and their performance in listening comprehension. The highest-ranking group are able to exercise a greater number of strategies (Chien and Wei 1998: 76)

> the findings suggest a strong relationship between the amount of strategy use and levels of success in language learning (Kojic-Sabo and Lightbown 1999: 189)

> effective language learners use strategies more appropriately than do less effective language learners (Chamot and El-Dinary 1999: 320)

> this study. . . . found evidence for a linear relationship between (self-rated) proficiency and the use of many learning strategies (Wharton 2000: 235)

> 'there is a positive linear relationship between memory strategy scores and overall composition grades' and a 'correlation between the use of memory strategies as measured by the SILL and the students' performances has been established' (Olivares-Cuhat 2002: 566)

> more proficient listeners were able to process the text in [a] knowledge-based manner, whereas less proficient readers seemed to rely on [a] data driven manner (Osada 2001: 84)

To summarize this section of correlation and causality between the two factors strategic behaviour and L2 proficiency:

1. There is clear evidence, if we combine the results of a number of studies, of a strong link between proficiency and differences in strategic behaviour. More proficient students deploy more sophisticated or complex combinations of strategies.

2. Less proficient students show evidence of being unable to deploy certain strategies, or strategy clusters as appropriate to tasks. However, we as yet do not know whether this inability is due to their lack of LKR, whether they are unaware of certain strategy clusters, refuse to use certain strategies, the task does not allow them sufficient time to deploy certain strategies, or they believe that the strategies that they use in L1 tasks are not transferable to L2 tasks.

3. There is as yet little evidence from the studies so far reviewed that strategic behaviour is the key independent variable in accelerating achievement or predicting ultimate attainment. I am not suggesting that there is no likelihood that this evidence will be found in the future, but simply that it has not yet been found.

4. In order to find that evidence we have to look to two types of studies. The first is where the relationship between linguistic knowledge, strategic behaviour and successful accomplishment of tasks (of various kinds) is tracked over a considerable period of time. The second type of study is the experimental intervention. In these, the researcher manipulates the strategic behaviour variable and measures pre- and post-treatment performance in an L2 task. In other words we are looking for the results of strategy-based instruction (SBI).

We will look at some SBI studies in a moment. Before we do this we need to take a look at the notion of the 'good language learner' as, what has been argued earlier, now requires us to reappraise this notion, particularly if we are to use the notion in connection with strategy-based interventions.

The Good Language Learner Problem

In a recent volume edited by Carol Griffiths (2008) called 'Lessons From Good Language Learners', twenty-three chapters each provide a characteristic that the authors believe a good language learner (GLL) might possess. A reader of the volume would probably conclude that therefore learners need to be motivated, have certain learning styles, possess a particular type of personality, on the whole preferably be females, use certain strategies, have high levels of meta-cognition, demonstrate autonomy, hold certain beliefs about learning, perhaps come from particular cultures which facilitate certain types of learning and score fairly highly on components of aptitude.

Fine. But what is a Good Language Learner? Not once in the book are we told *how to measure* a good language learner. In other words we are told a GLL's characteristics (and there seem to be a dauntingly great number of them!) but once again we do not know what the outcomes of those characteristics should

291

be. We are back at the dependent variable issue. Let us not forget how easy it is for practitioners to subjectively label learners as good and bad. If we include culture as a factor in judging good and poor learners we begin to run into problems of stereotyping. The five descriptions of a good listener provided in O'Malley et al.'s (1989) study may not transfer to different learning contexts. Mitchell and Hye-Won Lee (2003) found that teachers identified the GLL in very different ways in UK secondary classrooms when compared to Korean classrooms.

I hate to labour this point but I believe it to be a vital question that has to be resolved if we are to establish a solid theoretical foundation for SBI research (see next section). In other words, if we are going to take any lessons from the GLL we had better decide how that GLL got his or her badge of honour!

Is a GLL someone who has achieved a level 8 in the IELTS test? Is this a better GLL than someone who has achieved a level 6? Clearly not. Or at least not necessarily. As I have already hopefully demonstrated, proficiency tests are blind to the fact that the student with a level 6 may have reached that level in 6 months of L2 learning whereas their more proficient counterpart may have taken 10 years. The level 6 student may have reached their level 6 by studying alone, after a hard-day's work, and with a teach-yourself-English course, whereas their level 8 counterpart may have had all the benefits of a first-class private language school education. So clearly we cannot take any lessons from the level 8 students. Or at least not necessarily.

Is a GLL someone who is a language learning expert? Apart from the caveat about learning trajectory already discussed earlier, there are, compared to bilinguals, few of these around. I once taught applied linguistics to a student who claimed to speak more than 10 languages fluently, 5 languages adequately and was busily working on another three. I take my hat off to him. He almost certainly is a GLL. But should we take lessons from him? Or rather to put it less facetiously, should we be modelling SBI on him? Well, it would certainly do no harm to find out something of what he does to make language learning so easy *for him*. But I am not convinced that the totality of his strategic behaviour should be what we should be modelling the vast majority of our language learners on. Apart from anything else it would more than likely discourage the average learner. Trying to emulate such a language expert may be even more daunting than trying to emulate a native speaker!

Is a GLL someone who has achieved well in their language learning endeavour? A relatively high-achiever? Here I am using achievement (as already broached above) to describe someone who appears to be progressing more quickly in their language learning than his or her peers. We need to use this learner's peers as a comparison group otherwise our measurement of the progress will be unreliable if not downright meaningless. The peers will give us an indication of whether we have controlled for LKR, socio-economic status (SES), attendance at school/

university and so on. Two problems need to be resolved with this approach. If the group we are looking at has a whole range of LKR, how are we controlling for it? Well, this is the kind of problem that all researchers face and one way to resolve it is through stratification. The second problem is, why stop at these control variables? Why not include working memory capacity, aptitude components and motivation? The trouble with including these variables is that they have already been shown to be high correlates of strategic behaviour and/or correlates among themselves, whereas LKR, SES and attendance have not. So let us at least start with controlling for the latter. If we control for LKR, SES and attendance, at least we can say that learner X has achieved well 'against the odds'.

To some extent, Norton and Toohey (2001) in their 'changing perspectives on good language learners', seem to adhere to a position that we need to know a lot more about learners than simply a snapshot in time of their proficiency level. In their case studies of Eva (a Polish restaurant worker in Anglophone Canada) and Julie (a kindergarten child also in Canada) they take a socio-cultural perspective and conclude that 'the proficiencies of the good language learners in our studies were bound up not only with what they did individually but also in the possibilities their various communities offered them' (p. 318). However, while I very much welcome the fact that they mention progress relative to their peers, Eva is still judged an outstanding learner based on a snapshot in time (cloze passage, dictation, crossword, short essay) while Julie is judged to be a GLL on the basis of her teacher's subjective assessment of her. To be fair, more information about their trajectory is provided in the separate studies to which their 2001 summary refers. Nevertheless, the GLL's characteristics (how the two learners resisted the position that their environments had placed them in) are identified as leading to a higher proficiency end-point rather than on valid measurements of linguistic achievement over time.

To sum up my position, I would propose that an insight into the strategies used by the 'expert learner', and a thorough understanding of the strategic behaviour of the high-achiever, would provide us with a good basis for carrying out SBI. However, I would want to stress that there is no substitute for finding out what the individual learners we are teaching or researching are themselves actually doing and seeing how this is leading to success or failure in their language learning, no matter how we interpret success or failure.

We now come to the final section of the chapter where we examine the impact that SBI has had on improving performance and success.

Strategy-Based Instruction and Success

As I proposed earlier, one way of detecting a causal relationship between strategy use and success is to test a learner's performance in a language task or series of tasks, then provide instructional treatment based on strategic behaviour and then post-test in order to ascertain whether a significant difference has been made. If the study is carried out well and as many confounding variables have been eliminated as possible, then it is likely that the key variable in improving performance will have been a difference in strategic behaviour resulting from the treatment. Ideally, though, one would want to include a delayed test to see if the improvement in learning or performance was sustained over time. Additionally, we would want to measure strategic behaviour before and after. That way we not only discover 'that' SBI is effective, we also may glean a qualitative understanding of 'why' it is effective.

With this in mind let us examine a selection of SBI studies. Lack of space does not permit me to examine all four skills so I will look at general interventions into strategic behaviour, and reading and listening SBIs. This provides us with an insight if not a range of SBI evidence of effectiveness.

There have been a few interventions into general strategic behaviour, particularly in trying to raise metacognitive awareness, but the extent to which these have contributed to improving learning outcomes is not convincing. By general strategic behaviour I mean studies which encouraged learners to use a whole range of strategies which might underpin all four language skills as well as developing vocabulary and even possibly grammatical knowledge. In a study by Nunan (1997), subjects were randomly assigned to four different classes of which two received the SBI and two were used as controls. The SBI consisted essentially of an introduction to 'some of the key learning and study skills strategies underpinning the course' (p. 60). As the outcome measures were changes in strategic behaviour, perceived utility of a selection of strategies, and motivation, this is not an SBI in the currently accepted sense where some improvement of language knowledge or performance is being measured and attributed to the treatment. Nevertheless, Nunan reports that improvement in motivation was more detectable among the intervention students than the controls and that (unsurprisingly) the intervention group were more aware of strategies after the intervention. However, there was no significant difference in reported change in frequency of strategy use between the two conditions. Thus probably the most interesting finding was that a much higher proportion of intervention students 'placed a greater value' (p. 63) on strategies than the controls.

A much more successful general SBI was claimed by Flaitz and Feyten (1996). The study was carried out in two phases with first-year university students of Spanish involving both experimental and controls. The first phase consisted of metacognitive awareness raising (MAR) and 26 general strategies were encouraged. Significant differences were found between experimental and control students as measured by final grades. However, no measurement of pre-test proficiency appears to have been carried out. In the second phase both MAR and cognitive awareness raising was carried out and this time with students in a different educational context. Results for this phase appear less conclusive.

In reading comprehension, the overall results seem more conclusive. Carrell et al. (1989), Kusiak (2001), Raymond (1993), Talbot (1995), all report that students improved their reading comprehension as a result of SBI. The essential nature of these interventions was in encouraging students to identify text structure and to create a mental 'semantic map' while reading. The objective was also to encourage and enable inferencing of unknown or unfamiliar words and thus facilitate more detailed comprehension. However, in these studies there was no systematic measurement of differences in strategic behaviour prior to and after the intervention to support the findings and, although Kusiak's intervention was considerable (eight 45-minute sessions), *it was additional to the* students' normal language study, which may have favoured the experimental group.

In none of these studies was there an investigation of young learners and the general proficiency level was generally high. Positive results in a reading SBI involving young (11–12-year-olds) beginner-learners were found by Macaro and Erler (2008). In this study a series of age-specific strategies had first been identified by Erler (2002) using a grounded approach with a very similar cohort of students. The intervention measured both performance in reading comprehension and changing patterns in strategic behaviour. In the post-test experimental group readers significantly outperformed a comparison group with a reading text judged (by teachers) to be considerably above their level. Moreover, in the pre- and post-intervention strategies questionnaire, the experimental children appeared to become less reliant on the teacher and more able to engage with the text at both a word level and a global/inferential level. Unfortunately this study did not carry out delayed tests to measure sustained learning.

Fewer studies have been carried out to test whether SBI is effective in the skill of listening and those that have are less conclusive than in reading interventions. Three studies (McGruddy 1995; Ozeki 2000; Seo 2000) found only a relatively small improvement among listeners in the experimental group. In both Thompson and Rubin (1996) and Kohler (2002) more positive results were obtained and one differentiating feature may have been that these studies had a strong metacognitive element in the instruction, that is one which encouraged students to reflect and evaluate their strategic listening behaviour.

A positive impact of SBI on listening was found by Graham and Macaro (2008) in a study involving 68 lower intermediate learners of French with English L1. This study had four features which differentiated it from other listening SBIs: (1) it focused on very specific problem areas which had been identified in a previous phase of the project; (2) it linked the development of learner self-efficacy, with regard to a task, to the learners' evaluations of the effectiveness of the strategy clusters they were encouraged to try out; (3) the instruction included feedback to the learners on the strategies they reported using as the intervention progressed; and (4) it attempted to measured long-term learning by means of a delayed test. One of the specific problem areas previously elicited was the students' inability to recognize words they knew from the speech stream. This problem, the researchers hypothesized, might be due to an inability to segment groups of words in order to process them in phonological short-term memory as well as the different intonation patterns of French and English. Therefore a series of activities were included in the SBI to assist with this problem and listeners were encouraged to apply this knowledge as a strategy when problems arose. The intervention groups outperformed the controls both at post-test and delayed test and the intervention groups reported higher levels of self-efficacy with regard to listening.

This brief tour of the research on SBI would lead us to concur with other reviews of SBI (Hassan et al. 2005; Manchón 2008) that there is some limited evidence that strategy instruction can be effective. However, simply to demonstrate that language performance has improved at post-test following an intervention is not, in my view sufficient. As Manchón (2008) points out:

> perhaps the most telling feature of this research is that the proposed effects on 'learning' of strategy instruction were rarely discussed with reference to a model, theory, or hypothesis of second language acquisition. (p. 224)

So let us try to pull together what the ideal features of an SBI study report would be so that we can be confident about the effect of strategy instruction on knowledge and performance (but particularly the latter) in the L2.

1. Have the strategies been clearly defined by the researcher in the report and, more importantly, to the participants in the study? Specifically, following Macaro (2006), have they been described in terms of a cluster of mental actions, in relation to a specific task and with a clear aim as to how to accomplish that task? Moreover, is there a metacognitive dimension whereby the learner is encouraged to evaluate the effectiveness of the strategies against the task demands and his/her goals? I consider this to be a vital component of SBI in order to ensure that the independent variable (the treatment) is clearly isolated for its effect on the dependent variable (improved performance). Additionally, is the way the strategic behaviour is *supposed* to lead to learning or improved proficiency clear? In order for this to be the case, the strategies should not be described in abstract terms such as 'take notes whilst I am listening'.

2. Is there a clear relationship between the SBI (what the teacher did with the students) and what the students would be expected to do eventually as independent individual learners? Examples of the type of study which

appears to be about SBI but in fact are not are the so-called advance organizer studies (e.g., Herron et al. 1998; Teichert 1996). In these studies the researcher (or teacher) provided students with pre-listening activities designed to stimulate the schematic knowledge associated with the topic of the text they are about to hear or see. While these activities may help comprehension of the particular task at that particular time, they are no guarantee that they will improve comprehension in the long run because the independent variable is the teacher's manipulation of the task, not the student's change in strategic behaviour.

3. Is the intervention made explicit to the reader (even if it is not necessarily explicit to the learners)? Is there sufficient explanation about the way it was carried out; length of time; number of repeated exposure to examples of strategic behaviour; whether scaffolded or unscaffolded; monitored or unmonitored; whether it was evaluated or not? Apart from this transparency being essential to ensure a clear relationship between treatment and language learning improvement, it is useful to teachers to have a pedagogical intervention coherently set out so that they may be able to replicate it.

4. If the intervention is successful in terms of improvement in learning performance, is there also a measurement of change in strategic behaviour as a result of the intervention, *and* no change in other variables? The finding that the students improved in the task will be rendered even more believable if it is shown that their strategy use changed according to how the treatment intended it to change.

5. If the intervention is successful, is there any evidence that the students' motivation improved? As we have seen in at least one study above (Graham and Macaro 2008), a desirable link, in the students' mind, is: change in strategic behaviour, improvement in performance and greater self-efficacy with regard to future tasks of the same type. In this way learners can attribute success to their control of their learning rather than factors beyond their control.

6. Have delayed post-tests been carried out after a period of withdrawal from the SBI? Is there evidence that the intervention has retained its effectiveness over time and without learners being reminded by the teacher?

7. Is it clear that there is no equivalence between the strategies used in the SBI and the testing method used in the outcome measures? If there is equivalence, then the testing method may well be favouring the intervention group against the controls because they will have been prepared for the test.

8. Is there any further triangulation on the effectiveness of the SBI on improved learning, for example, by simply asking the learners' opinions?

9. Does the SBI time come out of normal teaching time? In other words is teaching time being 'sacrificed' for the purposes of improving strategic behaviour? It should not be additional time.

Many of these recommendations are not specific to SBI but to any form of intervention in the social sciences. However, they are particularly vital in LLS research if we are to show a clear causal link between strategic behaviour and improved performance.

Conclusions

In this chapter I have pursued a line of argument regarding a problem which I consider to be important in the research literature on language learner strategies, and particularly on the type of LLS research which examines relationships between variables. The argument has centred on my contention that the dependent variable 'success' has been under-theorized. This theoretical problem is not exclusive to LLS but pervades much of the individual differences literature. Gardner Tremblay and Masgoret (1997) in their examination of the relative impact of different IDs used proficiency as the outcome measure. My impression is that researchers have simply not considered this to be an issue whereas I believe that it is indeed a serious problem and lies at the heart of a number of unresolved questions linked to ID research. These unresolved questions are particularly thorny in LLS research which is a branch of ID. The over-arching claim of LLS research should be that strategic behaviour is an important ingredient in *becoming* a successful bilingual. I would be more than happy to subscribe to this claim if we could find sufficient evidence. My conclusion is that, after more than 30 years of research on LLS, we do not yet have enough evidence to make the claim. The reason for this lack of evidence results from a methodological problem. Many researchers have simply taken two measurements, strategic behaviour and proficiency, each at a single point in time, and argued that the variability of the former leads to variability in the latter. This method of describing the relationship between strategic behaviour and success is just not fit for purpose. All that this method has demonstrated so far is that learners at higher levels of proficiency use different strategy combinations to learners at lower levels of proficiency. I have therefore tried to offer solutions to the methodological problem.

I have proposed that, in a model of communicative competence which measures language in use, strategic behaviour must be the construct that adds value to the linguistic knowledge resources that the learner can draw upon during any kind of performance, be it skills based or learning based. To demonstrate that it adds value to LKR, researchers need to do two things.

First, if our resources permit it, we should be measuring achievement over time. In other words in order to isolate strategic behaviour as an independent variable which may relatively impact on *achievement* we have to control LKR at various time points during a learning/educational trajectory. The ideal design should be a longitudinal study which measures LKR, any changes in strategic behaviour and rate and type of performance progress. If our resources do not permit it, and we can only measure performance as a snapshot in time then we must *at the very least* measure LKR and stratify our samples accordingly. The research design in this case would be: divide the sample into groups with equal LKR, measure or identify strategic behaviour, then test performance.

Both these designs do raise the question of what components of LKR we should be measuring. Clearly it may be difficult to measure accurately all aspects referred to earlier and that is why I have suggested that the key components should be lexical knowledge and morpho-syntactic knowledge. However, it may be that for particular performance measures we need to focus on different aspects of LKR. For example, in a study of oral communication in a particular cultural context, it would be important to measure the component of LKR often referred to as 'pragmatic competence', but which I would call pragmatic knowledge. Does the Japanese learner/user of English *know* that British people have certain 'opening gambits' when meeting people for the first time and that 'silences' are unpleasant? (see Takaya 2007). This would be a useful component to measure under LKR in such a study. A measurement of strategic behaviour would then be whether the Japanese learner/user of English actually deploys this knowledge appropriately in a first time meeting with a British person.

The second methodological approach we need to further develop is a greater knowledge of our participants, even if the study is not a qualitative one based on a small sample. We need to have more information about the learners relative to their peers, to the environment they are learning in and to the specific language tasks they are engaged in. Only in this way can we control for confounding variables such as amount of exposure to the target language, type of teaching received and socio-economic status. This would entail a general rapprochement between educational research and applied linguistics research which I believe would be very welcomed.

Conclusions

Ernesto Macaro

This book has attempted to provide the reader with a number of insights into how researchers have gone about trying to solve the mysterious phenomenon that people, who can already speak one language, can learn other languages. It began, in Part 1, by presenting an overview of current research interests and agendas, attempting to explain key concepts, and by selecting aspects of SLA research methods which needed examination. It has tried to steer the reader through a complex landscape of books and journal articles, and enumerated the many research questions that are currently being asked. Part 2 complemented this overview by examining in some depth issues which have been in the foreground of SLA research and, within those issues, relationships between different concepts and variables.

The book did not set out to offer a comprehensive account of research in SLA, nor was its objective to arrive at an over-arching theory which explained second language acquisition. I believe the research community is still some way from being able to confidently do this. A theory of SLA would have to provide a series of logical and empirically based propositions which explained the processes through which learning, in any context, takes place and would predict that if certain circumstances pertained, a certain rate of learning would occur and/or a certain end state of learning would be attained. As we have seen from the chapters in Part 2, none of the authors, all experts in their own fields, have felt that we have arrived at a stage in the cumulative evidence which permitted the positing of a theory of SLA.

Vivian Cook has made a strong plea for SLA to be studied in its own right rather than as an adjunct to, or mirror image of, first language acquisition. Second language learners or users are not, as they develop their competence in the second language, 'doing the same thing' as first language acquirers. This is precisely because they have the knowledge and experience of a first language on which to draw as well as their greater metacognitive maturity. We have then a kind of paradox: SLA is a distinct human endeavour from L1 acquisition and development and one of the things that makes it distinct is the presence of the L1.

Perhaps this is nowhere better illustrated than in Victoria Murphy's exploration of the question of when it is best to start learning a second language. Her exploration finds little or no evidence that the early start is favourable. Here she argues that we have been largely mistaken in constantly trying to use the Critical Period (or even the so-called Sensitive Period) research agenda in order to make decisions about when children should start learning a language other than their home language. The Critical Period Hypothesis has been constructed on the basis of naturalistic evidence where exposure to the second language is extensive, deregulated and immediately applicable to communicative contexts. This is simply not the same as 'immersion' education. Let me provide a personal example. I began learning a second language (English) in an English-speaking environment (the UK) well before the offset of what is proposed as a critical period, after which, it is argued, native-like command of the language is impossible other than in a few exceptional cases. People tell me that they cannot detect any traces of my first language (Italian), although actually I can – but let's leave that aside. But my experience of being 'immersed' in the target language was entirely different from educational immersion, taking Murphy's example of a Japanese child going to immersion English in Japan. First, my contact with the L2 went far beyond history and maths lessons. It was a contact experience through the interaction with peers in the school playground, the football field and on the way home. There was language contact with shopkeepers, bus conductors and neighbours. None of these spoke my L1 just as during the school lessons there was no-one with whom to fall back on in Italian. This is entirely different from immersion classrooms where children share the L1 and in most cases the teacher knows the children's L1; where the interaction has nowhere near the communicative and emotional intensity brought about by surviving in a completely new environment. Little wonder then that the early immersion children neither make faster progress than the late immersion, nor do they provide evidence for the CPH.

Vivian Cook and Victoria Murphy's chapters also demand that we take cognizance of another growing branch of research evidence – the interaction between the second language and the first in the bilingual mind. Cook demonstrates, through the examination of experimental research, that the two systems are dynamic and symbiotic; Murphy provides evidence that some of the most effective early L2 learning occurs in settings where the child's first language is not cast aside. This once again suggests to me that attempting to suppress the L1, or pretending that an educational environment can be created whereby the L1 is untapped is virtually impossible. It also argues against the goal of SLA being projected as 'the monolingual second language speaker' (which is fascinating as an oxymoron!). As language teachers we should, of course, be trying to create bilinguals not native speakers of the L2. This requires a fundamental shift in how teachers need to conceptualize the L2 learning curriculum and pedagogy.

However (and it is a big 'however') there is another branch of research that both teachers and policy makers ignore at their peril. This branch of research is represented by Susan Gass in her exposition of how L2 input relates to L2 output. The research evidence makes it extremely hard to deny that through L2 input, L2 interaction and L2 feedback, acquisition can and does take place without any direct (or at least apparent) reference to the first language. The evidence is there even though we cannot see 'the black box' of the learner's brain in the process of converting input into output. It is because of this evidence that, despite the irrefutable presence of the L1 in L2 learning, the conclusion cannot be drawn, by practitioners, that the pedagogy should involve a constant comparison of the two languages – in other words a grammar-translation approach in instructed settings. We have abundant evidence that negotiation of meaning drives vocabulary acquisition. We have further evidence that negotiation of meaning and feedback (negative evidence) drives the development of the L2 rule-system. We have even more evidence that the cumulative effect of negotiation of meaning, feedback and forced output, provide the learner with the material and opportunities for considerable amounts of acquisition. What, in my view, we do not yet have evidence for is that this cumulative triumvirate is sufficient for the total acquisition of the target language. And that is why I believe that those authors working in the interaction hypothesis have not yet felt confident enough to posit it as an over-arching theory of acquisition.

In Chapter 1 (of Part 1) I have, in addition, argued that this area of research has concerned itself largely with *acquisition* resulting from oral interaction. It has concerned itself less with the development of *spoken performance*. In other words it has used the interaction microscope to examine the development of the *competence culture* not how input and output develop the skill of speaking. I can see why this should be so; researchers in this field are trying to develop a theory of competence not performance. However, I do believe that the time is ripe, and it would strengthen the interaction hypothesis, if research were to demonstrate both competence and performance as a result of differing features of interaction.

Instructed settings where interaction is highly prevalent have been the subject of Paul Seedhouse's contribution to this book. His examples demonstrate that there are huge gaps between the intended pedagogical objective of the teacher, the interactive activities that s/he sets up and what actually happens. Yet the reasons are not all down to either bad teaching or obstinate, uncooperative learners. It is in the interlocutors' interpretations of the objectives of the on-going talk that the breakdowns occurs. It is in that relationship between the simultaneous development of competence and performance that leads to misunderstandings. We have examples of teachers attempting to teach learners some language through encouraging them to speak, and teaching them to speak while covertly encouraging them to learn some language. In Seedhouse's chapter we are once again reminded of the difficulty of the language teaching task in that in no other subject is the L2 both the vehicle and the object of study to the same extent as in the languages classroom. It reminds us that interaction and learning are one and the same thing, and it is perhaps because of this difficulty that some practitioners resort to comparing the languages and treating the L2 purely as an object of study. In no other subject is asking beginner learners to 'write the date and underline the title' involve such a combination of language learning and language use. The 'mother tongue' teacher of English does not have to first teach the children the numbers from 1–31, at least five of the days of the week, the twelve months of the year, nor communicate the meaning of the noun 'title' or the imperative 'underline'. And it is in classroom interaction research that the intricacies of teaching both language knowledge and language use are so vividly displayed, Yet detailed analysis of classroom interaction, as we saw from the revue of the research methods of the past six years (by Andrew Cohen and Ernesto Macaro), has not been extensively used as a research tool. Indeed these authors have raised a number of concerns about some of the research instruments that are currently in vogue.

The challenges faced by the language teacher do not confine themselves to the paradoxes forced on them by the nature of interaction and acquisition, speaking and learning. They are also faced with not knowing how much each learner already 'knows' and the breadth and frameworks of that knowledge. We have been reminded of this by Paul Meara in that what it means to know vocabulary is not a straightforward question, and that it is a slightly different puzzle depending on the language you are teaching and the L1 of the learners. Take his FISH example. Apart from all lexemes associated with the word FISH, there is also the question that it is represented differently in different languages. In Spanish there is one word for the thing that swims in the sea and another for the thing you buy in the shop whereas in Italian, French and English there is only one. Moreover, the progression within vocabulary learning is a complex one rather than a simple progression from receptive knowledge to productive use. Hence teaching methodologies which place a strong emphasis on input when introducing new vocabulary and finish units of learning by eliciting productions may not be offering the range of connections needed for both breadth and depth of vocabulary learning.

So far, in these concluding remarks, we have considered SLA research entirely from a language perspective. Zoltán Dörnyei in this volume has explored two learner characteristics which are not directly language related: aptitude and motivation. Aptitude tests are not tests of the second language but tests of a stable and putative *ability to learn* a second language. Motivation is a complex trait which has been shown to be a very strong predictor of language learning success, but it is not language learning itself and you can be motivated to learn maths as well as languages. Dörnyei argues strongly that these two characteristics are anything but stable and highly unlikely to be traits – that is characteristics which are constant in the learner. Rather they are part of a complex constellation of individual differences in a constantly shifting kaleidoscope including how we see ourselves as possible bilinguals, and this in relation to our environment in general and the learning situation in particular. The motivation impulse does not, after all, occur in the heart, but in the brain. So why should it not be a series of cognitive mental actions and stages of processing which convince the learner to act in one way or another, to take one attitude or another?

My own difficulty with both aptitude and motivation literature in recent years has also been related to its putative stable and non-dynamic nature but from a slightly different perspective. In the case of aptitude, I find it difficult to accept that, say, phonological awareness and associative memory are as resistant to treatment as some of the literature suggests. There have been considerable efforts in the educational literature (albeit in mother tongue contexts) to intervene in these attributes of learners, with some success especially in the case of phonological awareness. In the case of motivation, I find there is something missing, and that is a *measure* of motivation itself. What I mean is that we have at least three major historical developments in the pursuit of the motivational construct – in what are its *characteristics*, and we have highly developed data elicitation instruments for those characteristics. What we do not seem to have is highly developed instruments which measure the motivational impulse, the drive, the effort and the sustainability of that effort. In other words we do not have motivational outcome measures. We simply compare the characteristics of motivation with language learning behaviour. Consequently, how is the teacher to judge the extent to which a learner is motivated? By observing the number of times they are willing to speak? By recording the promptness with which they deliver their homework? By asking the student on a scale of 1–10 how 'motivated' they are. It seems to me there is a big gap in the literature here.

An absence of a sufficiently defined outcome measure forms part of the central argument of my own chapter in this book which relates language learner strategies to successful learning. I hope I have demonstrated that there is considerable confusion about what we mean by successful language learning in the strategies literature and this clearly ties in with the absence of clear outcome measures in the individual differences literature more generally. In the case of strategies research I have argued for a more situated and longitudinal examination of this outcome measure. An understanding of the meaning of language learning success, just like an understanding of what it is to really know a word, is fundamental to language teaching pedagogy. For a teacher to have a clear idea of what the end and intermediate goals of learning are is crucial to the relationship s/he builds up with his/her students and to the possibility of adapting his/her language curriculum and pedagogy.

The reader will have noticed that I have tried in these concluding thoughts to raise some implications for the teacher and the learner of what has come earlier in this volume. What, after all, is the point of all this second language acquisition research? SLA is generally accepted to be a branch of applied linguistics which has been defined as the study of real world problems at the centre of which is language. In the case of SLA, who can these real world problems be for other than for teachers and learners of a second language? We should not forget this point. The real world problems are not in the process of being solved for the benefit of researchers. Researchers are merely part of the mechanism through which a problem might be solved. And I stress 'part of' because for too long teachers and learners have been left out of the SLA research equation.

Fortunately, many SLA researchers are also teachers. However, the vast majority (it seems from my scanning of the landscape in Chapter 1, Part 1) are teachers of adults. Or to be more precise, teachers of undergraduate students at university. Now I can understand why this might be so. There are pressures on university lecturers to carry out research and who better to carry out that research on than students in your own institution? But it does not get away from the fact that there is a scandalous (and I am treating myself to a highly charged adjective here) lack of research on adolescent and younger learners in 'foreign language' contexts. And there is even more of a scandalous lack of research on young *beginner* learners. This cannot continue. If we consider that the vast majority of second language learners in the world today are *not* adults and many of them are only just beginning to learn a language then we realize that we are failing in our duty to help them overcome their 'real world problems'.

So in second language acquisition research, if it is to make a real impact on teaching and learning, there are questions to be answered and issues to be addressed. These range from a far too researcher-dominated research agenda, through methodological problems identified, to a neglect of some language learning populations. I would hope that this Companion to SLA might not only serve as a source of knowledge and understanding for the scholar or reader, but also trigger in the reader a desire to address some of these issues and make a contribution to change.

References

Ackerman, P. L. (2003). Aptitude complexes and trait complexes. *Educational Psychologist, 38*, 85–93.

Ackerman, P. L. (2005). Personality, trait complexes and adult intelligence. In A. Eliasz, S. E. Hampson and B. De Raad (eds.), *Advances in personality psychology* (Vol. 2, pp. 91–112). Hove, East Sussex: Psychology Press.

Ackerman, P. L. and Heggestad, E. D. (1997). Intelligence, personality, and interests: Evidence for overlapping traits. *Psychological Bulletin, 121*, 219–245.

Ackerman, P. L. and Kanfer, R. (2004). Cognitive, affective, and conative aspects of adult intellect within a typical and maximal performance framework. In D. Y. Dai and R. J. Sternberg (eds.), *Motivation, emotion, and cognition: Integrative perspectives on intellectual functioning and development* (pp. 119–141). Mahwah, NJ: Lawrence Erlbaum.

Aitchison, J. (2003). *Words in the mind*. Oxford: Wiley-Blackwell. 3rd edition.

Alderson, J. C. and Hamp-Lyons, L. (1996). TOEFL preparation courses: A study of washback. *Language Testing, 13*, 280–297.

Al-jasser, F. (2008). The effect of teaching English phonotactics on the lexical segmentation of English as a foreign language. *System, 36*, 94–106.

Allen, L. Q. (2000). Form-meaning connections and the French causative. *Studies in Second Language Acquisition, 22*, 69–84.

Allwright, R. (1984). The importance of interaction in classroom language learning. *Applied Linguistics, 5*, 156–171.

Allwright, R. L. (1980). Turns, topics and tasks: Patterns of participation in language learning and teaching. In D. E. Larsen-Freeman (ed.), *Discourse analysis in second language research* (pp. 165–187). Rowley, MA: Newbury House.

Alptekin, C. (2002). Towards intercultural communicative competence in ELT. *ELT Journal, 56*, 57–64.

Alptekin, C. and Atakan, S. (1990). Field independence and hemisphericity as variables in L2 achievement. *Second Language Research, 6*, 135–149.

Ammar, A. and Spada, N. (2006). One size fits all? Recasts, prompts and L2 learning. *Studies in Second Language Acquisition, 28*, 543–574.

Anderson, J. R. (1983). *The architecture of cognition*. Cambridge, MA: Harvard University Press.

Anderson, L. W. and Krathwohl, D. R. (eds.) (2001). *A taxonomy for learning, teaching, and assessing: A revision of Bloom's taxonomy of educational objectives*. New York: Longman.

Anderson, N. (1991). Individual differences in strategy use in second language reading and testing. *Modern Language Journal, 75*, 4, 460–472.

Appel, J. (2007). Language teaching in performance. *International Journal of Applied Linguistics, 17*, 277–293.

Arteaga, D., Herschensohn, J. and Gess, R. (2003). Focusing on phonology to teach morphological form in French. *Modern Language Journal, 87*, 58–70.

Asher, J. J. (1986). *Learning another language through actions: The complete teacher's guidebook*. Los Gatos, CA: Sky Oaks Productions.

August, D. and Shanahan, T. (2008). *Developing reading and writing in second-language learners: Lessons from the report of the National Literacy Panel on language-minority children and youth*. New York: Routledge.

August, D. and Shanahan, T. (eds.) (2008). *Developing reading and writing in second-language learners*. NY/London: Routledge, International Reading Association, Center for Applied Linguistics.

Babaii, E. and Ansary, H. (2001). The C-test: A valid operationalization of reduced redundancy principle? *System, 29*, 209–219.

Bachman, L. F. (1990). *Fundamental considerations in language testing*. Oxford: Oxford University Press.

Bachman, L. F. and Cohen, A. D. (1998). Language testing – SLA interfaces: An update. In L. F. Bachman and A. D. Cohen (eds.), *Interfaces between second language acquisition and language testing research* (pp. 1–31). Cambridge, England: Cambridge University Press.

Baddeley, A. D. (2000). The episodic buffer: A new component of working memory? *Trends in Cognitive Sciences, 4*, 417–423.

Baddeley, A. D. and Hitch, G. J. (1974). Working memory. In G. A. Bower (ed.), *Recent advances in learning and motivation*. Volume 8 (pp. 47–89). New York: Academic Press.

Baddeley, A. D., Gathercole, S. E. and Papagno, C. (1998). The phonological loop as a language learning device. *Psychological Review, 105*, 158–173.

Baker, C. (2006). *Foundations of bilingual education and bilingualism*. Clevedon: Multilingual Matters.

Bardovi-Harlig, K. (1992). A second look at T-Unit Analysis: Reconsidering the sentence. *TESOL Quarterly, 26*, 2, 390–395.

Baron-Cohen, S. (1995). *Mindblindness: An essay on autism and theory of mind*. Cambridge, MA: MIT Press/Bradford Books.

Bartlett, F. C. (1932). *Remembering: A study in experimental and social psychology*.

Bates, E. and MacWhinney, B. (1987). Competition, variation and language learning. In B. MacWhinney (ed.), *Mechanisms of language acquisition*. Hillsdale, NJ: Erlbaum.

Bates, E. and MacWhinney, B. (1982). Functionalist approaches to grammar. In E. Wanner and L. Gleitman (eds.), *Language acquisition: The state of the art* (pp. 173–218). New York: Cambridge University Press.

Beeckmans, R., Eyckmans, J., Jansens, V., Dufranne, M. and van de Velde, H. (2001). Examining the Yes/No vocabulary test: Some methodological issues in theory and practice. *Language Testing, 18*, 235–274.

Beglar, D. and Hunt, A. (1999). Revising and validating the 2000 word level and university word level vocabulary tests. *Language Testing, 16*, 131–162.

Bellugi, U. and Brown, R. (eds.) (1964). *The acquisition of language*. Monographs of the Society for Research in Child Development, 29, 92.

Benati, A. (2001). A comparative study of the effects of processing instruction and output-based instruction on the acquisition of the Italian future tense. *Language Teaching Research, 5*, 95–127.

Benson, P. (2001). *Teaching and researching autonomy in language learning*. Harlow: Longman/Pearson Education.

Best, C. T., McRoberts, G. W. and Goodell, E. (2001). Discrimination of non-native consonant contrasts varying in perceptual assimilation to the listener's native phonological system, in *Journal of the Acoustical Society of America*, 109, 775–794.

Bialystock, E. (1979). Explicit and implicit judgements of L2 grammaticality. *Language Learning*, 29, 81–103.

Bialystok, E. (1993). 'Metalinguistic dimensions of bilingual language proficiency'. In E. Bialystok (ed.), *Language processing in bilingual children* (pp. 113–140). Cambridge: Cambridge University Press.

Bialystok, E. (2007). Acquisition of literacy in bilingual children: A framework for research. *Language Learning*, 57, 45–77.

Bialystok, E. and Miller, B. (1999). The problem of age in second-language acquisition: Influences from language, structure and task. *Bilingualism: Language and Cognition*, 2, 127–145.

Bickhard, M. H. (2003). An integration of motivation and cognition. In L. Smith, C. Rogers and P. Tomlinson (eds.), *Development and motivation: Joint perspectives* (pp. 41–56). Leicester: British Psychological Society.

Birdsong, D. (2005). Interpreting age effects in second language acquisition. In J. Kroll and A. de Groot (eds.), *Handbook of bilingualism: Psycholinguistic approaches* (pp. 109–127). Oxford: Oxford University Press.

Birdsong, D. (ed.) (1999). *Second language acquisition and the critical period hypothesis*. Mahwah, NJ: Erlbaum.

Bley-Vroman, R. (1988). The fundamental character of foreign language learning. In Rutherford, W. and Sharwood-Smith, M. (eds.), *Grammar and second language teaching: A book of readings*. New York: Newbury House/Harper and Row, 19–30.

Bley-Vroman, R. (1989). The logical problem of second language learning. In S. Gass and J. Schachter (eds.), *Linguistic perspectives on second language acquisition* (pp. 41–68). Cambridge: Cambridge University Press.

Block, E. (1986). The comprehension strategies of second language readers, *TESOL Quarterly*, 20, 463–491.

Bloom, P. (2002). *How children learn the meaning of words*. Cambridge, MA: MIT Press.

Bloomfield, L. (1933). *Language*. New York: Holt, Rinehart and Winston.

Blyth, C. (1997). A constructivist approach to grammar: Teaching teachers to teach aspect. *The Modern Language Journal*, 81, 50–66.

Bohannon, J. N. and Warren-Leubecker, A. (1988). Recent developments in speech to children: We've come a long way baby-talk. *Language Sciences*, 10, 89–110.

Bortfeld, H. and Whitehurst, G. J. (2001). Sensitive periods in first language acquisition. In D. B. Bailey, J. T. Bruer, F. J. Symons and J. W. Lichtman (eds.), *Critical thinking about critical periods*. Baltimore/London: Paul H. Brookes.

Bowles, M. A. and Leow, R. P. (2005). Reactivity and type of verbal report in SLA research methodology: Expanding the scope of investigation. *Studies in Second Language Acquisition*, 27, 415–440.

Braine, M. (1963). The ontogeny of English phrase structure: The first phase. *Language*, 39, 1–13.

Breen, M. (1985). Authenticity in the language classroom. *Applied Linguistics*, 6, 60–70.

Breen, M. (1989). The evaluation cycle for language learning tasks. In R. K. Johnson (ed.), *The second language curriculum*. Cambridge: Cambridge University Press, 187–206.

Brindley, G. (date). Outcomes-based assessment and reporting in language learning programmes: A review of the issues. *Language Testing,* 15, 45–85.

British Council (1985). *Teaching and learning in focus. Edited lessons* (Four Volumes). London: British Council.

Brock, C. (1986). The effects of referential questions in ESL classroom discourse. *TESOL Quarterly,* 20, 47–59.

Broeder, P., Extra, G., Van Hout, R., Stromqvist, S. and Voionmaa, K. (1988). *Processes in the developing lexicon.* Strasbourg: ESF *(Final Report, Volume 3* of the European Science Foundation project 'Second language acquisition by adult immigrants'). Tilburg:

Brown, J. D. (2004). Research methods for applied linguistics: Scope, characteristics, and standards (pp. 476–500). In A. Davies and C. Elder (eds.), *The handbook of applied linguistics.* Malden, MA: Blackwell.

Brown, J. D. and Rodgers, T. S. (2002). *Doing second language research.* Oxford, England: Oxford University Press.

Brown, R. (1973). *A first language: The early stages.* London: Allen and Unwin.

Brumfit, C. J. and Johnson, K. (eds.) (1979). *The communicative approach to language teaching.* Oxford: Oxford University Press.

Bruner, J. (1966). *Studies in cognitive growth.* London: Wiley.

Bruner, J. (1983). *Child's talk.* Oxford: Oxford University Press.

Bruton, A. (2007). Vocabulary learning from dictionary referencing and language feedback in EFL translational writing. *Language Teaching Research,* 11, 413–431.

Brutt-Griffler, J. (2002). *World English: A study of its development.* Clevedon: Multilingual Matters.

Buck, R. (2005). Adding ingredients to the self-organizing dynamic system stew: Motivation, communication, and higher-level emotions – and don't forget the genes! *Behavioral and Brain Science,* 28, 197–198.

Burstall, C. (1975). Factors affecting foreign-language learning: A consideration of some recent search findings. *Language Teaching and Linguistics Abstracts,* 8, 5–25.

Canagarajah, S. (1999). Interrogating the native-speaker fallacy: Non-linguistic roots, non-pedagogical results. In G. Braine, (ed.), *Non-native educators in English language teaching* (pp. 77–92). Mahwah, NJ: Erlbaum.

Canale, M. and Swain, M. (1980). Theoretical bases of communicative approaches to language teaching and testing. *Applied Linguistics,* 1, 1–47.

Carr, D. (ed.) (2006). *Teacher training DVD series* (Set of 15 DVDs). London: International House.

Carrell, P. L. (1982). Cohesion is not coherence. *TESOL Quarterly,* 16, 479–488.

Carrell, P. L. and Eisterhold, J. C. (1983). Schema theory and ESL reading pedagogy. In P. L. Carrell, J. Devine and D. E. Heskey (eds.), *Interactive approaches to second language reading.* Cambridge: Cambridge University Press.

Carrell, P. L., Pharis, B. G. and Liberto, J. C. (1989). Metacognitive strategy training for ESL reading. *TESOL Quarterly,* 20, 463–494.

Carroll, J. B. (1981). Twenty-five years of research in foreign language aptitude. In K. C. Diller (ed.), *Individual differences and universals in language learning aptitude* (pp. 83–118). Rowley, MA: Newbury House.

Carroll, J. B. and Sapon, S. (1959). *The modern language aptitude test.* San Antonio, TX: Psychological Corporation.

Carroll, S. (2001). *Input and evidence: The raw material of second language acquisition.* Amsterdam: John Benjamins.

Carroll, S. (2007). Autonomous induction theory. In B. VanPatten and J. Williams (eds.), *Theories in second language acquisition: An introduction* (pp. 155–173). Mahwah, NJ: Lawrence Erlbaum Associates.

Castagnaro, P. J. (2006). Audiolingual method and behaviourism: From misunderstanding to myth. *Applied Linguistics, 27,* 519–526.

Cenoz, J. (2003). The influence of age on the acquisition of English: General proficiency, attitudes and code-mixing. In M. García Mayo and M. García Lecumberri (eds.), *Age and the acquisition of English as a foreign language.* Clevedon: Multilingual Matters.

Chamot, A. and El-Dinary, P. (1999). Children's learning strategies in language immersion classrooms. *Modern Language Journal, 83,* 319–339.

Chaudron, C. (1988). *Second language classrooms: Research on teaching and learning.* Cambridge: Cambridge University Press.

Chien, C. and Wei, L. (1998). The strategy use in listening comprehension for EFL learners in Taiwan. *RELC Journal, 29,* 1, 66–91.

Chomsky, N. (1957). *Syntactic structures.* The Hague: Mouton.

Chomsky, N. (1965). *Aspects of the theory of syntax.* Boston, MA: MIT Press.

Chomsky, N. (1967). A review of B. F. Skinner's *Verbal Behavior.* In L. A. Jakobovits and M. S. Miron (eds.), *Readings in the psychology of language.* Prentice-Hall, pp. 142–143.

Chomsky, N. (1981). *Lectures on government and binding.* Dordrecht: Foris.

Chomsky, N. (1986). *Knowledge of language: Its nature, origin and use.* New York: Praeger.

Chomsky, N. (1990). *Some concepts and consequences of the theory of government and binding.* Boston, MA: MIT press.

Chomsky, N. (1995). *The minimalist program.* Cambridge, MA: MIT Press.

Chomsky, N. (2000). *New horizons in the study of language and mind.* Cambridge: Cambridge University Press.

Chouinard, M. M. and Clark, E. V. (2003). Adult reformulations of child errors as negative evidence. *Journal of Child Language, 30,* 637–669.

Christianson, K. (1997). Dictionary use by EFL writers: What really happens? *JSLW,* 6, 1, 23–43.

Clahsen, H. and Muysken, P. (1986). The availability of universal grammar to adult and child learners – a study of the acquisition of German word order. *Second Language Research, 2,* 93–119.

Clark, E. V. (2003). *First language acquisition.* Cambridge: Cambridge University Press.

Clément, R. and Gardner, R. C. (2001). Second language mastery. In H. Giles and W. P. Robinson (eds.), *The new handbook of language and social psychology* (2nd ed., pp. 489–504). London: Wiley.

Cobb, T. (2000). One size fits all? Francophone learners and English vocabulary tests. *Canadian Modern Language Review, 57,* 295–324.

Cohen, A. D. (1998). *Strategies in learning and using a second language.* Harlow, Essex: Longman.

Cohen, A. D. and Macaro, E. (eds.) (2007). *Language learner strategies: Thirty years of research and practice.* Oxford: Oxford University Press.

Cohen, L. and Manion, L. (1994). *Research methods in education*. 4th edition. London: Routledge.

Conklin, K. and Schmitt, N. (2008). Formulaic sequences: Are they processed more quickly than nonformulaic language by native and nonnative speakers? *Applied Linguistics*, 29, 72–89.

Cook, V. J. (1969). The analogy between first and second language learning. *International Review of Applied Linguistics*, 7, 207–216.

Cook, V. J. (1973). The comparison of language development in native children and foreign adults. *International Review of Applied Linguistics*, XI, 1, 13–28.

Cook, V. J. (1979). *Young children and language*. London: Edward Arnold.

Cook, V. J. (1986). Experimental approaches applied to two areas of second language learning research: Age and listening-based teaching methods. In V. J. Cook (ed.), *Experimental approaches to second language learning*. Oxford: Pergamon, 23–37.

Cook, V. J. (1992). Evidence for multi-competence. *Language Learning*, 42, 557–591.

Cook, V. J. (1993). *Linguistics and second language acquisition*. Basingstoke, UK: Macmillan.

Cook, V. J. (2001). *Second language learning and language teaching* (3rd edition). London: Arnold.

Cook, V. J. (2003a). The poverty-of-the-stimulus argument and structure-dependency in L2 users of English. *International Review of Applied Linguistics*, 41, 201–221.

Cook, V. J. (ed.) (2003b). *Effects of the second language on the first*. Clevedon: Multilingual Matters.

Cook, V. J. (2005). Written language and foreign language teaching. In V. Cook and B. Bassetti (eds.), *Second language writing systems* . Clevedon: Multilingual Matters, 424–442.

Cook, V. J. (2007). The goals of ELT: Reproducing native-speakers or promoting multi-competence among second language users? In J. Cummins and C. Davison (eds.), *International handbook on English language teaching*, Vol. 2 (pp. 237–248). Amsterdam: Kluwer.

Cook, V. J. (2008). *Second language learning and language teaching*. 4th edition. London: Hodder Educational.

Cook, V. J. (2009a). Multilingual Universal Grammar as the norm. In I. Leung (ed.), *Third language acquisition and universal grammar*. Bristol: Multilingual Matters, 55–70.

Cook, V. J. (2009b). Language user groups and language teaching. In V. J. Cook and Li Wei (eds.), *Contemporary Applied linguistics volume 1 language teaching and learning*. London: Continuum, t.a. 2009.

Cook, V. J. (2009c). *It's All in a Word*. London: Profile.

Cook, V. J. and Bassetti, B. (2005). An introduction to researching second language writing systems. In V. Cook and B. Bassetti (eds.), *Second language writing systems*. Clevedon: Multilingual Matters.

Cook, V. J. and Bassetti, B. (eds.) (2005). *Second language writing systems*. Clevedon: Multilingual Matters.

Cook, V. J. and Newson, M. (2007). *Chomsky's universal grammar. An introduction*, 3rd edition. Oxford: Blackwell.

Cook, V. J., Bassetti, B., Kasai, C., Sasaki, M. and Takahashi (2006). Do bilinguals have different concepts? The case of shape and material in Japanese L2 users of English. *International Journal of Bilingualism, 2,* 137–152.

Corder, S. P. (1967). The significance of learners' errors. *International Review of Applied Linguistics, 5,* 161–170.

Corder, S. P. (1971). Idiosyncratic dialects and error analysis, *International Review of Applied Linguistics, 9,* 147–159.

Corder, S. P. (1981). Language distance and the magnitude of the language learning task. In S. P. Corder (ed.), *Error analysis and interlanguage* (pp. 95–102). Oxford: Oxford University Press.

Corno, L., Cronbach, L. J., Kupermintz, H., Lohman, D. F., Mandinach, E. B., Porteus, A. W. and Talbert, J. E. (2002). *Remaking the concept of aptitude: Extending the legacy of Richard E. Snow.* Mahwah, NJ: Lawrence Erlbaum.

Coughlan, P. and Duff, P. (1994). Same task, different activities: Analysis of a second language acquisition task from an activity theory perspective, in J. P. Lantolf and G. Appel (eds.), pp. 173–194.

Creese, A. (2006). Supporting talk? Partnership teachers in classroom interaction. *International Journal of Bilingual Education and Bilingualism, 9,* 434–453.

Cromer, R. F. (1970), '"Children are nice to understand": Surface structure clues to the recovery of a deep structure', *British Journal of Psychology, 61,* 397–408.

Cromer, R. F. (1974). The development of language and cognition: The cognition hypothesis. In B. Foss (ed.), *New perspectives in child language.* London: Penguin.

Cross, S. E. and Markus, H. R. (1994). Self-schemas, possible selves, and competent performance. *Journal of Educational Psychology, 86*(3), 423–438.

Csikszentmihalyi, M. (1990). *Flow: The psychology of optimal experience.* New York: Harper and Row.

Cuervo, M. C. (2007). Double objects in Spanish as a second language: Acquisition of morphosyntax and semantics. *Studies in Second Language Acquisition, 29*(4), 583–615.

Cumming, A. (1989). 'Writing expertise and second language proficiency'. *Language Learning, 39,* 81–141.

Cummins, J. (1979). Cognitive/academic language proficiency, linguistic interdependence, the optimum age question and some other matters. *Working Papers on Bilingualism, 19,* 121–129.

Cummins, J. (1980). The cross-lingual dimensions of language proficiency: Implications for bilingual education and the optimal age issue. *TESOL Quarterly, 14,* 175–187.

Cummins, J. (1981). Age on arrival and immigrant second language learning in Canada. A reassessment. *Applied Linguistics, 11,* 132–149.

Cummins, J. (2000). *Language, power and pedagogy: Bilingual children in the crossfire.* Clevedon: Multilingual Matters.

Cummins, J. and Swain, M. (1986). *Bilingualism in education.* London: Longman.

Curtiss, S. (1977). *Genie: A psycholinguistic study of a modern-day 'Wild Child'.* New York: Academic Press.

Curtiss, S., Fromkin, V., Krashen, S., Rigler, R. and Rigler, M. (1974/2004). The linguistic development of Genie. In B. Lust and C. Foley (eds.), *First language acquisition: The essential readings.* Oxford: Blackwell.

Dai, D. Y. and Sternberg, R. J. (2004). Beyond cognitivism: Toward an integrated understanding of intellectual functioning and development. In D. Y. Dai and R. J. Sternberg (eds.), *Motivation, emotion, and cognition: Integrative perspectives on intellectual functioning and development* (pp. 3–38). Mahwah, NJ: Lawrence Erlbaum.

Daller, H., Van Hout, R. and Treffers-Daller, J. (2003). Lexical richness in the spontaneous speech of bilinguals. *Applied Linguistics, 24,* 197–222.

De Beaugrande, R. and Dressler, W. U. (1981). *Introduction to text linguistics.* London: Longman.

De Bot, K. and Weltens, B. (1995). Foreign language attrition. *Annual Review of Applied Linguistics, 15,* 151–164.

De Bot, K., Lowie, W. and Verspoor, M. (2005). *Second language acquisition: An advanced resource book.* Abingdon (UK): Routledge.

De Bot, K., Lowie, W, and Verspoor, M. (2007). A dynamic systems theory approach to second language acquisition. *Bilingualism: Language and Cognition, 10,* 7–21.

De Guerrero, M. (2005). *Inner speech – L2: Thinking words in a second language.* New York: Springer.

Deci, E. L. and Ryan, R. M. (1985). *Intrinsic motivation and self-determination in human behaviour.* New York: Plenum.

DeKeyser, R. (2007). The future of practice. In R. DeKeyser (ed.), *Practicing in a second language: Perspectives from applied linguistics and cognitive psychology.* New York: Cambridge University Press, 287–304.

DeKeyser, R. and Larson-Hall, J. (2005). What does the critical period really mean? In J. Kroll and A. de Groot (eds.), *Handbook of bilingualism: Psycholinguistic approaches.* Oxford: Oxford University Press, 88–108.

DeKeyser, R. and Larson-Hall, J. (2005). What does the Critical Period really mean? In J. Kroll and A. M. B. de Groot (eds.), *Handbook of bilingualism: Psycholinguistic approaches.* New York: Oxford University Press.

Dekeyser, R. Salaberry, R., Robinson, P. and Harrington, M. (2002). What gets processed in processing instruction? *Language Learning, 52,* 805–823.

Department of Education and Science (DES) (1990). *Modern foreign languages for ages 11 to 16.* London: Department of Education and Science and the Welsh Office.

Deprez, V. (1994). Underspecification, functional properties, and parameter setting. In B. Lut, M. Suner and J. Whitman (eds.), *Syntactic theory and first language acquisition.* Volume 1, New Jersey: Erlbaum.

Dewaele, J.-M., Petrides, K. V. and Furnham, A. (2008). The effects of trait emotional intelligence and sociobiographical variables on communicative anxiety and foreign language anxiety among adult multilinguals: A review and empirical investigation. *Language Learning, 58,* 911–960.

Donato, R. (2000). Sociocultural contributions to understanding the foreign and second language classroom, in J. P. Lantolf (ed.), *Sociocultural theory and second language learning.* Oxford: Oxford University Press, 27–50.

Dörnyei, Z. (2000). Motivation in action: Towards a process-oriented conceptualisation of student motivation. *British Journal of Educational Psychology, 70,* 519–538.

Dörnyei, Z. (2001). *Teaching and researching motivation.* Harlow: Longman.

Dörnyei, Z. (2002). The motivational basis of language learning tasks. In P. Robinson (ed.), *Individual differences in second language acquisition* (pp. 137–158). Amsterdam: John Benjamins.

Dörnyei, Z. (2003). Attitudes, orientations, and motivations in language learning: Advances in theory, research, and applications. In Z. Dörnyei (ed.), *Attitudes, orientations, and motivations in language learning* (pp. 3–32). Oxford: Blackwell.

Dörnyei, Z. (2003). *Questionnaires in second language research: Construction, administration, and processing.* Mahwah, NJ: Lawrence Erlbaum.

Dörnyei, Z. (2005). *The psychology of the language learner: Individual differences in second language acquisition.* Mahwah, NJ: Erlbaum.

Dörnyei, Z. (2007). *Research methods in applied linguistics.* Oxford, England: Oxford University Press.

Dörnyei, Z. (2009a). The L2 motivational self system. In Z. Dörnyei and E. Ushioda (eds.), *Motivation, language identity and the L2 self.* Clevedon: Multilingual Matters.

Dörnyei, Z. (2009b). *The psychology of second language acquisition.* Oxford: Oxford University Press.

Dörnyei, Z. and Ottó, I. (1998). Motivation in action: A process model of L2 motivation. *Working Papers in Applied Linguistics (Thames Valley University, London)*, 4, 43–69.

Dörnyei, Z. and Tseng, W.-T. (2009). Motivational processing in interactional tasks. In A. Mackey and C. Polio (eds.), *Multiple perspectives on interaction: Second language research in honor of Susan M. Gass* (pp. 117–134). Mahwah, NJ: Lawrence Erlbaum.

Dörnyei, Z. and Ushioda, E. (in press). *Teaching and researching motivation* (2nd ed.). Harlow: Longman.

Dörnyei, Z. (in press). Individual differences: Interplay of learner characteristics and learning environment. In N. C. Ellis and D. Larsen-Freeman (eds.), *Language as a complex adaptive system.* Oxford: Wiley Blackwell.

Doughty, C. and Long, M. H. (2003) (eds.), *The handbook of second language acquisition.* Oxford: Blackwell.

Doughty, C. and Varela, E. (1998). Communicative focus on form. In C. Doughty and J. Williams (eds.), *Focus on form in classroom second language acquisition*, 114–138. Cambridge: Cambridge University Press.

Doughty, P. S., Pearce, J. and Thornton, G. (1971). *Language in use.* London: Edward Arnold for the Schools Council.

Drew, P. and Heritage, J. (eds.) (1992a). *Talk at work: Interaction in institutional settings.* Cambridge: Cambridge University Press.

Drew, P. and Heritage, J. (1992b). Analyzing talk at work: An introduction, in P. Drew and J. Heritage (eds.), *Talk at work. Interactions in institutional settings.* Cambridge: Cambridge University Press, 3–65.

Dufva, M. and Voeten, M. J. M. (1999). Native language literacy and phonological memory as prerequisites for learning English as a foreign language. *Applied Psycholinguistics*, 20, 329–348.

Dulay, H. and Burt, M. (1974). A new perspective on the creative construct process in child second language acquisition. Working papers in bilingualism No. 4.

Dulay, H. C. and Burt, M. K. (1974). Natural sequences in child second language acquisition. *Language Learning*, 24, 37–53.

Dulay, H. C. and Burt, M. K. (1980). On acquisition orders. In S. Felix (ed.), *Second language development: Trends and issues* (pp. 245–257). Tübingen: Narr.

Dulay, H., Burt, M. K. and Krashen, S. (1982). *Language two.* New York: Oxford University Press.

Durrant, P. (2008). High-frequency collocations and second language learning. Unpublished Doctoral Thesis, University of Nottingham.

Dweck, C. S., Mangels, J. A. and Good, C. (2004). Motivational effects on attention, cognition, and performance. In D. Y. Dai and R. J. Sternberg (eds.), *Motivation, emotion, and cognition: Integrative perspectives on intellectual functioning and development* (pp. 41–55). Mahwah, NJ: Lawrence Erlbaum.

Eckman, F. R. (2004). Optimality Theory, markedness and second language syntax: The case of resumptive pronouns in relative clauses. *Studies in Phonetics, Phonology and Morphology,* 10, 89–110.

Edmondson, W. (1985). Discourse worlds in the classroom and in foreign language learning. *Studies in Second Language Acquisition,* 7, 159–168.

Egbert, J. (2003). A study of flow theory in the foreign language classroom. *Modern Language Journal,* 87, 499–518.

Ehrman, M. E. and Oxford, R. L. (1995). 'Cognition plus: Correlates of adult language proficiency'. *Modern Language Journal,* 79/1, 67–89.

Ellis, N. (2001). The processes of second language acquisition. In. B. VanPatten, J. Williams, S. Rott and M. Overstreet (eds.), *Form-meaning connections in second language acquisition.* London: Routledge.

Ellis, N. (2002). Frequency effects in language processing: A review with implications for theories of implicit and explicit language acquisition. *Studies in Second Language Acquisition,* 24, 143–188.

Ellis, N. (2003). Constructions, chunking, and connectionism: The emergence of second language structure. In C. Doughty and M. H. Long (eds.), *Handbook of second language acquisition* (pp. 33–68). Oxford: Blackwell.

Ellis, N. (2008). Usage-based and form-focused language acquisition: The associative learning of constructions, learned-attention, and the limited L2 endstate. In P. Robinson and N. Ellis (eds.), *Handbook of cognitive linguistics and second language acquisition* (pp. 372–405). London: Routledge.

Ellis, N. and Larsen-Freeman, D. (2006). Language emergence: Implications for applied linguistics – Introduction to the special issue. *Applied Linguistics,* 27, 558–589.

Ellis, R. (1985). Sources of variability in interlanguage. *Applied Linguistics,* 6, 118–131.

Ellis, R. (1994/2008). *The study of second language acquisition.* Oxford: Oxford University Press.

Ellis, R. (2003). *Task-based language learning and teaching.* Oxford: Oxford University Press.

Ellis, R. (2004). The definition and measurement of L2 explicit knowledge. *Language Learning,* 54, 227–275.

Ellis, R. (ed.) (2005). *Planning and task performance in a second language.* Amsterdam: John Benjamins.

Ellis, R. (2007). The differential effect of corrective feedback on two grammatical structures. In A. Mackey (ed.), *Conversational interaction and second language acquisition: A series of empirical studies* (pp. 339–360). Oxford, UK: Oxford University Press.

Ellis, R. and Sheen, Y. (2006). Re-examining the role of recasts in L2 acquisition. *Studies in Second Language Acquisition,* 28, 575–600.

Ellis, R., Basturkmen, H. and Loewen, S. (2001). Learner uptake in communicative ESL lessons. *Language Learning,* 51, 281–318.

315

Ellis, R., Loewen, S. and Erlam, R. (2006). Implicit and explicit corrective feedback and the acquisition of L2 grammar. *Studies in Second Language Acquisition, 28,* 339–368.

Ellis, R. Tanaka, Y. and Yamazaki, A. (1994). Classroom interaction, comprehension and the acquisition of L2 word meanings. *Language Learning, 44,* 449–491.

Emmorey, K. (2002). *Language, cognition and the brain: Insights from sign language research.* Mahwah, NJ: Erlbaum.

Ericsson, K. A. and Simon, H. A. (1993). *Protocol analysis: Verbal reports as data.* Cambridge, MA: Bradford/MIT Press.

Erlam, R. (2003). The effects of deductive and inductive instruction on the acquisition of Direct Object Pronouns in French as a second language. *The Modern Language Journal, 87,* 242–260.

Erler, L. (2002). Reading in a foreign language: Near-beginner adolescents' experiences of French in English secondary schools. Unpublished Doctoral Dissertation. University of Oxford.

Ervin-Tripp, S. (1974). Is second language learning like the first? *TESOL Quarterly, 8,* 111–127.

Escudero, P. and Boersma, P. (2004). Bridging the gap between L2 speech perception research and phonological theory. *Studies in Second Language Acquisition, 26,* 551–585.

Farrar, M. J. (1992). Negative evidence and grammatical morpheme acquisition. *Developmental Psychology, 28,* 90–98.

Felix, S. (1987). *Cognition and language growth,* Dordrecht: Foris.

Ferguson, C. (1971). Absence of copula and the notion of simplicity: A study of normal speech, baby talk, foreigner talk and pidgins. In D. Hymes (ed.), *Pidginization and creolization of languages* (pp. 141–150). Cambridge: Cambridge University Press.

Ferguson, C. H. (1959). Diglossia. *Word, 15,* 325–340.

Ferris, D. R. (2003). *Response to student writing: Implications for second language students.* Mahwah, NJ: Lawrence Erlbaum Associates.

Field, J. (2004). An insight into listeners' problems: Too much bottom-up or too much top-down? *System, 32,* 363–377.

Fitzpatrick, T. and Barfield, A. (eds.) (2009). *Lexical processing in second language learners: Essays in honour of Paul Meara.* Clevedon: Multilingual Matters.

Flaitz, J. and Feyten, C. (1996). A two phase study involving consciousness raising and strategy use for foreign language learners. In R. Oxford (ed.), *Language learning strategies around the world: Cross cultural perspectives* (Tech. Rep. No. 13, pp. 157–166). Honolulu: Second Language Teaching and Curriculum Center, University of Hawai`i.

Folse, K. (2006). The effect of type of written exercise on L2 vocabulary retention. *TESOL Quarterly, 14,* 182–177.

Foster, P. (1998). A classroom perspective on the negotiation of meaning. *Applied Linguistics, 19,* 1–23.

Fraser, B. (1999). What are discourse markers? *Journal of Pragmatics, 31,* 931–952.

Freed, B. (1980). Talking to foreigners versus talking to children; similarities and differences. In S. D. Krashen and R. C. Scarcella (eds.), *Issues in second language research* (pp. 19–27). Rowley, MA: Newbury House.

Freeman, D. and Richards, J. C. (1996) (eds.), *Teacher learning in language teaching*. Cambridge: Cambridge University Press.

Froehlich, M., Spada, N. and Allen, P. (1985). Differences in the communicative orientation of L2 classrooms. *TESOL Quarterly*, 19, 27–57.

Gan, Z., Humphreys, G. and Hamp-Lyons, L. (2004). 'Understanding successful and unsuccessful EFL students in Chinese universities'. *Modern Language Journal*, 88/3, 229–244.

Ganshow, L. and Sparks, R. (2001). Learning difficulties and FL learning: A review of research and instruction. *Language Teaching*, 34, 79–98.

García Lecumberri, M. and Gallardo, F. (2003). English FL sounds in school learners of different ages. In M. García Mayo and M. García Lecumberri (eds.). (pp?)

García Mayo, M. (2003). Age, length of exposure and grammaticality judgements in the acquisition of English as a foreign language. In M. García Mayo and M. García Lecumberri (eds.). *(pp?)*

García Mayo, M. and García Lecumberri, M. (eds.) (2003). *Age and the acquisition of English as a foreign language*. Clevedon: Multilingual Matters.

Gardener, H. (1993). *Multiple intelligences: The theory in practice*. New York: Basic Books.

Gardner, R. C. (1985). *Social psychology and second language learning: The role of attitudes and motivation*. London: Edward Arnold.

Gardner, R. C. (2005). *Integrative motivation and second language acquisition*. Paper presented at the Joint Convention of the Canadian Association of Applied Linguistics and the Canadian Linguistics Association in London, Canada. Retrieved on 9 September 2008 from http://publish.uwo.ca/~gardner/caaltalk5final.pdf

Gardner, R. C. and Lambert, W. E. (1959). Motivational variables in second language acquisition. *Canadian Journal of Psychology*, 13, 266–272.

Gardner, R. C. and MacIntyre, P. (1992). A student's contributions to second language learning. Part I: Cognitive variables. *Language Teaching*, 25, 211–220.

Gardner, R. C. and MacIntyre, P. D. (1993). A student's contributions to second-language learning. Part II: Affective variables. *Language Teaching*, 26, 1–11.

Gardner, R. C. and Tremblay, P. F. (1994). On motivation, research agendas and theoretical frameworks. *Modern Language Journal*, 78, 359–368.

Gardner, R. C., Tremblay, P. F. and Masgoret, A-M. (1997). Towards a full model of second language learning: An empirical investigation. *The Modern Language Journal*, 81, 3, 344–36.

Gass, S. (1979). Language transfer and universal grammatical relations. *Language Learning*, 29, 327–344.

Gass, S. (1988). Integrating research areas: A framework for second language studies. *Applied Linguistics*, 9, 198–217.

Gass, S. (1997). *Input, interaction and the second language learner*. Mahwah, NJ: Lawrence Erlbaum Associates.

Gass, S. (2003). Input and interaction. In C. Doughty and M. H. Long (eds.), *The handbook of second language acquisition* (pp. 224–255). Oxford, UK: Basil Blackwell.

Gass, S. and Varonis, E. (1985). Variation in native speaker speech modification to non-native speakers. *Studies in Second Language Acquisition*, 7, 37–57.

Gass, S. and Mackey, A. (2000). *Stimulated recall methodology in second language research*. Mahwah, NJ: Lawrence Erlbaum Associates.

Gass, S. and Mackey, A. (2006). Input, interaction and output: An overview. In K. Bardovi-Harlig and Z. Dörnyei (eds.), *AILA review* (pp. 3–17). Amsterdam: John Benjamins.

Gass, S. and Mackey, A. (2007). *Data elicitation for second and foreign language research.* Mahwah, NJ: Lawrence Erlbaum Associates.

Gass, S. and Schachter, J. (eds.) (1989). *Linguistic perspectives on second language acquisition.* Cambridge: Cambridge University Press.

Gass, S. and Selinker, L. (2008). *Second language acquisition: An introductory course* (3rd edition). London: Routledge.

Gass, S. and Varonis, E. (1989). Incorporated repairs in NNS discourse. In M. Eisenstein (ed.), *Variation and second language acquisition* (pp. 71–86). New York: Plenum.

Gass, S. and Varonis, E. (1994). Input, interaction and second language production. *Studies in Second Language Acquisition, 16,* 283–302.

Gass, S. Mackey, A. and Ross-Feldman, L. (2005). Task-based interaction in classroom and laboratory settings. *Language Learning, 55,* 575–561.

Gass, S., Behney, J. and Uzum, B. (in preparation). Inhibitory control, working memory, and L2 interaction gains.

Gathercole, S. E. and Baddeley, A. D. (1993). *Working memory and language.* New Jersey: Lawrence Erlbaum.

Gattegno, C. (1972). *Teaching foreign languages in schools – the silent way.* New York: Educational Solutions Inc.

Gattegno, C. (1976). *The common sense of teaching foreign languages.* New York: Educational Solutions Inc.

Genesee, F. (1981). A comparison of early and late second language learning. *Canadian Journal of Behavioral Science, 13,* 115–127.

Genesee, F. (1987). *Learning through two languages: Studies of immersion and bilingual education.* Rowley, MA: Newbury House.

Genesee, F. (1999). *Program alternatives for linguistically diverse students.* Educational Practice Report No. 1 Santa Cruz, CA and Washington, DC: Center for Research on Education, Diversity and Excellence. Available: http://www.cal.org/crede/pubs/edpractice/EPR1.htm

Genesee, F. (2004). What do we know about bilingual education for majority language students? In T. K. Bhatia and W. Ritchie (eds.), *Handbook of bilingualism and multiculturalism.* Malden, MA: Blackwell.

Genesee, F., Paradis, J. and Crago, M. (2004). *Dual language development and disorders: A handbook on bilingualism and second language learning.* Baltimore: Brookes.

Genesee, F., Lindholm-Leary, K., Saunders, W. M. and Christian, D. (2006). *Educating English language learners: A synthesis of research evidence.* Cambridge: Cambridge University Press.

Geva, E. and Wang, M. (2001). The development of basic reading skills in children: A cross language perspective. *Annual Review of Applied Linguistics, 21,* 182–204.

Gleick, J. (1993). *Chaos.* London: Abacus.

Gleitman, L. (1982). Maturational determinants of language growth. *Cognition, 10,* 103–114.

Goetz, P. J. (2003). The effects of bilingualism on theory of mind development. *Bilingualism, Language and Cognition, 6, 1,* 1–15.

Goh, C. M. (2000). A cognitive perspective on language learners' listening comprehension problems. *System*, 28, 55–75.

Goh, C. M. and Foong, K. P. (1997). Chinese ESL students' learning strategies: A look at frequency, proficiency, and gender. *Hong Kong Journal of Applied Linguistics*, 2, 1, 39–53.

Goldschneider, J. M. and DeKeyser, R. (2001). Explaining the natural order of L2 morpheme acquisition in English: A meta-analysis of multiple determinants. *Language Learning*, 51, 1–50.

Graham, S. and Macaro, E. (2008). Strategy instruction in listening for intermediate learners of French. *Language Learning*, 58, 747–783.

Graham, S., Santos, D. and Vanderplank, R. (2008). Listening comprehension and strategy use: A longitudinal study. *System*, 36, 52–68.

Green, A. (1998). *Verbal protocol analysis in language testing research: A handbook.* Cambridge: Cambridge University Press.

Green, J. M. and Oxford, R. (1995). A closer look at learning strategies, L2 proficiency, and gender. *TESOL Quarterly*, 29, 261–297.

Green, P. and Hecht, K. (1992). Implicit and Explicit Grammar: An empirical study. *Applied Linguistics*, 13, 168–184.

Greinadus, T., Beks, B. and Wakely, R. (2005). Testing the development of French word knowledge by advanced Dutch- and English-speaking learners and native speakers. *Modern Language Journal*, 89, 221–233.

Griffiths, C. (2003). Patterns of language learning strategy use. *System*, 31, 367–383.

Griffiths, C. (2008). *Lessons from the good language learner.* Cambridge: Cambridge University Press.

Gu, P. Y. (2004). 'Fine Brush and freehand: The vocabulary-learning art of two successful Chinese EFL learners'. *TESOL Quarterly*, 37/1, 73–104.

Guastello, S. J., Johnson, E. A. and Rieke, M. L. (1999). Nonlinear dynamics of motivational flow. *Nonlinear Dynamics, Psychology, and Life Sciences*, 3, 259–273.

Guasti, M. T. (2002). *Language acquisition: The growth of the grammar.* Cambridge, MA: Bradford Books.

Guthrie, E. (1983). Intake, communication and second-language teaching. In S. J. Savignon and M. S. Berns (eds.), *Communicative language teaching: Where are we going?* (pp. 33–53). Studies in Language Learning, 4, 2, (EDRS No. ED278226).

Haastrup, K. and Henriksen, B. (1998). Vocabulary acquisition: From partial to precise learning. In K. Haastrup and A. Viberg (eds.), *Perspectives on lexical acquisition in a second language* (pp. 97–124). Lund: Lund University Press.

Haastrup, K. and Henriksen, B. (2000). Vocabulary acquisition: Acquiring depth of knowledge through network building. *International Journal of Applied Linguistics*, 10, 61–80.

Hakuta, K. (1974). A preliminary report on the development of grammatical morphemes in a Japanese girl learning English as a second language. *Working Papers in Bilingualism*, 3, 18–43.

Hakuta, K. (2001). A critical period for second language acquisition? In D. B. Bailey, J. T. Bruer, F. J. Symons and J. W. Lichtman (eds.), *Critical thinking about critical periods*. Baltimore/London: Paul H. Brookes.

Halliday, M. A. K. (1975). *Learning how to mean.* London: Edward Arnold.

Hammond, K. (2006). More than a game: A critical discourse analysis of a racial inequality exercise in Japan. *TESOL Quarterly*, 40, 545–571.

Han, Z. (2002). A study of the impact of recasts on tense consistency in L2 output. *TESOL Quarterly*, 36, 543–572.

Han, Z. H. (2004). *Fossilization in adult second language acquisition*. Clevedon: Multilingual Matters.

Hanaoka, O. (2007). Output, noticing, and learning: An investigation into the role of spontaneous attention to form in a four-stage writing task. *Language Teaching Research*, 11, 459–479.

Hannan, M. (2004). A study of the development of the English verbal morphemes in the grammar of 4–9 year old Bengali-speaking children in the London borough of Tower Hamlets. Unpublished doctoral dissertation, University of Essex.

Harmer, J. (1998). *How to teach English*. Harlow: Longman.

Hassan, X., Macaro, E., Mason, D., Nye, G., Smith, P. and Vanderplank, R. (2005). Strategy training in language learning – a systematic review of available research. In *Research evidence in education library*. London: EPPI-Centre, Social Science Research Unit, Institute of Education, University of London.

Hatch, E. (1978). Discourse analysis and second language acquisition. In E. Hatch (ed.), *Second language acquisition: A book of readings*. Rowley, MA: Newbury House, 401–435.

Hatch, E. (1983). Simplified input and second language acquisition. In R. Andersen (ed.), *Pidginization and creolization as language acquisition* (pp. 64–86). Rowley, MA: Newbury House.

Have, P. Ten. (2005). *Doing conversation analysis*. London: Sage.

Hawkins, E. (1984). *Awareness of language. An introduction*. Cambridge: Cambridge University Press.

Hawkins, R. and Chen, C. (1997). The partial availability of Universal Grammar in second language acquisition: The 'failed functional features' hypothesis. *Second Language Research*, 13, 187–226.

Henriksen, B. (1999). Three dimensions of vocabulary development. *Studies in Second Language Acquisition*, 21, 303–317.

Heritage, J. (1984). *Garfinkel and ethnomethodology*. Cambridge: Polity Press.

Herron, C., Cole, P., York, H. and Linden, P. (1998). A comparison study of student retention of foreign language video: Declarative versus interrogative advance organizer. *Modern Language Journal*, 82, 237–247.

Herschensohn, J. (2007). *Language development and age*. Cambridge: Cambridge University Press.

Hesse-Biber, N. S. and Leavy, P. (2006). *The practice of qualitative research*. Thousand Oaks, CA: Sage.

Hidi, S., Renninger, K. A. and Krapp, A. (2004). Interest, a motivational variable that combines affective and cognitive functioning. In D. Y. Dai and R. J. Sternberg (eds.), *Motivation, emotion, and cognition: Integrative perspectives on intellectual functioning and development* (pp. 89–115). Mahwah, NJ: Lawrence Erlbaum.

Higgins, E. T. (1987). Self-discrepancy: A theory relating self and affect. *Psychological Review*, 94, 319–340.

Higgins, E. T. (1998). Promotion and prevention: Regulatory focus as a motivational principle. *Advances in Experimental Social Psychology*, 30, 1–46.

Holec, H. (1981). *Autonomy and foreign language learning*. Oxford: Pergamon.

Hosenfeld, C. (1997). A preliminary investigation of the reading strategies of successful and nonsuccessful second language learners. *System*, 5, 110–123.

Howatt, A. (2004). *A history of English language teaching,* 2nd edition. Oxford: Oxford University Press.

Howatt, A. and Widdowson, H. G. (2004). *A history of English language teaching,* 2nd edition. Oxford: Oxford University Press.

Hu Guangwei (2002). Psychological constraints on the utility of metalinguistic knowledge in second language production. *Studies in Second Language Acquisition,* 24, 347–386.

Huibregtse, I., Admiraal, W. and Meara, P. M. (2002). Scores on a Yes/No vocabulary test: Correction for guessing and response style. *Language Testing,* 19, 227–245.

Hunt, K. W. (1965). *Grammatical structures written at three grade levels.* (Research Report No. 3). Urbana. IL: National Council of Teachers of English.

Hunt, K. W. (1970). Recent measures in syntactic development. In M. Lester (ed.), *Readings in applied transformation grammar.* New York: Holt, Rinehart and Winston.

Hutchby, I. and Wooffitt, R. (1998). *Conversation analysis.* Cambridge: Polity Press.

Hyland, K. and Tse, P. (2004). Metadiscourse in academic writing: A reappraisal. *Applied Linguistics,* 25, 156–177.

Hyltenstam, K. and Abrahamsson, N. (2003). Maturational constraints in SLA. In C. J. Doughty and M. H. Long (eds.), *The handbook of second language acquisition.* Oxford: Blackwell.

Hymes, D. (1972). On communicative competence. In J. B. Pride and J. Holmes (eds.), *Sociolinguistics.* Harmondsworth: Penguin.

Ingram, D. (1989). *First language acquisition.* Cambridge: Cambridge University Press.

Ishida, M. (2004). Effects of recasts on the acquisition of the aspectual form *-te i-(ru)* by learners of Japanese as a foreign language. *Language Learning,* 54, 311–394.

Izumi, S., Bigelow, M., Fujiwara, M. and Fearnow, S. (1999). Testing the output hypothesis: Effects of output on noticing and second language acquisition. *Studies in Second Language Acquisition,* 21, 421–452.

Jackendoff, R. (2002). *Foundations of language: Brain, meaning, grammar, evolution.* Oxford, UK: Oxford University Press.

Jackson, C. (2007). The use and non-use of semantic information, word order, and case markings during comprehension by L2 learners of German. *Modern Language Journal,* 91, 418–432.

Jarvis, S. (2002). Short texts, best-fitting curves and new measures of lexical diversity. *Language Testing,* 19, 57–84.

Jarvis, S. and Pavlenko, A. (eds.) (2008). *Crosslinguistic influence in language and cognition.* Abingdon: Routledge.

Johnson, J. and Newport, E. (1989). Critical period effects in second language learning: The influence of maturational state on the acquisition of ESL. *Cognitive Psychology,* 21, 60–99.

Johnson, J. Prior, S. and Artuso, M. (2002). Field dependence as a factor in second language communicative production. *Language Learning,* 50, 529–567.

Johnson, K. (2005). *Expertise in second language learning and teaching.* Basingstoke, UK: Palgrave Macmillan.

Johnson, K. E. (1995). *Understanding communication in second language classrooms.* Cambridge: Cambridge University Press.

Johnson, R. K. and Swain, M. (1997). *Immersion education: International perspectives.* Cambridge: Cambridge University Press.

Johnstone, B. (2000). *Qualitative methods in sociolinguistics.* New York: Oxford.

Kang, H-W. and Golden, A. (1994). Vocabulary learning and instruction in a second or a foreign language. *International Journal of Applied Linguistics, 4,* 57–77.

Karmiloff, K. and Karmiloff-Smith, A. (2001). *Pathways to language: From foetus to adolescent.* Harvard: Harvard University Press.

Kasper, G. and Kellerman, E. (eds.) (1997). *Communication strategies: Psycholinguistic and sociolinguistic perspectives.* London: Longman.

Keenan, E. and Comrie, B. (1977). Noun phrase accessibility and Universal Grammar. *Linguistic Inquiry, 8,* 63–99.

Kellerman, E., Koonen, H. and van der Haagen, M. (2005). 'Feet speak louder than words': A preliminary analysis of language provisions for professional footballers in the Netherlands. In M. H. Long (ed.), *Second language needs analysis* (pp. 200–224). Cambridge: Cambridge University Press.

Kelly, G. A. (1955). *The psychology of personal constructs: A theory of personality.* New York: W. E. Norton and Co. Inc.

Kern, R., Ware, P. and Warschauer, M. (2004). Crossing frontiers: New directions in online pedagogy and research. *Annual Review of Applied Linguistics,* 243–260.

Khaldieh, S. A. (2000). 'Learning strategies and writing process of proficient vs. less-proficient learners of Arabic'. *Foreign Language Annals, 33,* 522–533.

Kim, J.-H. and Han, Z. (2007). Recasts in communicative EFL classes: Do teacher intent and learner interpretation overlap? In A. Mackey (ed.), *Conversational interaction in second language acquisition.* Oxford: Oxford University Press.

Kim, S.-H. (2008). Noticeability of feedback: The effects of noticing in reformulation of L2 writing. Paper presented at SLRF, Honolulu.

Klein, W. and Perdue, C. (1997). 'The basic variety (or: couldn't natural languages be much simpler?)', *Second Language Research, 13,* 301–347.

Knell, E., Qiang, H., Pei, M., Chi, Y., Siegel, L. S., Zhao, L. and Zhao, W. (2007). Early English immersion and literacy in Xi'an, China. *The Modern Language Journal, 91,* 395–417.

Kohler, D. B. (2002). *The effects of metacognitive language learning strategy training on lower-achieving second language learners.* Unpublished doctoral dissertation, Department of Instructional Psychology and Technology, Brigham Young University, USA.

Kojic-Sabo, I. and Lightbown, P. M. (1999). 'Students' approaches to vocabulary learning and their relationship to success.' *Modern Language Journal, 83/2,* 176–192.

Kormos, J. (2000). The role of attention in monitoring second language speech production. *Language Learning, 50,* 343–384.

Kormos, J. and Dörnyei, Z. (2004). The interaction of linguistic and motivational variables in second language task performance. *Zeitschrift für Interkulturellen Fremdsprachenunterricht [Online], 9,* p. 19.

Kosslyn, S. M. and Smith, E. E. (2000). Introduction to Part VIII: Higher cognitive functions. In M. S. Gazzaniga (ed.), *The new cognitive neurosciences* (2nd edition, pp. 961–963). Cambridge, MA: MIT Press.

Kramsch, C. (1993). *Context and culture in language teaching.* Oxford: Oxford University Press.

Kramsch, C. (2002) (ed.). *Language acquisition and language socialization: Ecological perspectives*. London: Continuum.

Krashen, S. (1982). *Principles and practice in second language acquisition*. New York: McGraw-Hill.

Krashen, S. D. (1981). *Second language acquisition and second language learning*. Oxford, UK: Pergamon.

Krashen, S. D. (1985). *The input hypothesis: Issues and implications*. London: Longman.

Krashen, S. D. and Terrell, T. D. (1983). *The natural approach: Language acquisition in the classroom*. London: Prentice Hall.

Krathwohl, D. R., Bloom, B. S. and Massia, B. B. (1964). Taxonomy of educational objectives. Handbook 2: Affective domain. New York: David McKay Company.

Kuiken, F. and Vedder, I. (2002). The effect of interaction in acquiring the grammar of a second language. *International Journal of Educational Research, 37*, 343–358.

Kusiak, M. (2001). The effect of metacognitive strategy training on reading comprehension and metacognitive knowledge. *EUROSLA Yearbook, 255*–274.

Labov, W. (1984). Field methods of the project on linguistic change and variation. In Baugh, J. and Sherzer, J. (eds.), *Language in use: Readings in sociolinguistics, 28*–53. Englewood Cliffs: Prentice Hall.

Lado, R. (1957). *Linguistics across cultures, applied linguistics language teachers*. Ann Arbor, MI: University of Michigan Press.

Lamb, T. and Reinders, H. (2008). *Learner and teacher autonomy: Concepts, realities and responses*. Amsterdam: John Benjamins.

Lambert, W. E. and Tucker, G. R. (1972). *Bilingual education of children: The St. Lambert experiment*. Rowley MA: Newbury House.

Lantolf, J. (ed.) (2000). *Sociocultural theory and second language learning*. Oxford: Oxford University Press.

Lantolf, J. (2007). Sociocultural theory and second language learning. In B. VanPatten and J. Williams (eds.), *Theories in second language acquisition: An introduction* (pp. 201–224). Mahwah, NJ: Lawrence Erlbaum Associates.

Lantolf, J. and Appell, G. (1994) (eds.), *Vygotskian approaches to second language research*. Norwood, NJ: Ablex.

Lantolf, J. P. and Thorne, S. (2006). *Sociocultural theory and the genesis of second language development*. Oxford, UK: Oxford University Press.

Larsen-Freeman (1997). Chaos/complexity science and second language acquisition. *Applied Linguistics, 18*, 141–165.

Larsen-Freeman, D. and Cameron, L. (2008). *Complex systems and applied linguistics*. Oxford: Oxford University Press.

Larsen-Freeman, D. and Long, M. H. (1991). *An introduction to second language acquisition research*. London: Longman.

Larson-Hall, J. (2008). Weighing the benefits of studying a foreign language at a younger starting age in a minimal input situation. *Second Language Research, 24*, 35–63.

Lasagabaster, D. and Doiz, A. (2003). Maturational constraints on foreign-language written production. In M. García Mayo and M. García Lecumberri (eds.) 136–160.

Laufer, B. (1994).The lexical profile of second language writing: Does it change over time? *RELC Journal, 25*, 21–33.

Laufer, B. (1995). Beyond 2000: A measure of productive lexicon in second language. In L. Eubank and M. Sharwood-Smith (eds.), *The current state of interlanguage* (pp. 265–272). Philadelphia, PA: John Benjamins.

Laufer, B. (1998). The development of passive and active vocabulary in a second language: Same or different? *Applied Linguistics, 19, 2, 255–271.*

Laufer, B. (2001). Quantitative evaluation of vocabulary: How it can be done and what it is good for. In C. Elder, A. Brown, E. Grove, K. Hill, N. Iwashita, T. Lumley, T. McNamara and K. O.'Loughlin (eds.), *Experimenting with uncertainty* (pp. 241–250). Cambridge: Cambridge University Press.

Laufer, B. (2005). Lexical frequency profiles: From Monte Carlo to the Real World. A response to Meara. *Applied Linguistics, 26, 581–587.*

Laufer, B. and Nation, I. S. P. (1995). Vocabulary size and use: Lexical richness in L2 written production. *Applied Linguistics, 16, 307–322.*

Laufer, B. and Nation, P. (1999). A vocabulary size test of controlled productive ability. *Language Testing, 16, 33–51.*

Lazaraton, A. (2002). Quantitative and qualitative approaches to discourse analysis. *Annual Review of Applied Linguistics, 22, 32–51.*

Lazaraton, A. (2005). Quantitative research methods. In Hinkel, E. (ed.), *Handbook of research in second language teaching and learning* (pp. 209–224). Mahwah, NJ: Lawrence Erlbaum.

Lee, J. and Shallert, D. L. (1997). The relative contribution of L2 langauge proficiency and L1 reading ability to L2 reading performance: A test of the threshold hypothesis in an EFL context. *TESOL Quarterly, 31, 4, 713–739.*

Leeman, J. (2003). Recasts and second language development: Beyond negative evidence. *Studies in Second Language Acquisition, 25, 37–63.*

Leeser, M. J. (2004). The effects of topic familiarity, mode, and pausing on second language learners' comprehension and focus on form. *Studies in Second Language Acquisition, 26, 587–615.*

Leeser, M. J. (2007). Learner-based factors in L2 reading comprehension and processing grammatical form: Topic familiarity and working memory. *Language Learning, 57, 229–270.*

Lenneberg, E. H. (1967). *Biological foundations of language.* New York: Wiley.

Lennon, P. (1990). Error: Some problems of definition, identification, and distinction. *Applied Linguistics, 12, 180–195.*

Lennon, P. (1990). Investigating fluency in EFL: A quantitative approach. *Language Learning, 40, 387–417.*

Leow, R. P. and Morgan-Short, K. (2004). To think aloud or not to think aloud: The issue of reactivity in SLA research methodology. *Studies in Second Language Acquisition, 26, 35–57.*

Leung, C. and Mohan, B. (2004). Teacher formative assessment and talk in classroom contexts: Assessment as discourse and assessment of discourse. *Language Testing, 21, 335–359.*

Levinson, S. (1983). *Pragmatics.* Cambridge: Cambridge University Press.

Lewis, M. (1993). *The lexical approach: The state of ELT and a way forward.* Hove, England: Language Teaching Publications.

Lewis, M. (1997). *Implementing the lexical approach.* Hove, England: Language Teaching Publications.

Lewis, M. D. (2005). Bridging emotion theory and neurobiology through dynamic systems modelling. *Behavioral and Brain Science*, 28, 169–245.

Lightbown, P. and Spada, N. (1993/2006). *How languages are learned*. Oxford: Oxford University Press.

Lindholm-Leary, K. and Borsato, G. (2007). Academic achievment. In F. Genesee, K. Lindholm-Leary, W. M. Saunders and D. Christian (eds.), *Educating English language learners: A synthesis of research evidence*. New York: Cambridge University Press.

Linnenbrink, E. A. and Pintrich, P. R. (2004). Role of affect in cognitive processing in academic contexts. In D. Y. Dai and R. J. Sternberg (eds.), *Motivation, emotion, and cognition: Integrative perspectives on intellectual functioning and development* (pp. 57–87). Mahwah, NJ: Lawrence Erlbaum.

Littlemore, J. (2001). An empirical study of the relationship between cognitive style and the use of communication strategy. *Applied Linguistics*, 22, 241–265.

Littlewood, W. (1981). *Communicative language teaching: An introduction*. Cambridge: Cambridge University Press.

Locke, E. A. (2000). Motivation, cognition, and action: An analysis of studies of task goals and knowledge. *Applied Psychology: An International Review*, 49, 408–429.

Loewen, S. (2005). Incidental focus on form and second language learning. *Studies in Second Language Acquisition*, 27, 361–386.

Long, M. (1981). Input, interaction and second language acquisition. In Winitz, H. (ed.), *Native Language and Foreign Language Acquisition, Annals of the New York Academy of Sciences*, 379, 259–278.

Long, M. (1983). 'Inside the "Black Box"'. In H. Seliger and M. Long (eds.), *Classroom oriented research in second language acquisition* (pp. 3–36). Rowley: Newbury House.

Long, M. (1985). Input and second language acquisition theory, in S. Gass and C. Madden (eds.), *Input in second language acquisition* (pp. 377–393). Rowley: Newbury House.

Long, M. H. (1991). Focus on form: A design feature in language teaching methodology. In K. de Bot, R. Ginsberg and C. Kramsch (eds.), *Foreign language research in cross-cultural perspective* (pp. 39–52). Amsterdam: John Benjamins.

Long, M. H. (1996). The role of the linguistic environment in second language acquisition. In W. Ritchie and T. Bhatia (eds.), *Handbook of second language acquisition* (pp. 413–468). San Diego, CA: Academic Press.

Long, M. H. (1996). The Role of the Linguistic Environment in Second Language Acquisition, in W. C. Ritchie and T. K. Bhatia (eds.), *Handbook of second language acquisition*. New York: Academic Press, 414–468.

Long, M. H. (2007). *Problems in SLA*. Mahwah, NJ: Lawrence Erlbaum Associates.

Lubelska, D. and Matthews, M. (1997). *Looking at language classrooms*. Cambridge: Cambridge University Press.

Lubinski, D. and Webb, R. M. (2003). Individual differences. In L. Nadel (ed.), *Encyclopedia of cognitive science* (Vol. 2, pp. 503–510). London: Nature Publishing.

Luria, A. R. (1976). *Cognitive development: Its cultural and social foundations*. Boston: Harvard University Press.

Lyons, J. (1971) (ed.). *New horizons in linguistics*. Harmondsworth: Penguin.

Lyster, R. (1998). Recasts, repetition and ambiguity in L2 classroom discourse. *Studies in Second Language Acquisition*, 20, 51–80.

Lyster, R. (2004). Differential effects of prompts and recasts in form-focused instruction. *Studies in Second Language Acquisition, 26, 399–432.*

Lyster, R. and Ranta, L. (1997). Corrective feedback and learner uptake: Negotiation of form in communicative classrooms. *Studies in Second Language Acquisition, 19,* 37–66.

Macaro, E. (2003). *Teaching and learning a second language: A guide to current research and its applications.* London: Continuum.

Macaro, E. (2005). Codeswitching in the L2 classroom: A communication and learning strategy. In E. Llurda (ed.), *Non-native language teachers: Perceptions, challenges, and contributions to the profession* (pp. 63–84). Boston, MA: Springer.

Macaro, E. (2006). Strategies for language learning and for language use: Revising the theoretical framework. *Modern Language Journal, 90, 320–337.*

Macaro, E. and Erler, L. (2008). Raising the achievement of young-beginner readers of French through strategy instruction. *Applied Linguistics, 29, 90–119.*

Macaro, E. and Graham, S. (2008). The development of the passé composé in lower intermediate learners of French. *Language Learning Journal, 36, 5–20.*

Macaro, E. and Masterman, E. (2006). Does intensive explicit grammar instruction make all the difference? *Language Teaching Research, 10, 297–327.*

MacIntyre, P. D. (2002). Motivation, anxiety and emotion in second language acquisition. In P. Robinson (ed.), *Individual differences in second language acquisition* (pp. 45–68). Amsterdam: John Benjamins.

MacIntyre, P. D., Baker, S. C., Clément, R. and Donovan, L. A. (2003). Talking in order to learn: Willingness to communicate and intensive language programs. *Canadian Modern Language Review, 59, 589–607.*

MacIntyre, P. D., Clément, R., Dörnyei, Z. and Noels, K. A. (1998). Conceptualizing willingness to communicate in a L2: A situated model of confidence and affiliation. *Modern Language Journal, 82, 545–562.*

MacIntyre, P. D., MacKinnon, S. P. and Clément, R. (2009). From integrative motivation to possible selves: The baby, the bathwater, and the future of language learning motivation research. In Z. Dörnyei and E. Ushioda (eds.), *Motivation, language identity and the L2 self.* Bristol: Multilingual Matters.

MacIntyre, P. D., Baker, S. C., Clement, R., Conrod, S. (2001). Willingness to communicate, social support, and language-learning orientations of immersion students. *Studies in Second Language Acquisition, 23, 369–388.*

Mackey, A. (1999). Input, interaction and second language development. *Studies in Second Language Acquisition, 21, 557–587.*

Mackey, A. (2002). Beyond production: Learners' perceptions about interactional processes. *International Journal of Educational Research, 37, 379–394.*

Mackey, A. (ed.) (2007). *Conversational interaction in second language acquisition.* Oxford: Oxford University Press.

Mackey, A. and Gass, S. M. (2005). *Second language research: Methodology and design.* Mahwah, NJ: Lawrence Erlbaum.

Mackey, A. and Philp, J. (1998). Conversational interaction and second language development: Recasts, responses and red herrings? *The Modern Language Journal, 82, 338–356.*

Mackey, A. and Goo, J. (2007). Interaction research in SLA: A meta-analysis and research synthesis. In A. Mackey (ed.), *Conversational interaction in second language acquisition: A series of empirical studies* (pp. 407–452). Oxford, UK: Oxford University Press.

Mackey, A. and Philp, J. (1998). Conversational interaction and second language development: Recasts, responses, and red herrings. *The Modern Language Journal,* 82, 338–356.

Mackey, A., Gass, S. and McDonough, K. (2000). Learners' perceptions about feedback. *Studies in Second Language Acquisition,* 22, 471–497.

Mackey, W. F. (1972). The description of bilingualism. In J. A. Fishman (ed.), *Readings in the sociology of language* (pp. 554–584). The Hague: Mouton.

MacWhinney, B. (1987). The competition model. In B. MacWhinney (ed.), *Mechanisms of language acquisition.* Hillsadale, NJ: Erlbaum.

Mainzer, K. (1997). *Thinking in complexity* (3rd edition). Berlin: Springer-Verlag.

Major, R. (1994). Chronological and stylistic aspects of second language acquisition of consonant clusters. *Language Learning,* 44, 655–680.

Malvern, D., Richards, B., Chipere, N. and Duran, P. (2004). *Lexical diversity and language development.* New York: Palgrave Macmillan.

Malvern, D. D. and Richards, B. J. (1997). A new measure of lexical diversity. In A. Ryan and A. Wray (eds.), *Evolving models of language* (pp. 58–71). Clevedon: Multilingual Matters.

Manchón, R. M. (2008). Taking strategies to the foreign language classroom: Where are we now in theory and research? *IRAL,* 46, 233.

Mann, V. A. (1986). 'Temporary memory for linguistic and non-linguistic material in relation to the acquisition of Japanese kanji and kana'. In H. S. R. Kao and R. Hoosain (eds.), *Linguistics, psychology, and the Chinese language* (pp. 55–167). Hong Kong: University of Hong Kong Press.

Marcus, G. (1993). Negative evidence in language acquisition. *Cognition,* 46, 53–85.

Markee, N. (2000). *Conversation analysis.* Lawrence Erlbaum Associates.

Markee, N. (2005). The organization of off-task classroom talk in second language classrooms, in K. Richards and P. Seedhouse (eds.), *Applying conversation analysis* (pp. 197–213). Basingstoke: Palgrave Macmillan.

Markus, H. R. (2006). Foreword. In C. Dunkel and J. Kerpelman (eds.), *Possible selves: Theory, research and applications* (pp. xi–xiv). New York: Nova Science.

Markus, H. and Nurius, P. (1986). Possible selves. *American Psychologist,* 41, 954–969.

Markus, H. and Ruvolo, A. (1989). Possible selves: Personalized representations of goals. In L. A. Pervin (ed.), *Goal concepts in personality and social psychology* (pp. 211–241). Hillsdale, NJ: Lawrence Erlbaum.

Marsden, E. and David A. (2008). Vocabulary use during conversation: A cross-sectional study of development from year 9 to year 13 among learners of Spanish and French. *Language Learning Journal,* 36, 181–198.

McCafferty, S. G. and Stam, G. (eds.) (2008). *Gesture: Second language acquisition and classroom research.* Abingdon (UK): Routledge.

McCafferty, S. Roebuck, R. F. and Wayland, R. P. (2001). Activity theory and the incidental learning of second-language vocabulary. *Language Awareness,* 10, 289–294.

McDaniel, D., McKee, C. and Cairns, H. S. (1996). *Methods for assessing children's syntax,* Cambridge, MA: MIT Press.

McDonough, K. (2005). Identifying the impact of negative feedback and learners' responses on ESL question development. *Studies in Second Language Acquisition*, 27, 79–103.

McDonough, K. (2007). Interactional feedback and the emergence of simple past activity verbs in L2 English. In A. Mackey (ed.), *Conversational interaction and second language acquisition: A series of empirical studies* (pp. 323–338). Oxford, UK: Oxford University Press.

McDonough, S. (1981). *Psychology in foreign language teaching*. London: George Allen and Unwin.

McDonough, S. (2005). Training language learning expertise. In K. Johnson (ed.), *Expertise in second language learning and teaching*. London: Palgrave Macmillan.

McDonough, K. and Mackey, A. (2006). Responses to recasts: Repetitions, primed production, and linguistic development. *Language Learning*, 56, 693–720.

McDonough, K. and Mackey, A. (2008). Syntactic priming and ESL question development. *Studies in Second Language Acquisition*, 30, 31–47.

McEnery, T. Xiao, R. and Tono, Y. (2006). *Corpus-based language studies*. London: Routledge.

McGruddy, R. (1995). The effect of listening comprehension strategy training with advanced level ESL students. Unpublished doctoral dissertation, Georgetown University: Washington, DC, USA.

McLaughlin, B. (1987). *Theories of second-language learning*. London: Arnold.

McLaughlin, B. (1990). Restructuring. *Applied Linguistics*, 11, 113–128.

McLaughlin, B. and Nayak, N. (1989). Processing a new language: Does knowing other languages make a difference? In H. W. Dechert and M. Raupach (eds.), *Interlingual processes* (pp. 5–16). Tubingen, Germany: Gunter Narr Verlag.

McLaughlin, B., Rossman, T. and McLeod, B. (1983). 'Second language learning: An information-processing perspective'. *Language Learning*, 36, 109–123.

McNeill, D. (1965). *Some thoughts on first and second language acquisition*. Mimeo: Harvard University.

McNeill, D. (1966). Developmental psycholinguistics. In F. Smith and G. A. Miller (eds.), *The Genesis of Language: A Psycholinguistic Approach*, (pp. Cambridge, MA: MIT Press.

Meara, P. M. (1994). The complexities of simple vocabulary tests. In F. G. Brinkman, J. A. van der Schee and M. C. Schouten-van Parreren (eds.), *Curriculum research: Different disciplines and common goals*. Amsterdam: Vrije Universiteit.

Meara, P. M. (2007). Simulation word associations in an L2: Approaches to lexical organisation. *International Journal of English Studies*, 7, 1–20.

Meara, P. M. and Buxton, B. (1987). An alternative to multiple choice vocabulary tests. *Language Testing*, 4, 142–154.

Meara, P. M. and Jones, G. (1990). *The Eurocentres vocabulary size test*. 10KA. Zurich: Eurocentres.

Meara, P. M. and Milton, J. L. (2003). *X_Lex: The Swansea vocabulary levels test*. Newbury: Express Publishing.

Meara, P. M. and Miralpeix, I. (2008). V_Size v2.00. Swansea: Lognostics.

Meara, P. M. and Wolter, B. (2004). V_Links: Beyond vocabulary depth. *Angles on the English Speaking World*, 4, 85–97.

Meristo, M., Falkman, K. W., Hjelmquist, E., Tedoldi, M., Surian, L. and Siegal, M. (2007). 'Language access and theory of mind reasoning: Evidence from deaf children in bilingual and oralist environments'. *Developmental Psychology*, 43, 1156–1169.

Meschhyan, G. and Hernandez, A. (2002). Is native language decoding skill related to second language learning? *Journal of Educational Psychology*, 94, 14–22.

Met, M. (1991). Learning language through content: Learning content through language. *Foreign Language Annals*, 24, 281–295.

Miralpeix, I. (2007). Lexical knowledge in instructed language learning: The effects of age and exposure. *International Journal of English Studies*, 7, 61–83.

Mitchell, R. and Hye-Won Lee, J. (2003). Sameness and difference in classroom learning cultures: Interpretations of communicative pedagogy in the UK and Korea. *Language Teaching Research*, 7, 35–63.

Mitchell, R. and Myles, F. (1998). *Second language learning theories*. London: Arnold.

Miyake, A. and Friedman, D. (1998). Individual differences in second language proficiency: Working memory as language aptitude. In A. F. Healy and L. E. Bourne (eds.), *Foreign language learning: Psycholinguistic studies on training and retention* (pp. 339–364). Mahwah, NJ: Lawrence Erlbaum.

Mochida, A. and Harrington, M. (2006). The Yes/No test as a measure of receptive vocabulary knowledge. *Language Testing*, 23, 73–98.

Montrul, S. and Sablakova, R. (2003). Competence similarities between native and near-native speakers: An investigation of the preterite-imperfect contrast in Spanish. *Studies in Second Language Acquisition*, 25, 351–398.

Mori, J. (2001). Border crossings? Exploring the intersection of second language acquisition, conversation analysis and foreign language pedagogy. *The Modern Language Journal*, 91, 849–862.

Mori, J. (2002). Task design, plan and development of talk-in-interaction: An analysis of a small group activity in a Japanese language classroom. *Applied Linguistics*, 23, 323–347.

Moskowitz, G. (1976). The classroom interaction of outstanding language teachers. *Foreign Language Annals*, 9, 135–157.

Moussu, L. and Llurda, E. (2008). Non-native English-speaking English language teachers: History and research. *Language Teaching*, 41, 315–348.

Moyer, A. (2004). *Age, accent and experience in second language acquisition*. Clevedon: Multilingual Matters.

Muñoz, C. (2006a) (ed.), *Age and the rate of foreign language learning*. Clevedon: Multilingual Matters.

Muñoz, C. (2006b). The effects of age on foreign language learning: The BAF project. In C. Muñoz (ed.), *Age and rate of foreign language learning*. page Clevedon: Multilingual Matters.

Myers-Scotton, C. (1989). Code-switching with English: Types of switching, types of communities. *World Englishes*, 8, 333–346.

Nassaji, H. (2003). 'L2 vocabulary learning from context: Strategies, knowledge sources, and their relationship with success in L2 lexical inferencing'. *TESOL Quarterly*, 37/4, 645–670.

Nation, I. S. P. (2001). *Learning vocabulary in another language*. Cambridge: Cambridge University Press.

Nation, I. S. P. (1990). *Teaching and learning vocabulary*. Rowley, MA: Newbury House.

Nation, I. S. P. (2009). 'New roles for L2 vocabulary in language teaching'. In V. J. Cook and Li Wei (eds.), *Contemporary applied linguistics volume 1 language teaching and learning*. London: Continuum.

Nation, R. and McLaughlin, B. (1986). Novices and experts: An information processing approach to the 'good language learner' problem. *Applied Psycholinguistics, 7*, 41–56.

Newport, E. (1990). Maturational constraints on language learning. *Cognitive Science, 14*, 11–28.

Newport, E. L., Gleitman, H. and Gleitman, C. R. (1977). Mother, I'd rather do it myself: Some effects and non-effects of maternal speech style. In C. E. Snow and C. A. Ferguson (eds.), *Talking to children: Language input and acquisition* (pp. 9–149). Cambridge: Cambridge University Press.

Nicholas, H. Lightbown, P. and Spada, N. (2001). Recasts as feedback to language learners. *Language Learning, 51*, 4, 719–758.

Nicholas, H., Lightbown, P. and Spada, N. (2002). Recasts as feedback to language learners. *Language Learning, 51*, 4, 719–758.

Nikolov, M. (2006). Test-taking strategies of 12- and 13-year-old Hungarian learners of EFL: Why whales have migraines. *Language Learning, 56*, 1, 1–51.

Nisbet, D. L., Tindall, E. R. and Arroyo, A. A. (2005). 'Language learning strategies and English proficiency of Chinese university students'. *Foreign Language Annals, 38*, 100–107.

Noels, K. A. (2003). Learning Spanish as a second language: Learners' orientations and perceptions of their teachers' communication style. In Z. Dörnyei (ed.), *Attitudes, orientations, and motivations in language learning* (pp. 97–136). Oxford: Blackwell.

Noels, K. A. (2009). The internalisation of language learning into the self and social identity. In Z. Dörnyei and E. Ushioda (eds.), *Motivation, language identity and the L2 self*. Bristol: Multilingual Matters.

Noels, K. A., Clément, R. and Pelletier, L. G. (1999). Perceptions of teachers' communicative style and students' intrinsic and extrinsic motivation. *Modern Language Journal, 83*, 23–34.

Noels, K. A., Clément, R. and Pelletier, L. G. (2001). Intrinsic, extrinsic, and integrative orientations of French Canadian learners of English. *Canadian Modern Language Review, 57*, 424–444.

Norton, B. (2000). *Identity and language learning: Gender, ethnicity and educational change*. London: Longman.

Norton, B. (2000). *Identity and language learning: Social processes and educational practice*. Harlow: Pearson.

Norton, B. (2001). Non-participation, imagined communities and the language classroom. In M. P. Breen (ed.), *Learner contributions to language learning: New directions in research* (pp. 159–171). Harlow, England: Longman.

Norton, B. and Toohey, K. (2001). Changing perspectives on good language learners. *TESOL Quarterly, 35*, 307–321.

Nowak, A., Vallacher, R. R. and Zochowski, M. (2005). The emergence of personality: Dynamic foundations of individual variation. *Developmental Review, 25*, 351–385.

Nunan, D. (1992). *Research methods in language learning*. Cambridge: Cambridge University Press.

Nunan, D. (1997). Strategy training in the languages classroom: An empirical investigation. *RELC Journal*, 28, 56–81.

O'Grady, W. (2005). *How children learn language*. Cambridge: Cambridge University Press.

O'Malley, J. M. and Chamot, A. U. (1990). *Learning strategies in second language acquisition*. Cambridge: Cambridge University Press.

O'Malley, J. M., Chamot, A. U. and Küpper, L. (1989). Listening comprehension strategies in second language acquisition. *Applied Linguistics*, 10, 4, 418–437.

Ochs, E. and Schieffelin, B. (1984). Language acquisition and socialisation: Three developmental stories and their implications. In R. Shweder and R. Levine (eds.), *Culture and its acquisition*. New York: Cambridge University Press.

Ohta, A. S. (2001). *Second language acquisition processes in the classroom*. Mahwah, NJ: Lawrence Erlbaum.

Olivares-Cuhat, G. (2002). 'Learning strategies and achievement in the Spanish writing classroom: A case study'. *Foreign Language Annals*, 35/5, 561–570.

Oliver, R. (1995). Negative feedback in child NS–NNS conversation. *Studies in Second Language Acquisition*, 17, 459–481.

Osada, N. (2001). 'What strategy do less proficient learners employ in listening comprehension?: A reappraisal of bottom-up and top-down processing'. *Pan-Pacific Association of Applied Linguistics*, 5/1, 73–90.

Otomo, K. (2001). Maternal responses to word approximations in Japanese children's transition to language. *Journal of Child Language*, 28, 29–57.

Oxford, R. L. (1990). *Language learning strategies: What every teacher should know*. Boston, MA: Heinle.

Oxford and Nyikos, M. (1989). Variables affecting choice of language learning strategies by university students. *MLJ*, 73, 3, 291–300.

Oxford, R. L., Park-Oh, Y. Y., Ito, S. and Sumrall, M. (1993). 'Learning a language by satellite television: What influences student achievement?' *System*, 21, 31–48.

Ozeki, N. (2000). Listening strategy instruction for female EFL college students in Japan. Unpublished doctorial dissertation, Indiana University of Pennsylvania, The Graduate School and Research Department of English.

Palmberg, R. (1987). Patterns of vocabulary development in foreign language learners. *Studies in Second Language Acquisition*, 9, 201–220.

Paribakht, T. (1985). 'Strategic competence and language proficiency'. *Applied Linguistics*, 6/2, 132–146.

Paribakht, S. (2005). The influence of first language lexicalization on second language lexical inferencing: A Study of Farsi speaking learners of English as a foreign language. *Language Learning*, 55, 701–748.

Paribakht, S. and Wesche, M. (1993). The relationship between reading comprehension and second language development in a comprehension-based ESL program. *TESL Canada Journal*, 11, 9–29.

Park, G. P. (1997). Language learning strategies and English proficiency in Korean University students. *Foreign Language Annals*, 30, 211–221.

Parrott, W. G. (2004). The nature of emotion. In M. B. Brewer and M. Hewstone (eds.), *Emotion and motivation* (pp. 5–20). Oxford: Blackwell.

Paulus, T. (1999). The effect of peer and teacher feedback on student writing. *Journal of Second Language Writing*, 8, 265–290.

Pavlenko, A. (2002). Poststructuralist approaches to the study of social factors in second language learning and use. In V. Cook (ed.), *Portraits of the L2 user* (pp. 277–302). Clevedon: Multilingual Matters.

Pawlak, M. (2008). The effect of corrective feedback on the acquisition of the English third-person –*s* ending. In D. Gabryś-Barker (ed.), *Morphosyntactic issues in second language acquisition* (pp. 182–202). Clevedon, UK: Multilingual Matters.

Penfield, W. and Roberts, L. (1959). *Speech and brain mechanisms*. Princeton, NJ: Princeton University Press.

Petersen, K. M., Reis, A., Askelöf, S., Castro-Caldas, A. and Ingvar, M. (2000). Language processing modulated by literacy: A network analysis of verbal repetition in literate and illiterate subjects. *Journal of Cognitive Neuroscience*, 12, 364–382.

Philp, J. (2003). Constraints on noticing the gap: Nonnative speakers' noticing of recasts in NS-NNS interaction. *Studies in Second Language Acquisition*, 25, 99–126.

Piaget, J. and Inhelder, B. (1969). *The psychology of the child*. New York: Basic Books.

Pica, T. (1984). Methods of morpheme quantification: Their effect on the interpretation of second language data. *Studies in Second Language Acquisition*, 6, 69–78.

Pica, T. Young, R. and Doughty, C. (1987).The impact of interaction on comprehension. *TESOL Quarterly*, 21, 737–758.

Pica, T. Holliday, L., Lewis, N. and Morgenthaler, L. (1989). Comprehensible output as an outcome of linguistic demands on the learner. *Studies in Second Language Acquisition*, 11, 63–90.

Pienemann, M. (1984). Psychological constraints on the teachability of languages. *Studies in Second Language Acquisition*, 6, 186–214.

Pienemann, M. (1998). *Language processing and second-language development: Processability theory*. Amsterdam: John Benjamins.

Piller, I. (2002). *Bilingual couples talk: The discursive construction of hybridity*. Amsterdam: John Benjamins.

Pimsleur, P. (1966). *The Pimsleur language aptitude battery*. New York: Harcourt, Brace, Jovanovic.

Pizzolato, J. E. (2006). Achieving college student possible selves: Navigating the space between commitment and achievement of long-term identity goals. *Cultural Diversity and Ethnic Minority Psychology*, 12, 57–69.

Platt, E. and Brooks, F. (1994). The acquisition rich environment revisited. *Modern Language Journal*, 78, 497–511.

Plunkett, K. (1998). Language acquisition and connectionism. *Language and Cognitive Processes*, 13, 97–104.

Poeppel, D. and Wexler, K. (1993). The full competence hypothesis of clause structure in early German. *Language*, 69, 1–33.

Polio, C. (2007). A history of input enhancement: Defining an evolving concept. In C. Gascoigne (ed.), *Assessing the impact of input enhancement in second language education* (pp. 1–17). Stillwater, OK: New Forums Press.

Politzer, R. L. (1983). 'An exploratory study of self-reported language learning behaviours and their relation to achievement'. *Studies in Second Language Acquisition*, 6, 54–68.

Porte, G. (2002). *Appraising research in second language learning: A practical approach to critical analysis of quantitative research*. Amsterdam: John Benjamins.

Posner, M. (1988). Structures and functions of selective attention. In T. Boll and B. Bryand (eds.), *Master lectures in clinical neuropsychology and brain function: Research, measurement, and practice* (pp. 171–202). Washington, DC: American Psychological Association.

Posner, M. (1992). Attention as a cognitive system. *Directions in Psychology Science, 1*, 11–14.

Posner, M. and Petersen, S. E. (1990). The attention system of the human brain. *Annual Review of Neuroscience, 13*, 25–42.

Poulisse, N. and Schils, E. (1989). 'The influence of task- and proficiency-related factors on the use of compensatory strategies: A quantitative analysis'. *Language Learning, 39*, 15–48.

Prince, A. and Smolensky, P. (1993). *Optimality theory: Constraint interaction in generative grammar*. Rutgers University Center for Cognitive Science Technical Report 2.

Raatz, U. and Klein-Braley, C. (1981). The C-test – a modification of the cloze procedure. In T. Culhane, C. Klein-Braley and D. Stevenson (eds.) (1981). *Practice and problems in language testing*, pp. 113–148. *University of Essex Occasional Paper*, University of Essex, Colchester.

Raatz, U. and Klein-Braley, C. (1998). *Introduction to language testing and C-Tests*. Accessed at: http://www.uniduisburg.de/fb3/angling/forschung/howtodo.htm

Raimes, A. (1987). 'Language proficiency, writing ability, and composition strategies: A study of ESL college student writers'. *Language Learning, 37*, 439–467.

Ranta, L. (2008). Aptitude and good language learners. In C. Griffiths (ed.), *Lessons from good language learners* (pp. 142–155). Cambridge: Cambridge University Press.

Raymond, P. M. (1993). The effects of structure strategy training on the recall of expository prose for university students reading French as a second language. *The Modern Language Journal, 77*, 445–458.

Read, J. (1993). The development of a new measure of L2 vocabulary knowledge. *Language Testing, 10*, 355–371.

Read, J. (1995). Refining the word associates format as a measure of depth of vocabulary knowledge. *New Zealand Studies in Applied Linguistics, 1*, 1–17.

Read, J. (1997). Vocabulary and testing. In N. Schmitt and M. McCarthy (eds.), *Vocabulary: description, acquisition and pedagogy* (pp. 303–320). Cambridge: Cambridge University Press.

Read, J. (1998). Validating a test to measure depth of vocabulary knowledge. In A. Kunnan (ed.), *Validation in language assessment*, pp. 41–60. Mahwah, NJ: Lawrence Erlbaum.

Read, J. (2007). Second language vocabulary assessment: Current practice and new directions. *International Journal of English Studies, 7*, 105–125.

Richards, J. C. (1976). The role of vocabulary teaching. *TESOL Quarterly, 10*, 77–89.

Richards, B. J. and D. D. Malvern (2000). Accommodation in oral interviews between foreign language learners and teachers who are not native speakers. *Studia Linguistica, 54*, 2, 260–271.

Richards, J. and Rodgers, T. (1986). *Approaches and methods in language teaching: A description and analysis*. Cambridge: Cambridge University Press.

Richards, K. and Seedhouse, P. (eds.) (2005). *Applying conversation analysis*. Basingstoke: Palgrave Macmillan.

Riding, R. J. and Sadler-Smith, E. (1992). Type of instructional material, cognitive style and learning performance. *Educational Studies*, 18, 323–340.

Rivers, W. P. (2001). Autonomy at all costs: An ethnography of metacognitive self-assessment and self-management among experienced language learners. *Modern Language Journal*, 85, 279–290.

Rizzi, L. (2004). On the study of the language faculty: Results, developments and perspectives. *Linguistic Review*, 21, 323–344.

Robinson, P. (1995). Attention, memory, and the 'noticing' hypothesis. *Language Learning*, 45, 283–331.

Robinson, P. (2001). Individual differences, cognitive abilities, aptitude complexes and learning conditions in second language acquisition. *Second Language Research*, 17, 368–392.

Robinson, P. (ed.) (2001). *Cognition and second language instruction*. Cambridge: Cambridge University Press.

Robinson, P. (2002). Learning conditions, aptitude complexes and SLA: A framework for research and pedagogy. In P. Robinson (ed.), *Individual differences and instructed language learning* (pp. 113–133). Amsterdam: John Benjamins.

Robinson, P. (2007). Aptitudes, abilities, contexts, and practice. In R. M. DeKeyser (ed.), *Practice in second language learning: Perspectives from linguistics and cognitive psychology* (pp. 256–286). Cambridge: Cambridge University Press.

Robinson, P. (in press). *Aptitude in second language learning*. Oxford: Oxford University Press.

Robinson, R. D. (1973). The cloze procedure: A new tool for adult education. *Adult Education Quarterly*, 23, 97–98.

Roebuck, R. (2000). Subjects speak out: How learners position themselves in a psycholinguistic task, in J. Lantolf (ed.), *Sociocultural theory and second language learning* (pp. 79–95). Oxford: Oxford University Press.

Roehr, K. (2008). Metalinguistic knowledge and language ability in university-level L2 learners. *Applied Linguistics*, 29, 173–199.

Rott, S. (2005). Processing glosses: A qualitative exploration of how form-meaning connections are established and strengthened. *Reading in a Foreign Language*, 17, 95–124.

Rubin, J. (1975). What the 'Good Language Learner' can teach us. *TESOL Quarterly*, 41–51.

Sanaoui, R. (1995). Adult learners' approaches to learning vocabulary in second languages. *The Modern Languages Journal*, 79, 1, 15–28.

Satterfield, T. (2003). Economy of interpretation: Patterns of pronoun selection in transitional bilinguals. In V. J. Cook (ed.), *L2 effects on the L1*, 214–233. Clevedon: Multilingual Matters.

Saxton, M. (1997). The contrast theory of negative input. *Journal of Child Language*, 24, 139–161.

Saxton, M. (2000). Negative evidence and negative feedback: Immediate effects on the grammaticality of speech. *First Language*, 20, 221–252.

Saxton, M. (2005). 'Recast' in a new light: Insights for practice from typical language studies. *Child Language Teaching and Therapy*, 21, 23–38.

Saxton, M., Backley, P. and Gallaway, C. (2005). Negative input for grammatical errors: Effects after a lag of 12 weeks. *Journal of Child Language*, 32, 643–672.

Saxton, M., Houston-Price, C. and Dawson, N. (2005). The prompt hypothesis: Clarification requests as corrective input for grammatical errors. *Applied Psycholinguistics*, 26, 393–413.

Saxton, M., Kulcsar, B., Marshall, G. and Rupra, M. (1998). The longer term effects of corrective input: An experimental approach. *Journal of Child Language*, 25, 701–721.

Scherer, K. R. (1995). Plato's legacy: Relationships between cognition, emotion, and motivation. *Geneva Studies in Emotion and Communication*, 9, 1–7.

Schiff, R. and Calif, R. (2007). Role of phonological and morphological awareness in L2 oral word reading. *Language Learning*, 57, 271–298.

Schiffrin, D. (1987). *Discourse markers*. Cambridge: Cambridge University Press.

Schiffrin, D., Tannen, D. and Hamilton, H. E. (eds.) (2003). *A handbook of discourse analysis*. Oxford: Blackwell.

Schmid, M., Kopke, B., Keijzer, M. and Weilemar, L. (eds.) (2004). *First language attrition*. Amsterdam: John Benjamins.

Schmidt, R. (1995) (ed.). *Attention and awareness in foreign language teaching and learning. (Technical Report, No. 9)*. Honolulu: University of Hawaii at Manoa.

Schmitt, N. (ed.) (2004). *Formulaic sequences: Acquisition, processing and use*. Amsterdam: John Benjamins.

Schmitt, N., Schmitt, D. and Clapham, C. (2001). Developing and exploring the behaviour of two new versions of the Vocabulary Levels Test. *Language Testing*, 18, 55–89.

Schumann, J. H. (1978). The acculturation model for second-language acquisition. In R. C. Gingras (ed.), *Second language acquisition and foreign language teaching* (pp. 27–50). Washington, DC: Center for Applied Linguistics.

Schumann, J. H. (1986). Research on the acculturation model for second language acquisition. *Journal of Multilingual and Multicultural Development*, 7, 379–392.

Schumann, J. H. (2004). Introduction. In J. H. Schumann, S. E. Crowell, N. E. Jones, N. Lee, S. A. Schuchert and L. A. Wood (eds.), *The neurobiology of learning: Perspectives from second language acquisition* (pp. 1–6). Mahwah, NJ: Lawrence Erlbaum.

Schwartz, B. D. and Sprouse, R. A. (1996). L2 cognitive states and the full transfer/Full Access model. *Second Language Research*, 12, 40–72.

Scovel, T. (2000). A critical review of the critical period research. *Annual Review of Applied Linguistics*, 20, 213–223.

Scovel, T. (2002). *Learning new languages: A guide to second language acquisition*. Boston: Heinle and Heinle.

Seedhouse, P. (1996). *Learning Talk: A Study of the Interactional Organisation of the L2 Classroom from a CA Institutional Discourse Perspective*. Unpublished doctoral thesis, University of York, U.K.

Seedhouse, P. (2004). *The interactional architecture of the language classroom: A conversation analysis perspective*. Malden, MA: Blackwell.

Seedhouse, P. (2005). 'Task' as research construct. *Language Learning*, 55, 533–570.

Segal, H. G. (2006). Possible selves, fantasy distortion, and the anticipated life history: Exploring the role of imagination in social cognition. In C. Dunkel and J. Kerpelman (eds.), *Possible selves: Theory, research and applications* (pp. 79–96). New York: Nova Science Publishers Inc.

Seidlhofer, B. (2003). *Controversies in applied linguistics.* Oxford: Oxford University Press.

Seliger, H. W. and Shohamy, E. (1989). *Second language research methods.* Oxford: Oxford University Press.

Selinker, L. (1972). Interlanguage. *International Review of Applied Linguistics,* 10, 209–231.

Selinker, L. and Lakshmanan, U. (1992). Language transfer and fossilization: The 'Multiple Effects Principle'. In S. Gass, and L. Selinker (eds.), *Language transfer in language learning.* Amsterdam: John Benjamins, pp. 197–216.

Seo, K. (2000). Intervening in tertiary students' strategic listening in Japanese as a foreign language. Unpublished doctorial dissertation, Griffith University, Australia.

Shank, G. (1993). Qualitative research? Quantitative research? What's the problem? Resolving the dilemma via a postconstructivist approach. In Proceedings of Selected Research and Development Presentations at the Convention of the Association for Educational Communications and Technology Sponsored by the Research and Theory Division (15th, New Orleans, Louisiana, 13–17 January 1993). ERIC ED 362202.

Sharwood-Smith, M. (1994). *Second language learning: Theoretical foundations.* London: Longman.

Sheen, Y. (2007). Exploring the relationship between characteristics of recasts and learner uptake. *Language Teaching Research,* 19, 361–392.

Shiotsu, T. (2001). An analysis of the vocabulary levels test. *Bulletin of the Institute of Foreign Language Education Kurume University* 8, 27–49.

Sinclair de Zwart, H. (1969). Developmental psycholinguistics. In Elkind, D. and Flavell, J. H. (eds.), *Studies in cognitive development.* New York: Oxford University Press, 315–366.

Sinclair, J. and Coulthard, R. M. (1975). *Toward an analysis of discourse.* Oxford: Oxford University Press.

Singleton, D. (2005). The critical period hypothesis: A coat of many colours. *IRAL,* 43, 269–285.

Singleton, D. (2007). The critical period hypothesis: Some problems. *Interlingüistica,* 17, 48–56.

Singleton, D. and Ryan, L. (2004). *Language acquisition: The age factor.* Clevedon: Multilingual Matters.

Skehan, P. (1989). *Individual differences in second-language learning.* London: Arnold.

Skinner, B. (1957). *Verbal behaviour.* New York: Appleton-Century-Crofts.

Skinner, B. F. (1975). *Verbal behavior.* Acton, MA: Copley Publishing Group.

Slimani-Rolls, A. (2003). Exploring a world of paradoxes: An investigation of group work. *Language Teaching Research,* 7, 221–239.

Slobin, D. I. (ed.) (1985). *The crosslinguistic study of language acquisition* (Vols 1–2). Hillsdale, NJ: Lawrence Erlbaum.

Slobin, D. I. and Welsh, C. (1973). Elicited imitation as a research tool in developmental psycholinguistics. In Ferguson, C. and Slobin, D. (eds.), *Studies of child language.* New York: Holt Rinehart Winston.

Snow, C. (1987). Relevance of a critical period to language acquisition. In M. Bornstein (ed.), *Sensitive periods in development: Interdisciplinary perspectives.* pp. 183–210. Hillsdale, NJ/London: Erlbaum.

Snow, C. (2002). Second language learners and understanding the brain. In A. Galaburda, S. M. Kosslyn and Y. Christen (eds.), *The Languages of the brain.* Cambridge, MA: Harvard University Press.

Snow, C. and Hoefnagel-Höhle, M. (1978). The critical period for language acquisition: Evidence from second language learning. *Child Development, 49,* 1114–1128.

Snow, C. E. and Ferguson, C. A. (eds.) (1977). *Talking to children.* Cambridge: Cambridge University Press.

Sorace, A. (2004). Native language attrition and developmental instability at the syntax-discourse interface: Data, interpretations and methods. *Bilingualism: Language and Cognition, 7,* 143–145.

Spada, N. and Lightbown, P. M. (1999). Instruction, first language influence, and developmental readiness in second language acquisition. *Modern Language Journal, 83,* 1–22.

Spolsky, B. (1995). Prognostication and language aptitude testing, 1925–1962. *Language Testing, 12,* 321–340.

Stanovich, K. E. (1980). Toward an interactive-compensatory model of individual differences in the development of reading fluency. *Reading Research Quarterly, 16,* 32–71.

Stern, H. (1967). Foreign language learning and the new view of first language acquisition. *Child Study, 30,* 25–36.

Stern, H. H. (1983). *Fundamental concepts of language teaching.* Oxford: Oxford University Press.

Stevens, F. (1983). Activities to promote learning and communication in the second language classroom. *TESOL Quarterly, 17,* 259–272.

Stockwell, R., Bowen, D. and Martin, J. W. (1965). *The grammatical structures of English and Spanish: An analysis of structural differences between the two languages.* Chicago: University of Chicago Press.

Strapp, C. M. (1999). Mothers', fathers', and siblings' responses to children's language errors: Comparing sources of negative evidence. *Journal of Child Language, 26,* 373–391.

Strapp, C. M. and Federico, A. (2000). Imitations and repetitions: What do children say following recasts? *First Language, 20,* 273–290.

Su, I-Ru (2001). Transfer of sentence processing strategies: A comparison of L2 learners of Chinese and English. *Applied Psycholinguistics, 22,* 83–112.

Sullivan, P. (2000). Spoken artistry: Performance in a foreign language classroom, in J. K. Hall and L. S. Verplaetse (eds.), *Second and foreign language learning through classroom interaction.* Mahwah, NJ: Lawrence Erlbaum Associates, 73–90.

Sunderman, G. and Kroll, J. (2006). First language activation during second language lexical processing: An investigation of lexical form, meaning and grammatical class. *Studies in Second Language Acquisition, 28,* 387–422.

Swain, M. (1972). Bilingualism as a first language. PhD Dissertation. Irvine: University of California .

Swain, M. (1985). Communicative competence: Some roles of comprehensible input and comprehensible output in its development. In S. Gass and C. Madden (eds.), *Input in second language acquisition* (pp. 235–253). Rowley, MA: Newbury House.

Swain, M. (1995). Three functions of output in second language learning. In G. Cook and B. Seidlhofer (eds.), *Principle and practice in applied linguistics* (pp. 125–144). Oxford, UK: Oxford University Press.

Swain, M. (2005). The output hypothesis: Theory and research. In E. Hinkel (ed.), *Handbook of research in second language teaching and learning* (pp. 471–483). Mahwah, NJ: Lawrence Erlbaum Associates.

Swales, J. (1990). *Genre analysis: English in academic and research settings.* Cambridge: Cambridge University Press.

Taillefer, G. F. (1996). L2 reading ability: Further insight into the short-circuit hypothesis. *Modern Language Journal,* 80, 461–477.

Takaya, K. (2007). Knowledge and performance of small talk by Japanese users of English. Unpublished doctoral dissertation. University of Oxford, Department of Education.

Talbot, D. C. (1995). Metacognitive strategy training for reading: Developing second language learners' awareness of expository text patterns. Unpublished Doctoral Dissertation, University of Hong Kong.

Tarone, E. and Swain, M. (1995). A sociolinguistic perspective on second language use in immersion classrooms. *Modern Language Journal ,* 79, 166–178.

Taylor, W. (1956). Recent developments in the use of 'Cloze Procedure'. *Journalism Quarterly,* 33, 42–48.

Tedick, D. (2004). *Second language teacher education: International perspectives.* London: Routledge.

Teichert, H. U. (1996). A comparative study using illustrations, brainstorming, and questions as advance organizers in intermediate college German conversation classes. *Modern Language Journal,* 80, 509–517.

Thomas, W. and Collier, V. P. (1997). *School effectiveness for language minority students.* Washington: National Clearinghouse for Bilingual Education. (www.ncbe.gwu. edu)

Thompson, I. and Rubin, J. (1996). Can strategy instruction improve listening comprehension? *Foreign Language Annals,* 29, 3, 331–342.

Tomasello, M. (1999). *The cultural origins of human cognition.* Cambridge, MA: Harvard University Press.

Tomasello, M. (2003). *Constructing a language.* Cambridge, MA: Harvard University Press.

Tomlin, R. S. and Villa, V. (1994). Attention in cognitive science and second language acquisition. *Studies in Second Language Acquisition,* 16, 183–203.

Towell, R., Hawkins, R. and Bazergui, N. (1996). The development of fluency in advanced learners of French. *Applied Linguistics,* 17, 1, 84–119.

Tragant, E. and Victori, M. (2006). Reported strategy use and age. In C. Muñoz (ed.), *Age and rate of foreign language learning.* Clevedon: Multilingual Matters.

Tremaine, R. V. (1975). *Syntax and Piagetian operational thought.* Washington, D.C.: Georgetown U.P.

Trevarthen, C. (1974). Conversations with a two month old. *New Scientist,* 62.

Trofimovich, P. and Baker W. (2007). Learning prosody and fluency characteristics of second language speech: The effect of experience on child learners' acquisition of five suprasegmentals. *Applied Psycholinguistics*, 28, 251–276.

Truscott, J. (1996). The case against grammar correction in L2 writing classes. *Language Learning*, 46, 327–369.

Truscott, J. (1998). Noticing in second language acquisition: A critical review. *Second Language Acquisition Research*, 14, 103–135.

Tseng, W. Dornyei, Z. and Schmitt, N. (2005). A new approach to assessing strategic learning: The case of self-regulation in vocabulary acquisition. *Applied Linguistics*, 27, 78–102.

Tsui, A. B. M. and Fullilove, J. (1998). Bottom-up or top-down processing as a discriminator of L2 listening performance. *Applied Linguistics*, 19, 432–451.

Tsui, A. B. M. and Ng, M. (2000). Do secondary L2 writers benefit from peer comments? *Journal of Second Language Writing*, 9, 147–170.

Tversky, B., Kugelmass, S. and Winter, A. (1991). 'Cross-cultural and developmental trends in graphic productions'. *Cognitive Psychology*, 23, 515–557.

Ullman, R. and Geva, R. (1984). Approaches to observation in second language classes, in C. Brumfit (ed.), *Language issues and education policies*. Oxford: Pergamon, 113–128.

Ushioda, E. (2001). Language learning at university: Exploring the role of motivational thinking. In Z. Dörnyei and R. Schmidt (eds.), *Motivation and second language acquisition* (pp. 91–124). Honolulu, HI: University of Hawaii Press.

Ushioda, E. (2007). Motivation, autonomy and sociocultural theory. In P. Benson (ed.), *Learner autonomy 8: Teacher and learner perspectives* (pp. 5–24). Dublin: Authentik.

Ushioda, E. and Dörnyei, Z. (2009). Motivation, language identities and the L2 self: A theoretical overview. In Z. Dörnyei and E. Ushioda (eds.), *Motivation, language identity and the L2 self*. Bristol: Multilingual Matters.

Üstünel, E. (2003). *The sequential organisation of teacher-initiated and teacher-induced code-switching in a Turkish University EFL setting*. Unpublished PhD thesis, the University of Newcastle upon Tyne, UK.

Üstünel, E. and Seedhouse, P. (2005). Why that, in that language, right now?: Code-switching and pedagogical focus. *International Journal of Applied Linguistics*, 15, 302–325.

Van Geert, P. (2008). The Dynamic systems approach in the study of L1 and L2 acquisition: An introduction. *Modern Language Journal*, 92, 179–199.

Van Lier, L. (1996). *Interaction in the language curriculum: Awareness, autonomy and authenticity*. London: Longman.

Van Lier, L. (1988). *The classroom and the language learner*. New York: Longman.

Vandergrift, L. (1998). 'Successful and less successful listeners in French: What are the strategy differences?' *The French Review*, 71/3, 370–394.

Vandergrift, L. (2003). Orchestrating strategy use: Toward a model of the skilled second language listener. *Language Learning*, 53, 3, 463–496.

Vanderplank, R. (2008). The significance of first language development in five to nine year old children for second and foreign language learning. *Applied Linguistics*, 29, 717–722.

Vann, J. R. and Abraham, R. G. (1990). 'Strategies of unsuccessful language learners'. *TESOL Quarterly*, 24/2, 177–198.

VanPatten, B. (1996). *Input processing and grammar instruction in second language acquisition*. Norwood, NJ: Ablex.

VanPatten, B. (2007). Input processing in adult second language acquisition. In B. VanPatten and J. Williams (eds.) (pp. 115–135).

VanPatten, B. and Williams, J. (eds.) (2006). *Theories in second language acquisition*. London: Routledge.

Varonis, E. and Gass, S. (1985). Non-native/non-native conversations: A model for negotiation of meaning. *Applied Linguistics*, 6, 71–90.

Verhoeven, L. and de Jong, J. (1992). *The construct of language proficiency: Applications of psychological models to language assessment*. Amsterdam: John Benjamins.

Vickers, C. H. (2007). Second language socialization through team interaction among electrical and computer engineering students. *The Modern Language Journal*, 91, 621–640.

Victori, M. and Tragant, E. (2003). Learner strategies: A cross-sectional and longitudinal study of primary and high-school EFL learners. In M. García Mayo and M. García Lecumberri (eds.), *Age and the acquisition of English as a foreign language*. Clevedon: Multilingual Matters.

Vygotsky, L. S. (1934/1962). *Thought and language*. Cambridge, MA: MIT Press.

Vygotsky, L. S. (1935/1978). *Mind in society*. Cambridge, MA: Harvard University Press.

Waters, G. S. and Caplan, D. (1996). The measurement of verbal working memory capacity and its relation to reading comprehension. *The Quarterly Journal of Experimental Psychology*, 49A, 51–79.

Webb, S. (2008). Receptive and productive vocabulary size of L2 learners. *Studies in Second Language Acquisition*, 30, 79–95.

Weber, A. and Cutler, A. (2006). First-language phonotactics in second-language listening. *Journal of the Acoustical Society of America*, 119, 597–607.

Weeks, T. E. (1971). Speech registers in young children. *Child Development*, 42, 1119–1131.

Weinert, R. (1995). The role of formulaic language in second language acquisition: A review. *Applied Linguistics*, 16, 180–205.

Weinreich, U. (1953). *Languages in contact*. The Hague: Mouton.

Wells, G. (1981). *Learning through interaction*. Cambridge: Cambridge University Press.

Wenger, E. (1998). *Communities of practice: Learning, meaning, and identity*. Cambridge: Cambridge University Press.

Wesche, M. B. (1981). 'Learning behaviors of successful adult learners in intensive language training'. *Canadian Modern Language Review*, 37, 415–430.

Wesche, M. and Paribakht, T. S. (1996). Assessing vocabulary knowledge: Depth vs. breadth. *Canadian Modern Language Review*, 53, 13–40.

Wesche, M., Toews-Janzen, M. and MacFarlane, A. (1996). *Comparative outcomes and impact of early, middle and late entry French immersion options: Review of recent research and annotated bibliography*. Toronto: OISE/UT Press.

Wharton, G. (2000). Language learning strategy use of bilingual foreign language learners in Singapore. *Language Learning*, 50, 203–243.

White, J. and Lightbown, P. M. (1984). Asking and answering in ESL classes. *Canadian Modern Language Review*, 40, 228–244.

White, L. (1989). *Universal Grammar and second language acquisition*. Amsterdam: John Benjamins.

White, L. (2003). *Second language acquisition and Universal Grammar*. Cambridge: Cambridge University Press.

White, L. (2007). Linguistic theory, universal grammar, and second language acquisition. In B. VanPatten and J. Williams (eds.), *Theories in second language acquisition: An introduction* (pp. 37–55). Mahwah, NJ: Lawrence Erlbaum Associates.

Widdowson, H. G. (1978). *Teaching language as communication*. Oxford: Oxford University Press.

Wikberg, K. (1979). Lexical competence and the Swedish learner's problems with English vocabulary. In B. Hammarberg (ed.), *Kontrastiv lingvistik och sekundär-spraksforskning*: Stockholm Universitet.

Wilkins, D. A. (1976). *Notional syllabuses*. London: Oxford University Press.

Williams, J. N. and Lovatt, P. (2003). Phonological memory and rule learning. *Language Learning, 53*, 67–121.

Williams, M. and Burden, R. (1997). *Psychology for language teachers*. Cambridge: Cambridge University Press.

Williams, R. (1975). 'The BITCH-100: A culture-specific test', *Journal of Afro-American Issues, 3*, 103–116.

Willis, J. (1992). Inner and Outer: Spoken discourse in the language classroom, in M. Coulthard (ed.), *Advances in spoken discourse analysis* (pp. 161–182). London: Routledge.

Wode, H. (1981). *Learning a second language*. Tübingen: Narr.

Wood, D. (2002). Formulaic language in thought and word: Vygotskyan interpretations. *Cahiers Linguistiques d'Óttawa, 3*, pp. 26–55.

Wray, A. (2002). *Formulaic language and the lexicon*. Cambridge: Cambridge University Press.

Zipf, G. K. (1935). *The psychobiology of language*. New York: Houghton-Mifflin.

Zobl, H. (1985). Grammars in search of input and intake. In S. Gass and C. Madden (eds.), *Input and second language acquisition*, 329–344. Rowley, MA: Newbury House.

Zobl, H. (1995). Converging evidence for the 'Acquisition-Learning' distinction. *Applied Linguistics, 16*, 35–56.

Zobl, H. and Liceras, J. (1994). Functional categories and acquisition orders. *Language Learning, 44*, 159–180.

Zuckernick, H. (1996). Second language word decoding strategies. *Canadian Modern Language Review, 53*, 76–96.

Index

Note: Page references in **bold** refer to brief exposition of concept; page references in *italics* refer to figures, tables.